Karimah Ashadu: Tendered

Edited by Bianca Stoppani with
Alessandro Rabottini and Leonardo Bigazzi

Camden Art Centre
Fondazione In Between Art Film
The Renaissance Society at the University of Chicago

Mousse Publishing

Karimah Ashadu

Tendered

FOREWORD

Karimah Ashadu's solo exhibition *Tendered* marks the second project launched under the auspices of *Unison*, a biennial programme initiated by Fondazione In Between Art Film. This initiative aims to forge partnerships with international institutions to co-commission newly conceived exhibitions showcasing contemporary artists working with moving images.

After inaugurating the series with Ali Cherri in 2023, I am delighted to continue with Ashadu, an artist whose work has marked both key moments in her own creative development and in the history of the Fondazione. In 2022, Ashadu was among the artists invited to *Penumbra*, the group exhibition that introduced the Fondazione to an international audience at the Venice Biennale. I still remember the emotion of unveiling *Plateau*, the two-channel video installation we commissioned and produced for that occasion. Just two years later, we returned to Venice together, when the Fondazione produced *Machine Boys*, the work that earned Ashadu the Silver Lion for a Promising Young Participant at the 60th International Art Exhibition of the Venice Biennale. The joyful atmosphere of the awards ceremony, and Ashadu's moving words as she accepted the prize, remain etched in my memory.

Supporting artists throughout their creative journeys is a cornerstone of the Fondazione's mission, and I was thrilled to have the opportunity to co-commission and produce *MUSCLE*, the video work at the heart of *Tendered*. This powerful piece exemplifies Ashadu's gift for capturing ordinary aspects of daily life in her native Nigeria and transforming them into profound reflections on existential, social and political realities that resonate deeply with our times.

I am deeply grateful to Ashadu for creating the exhibition that inspired this publication, and for offering us such compelling, critical and imaginative portrayals of strength and vulnerability, persistence and survival.

MUSCLE was commissioned and produced by Fondazione In Between Art Film together with Camden Art Centre in London and the Renaissance Society at the University of Chicago. I would like to thank Martin Clark and Myriam Ben Salah, the respective directors of these institutions, for fostering the dialogue that made this collaboration possible. I conceived the Fondazione as a dynamic and fluid platform, much like the medium of moving images itself, and it is essential for us to build meaningful cultural and creative relationships with institutions such as these, whose distinguished histories continue to embrace the diversity of contemporary artistic languages.

As with every exhibition and the publication that accompanies it, a project like this is the result of many individuals whose dedication and expertise come together in service of a shared vision. I wish to thank the teams at Camden Art Centre and the Renaissance Society for creating the conditions that allow such dialogue to flourish.

Karimah Ashadu's work carries both clarity of vision and courage of intent – qualities we need now more than ever. I hope this exhibition, and this book, will offer a space to come together, to reflect and to engage with those very qualities.

Beatrice Bulgari, President
Fondazione In Between Art Film

DIRECTORS' FOREWORD

Tendered is published on the occasion of Karimah Ashadu's first solo exhibitions in London and Chicago, marking an important moment of recognition for a young artist and filmmaker of exceptional talent. Ashadu grew up between the United Kingdom and Nigeria, and she situates both herself and her work within a constant negotiation of proximity and distance. Engaging with contemporary manifestations of Nigerian history borne by its people and landscapes, her singular artistic vision often centres on the struggles and stories of men as they go about life and work. Foregrounding ideas of resilience and value – key themes in Nigeria's history – Ashadu's nuanced and intimate portraits, whether of individuals or communities, probe multifaceted reflections on the cultural context of West Africa, a context that is inextricably shaped by conditions of economic independence and exploitation in the aftermath of British colonial rule.

This exhibition has two iterations, first at Camden Art Centre, London, in October 2025, followed by the Renaissance Society, Chicago, in autumn 2026. Both exhibitions will include Ashadu's most recent work, *MUSCLE* (2025), co-commissioned and produced by the two institutions with Fondazione In Between Art Film. This intimate portrait of bodybuilders, shot in the heart of Lagos's slums, features a community of men striving to attain a hypermasculine ideal, and continues the artist's research into issues of socioeconomic independence and patriarchy within the context of West African culture and society.

Ashadu's first artistic medium was painting, and that sensibility carries through to the visual language of her films, combining a strong sense of colour, composition and form, which extends into the design of the viewing environment. The exhibitions also showcase a series of sculptures, conceived especially for *MUSCLE* that reference the objects and environments within. Together with a careful selection of previous films, the exhibitions take visitors on a journey through the range of Ashadu's practice, from the intimate to the expansive, featuring works that form a cinematic narrative of bodies and land – an undulating scenario of urban subcultures, quotidian labour and our relationship to nature.

The exhibition's title carries a quiet complexity. 'Tendered' suggests economic exchange, as something formally offered at a price. It speaks to systems of value – Black value, African value, diasporic value, labour value – and how these are measured and by whom. Such central questions run throughout Ashadu's practice. But they might also speak to the inherited hierarchies that implicate Nigeria, West Africa and the Global South in systems that are shaped by colonial histories and exploitative structures while still playing out in how bodies, borders and resources are treated today. At the same time, 'to tend' alludes to care and cultivation, as well as the body itself as a site of tenderness – something vulnerable, fragile and a place of intimacy and relationships with others. This duality holds within it complementary qualities, including the emotional and the transactional, the intimate and the systemic. It speaks to resistance, and to the care, strength and dignity that persist despite systems that try to devalue all these human qualities. In the artist's own words, "It positions the viewer, and perhaps even the subject, in consideration of their role within these negotiations of worth."

This is the first reference monograph on Ashadu's practice, and it will be a rich resource for readers who hope to gain an understanding of the breadth of her work to date, spanning more than a decade from *Lagos Island*, made in 2012, through to *MUSCLE*, made in 2025. It features contributions from the artist herself; Myriam Ben Salah, executive director and chief curator at the Renaissance Society, Chicago; Leonardo Bigazzi, curator at Fondazione In Between Art Film; Gina Buenfeld-Murley, curator at Camden Art Centre, London; Martin Clark, director of Camden Art Centre; Dr. Clive Chijioke Nwonka, associate professor of film, culture and society at University College London; Alessandro Rabottini, artistic director of Fondazione In Between Art Film; Bettina Steinbrügge, director of Mudam Luxembourg; and Arese Uwuoruya, assistant curator at Camden Art Centre. We are also enormously grateful to Bianca Stoppani, editor at Fondazione In Between Art Film, for all of their work on this publication.

Tendered is curated by Alessandro Rabottini and Leonardo Bigazzi. Their commitment has been abundantly evident since the inception of this project, from the selection of works, to supporting the new commission, to conceptualising the exhibition design at each venue, to the vision for this book. In each and every aspect, they have demonstrated the deepest concern and understanding of what is at stake in Ashadu's practice. At Camden Art Centre, the exhibition is curated in dialogue with Martin Clark and Gina Buenfeld-Murley. The iteration at the Renaissance Society is curated with Myriam Ben Salah and Karsten Lund and will see a different configuration of the works in response to that space.

Tendered would not have been possible without the immense generosity of Fondazione In Between Art Film. Founded in Rome in October 2019, its mission is the promotion of a culture of moving images and the support of international artists, institutions and research centres that explore dialogues between the disciplines of film, video, performance and installation. Under the guidance of its founder and president, Beatrice Bulgari, Fondazione In Between Art Film aims to contribute to international artistic debates by furthering the role and potential of moving images in our time. *Tendered* is the second of its *Unison* projects, and we are honoured to be part of this ongoing programme.

Additionally, the exhibition at Camden Art Centre is supported by the Karimah Ashadu Exhibition Circle, supporters of Ashadu's work and practice, as well as the Artists' Circle, patrons of the gallery who support a selected exhibition each year. We would like to thank both groups of committed and passionate advocates for their enthusiasm around Camden's core vision of platforming and commissioning exciting new talent.

We would also like to thank Sadie Coles, together with Laura Lord and Connor Linskey, and Sadie Coles HQ, for their support of the exhibition in London.

At the Renaissance Society, all publications are made possible by The Mansueto Foundation Publications Program.

Most importantly, we would like to extend our deepest gratitude to Karimah Ashadu for her dedication to *Tendered*, and her courageous determination to journey into physical and thematic *terra incognita*, to reveal worlds and personal stories with grace and respect. It has been a privilege to be part of this vital work and to bring it to our audiences in London and Chicago.

Martin Clark, Director
Camden Art Centre

Myriam Ben Salah, Executive
Director and Chief Curator
The Renaissance Society at
the University of Chicago

CONTENTS

Editors' Note

Bianca Stoppani with Alessandro Rabottini and Leonardo Bigazzi

This reference monograph reviews, for the first time, Karimah Ashadu's career to date. Its detailed overview of her filmic practice is both illustrative and interpretive, with newly commissioned written contributions and an extended conversation with the artist.

Conceived to highlight the fact that form and content are inextricable in Ashadu's production, the publication is paced through images and texts in a manner that echoes the artist's use of silence and sound to produce rhythm in her films. It puts particular emphasis on the films' composition and framing aspects through visual essays authored by Ashadu, which take the reader on a time travel across her work, highlighting some of its recurring formal concerns – namely colour, the body (whether human, animal or machinic), gazes that break the fourth wall, the movement of goods, collectivity and landscape, from the industrial areas of Hamburg to the busy streets of Lagos.

A fully illustrated section at the centre of the book includes documentation of Ashadu's most significant works realised between 2012 and 2025. It stands as the most comprehensive record of her production to date, and not only visually brings forward the vibrancy of each film, but also offers a key reference for further study. To this end, it includes original synopses carefully penned by Arese Uwuoruya (assistant curator at Camden Art Centre, London) and the films' production credits.

In his role as co-curator of the exhibition *Tendered*, Alessandro Rabottini authored 'Saturated Proximity: Rhythm, Porosity and Distance in the Films of Karimah Ashadu', an essay that expands upon the curatorial concept while suggesting poetic and spatial relationships between Ashadu's works and their display.

A far-reaching conversation between the artist, Myriam Ben Salah (executive director and chief curator of the Renaissance Society at the

University of Chicago), Martin Clark (director of Camden Art Centre, London) and Gina Buenfeld-Murley (curator at Camden Art Centre), moderated by Leonardo Bigazzi (co-curator of the exhibition), discusses key points in Ashadu's practice, such as the entanglements between socio-economic precarity and self-determination, masculinity and performance, labour and desire.

Bettina Steinbrügge (director of Mudam Luxembourg) composes the essay 'Reclaiming the Image from a History of Extraction', where she passionately conjures Ashadu's themes and cinematography choices, ultimately observing that the work is "a profoundly social act" in which the camera "listens, lingers and reveals, becoming an engaging, and engaged, witness" of "marginalised voices and informal economies."

'Muscle Memory: The Black Atlanticist Form of *MUSCLE*', written by Dr. Clive Chijioke Nwonka (associate professor in film, culture and society at University College London), proposes a novel reading of Ashadu's filmmaking, and in particular her newly commissioned film *MUSCLE*, through Paul Gilroy's concept of the Black Atlantic: that the hypermasculinity sought and performed by the film's protagonists bears the weight of the aftermath of colonialism, transatlantic slavery and the white racial imaginary.

Throughout the book, images are displayed in dynamic grids, proposing zooms in and out from the formal aspects of the artist's practice, while words are meant to be moments of dwelling and repose into what lies both within and beyond the frame. Our heartfelt appreciation goes to Lorenzo Mason Studio (Michele Bellinaso, Lorenzo Mason and Simone Spinazzè) for the ongoing, cross-pollinating dialogue that made such a layered layout possible, and to Agnese Cantelmi of Mousse Publishing for her editorial support throughout the production process.

We are thankful to the authors who contributed to this volume with such purpose and dedication, and to the teams at Karimah Ashadu's studio, Camden Art Centre, the Renaissance Society and Sadie Coles HQ, who have sustained us from the beginning in the book's realisation.

Last but not the least, our deepest gratitude goes to Karimah Ashadu, who has entrusted us with the task of imagining, together, such an important agent for her career to come.

Colours
Karimah Ashadu

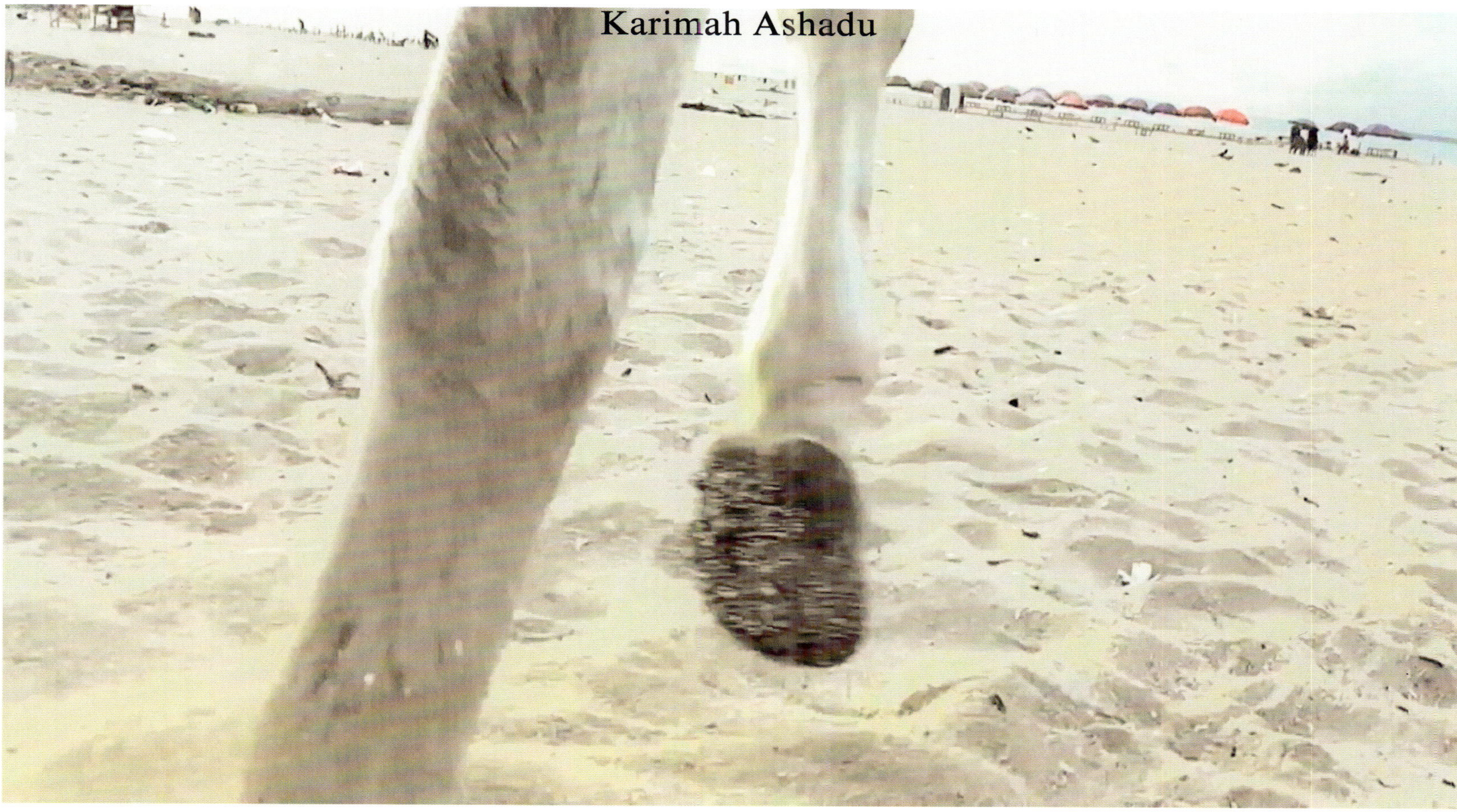

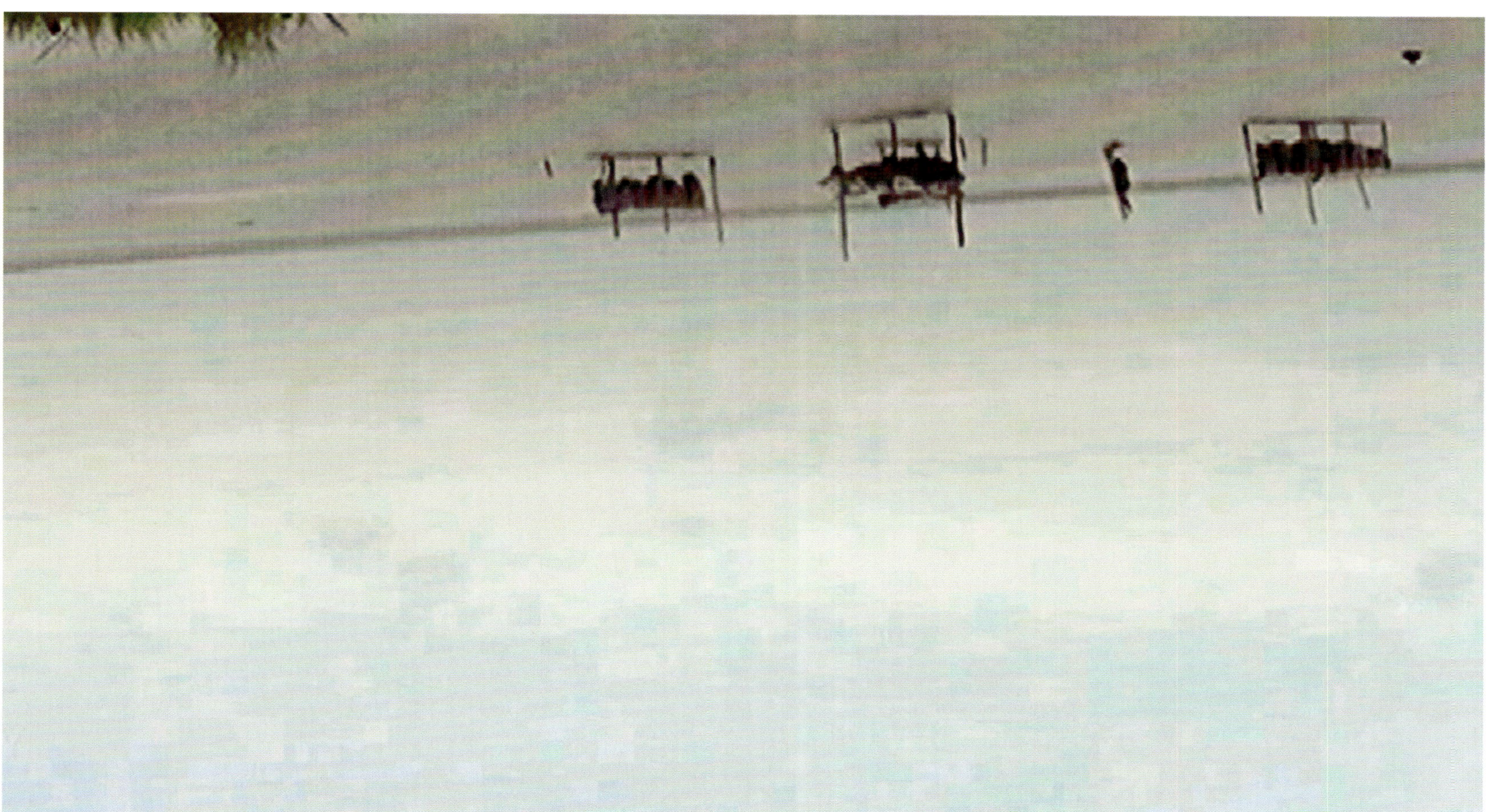

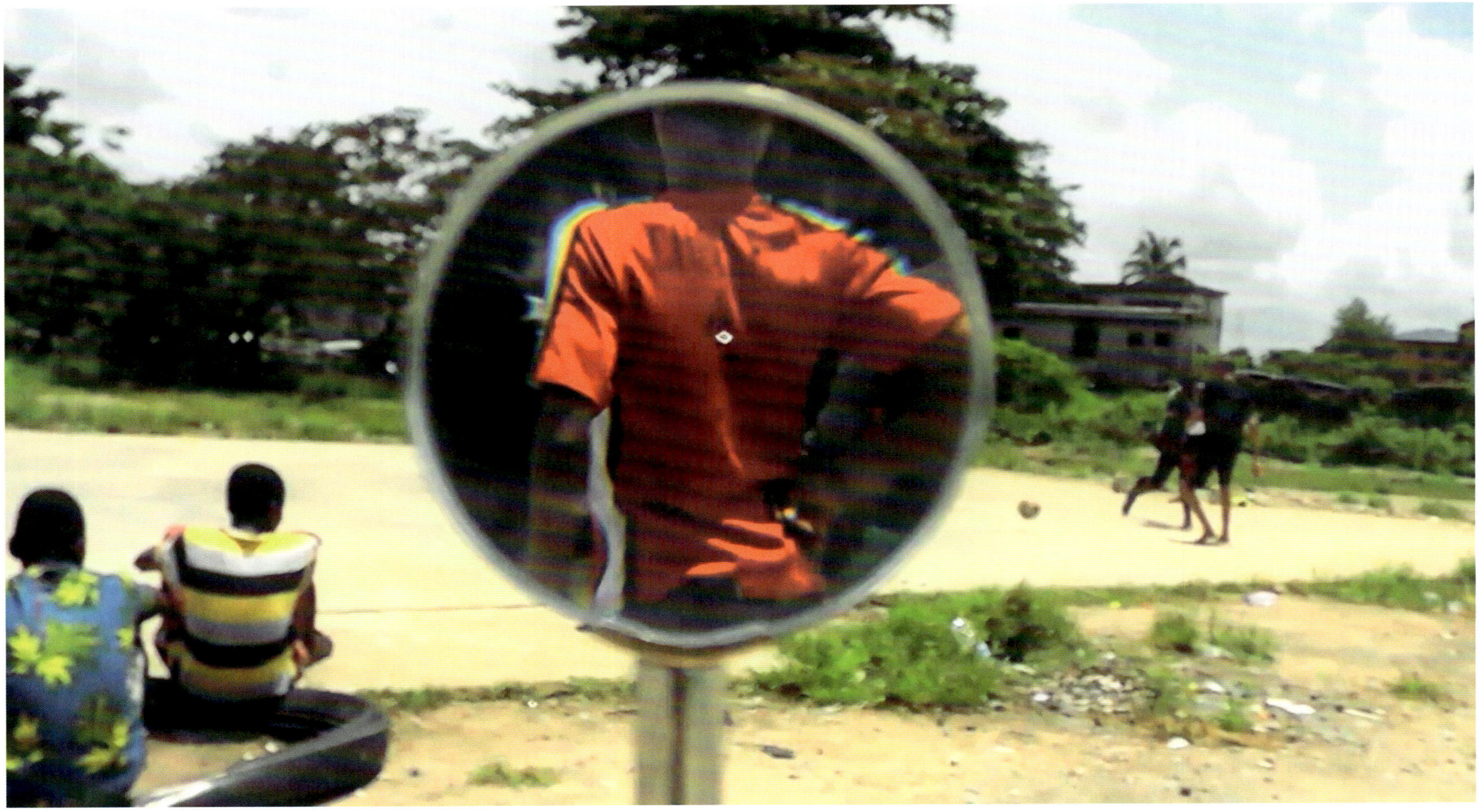

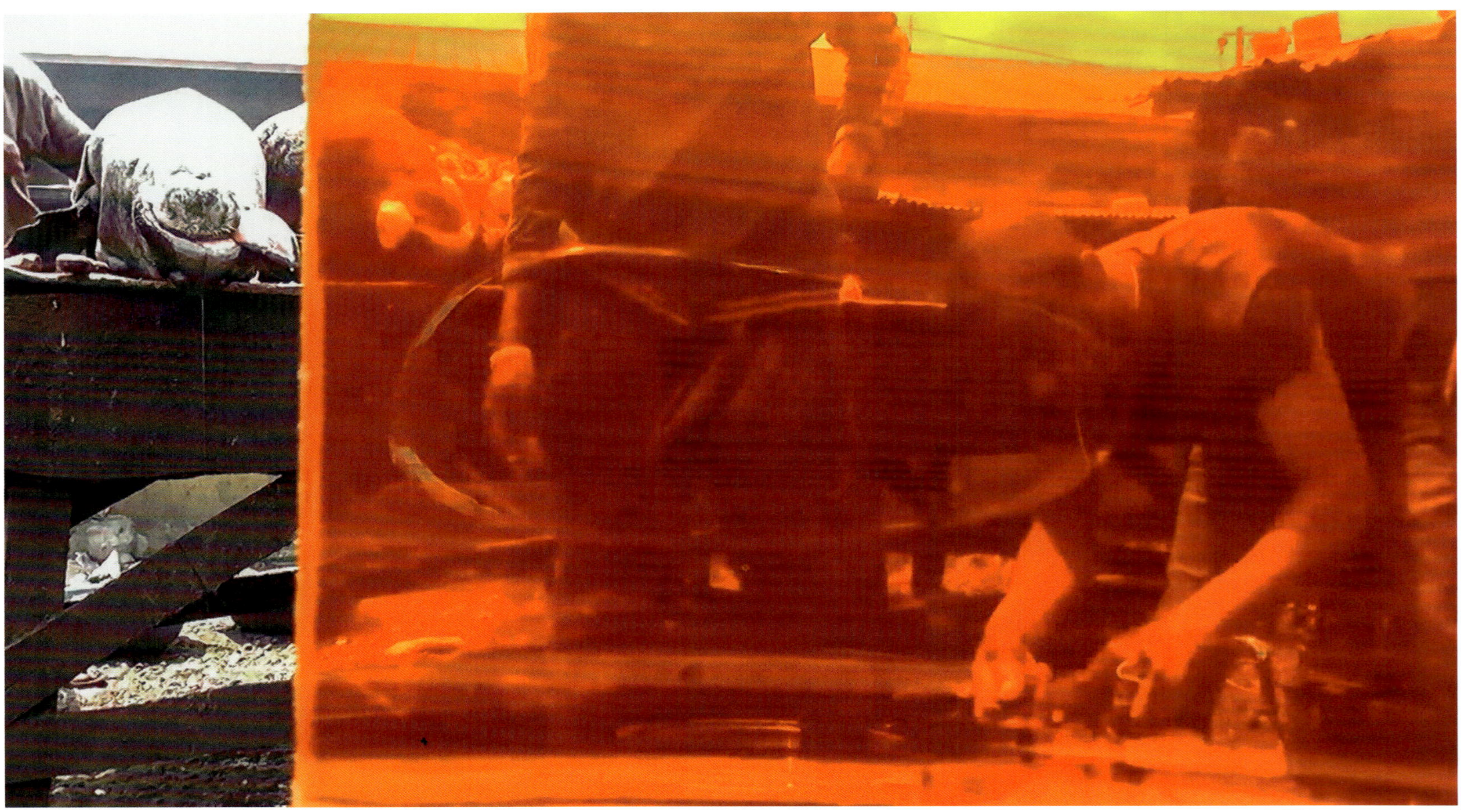

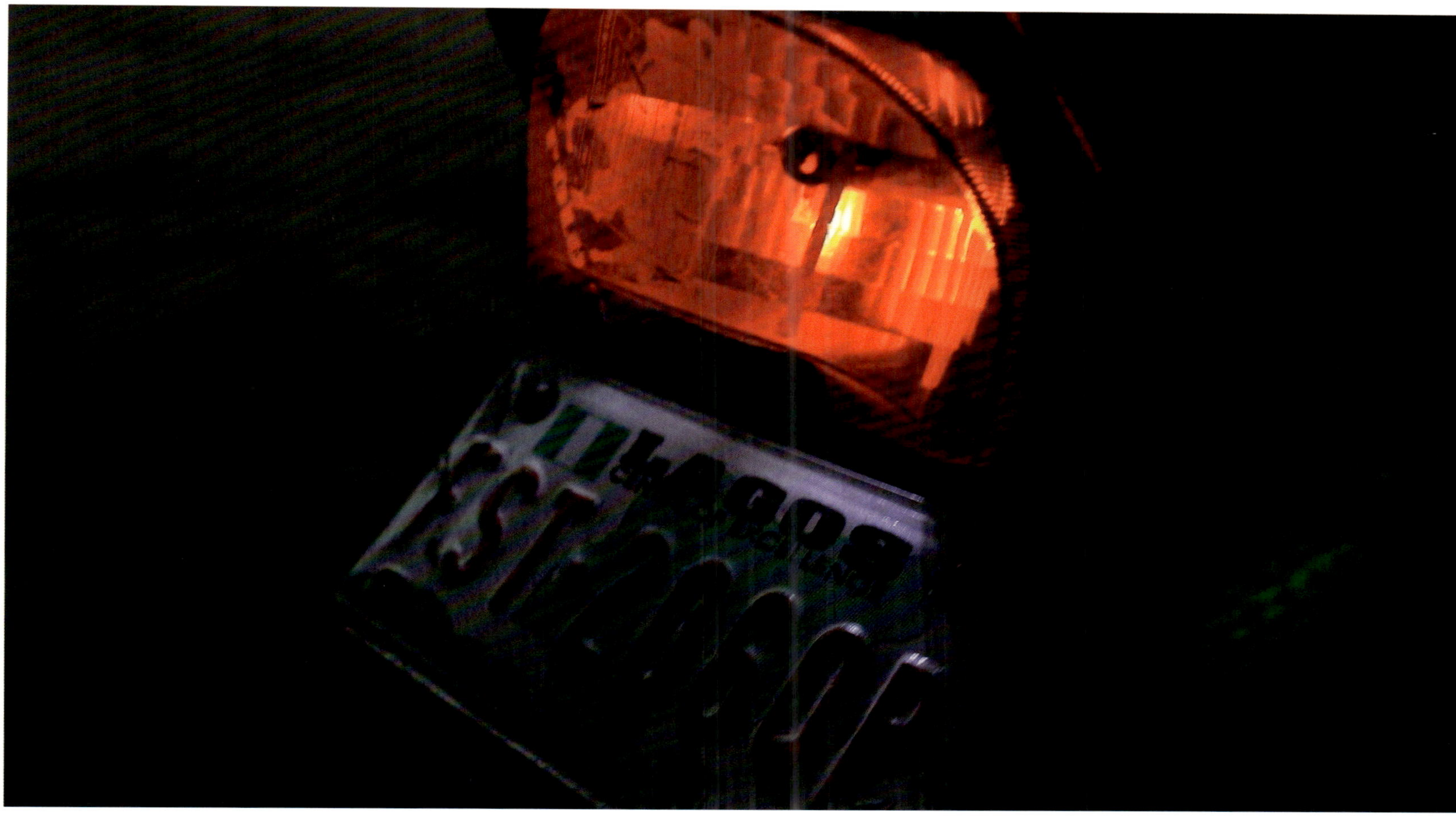

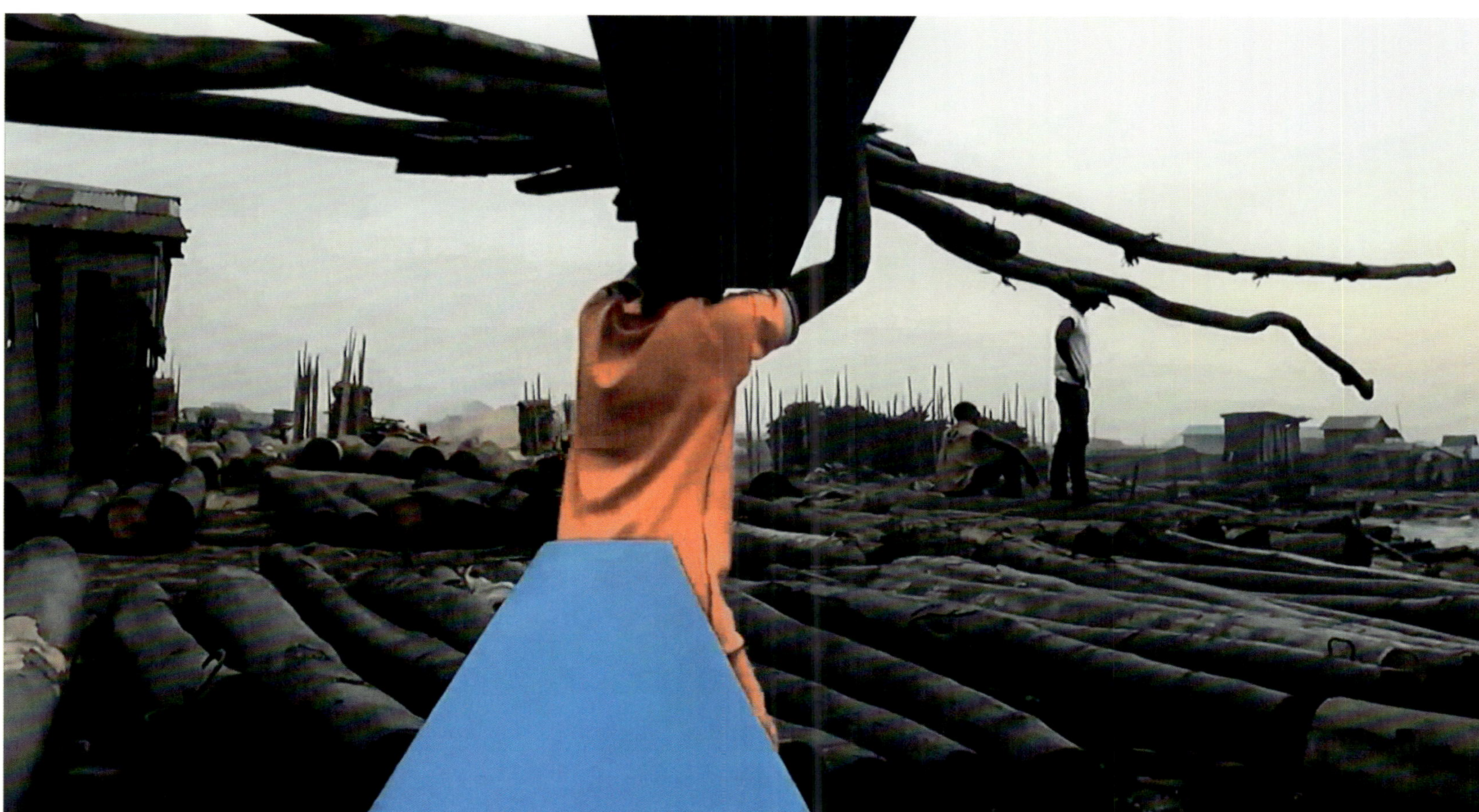

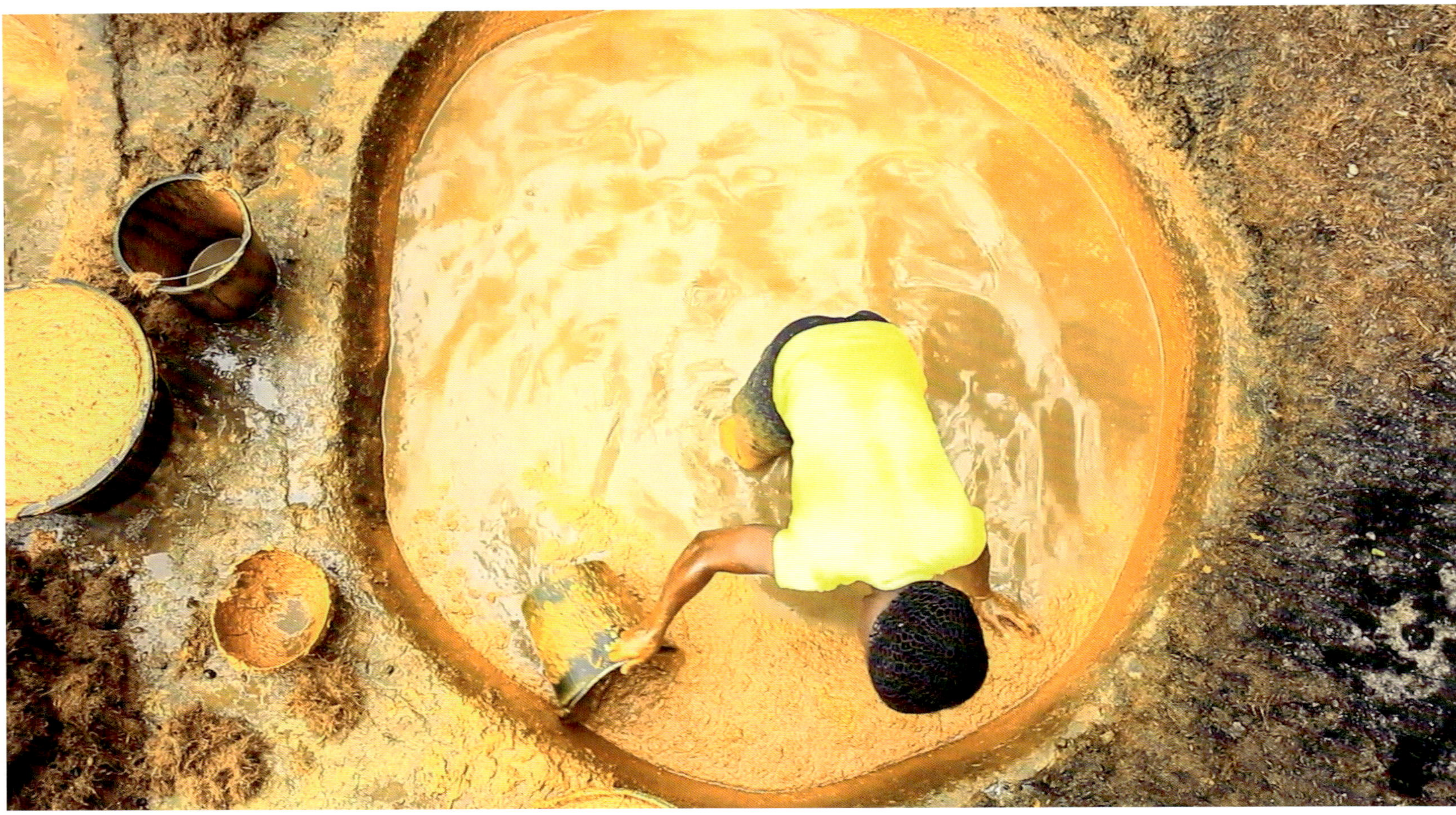

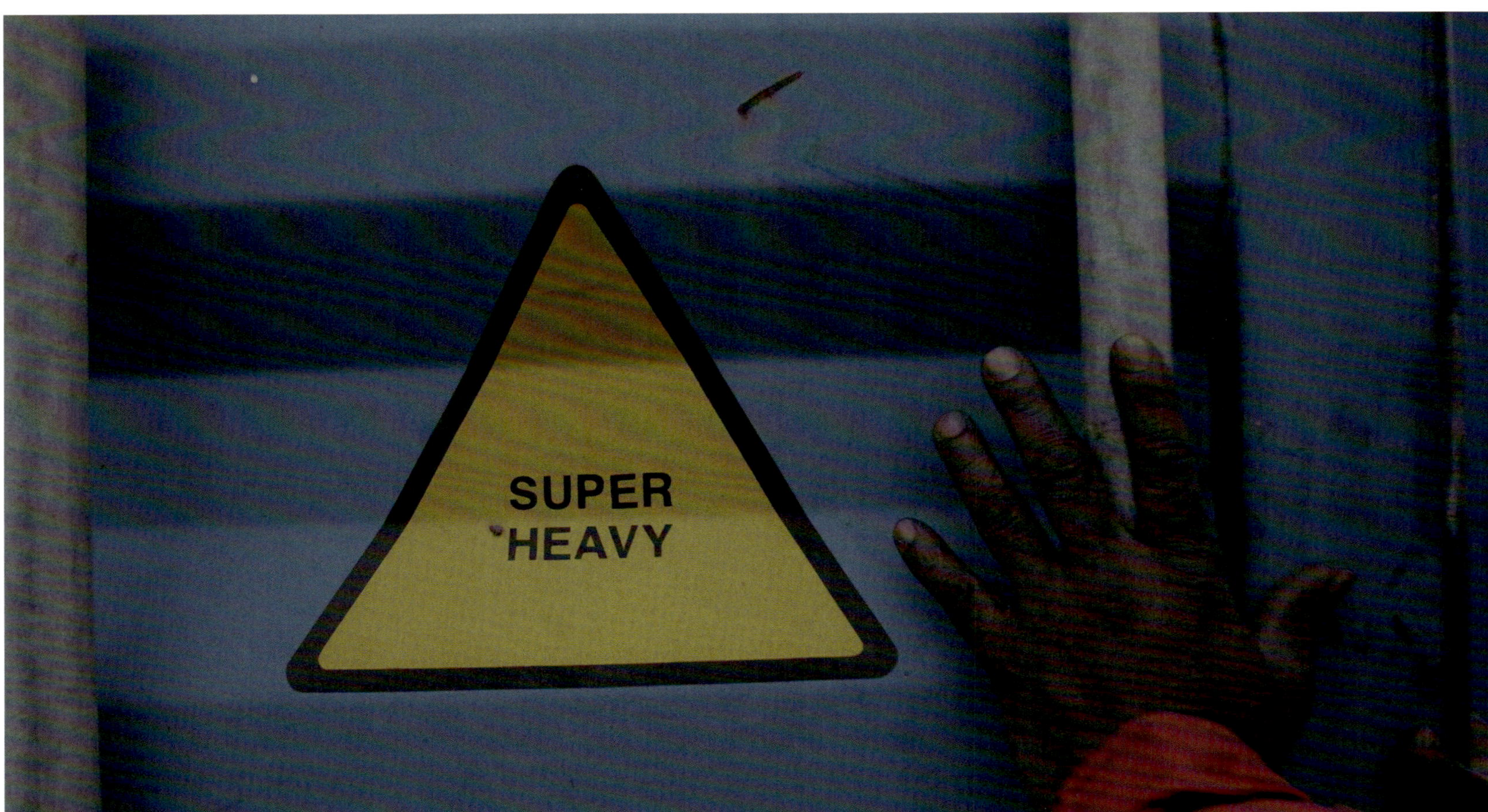
SUPER
HEAVY

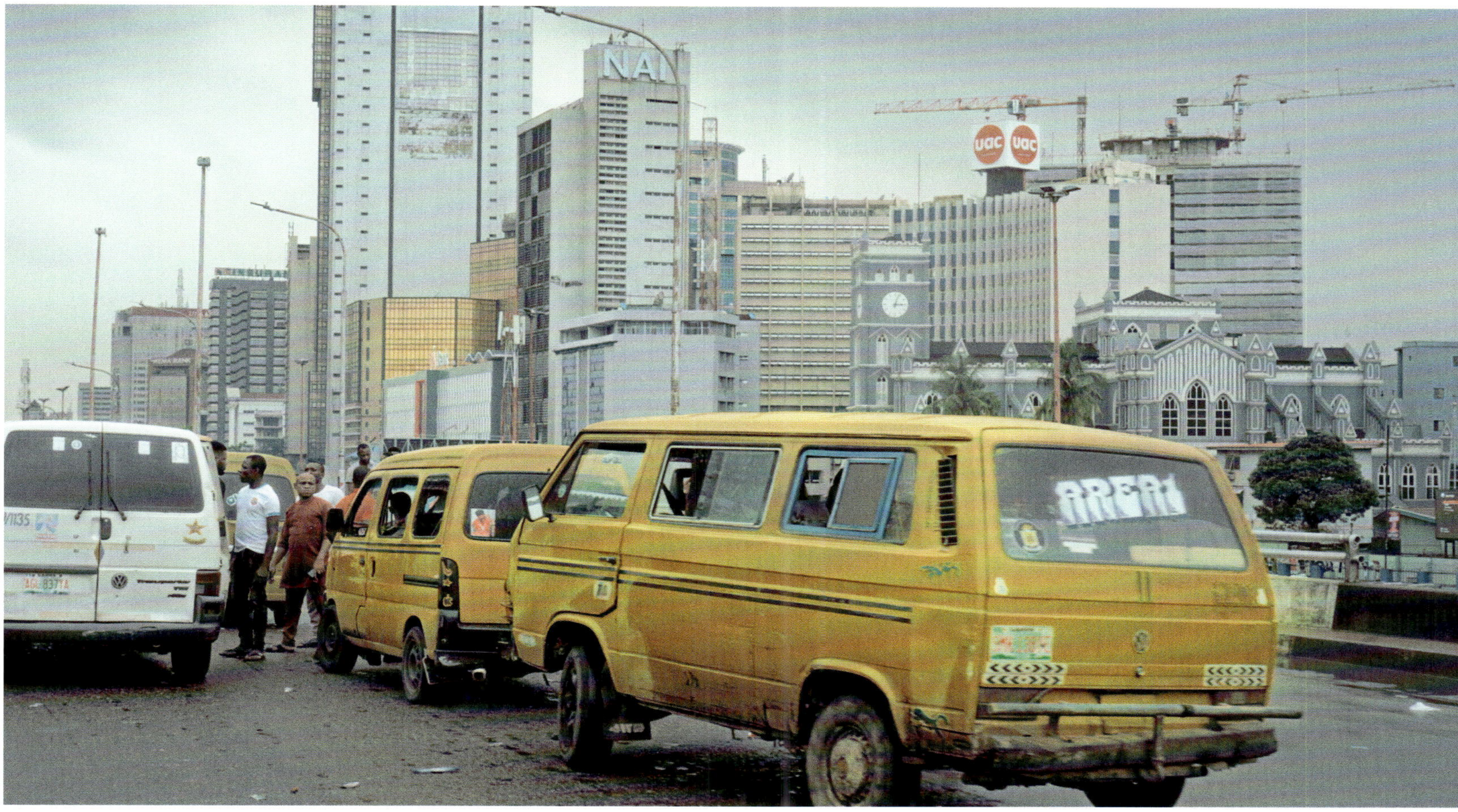
NAI
uac
uac
AREA1

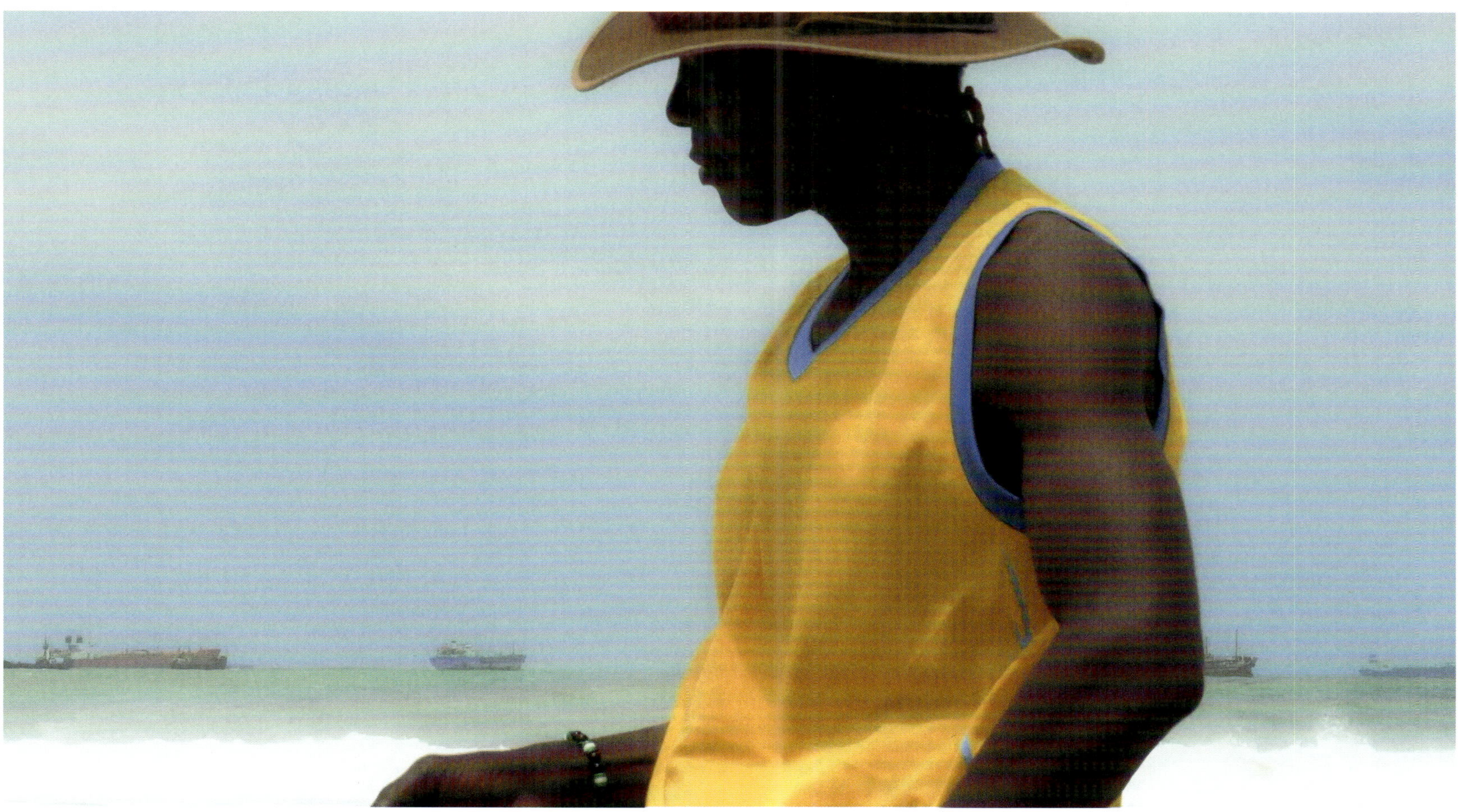

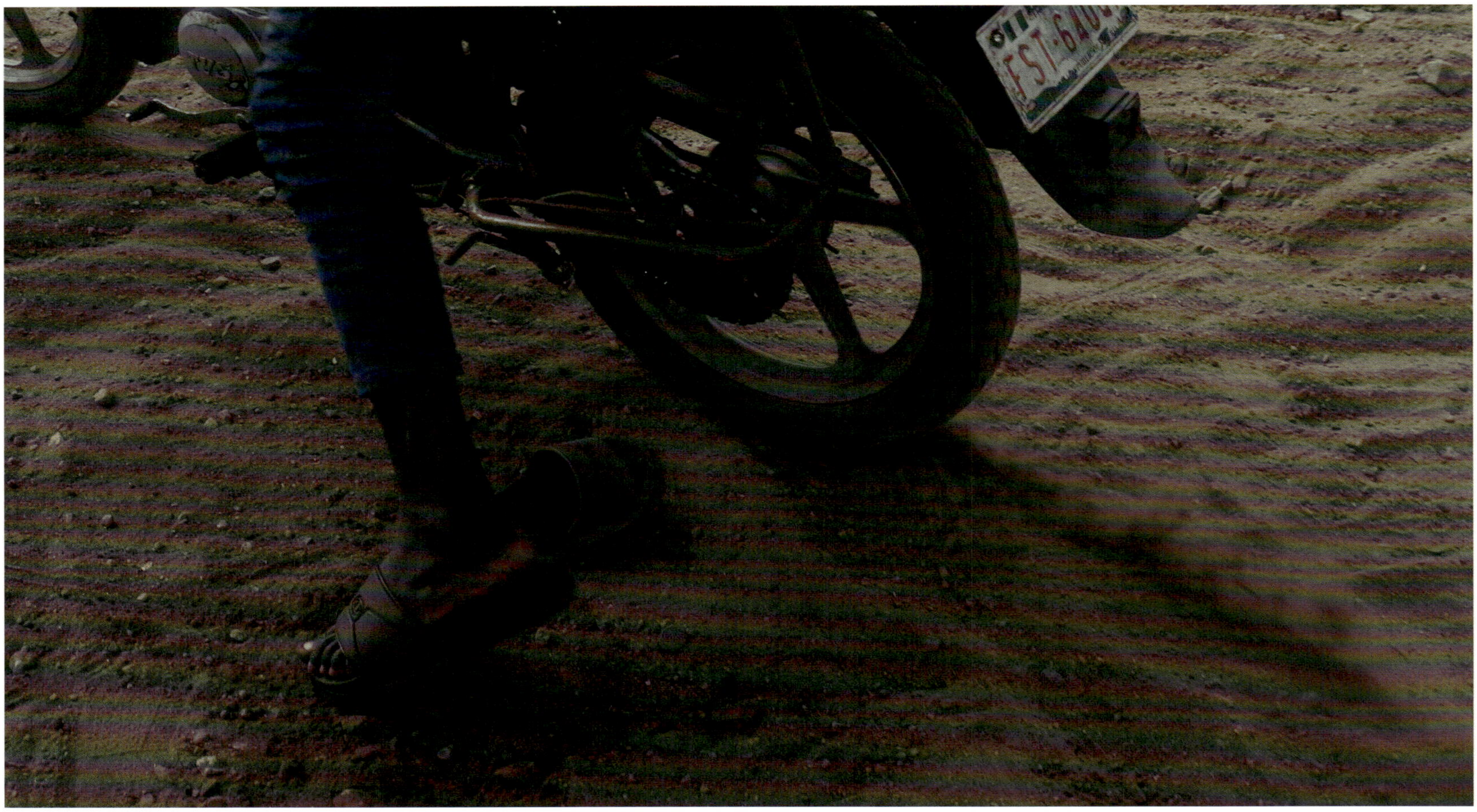

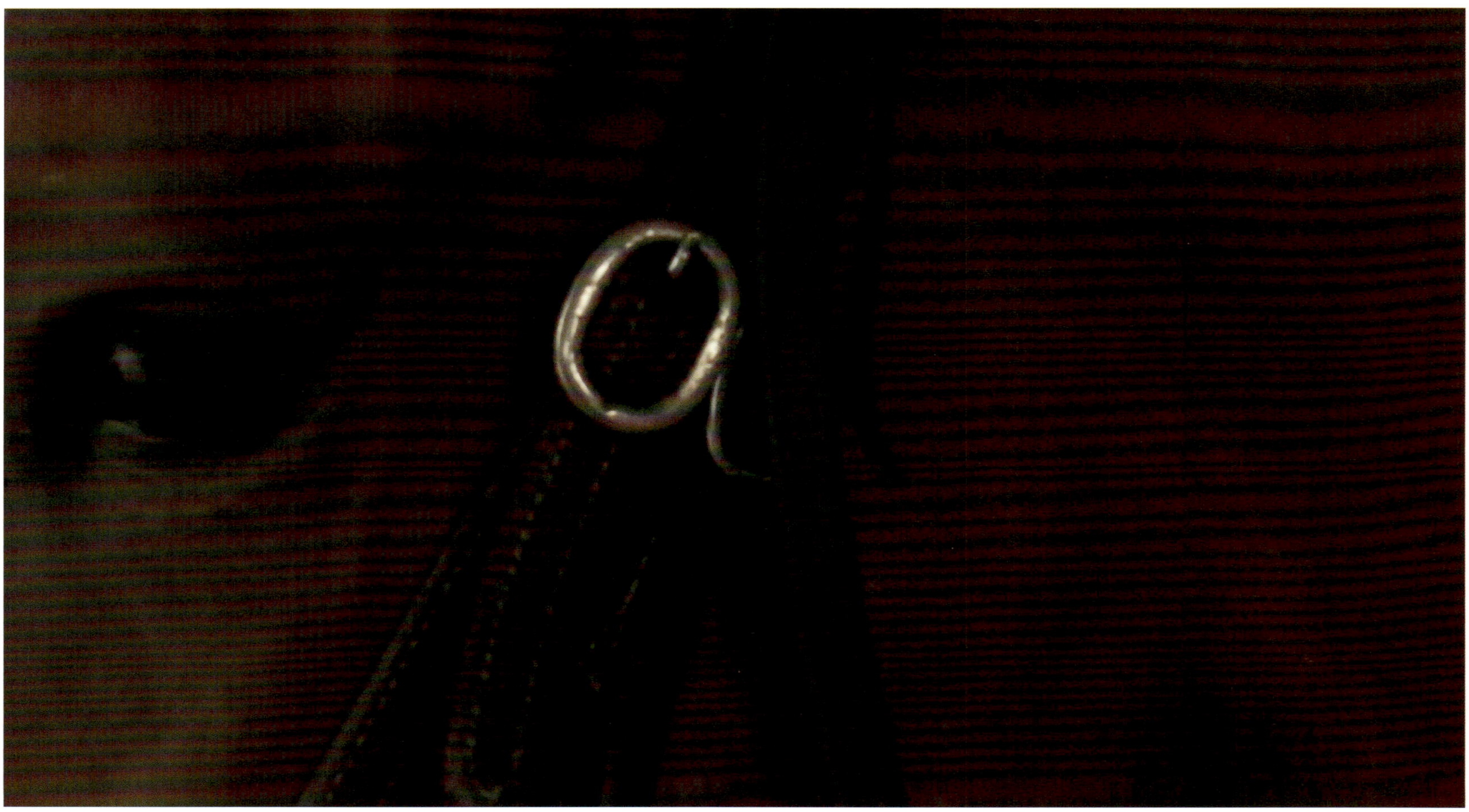

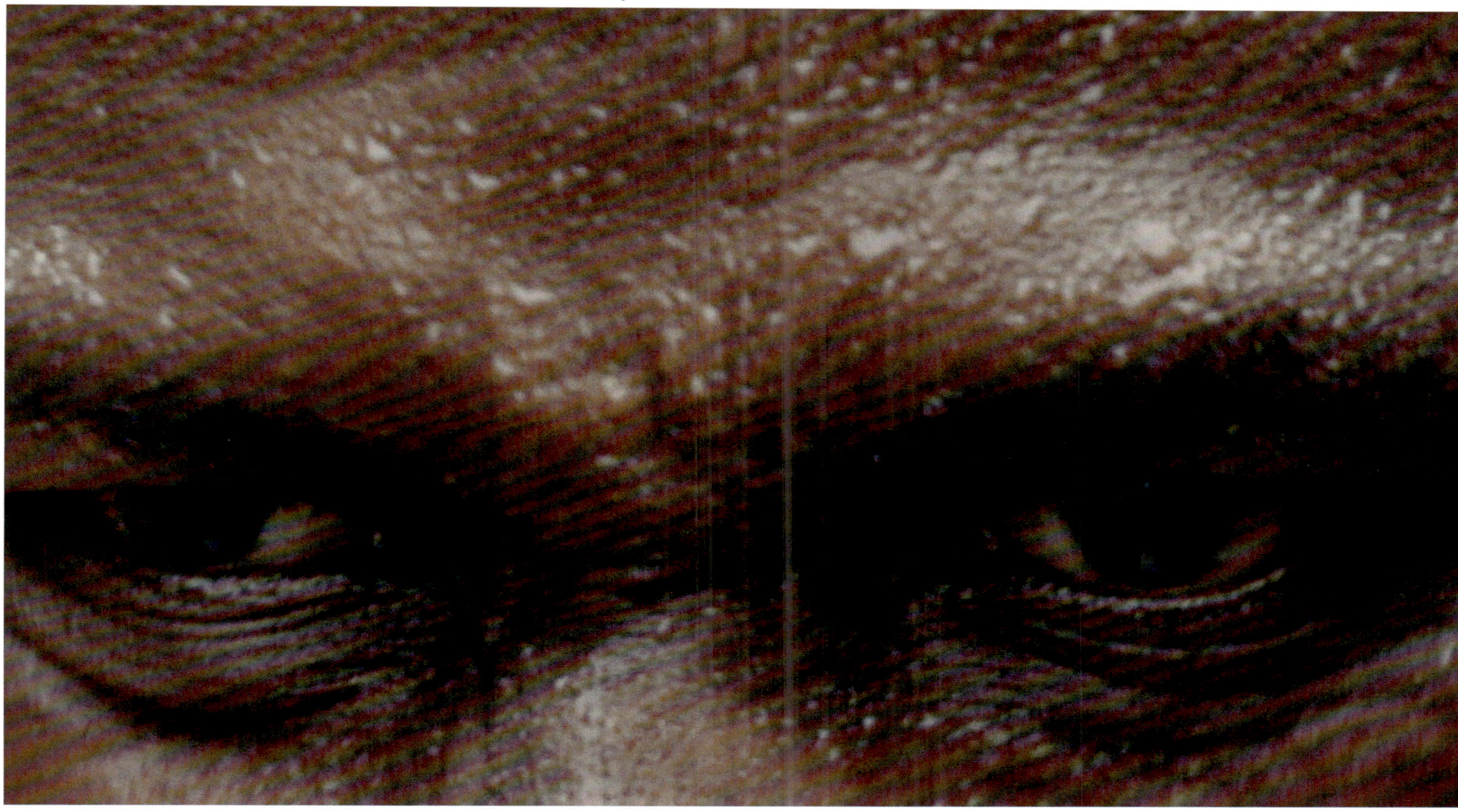

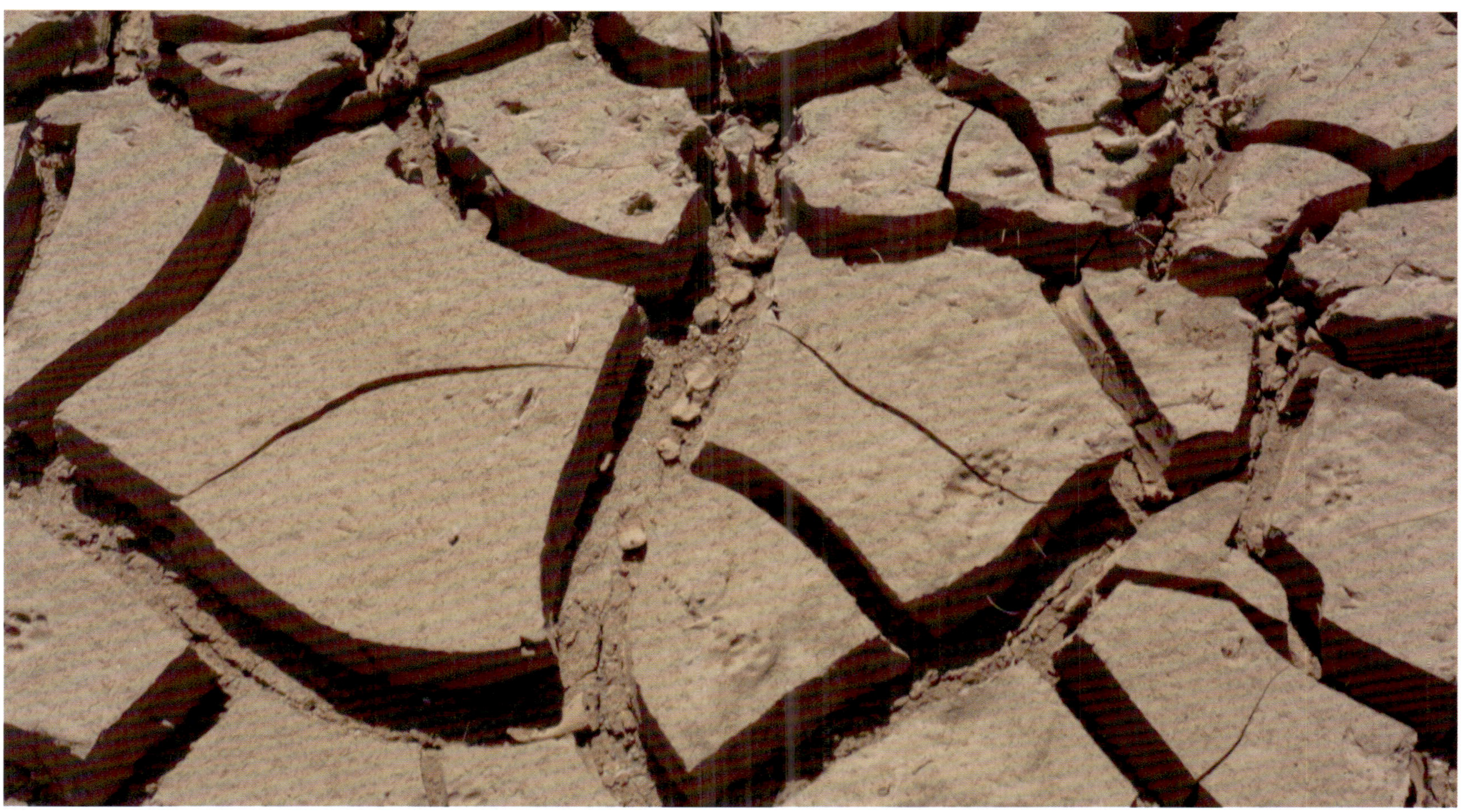

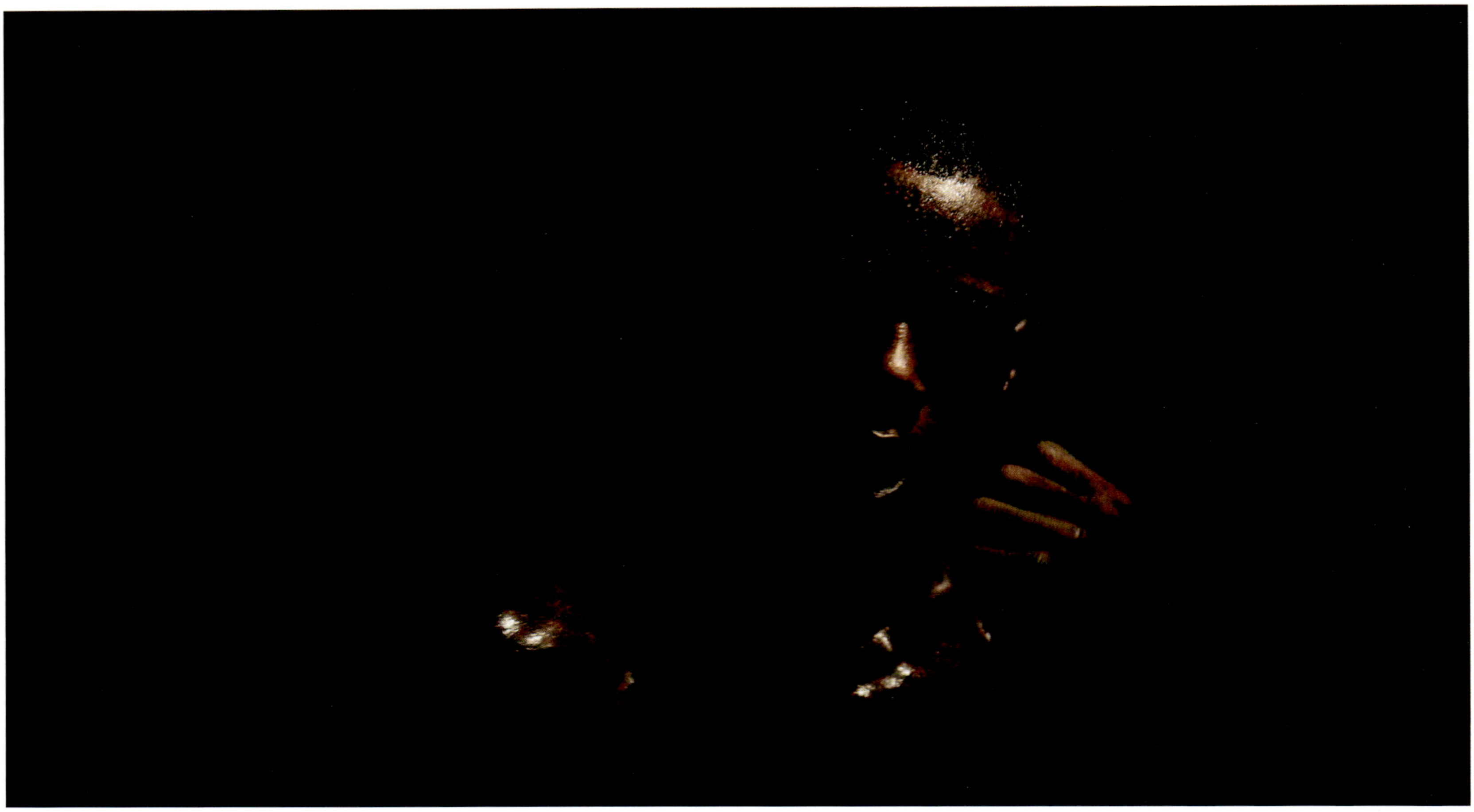

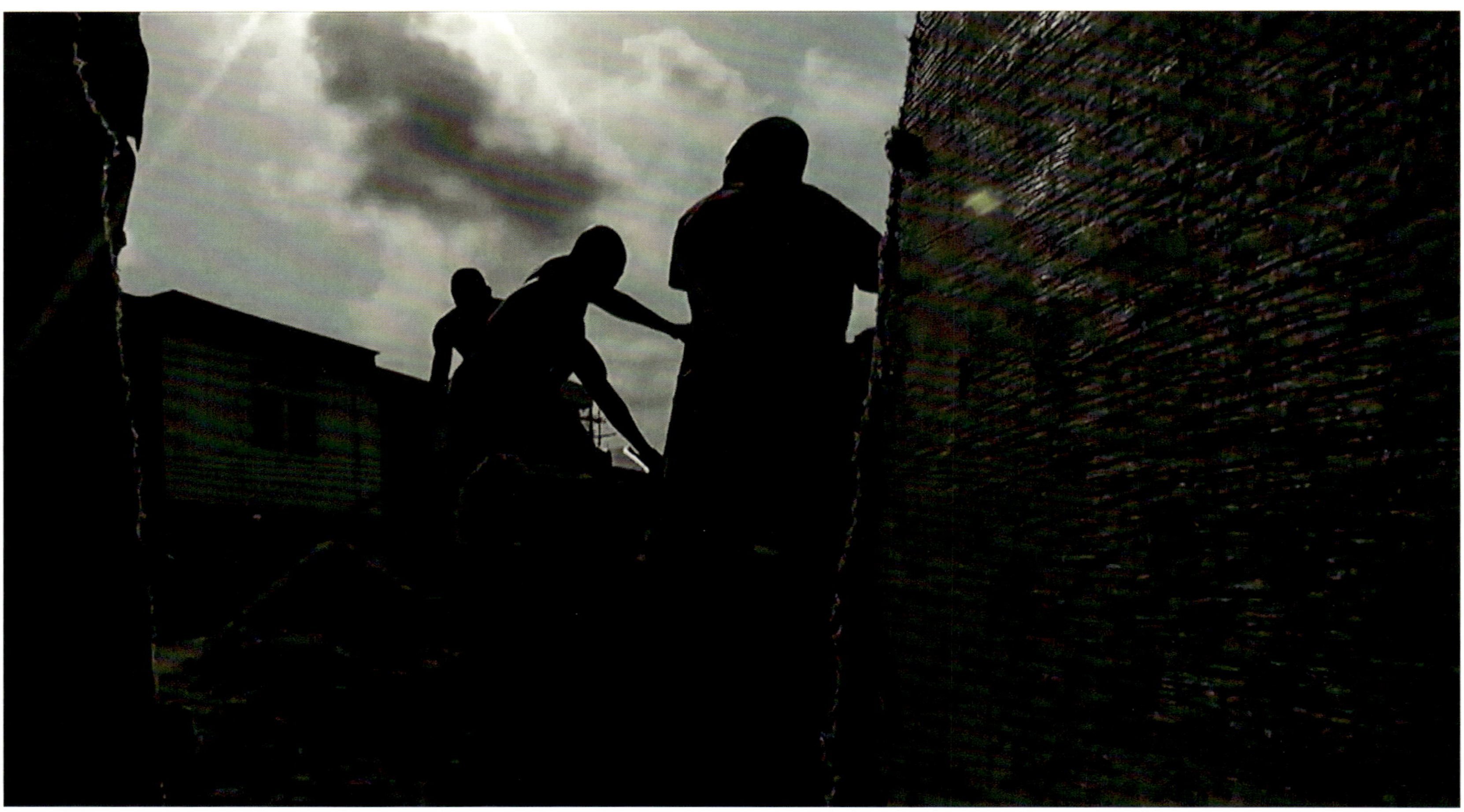

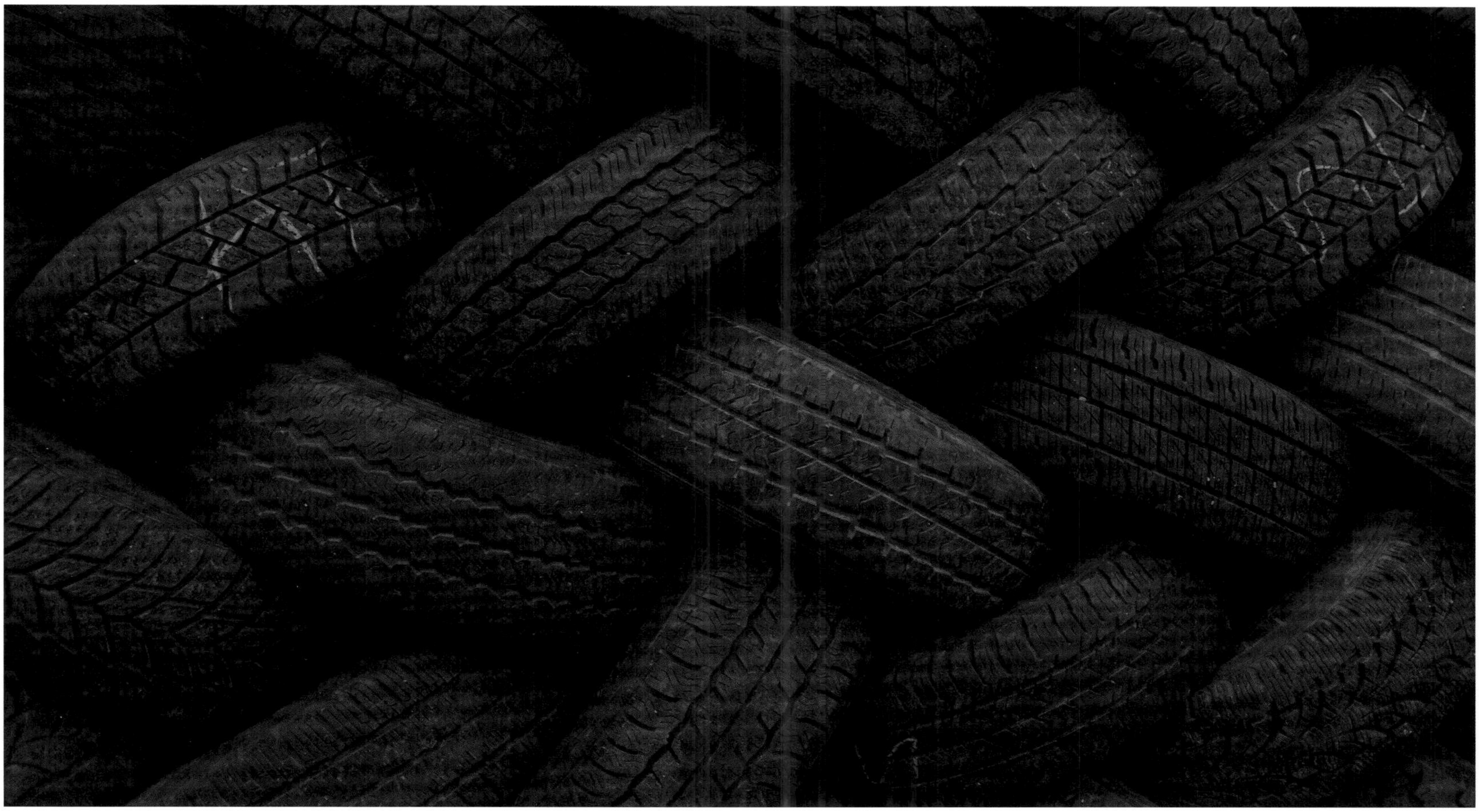

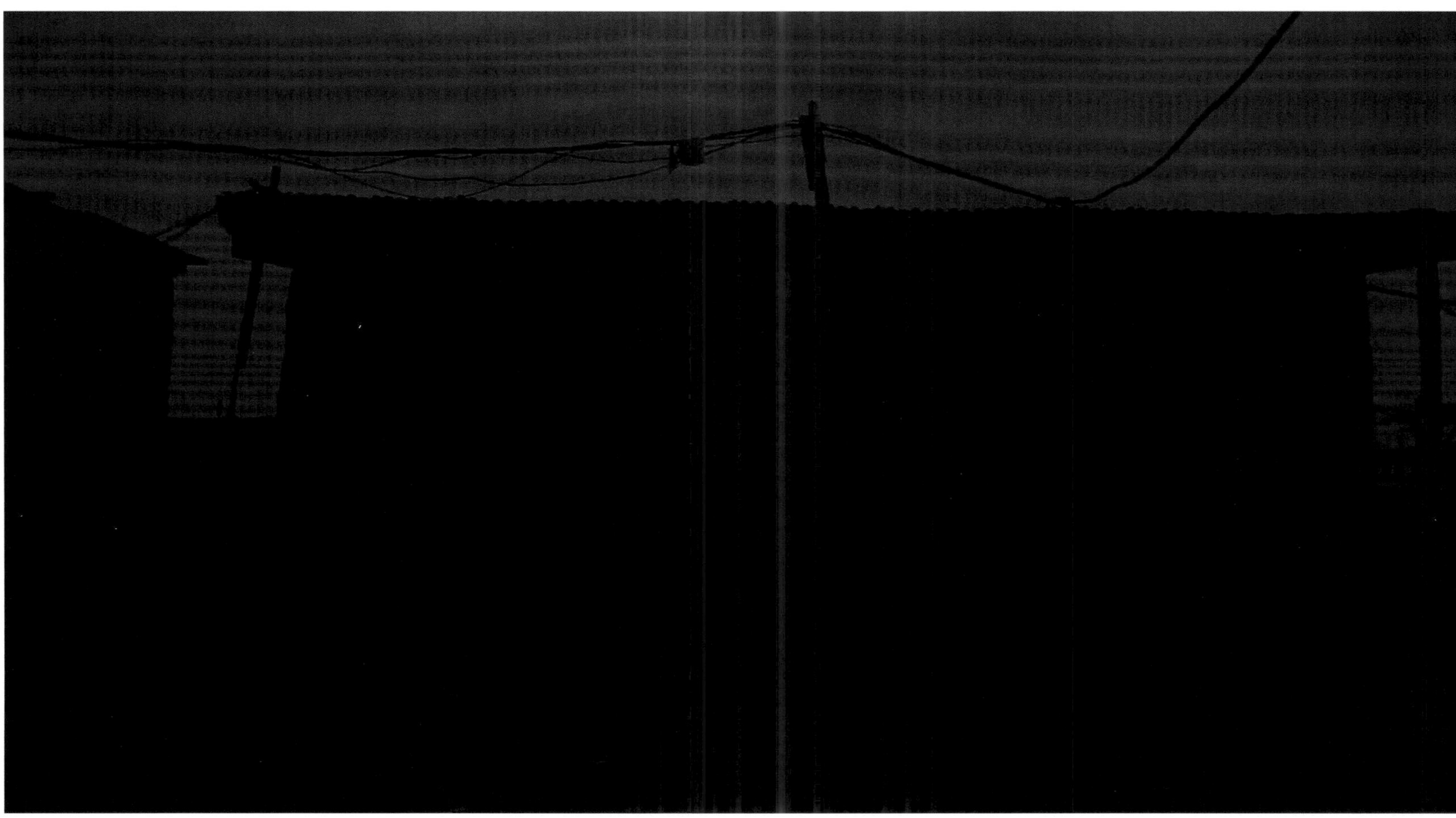

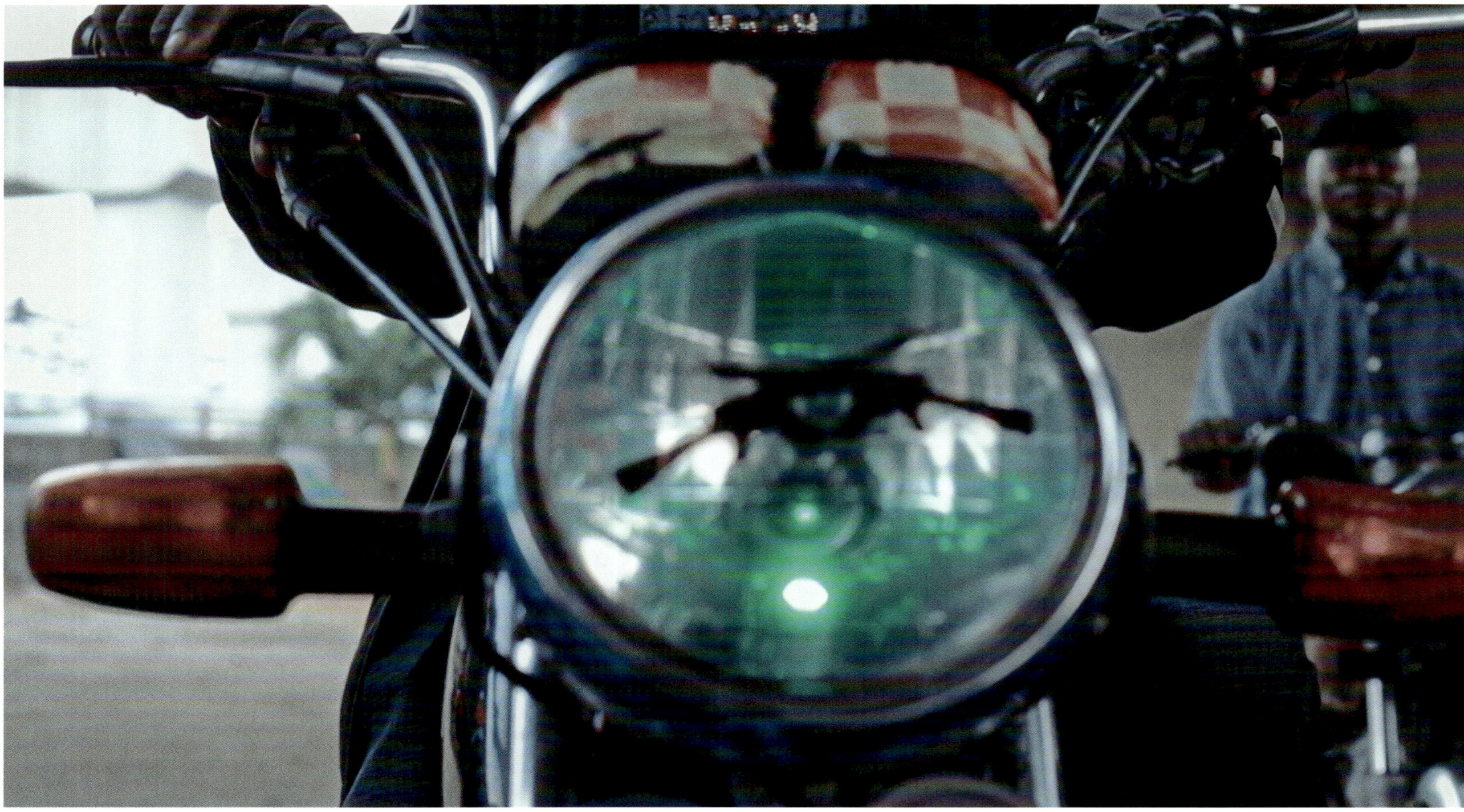

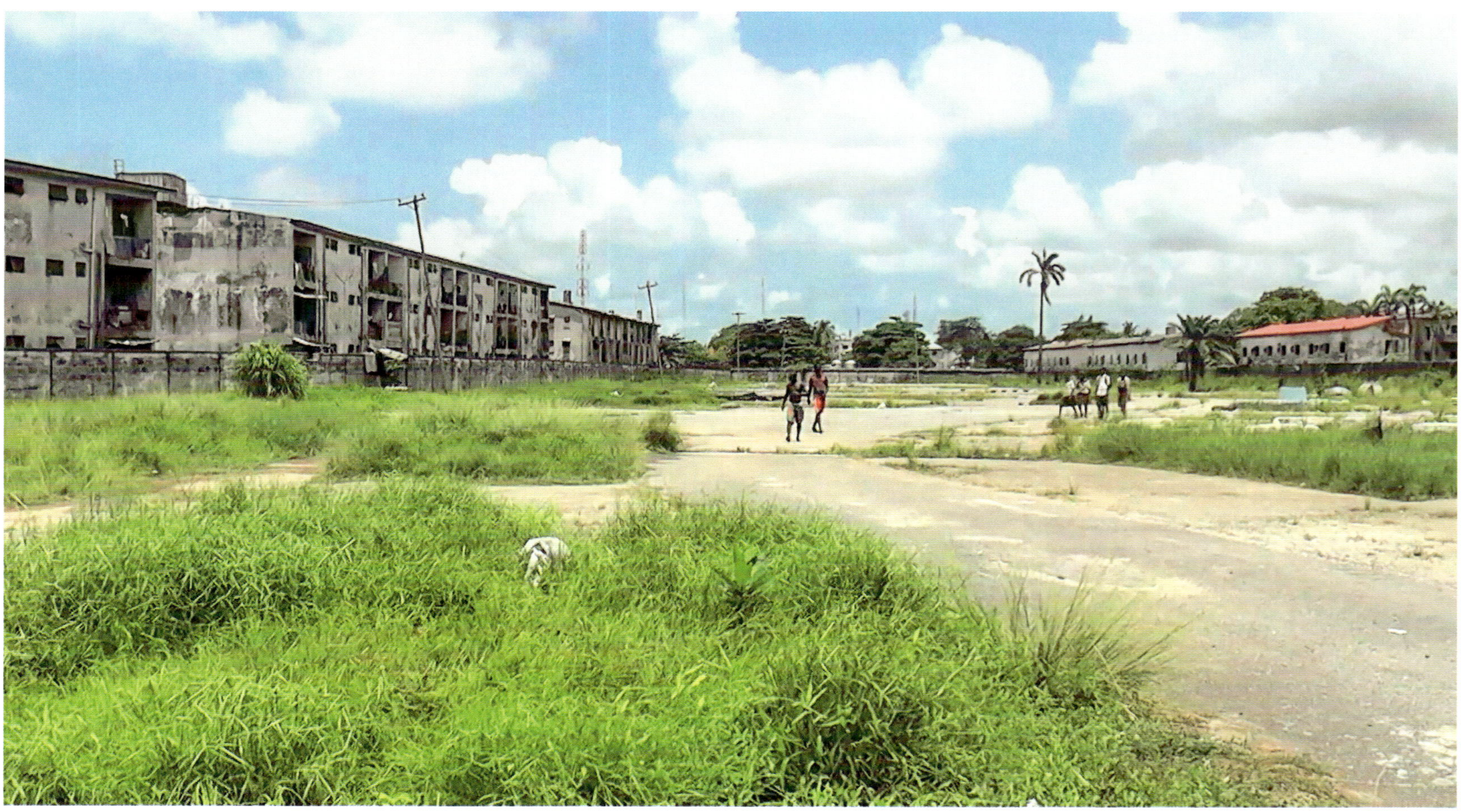

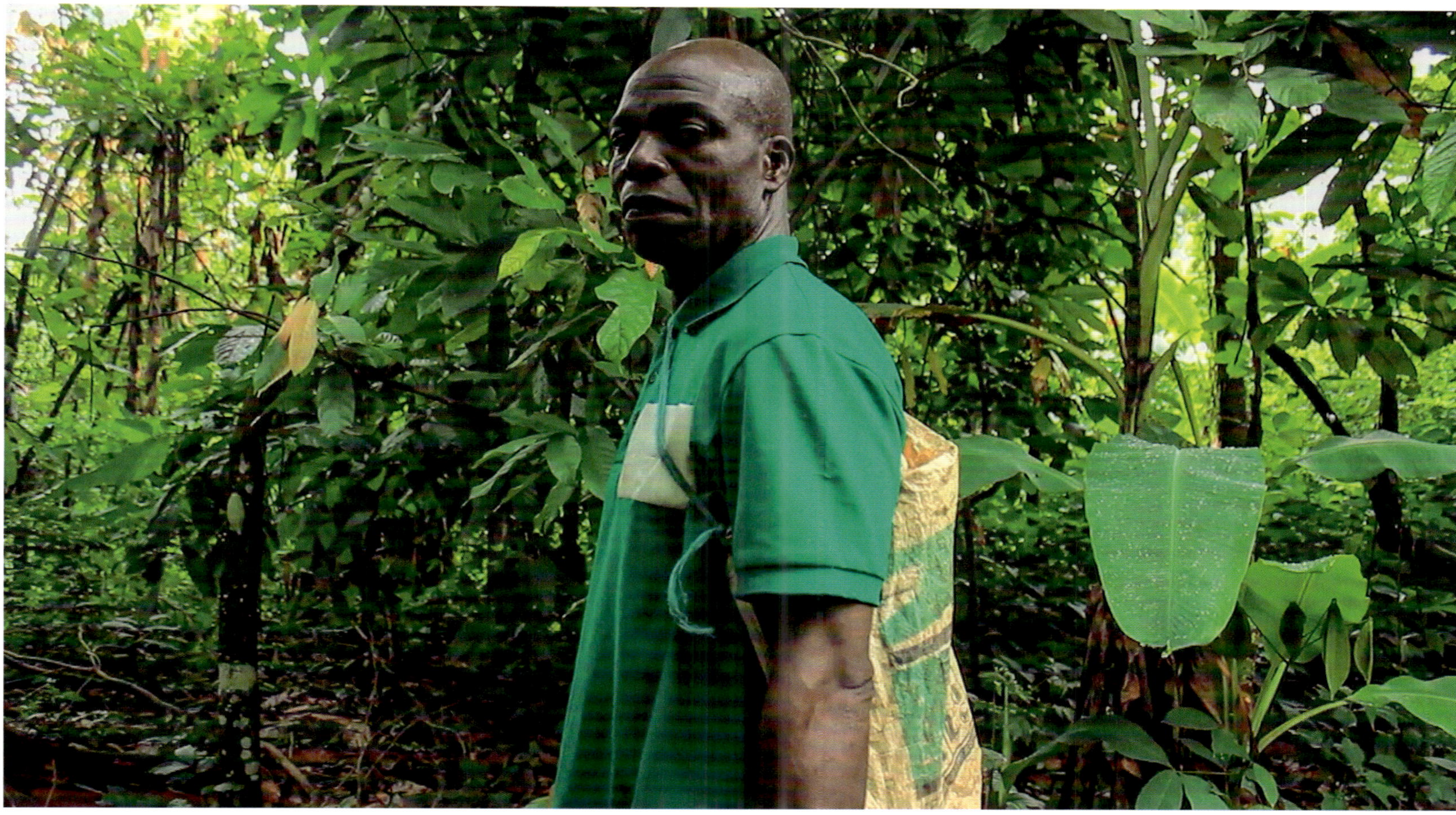

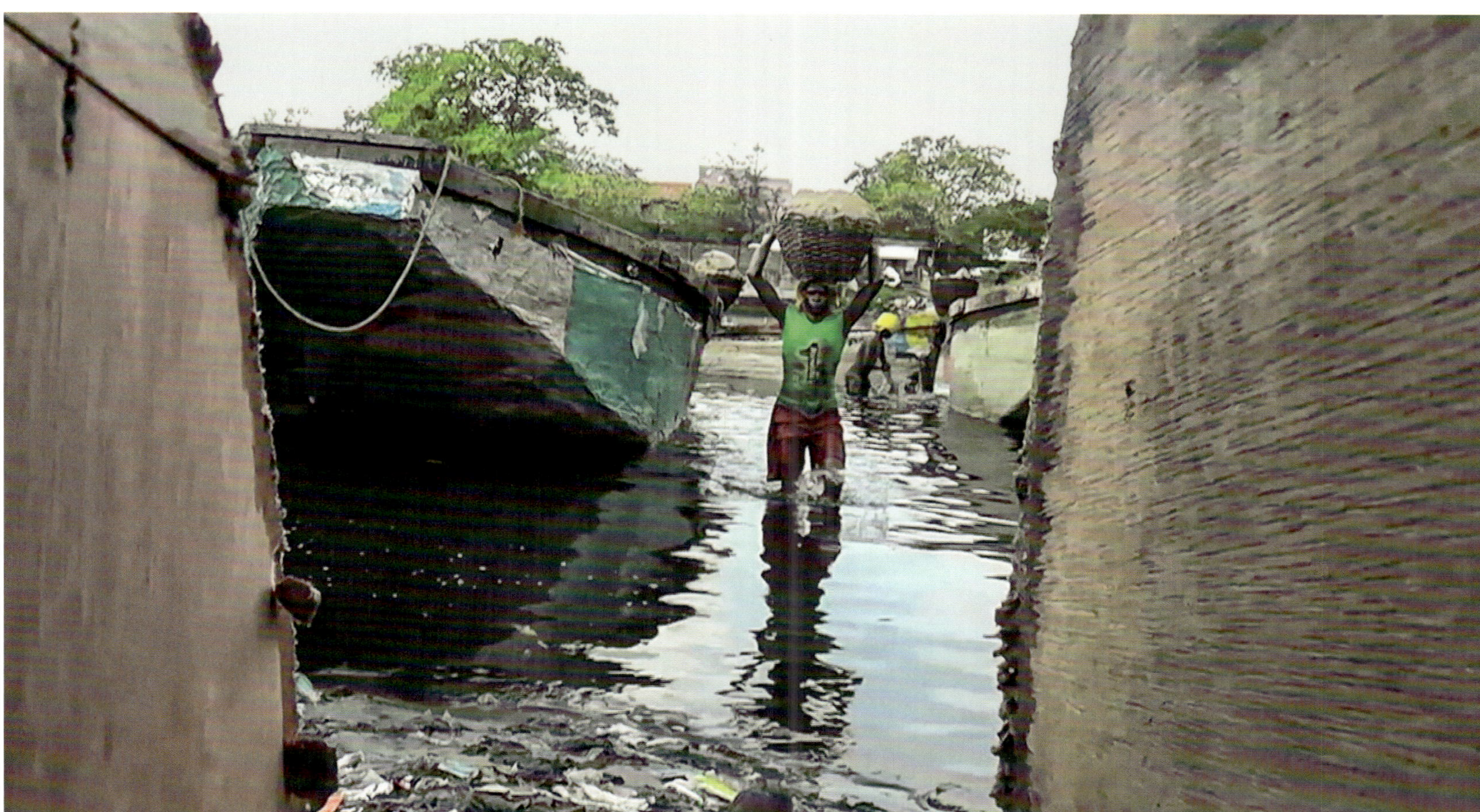

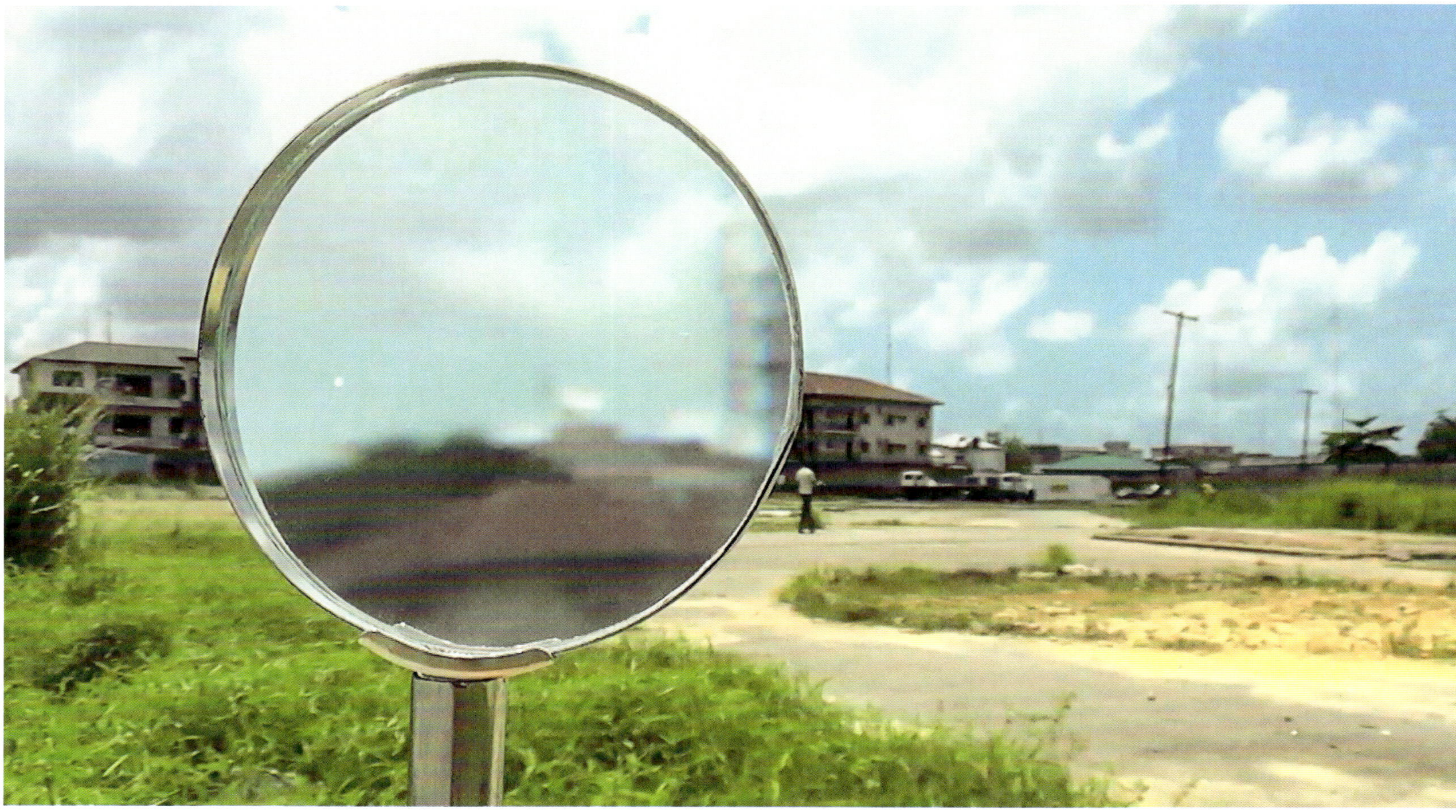

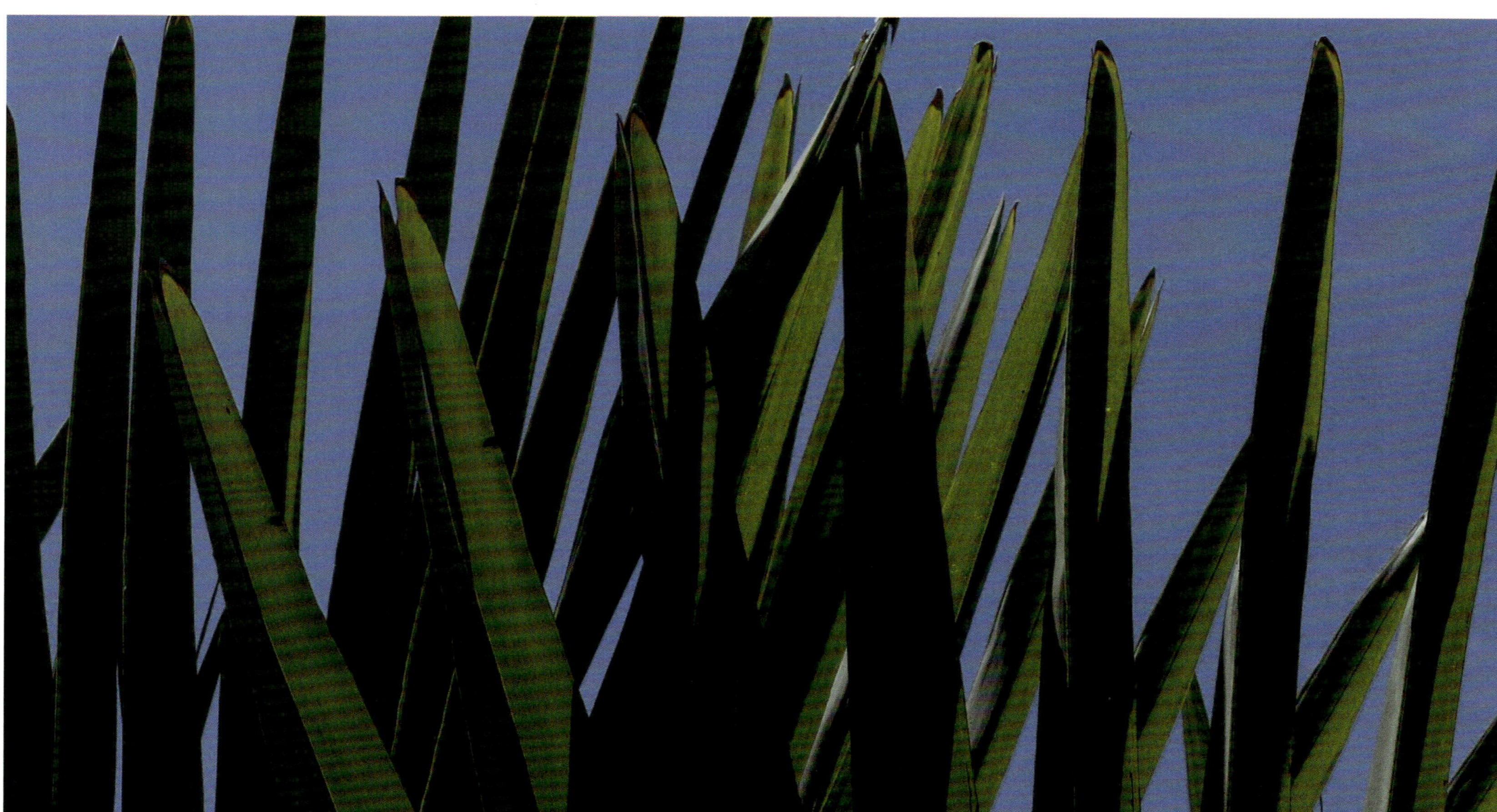

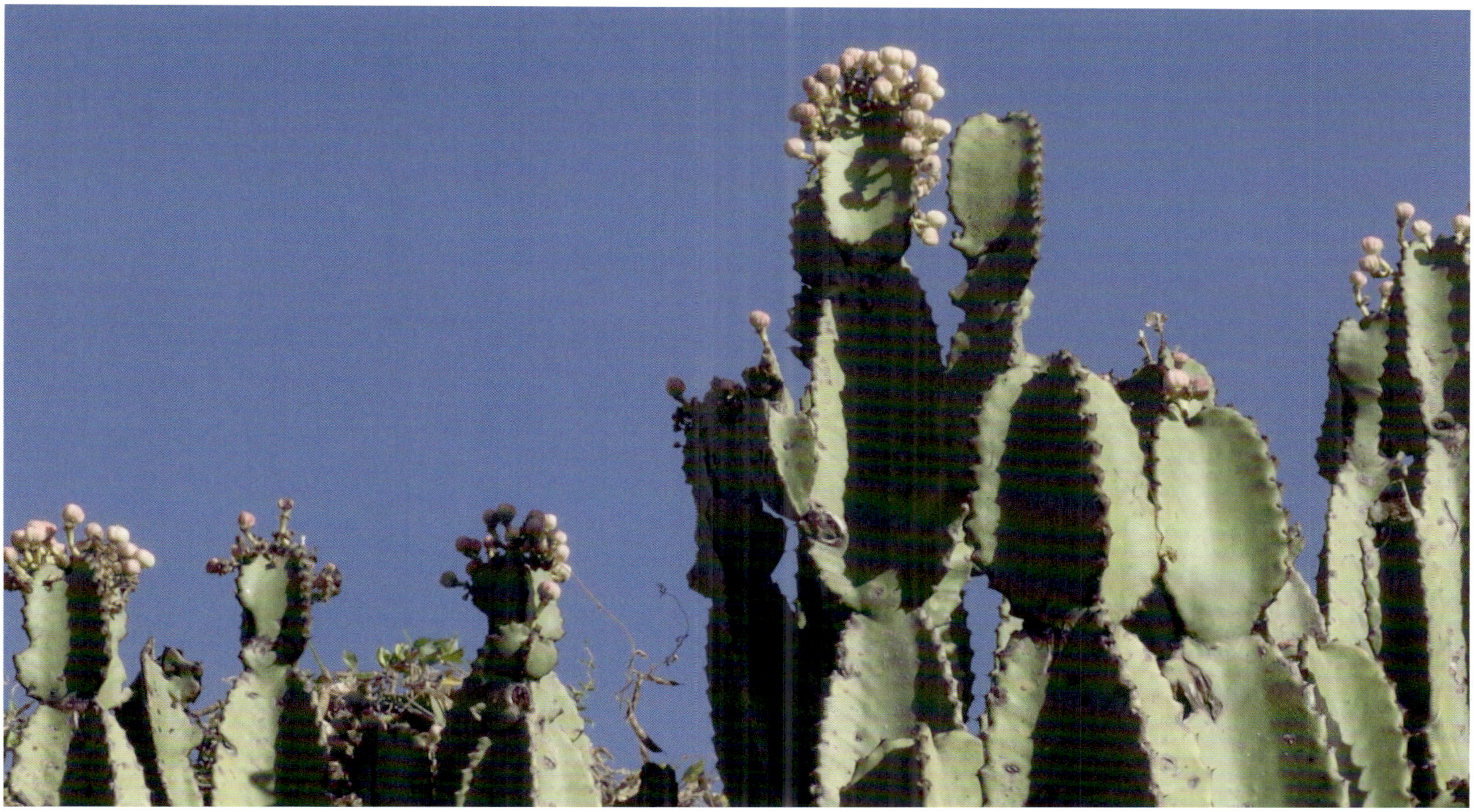

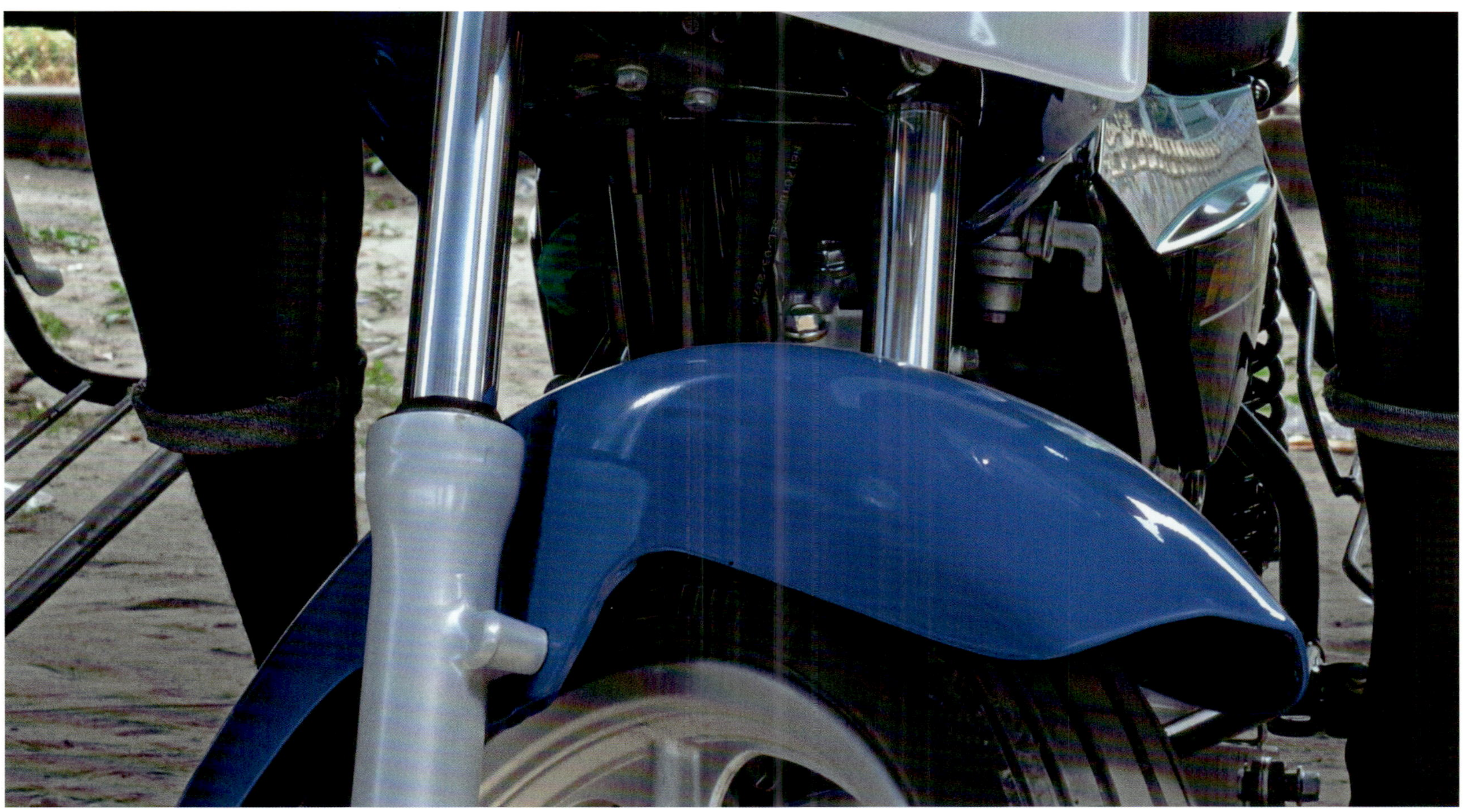

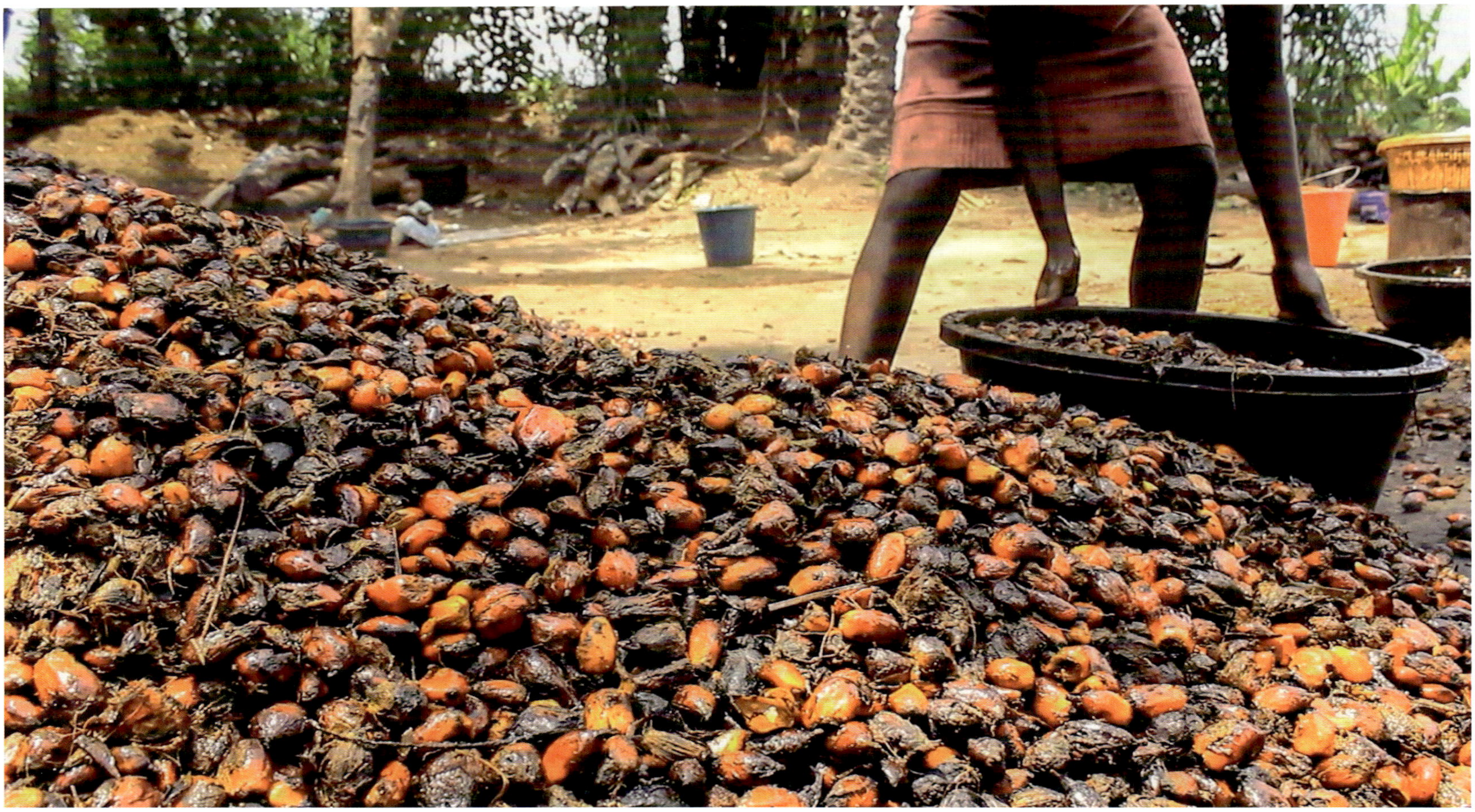

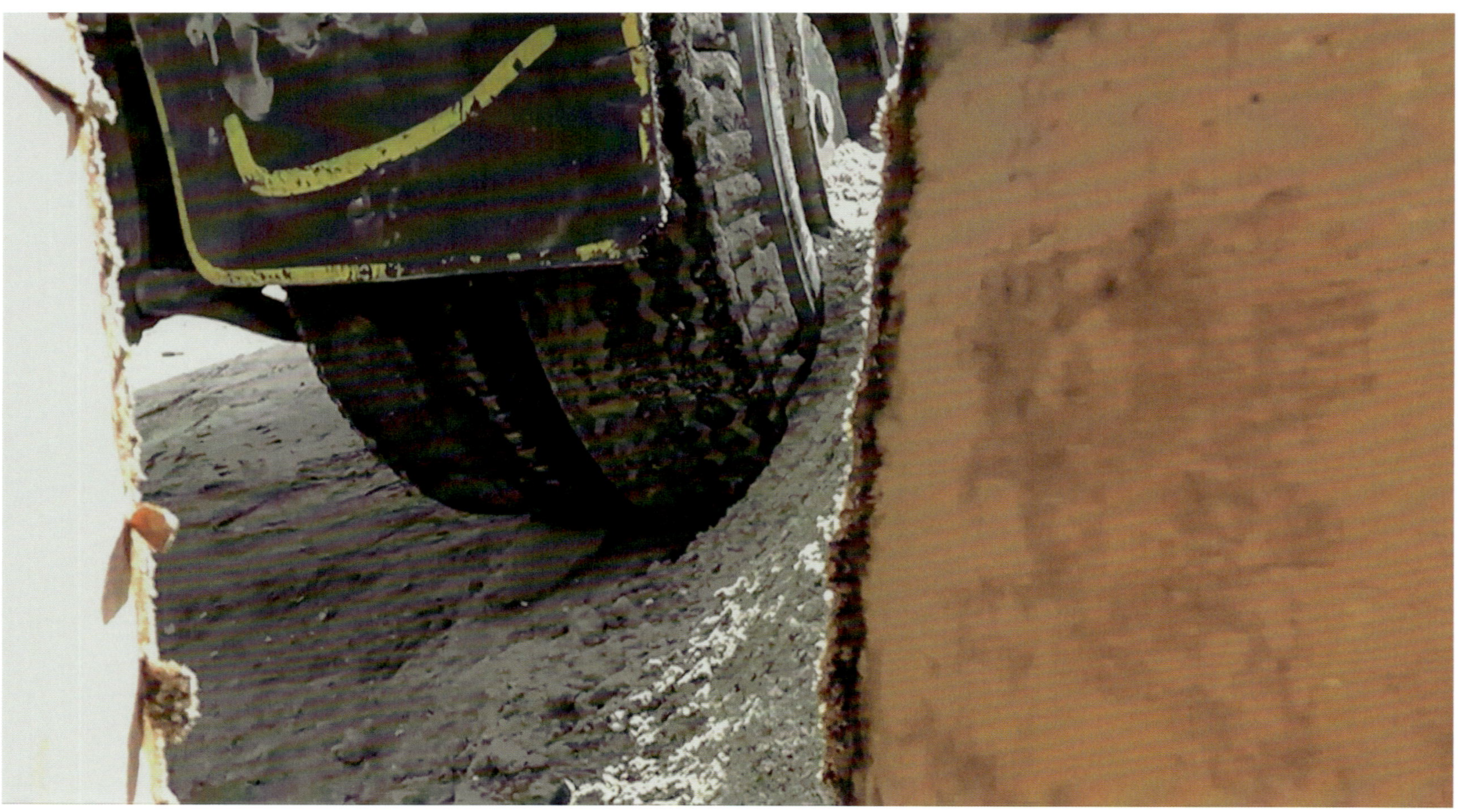

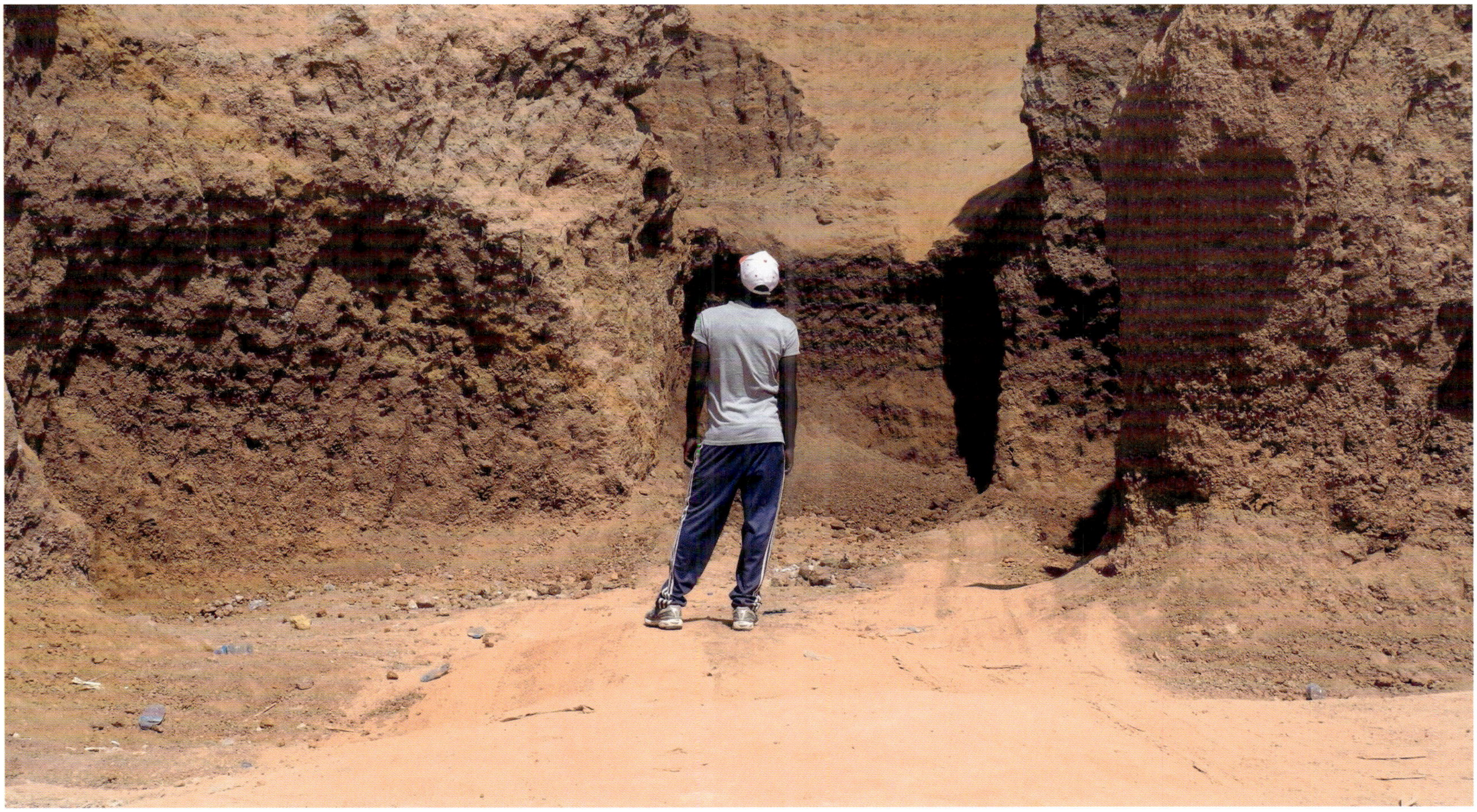

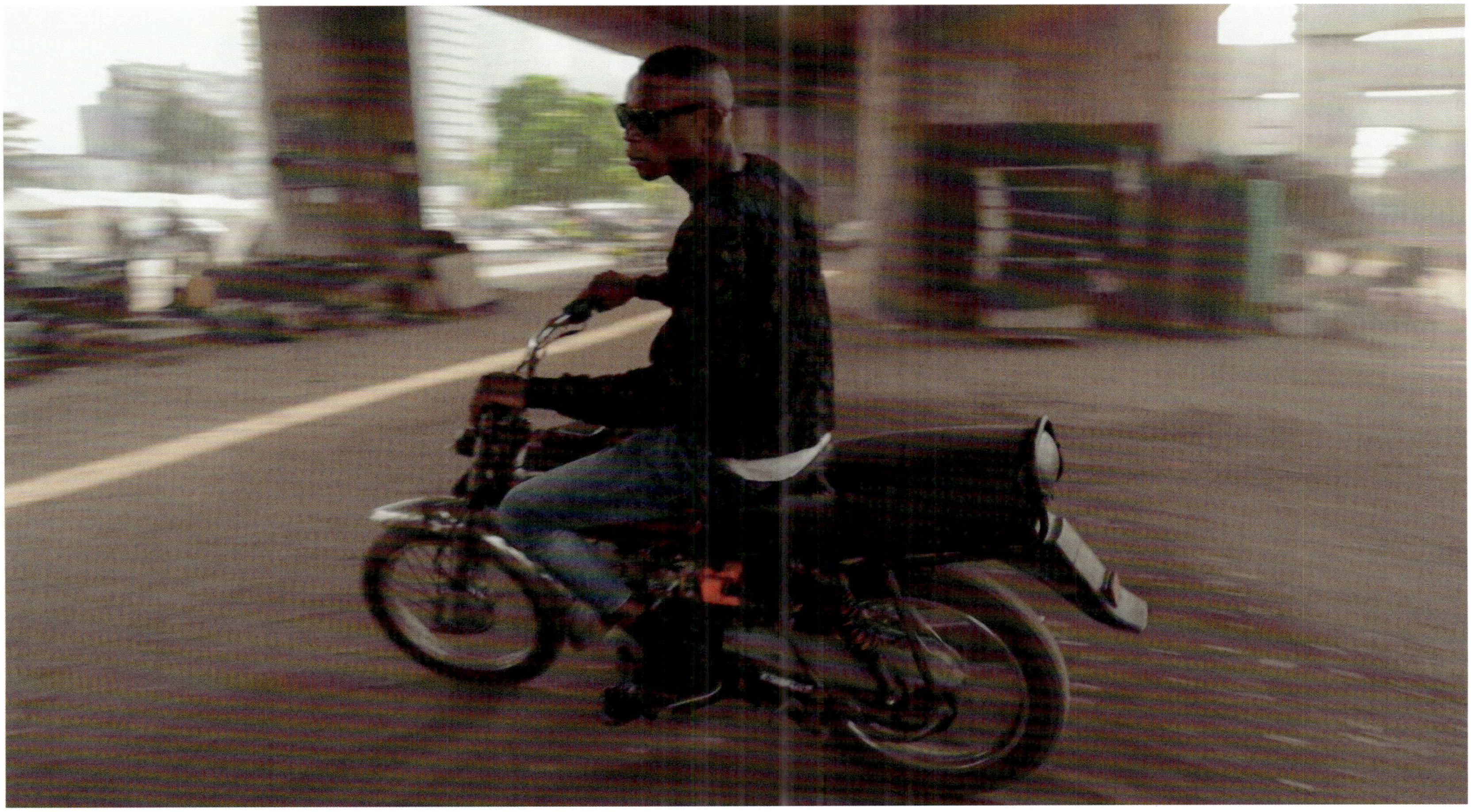

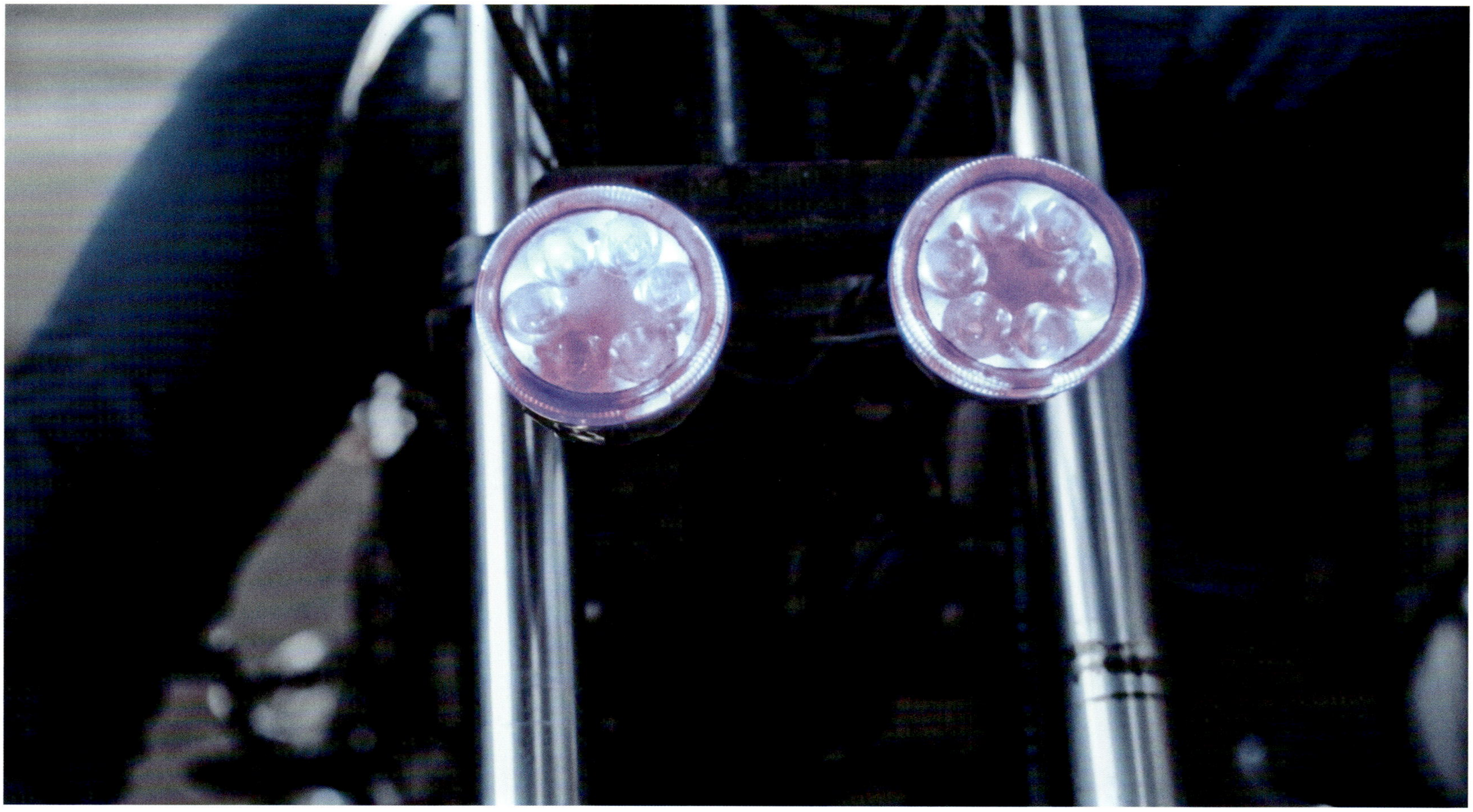

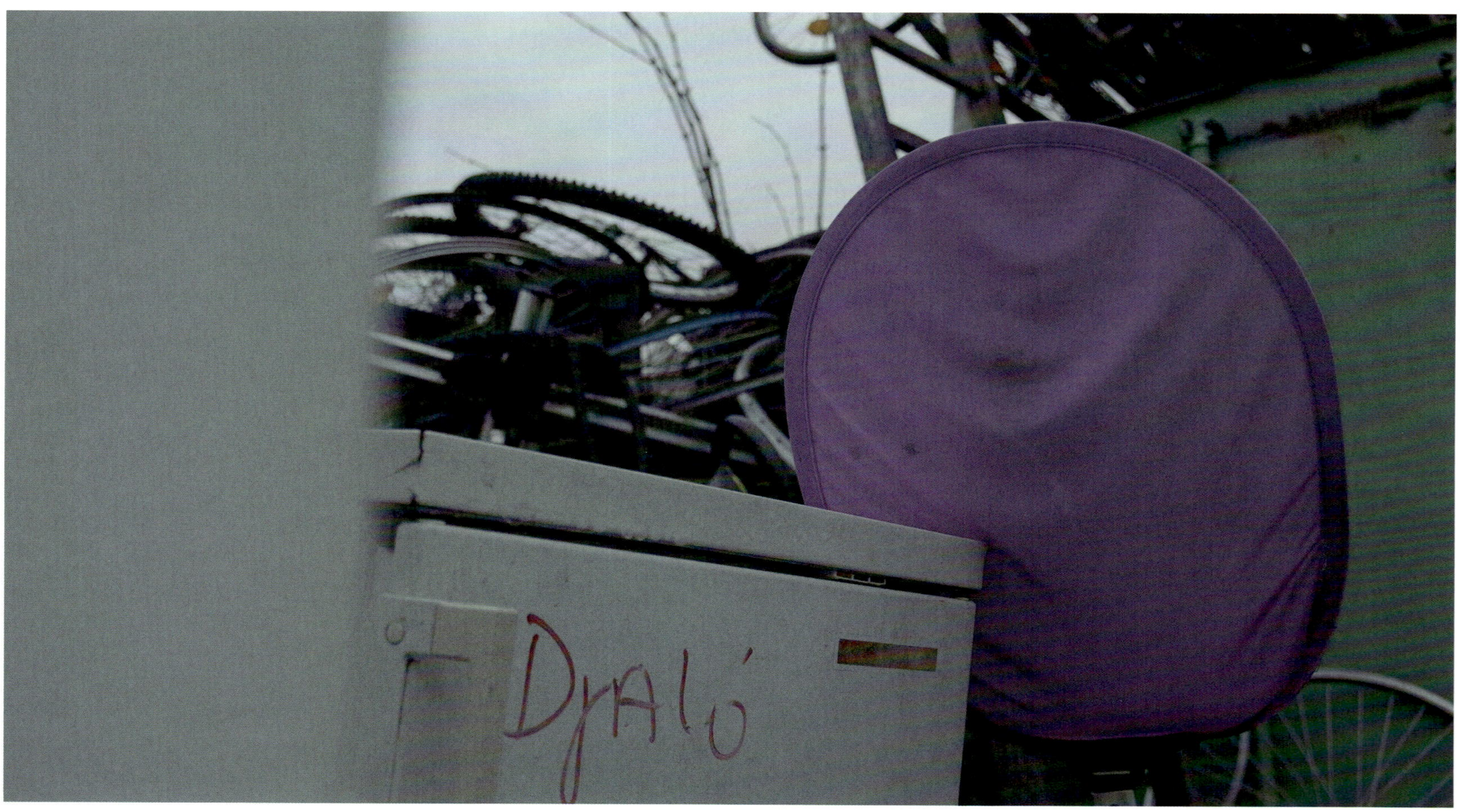
DjAló

Saturated Proximity: Rhythm, Porosity and Distance in the Films of Karimah Ashadu

Alessandro Rabottini

> I direct very heavily. I'm very specific about what I want.
> —Karimah Ashadu[1]

The Red Room of Persistence

An abattoir, a place where animals are slaughtered by human hand. A space of toil and massacre, a hive of severance. The space and the passing days are punctuated by a perpetual cadence, as precise as the chop itself: regular thuds, falling one after the next. We are in the open-air slaughterhouse of Makoko, a slum in Lagos, on the coast of Nigeria, and we are led here by *King of Boys (Abattoir of Makoko)* (2015), the first video work by Karimah Ashadu that we encounter along the path of her solo show *Tendered*.

The camera view is inspective – a mechanical gaze rotating on its own axis, scanning the space. A 360-degree visual survey of this laborious horizon, one of gestures and carcasses, tools and people. This is a place of extreme proximity, and thus a vital one. Death stands beside nourishment, dismemberment beside innocence. Childhood, indeed, is a key presence here, a witness to the daily grind and a participant in it. We see kids passing through the abattoir on their way to school, and kids who play an active role in the work. In more than one case, they are the only ones who acknowledge the presence of the camera, returning its gaze. There is something impassive in the way the lens records the toil that pervades the Makoko slaughterhouse, an observational quality arising from the way its movement seems predetermined. Reality is right there for the documenting, an accessible hustle and bustle, or perhaps accessible precisely because it is too busy existing.

1 'Karimah Ashadu with Toby Kamps', *The Brooklyn Rail*, June 2024, https://brooklynrail.org/2024/06/art/Karimah-Ashadu-with-Toby-Kamps/.

In this gaze that Ashadu fabricates and deploys, there is a sensitivity imbued with immediacy. It is something that defines Ashadu's entire practice, not just this specific work – namely a propensity towards forms of truth capable of saturating the visual field. There is an idea here of how to manoeuvre the lens that is also symptomatic of how to make it exist in the world, meaning, without calling on her subjects to do something they wouldn't in the absence of the camera. This is a trait that Ashadu's work has had since its inception (*King of Boys [Abattoir of Makoko]* is a work from ten years ago), and which leads to the atmosphere of truthfulness that envelops her images – a feeling of total adherence to those who are the subjects of representation, who are never called upon to pose or perform any hint of a script.

For Ashadu, the camera is a site of extreme proximity, often very close to the bodies it portrays and immersed in the spaces they inhabit. Extreme proximity insofar as it is the place where the artist explores the meaning and implications of an intermittent geographical and autobiographical distance: between the city of London, where she was born, and the city of Lagos, where she lived until the age of ten, before returning to England; between Nigeria, where almost all of her works have been shot to date, and Germany, where she now resides. But above all, the camera is the place where her work takes place and unfolds, in keeping with an inextricable process of identification between the formal and narrative planes.

At irregular intervals, the image suddenly turns bright red, sometimes veering towards orange, and the rest of the room where the work is installed follows suit. After a short while, the image and the room return to their original shades, only to sink back once more into a reddish hue, cyclically. This recurring alteration, of both the image and the projection

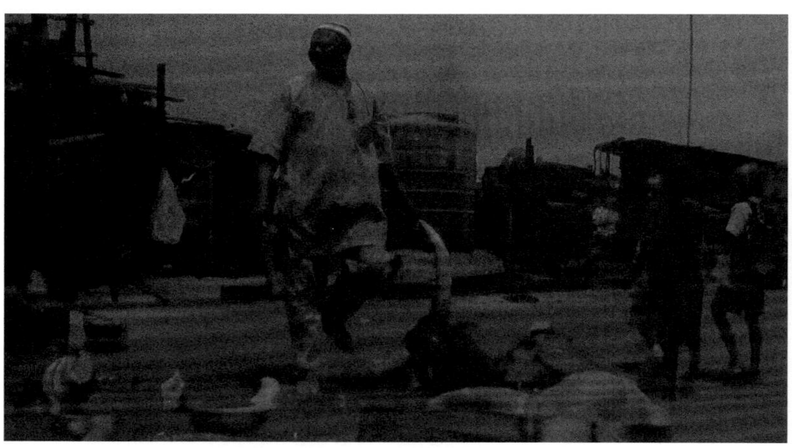

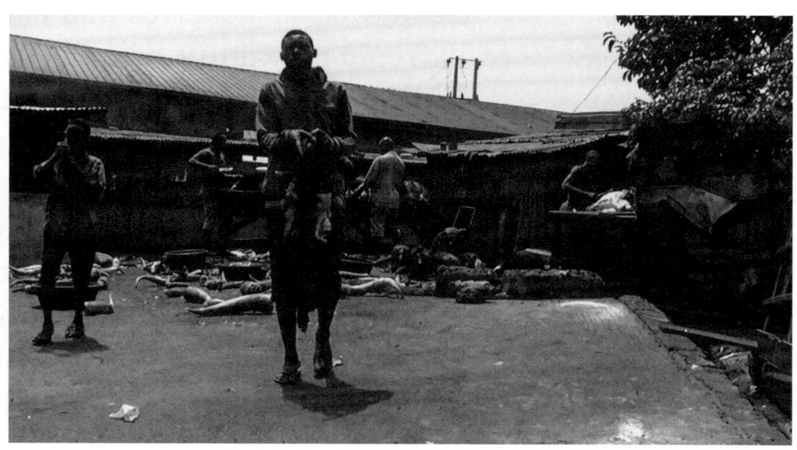

space, informs the few minutes of the work's duration, and at the same time its experiential nature. It is the result of a handmade modification to the camera, which is encased within a filter made out of an object, namely a plastic beer cask, found on the streets of Amsterdam, where Ashadu also lived. The materiality of this filter, moved by the artist in a rapid and rhythmic manner as if it were a shutter, reverberates in the tactility with which its movement shapes the experience of the image, giving rise to manifold effects. We are, at the same time, inside the Makoko abattoir and inside the camera filming it. The cadence of the machetes are as rhythmic as the presence of the filter is inexorable. The sound of the tools shearing up the carcasses is just as sharp as the colour to which everything veers is visceral and internal.

As spectators – along with some of the people passing through the frame – we are exposed to the presence of the camera as a device, made aware not only of its status as an object, but also of the nature of its gaze, one that is structurally selective, and intentional even when it appears to be objective. We are made witnesses – and once you are a witness, there is no turning back – to the fact that images are a matter of persistence and retreat, places where perception and knowledge are continuously saturated and desaturated throughout the historical process.

There are no words in *King of Boys (Abattoir of Makoko)*. Here, eloquence lies entirely in the auditory tapestry that weaves together voices and repetitive gestures. In the sensory vividness this work exudes, *King of Boys (Abattoir of Makoko)* becomes the specific yet oblique portrait of a local community engaged in everyday activities and, at the same time, the echo of something universal: the cacophonous, often tiring, sometimes painful rhythm of human existence on Earth.

In this early work, Ashadu already pursues an effect that would become a defining trait in her practice, namely that of achieving a very subtle, vibrant, albeit indefinable balance, a loose lyrical tension between the observational quality of the images and their experimental temperature – between something that is pulsating because it is true, and something that is imprinted on the retina and in the memory because it is visually penetrating. Neither documentary nor pure invention, Ashadu's work lies across a territory where the prosaic speaks with new words, and where the everyday does not pass by, but remains almost sculpted.

The Brown Room of Pressure

A room of proximity, of an excess of proximity. A saturated room, one with a dense atmosphere. The space is filled with sound, its capacity pushed almost to the limit. Like an oversized machine that contracts and exhales, a clamour of iron and breathlessness fills the air. All this takes place before the image is even fully distinguishable. With *MUSCLE* (2025) – the second video work on display and the beating heart of the exhibition – we find ourselves once more at the centre of things, in the midst of bodies. And once again, we find ourselves in a room whose colour is an extension of the dominant hue of the film projected within it. Filmed at Lagos Island, *MUSCLE* records the rhythmic movements, spasms and stretches of male bodies training outdoors with weights and gym equipment assembled in a makeshift fashion.[2] In what appears to be a radical absence of depth in the image, the camera sticks to the faces, biceps and pectorals of the protagonists to such an extent that it cancels out the space in which they move, the very perception of the context. When two different bodies occupy the frame, they seem to collide and consume all the air around them.

While *King of Boys (Abattoir of Makoko)* takes us into the congested daily life of the Makoko slaughterhouse and into the camera that filmed it, *MUSCLE* leads us into intimate, even epidermal contact with a group ritual that takes place in and for the urban space. In both works, the sound is incessant, a product of gestures repeated daily in a close, rhythmic and serial confrontation between bodies and tools, actions and materials. If *King of Boys (Abattoir of Makoko)* evokes nourishment and its commercialisation, *MUSCLE* highlights the trained body as an instrument of social redemption and economic salvation, and it is perhaps no coincidence that both actions – feeding and training – require daily commitment, and thus the works draw on themes of dedication, sacrifice and survival. Ashadu seems interested in tracing the elements of an optical and sonic regime of fatigue in everyday gestures, one that pulsates incessantly, like existence itself. Ten years apart, *King of Boys (Abattoir of Makoko)* and *MUSCLE* place forms of corporeality that the artist focuses on at the heart of the representation by virtue of their being intrinsically 'cinematic':

> I am interested in the physicality of labour. When a person has done something for so long, the body moves in a particular way that is very beautiful. It has a memory, it becomes automatic. I am really drawn to that, and I am interested in how the camera can communicate this physicality.[3]

2 The motif of weights assembled by hand echoes a theme central to Ashadu's practice, namely the idea of making do with what is at hand and, by extension, an interest in spontaneous and informal economies. We find references to ideas displaying great resource, independence and resistance in works like *Brown Goods* (2020), which gives voice to a Nigerian migrant living in Hamburg trading in secondhand electrical goods; *Plateau* (2021–22), which portrays undocumented tin miners in Nigeria's Jos Plateau and *Machine Boys* (2024), which focuses on the now-illegal phenomenon of motorcycle taxis in Lagos.

Here, once again, the camera lens is not the means to provide a documentary representation of physicality – in this case, Black male physicality – but rather a tool to amplify and magnify it, transforming it into a presence so visual and tactile that it complicates the relationship between these images and the principle of realism. Remaining almost glued to the tense muscles, sweaty skin and gritted teeth, the lens saturates the room in which the work is projected with absolute concreteness, in a constant tension between veracity and abstraction. Through constant, repeated and exhausting close-ups, *MUSCLE* achieves a form of naturalism that is as overflowing as it is

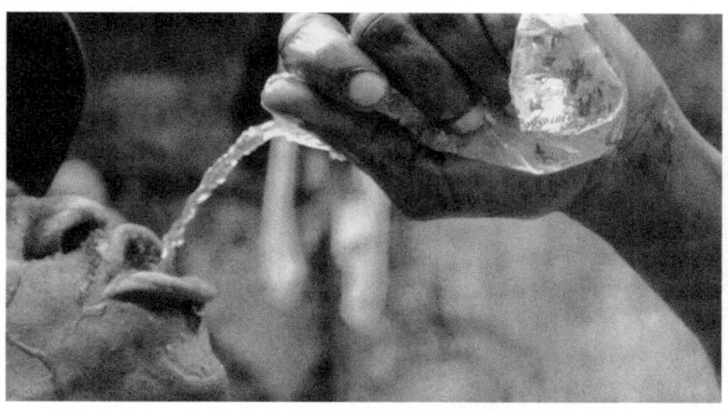

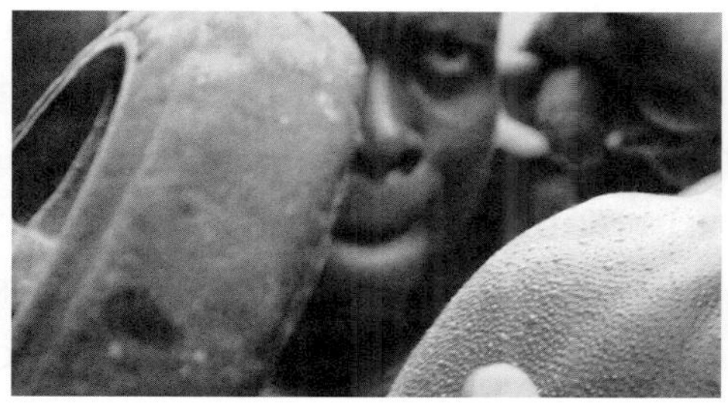

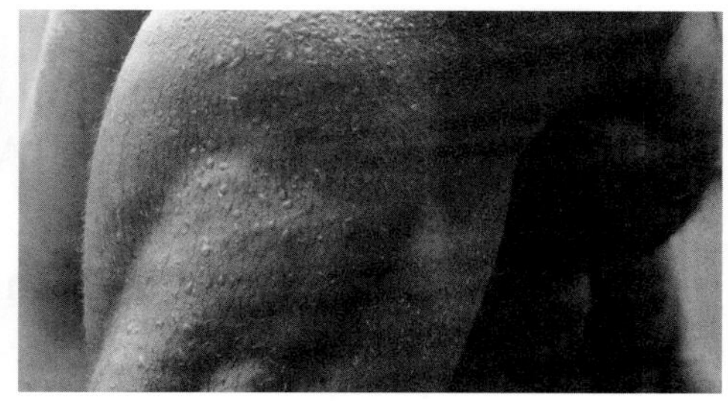

paradoxical – overflowing insofar as it tests the limits of the image itself, and paradoxical because, despite the absence of full figures, it is effective in making the veracity of the bodies palpable and present.

Of the image and its sensory fullness, Ashadu makes a use so exasperated that we might even describe it as distorted, yet one that ultimately frees her subjects from the weight of representation and the politics behind it. Her subjects inhabit the space of the screen in a spontaneous manner. They are not the subject of metaphorisation, nor is any narrative ascribed to the movement of their bodies or the words with which they say more about themselves. Their 'story' – that of a physique necessarily honed if it is to emancipate oneself from one's disadvantaged starting point and take a stand in a society that rewards virility – is entrusted to short yet telling sentences uttered by the subjects themselves throughout the over twenty minutes of the work. The rest is done by the camera, with a gaze that is as participatory as it is interrogatory, a gaze that knows how to capture – be it tenderly or abrasively – the contradictions of a society like Nigeria's without flattening them onto the individual bodies portrayed.

A complex and nuanced portrait of a certain way of experiencing masculinity in contemporary Nigeria, *MUSCLE* demonstrates the layered sensitivity with which Ashadu films her subjects after gaining their trust and nurturing their willingness to open up. Despite its congested aesthetic, the

3 Karimah Ashadu in conversation with Mark Rappolt, 'Labour, Hierarchy and Hypermasculinity within Nigerian Culture', part of the public programme *Thick Atmospheres*, curated by Bianca Stoppani in the context of the exhibition *Nebula*, Complesso dell'Ospedaletto, Venice, April 17–November 24, 2024. *Thick Atmospheres* took place at the Teatrino di Palazzo Grassi, Venice, October 17–18, 2024. A recording of the conversation is available at https://inbetweenartfilm.com/en/thick-atmospheres/.

pressure of its emotional temperature and the contractions of its rhythm, this work contains and exudes a dense repertoire of emotions and implications – one that is at times contradictory, at others impalpable. This complexity is the result of an intention that is as much intuitive as it is precise: to make the lens not only a site of proximity but, above all, a porous place of coexistence. Showing how bodies reflect the expectations of a patriarchal society doesn't exclude the possibility of empathising with the fragility of the psychologies that those same bodies harbour. Manifesting the limits of a certain conception of physical strength doesn't exclude the contemplation of tenderness in one's gaze. Questioning the cultural reasons for discipline and sacrifice doesn't mean censoring the dimension of seduction and desire. And hinting at aggressiveness doesn't stop Ashadu from trying to read the vulnerability that lies at its core.

MUSCLE takes the concept of 'pressure' – be it social pressure or that of pumping iron – and materialises it in a projection space where moving images and sounds take on a physical but also a gravitational nature, a weight that pushes downwards. All of Ashadu's works possess this quality. They are oblique and elliptical portraits and, precisely for this reason, radically eloquent. They evoke cultural, historical and political meanings through the experience of the images in space, without stating them directly. Despite the careful planning that goes into their production, Ashadu's film portraits seem almost fleeting, sketched with an awareness of how difficult, and ultimately futile, it is to ask existence to stand still and pose. They make very sparing use of the spoken word, and seem to respond to an impressionistic economy of framing and editing, to a phrasing made more of silent understanding than of arguments.

The Green Room of Release

Something slows down, and the horizon opens up. There is finally a breeze, a change of pace and temperature. A different landscape. A certain degree of breathing space and depth. *Cowboy* (2022) is the third and final video work in *Tendered*: from the urban spaces dense with community in *King of Boys (Abattoir of Makoko)* and *MUSCLE*, we move into the natural and narrative landscape of a single man. From the stubborn, hammering friction of tools, we move to arrhythmic expanses of wind and waves. From the red and brown in which we were immersed in the previous two rooms, we find ourselves in a green that offers a sense of decongestion.

The work in the exhibition that most draws on the spoken word, *Cowboy* is the first-person tale of a life spent since childhood with horses, a monologue by a man about his daily familiarity with the equestrian world. Whereas *King of Boys (Abattoir of Makoko)* is a kinetic cacophony of slaughter and commerce, *Cowboy* is a solo piece about coexistence and mutual care ("I have learned that they can take care of humans", says the protagonist about his horses). And while in *MUSCLE*, the body experiences daily intimacy with contraction and effort, in *Cowboy*, the days are accompanied by the supple actions of horses. The camera's soft movements in *Cowboy* alternate between close-ups and long tracking shots. When the lens lingers on a horse's head, the other screen opens up to the vastness of the stormy sea of Tarkwa Bay, near Lagos, where the film was made. And whereas in *MUSCLE*, space was banished and a sense of constraint prevailed, the narrative of *Cowboy* unfolds along lines of distance and depth. The immersion in lush nature is total.

Once again, it is the camera's gaze, its position in relation to the subject and its own movements, that reveals the intentions behind Ashadu's practice, producing in this case a portrait that is (if possible) even more oblique than the others, a story that seems to slip through our fingers. In this idyllic and meditative work, in the atmosphere of a minimal and subdued epic about freedom, symbols unfold that have the silent and threatening character of clouds gathering on the horizon. For a long time, the camera follows the protagonist on horseback through the thick vegetation to the coast, always from behind. What at first appears to be a peaceful trot gradually gives way to a sense of unease, as if someone is following him. As distant as an echo, evoking the trope of the Black man being hunted down, Ashadu handles the feeling of unease with the subtle persistence of an arpeggio.[4] With equal formal control and a minimalist approach to storytelling, she repeatedly frames an ocean horizon crowded with cargo ships, closing on this view with what increasingly appears to be a symbolic meditation on freedom, liberation from restrictions and a gaze set on the future.

With *Cowboy*, Ashadu gives voice to a landscape that, going back centuries, has been a silent witness to the commerce of humans through the slave trade, and the exploitation of social and environmental resources through European colonialism, where sea routes have been ploughed by the disintegration of generations. The landscape is, to this day, mindful of all this: of the slaughter and separation of entire communities, of physical strength as the only chance for survival and of the promise of a distant freedom. When, in the opening minutes of *Cowboy*, the protagonist lists the many countries around the world where his life with horses has taken him – Argentina, Ethiopia, Brazil, Libya and beyond – we as viewers

4 On the recurrence of the figure of the fugitive in other works by Ashadu, especially in *Machine Boys*, see the essay by Dr. Clive Chijioke Nwonka in this volume, at pages 113–21.

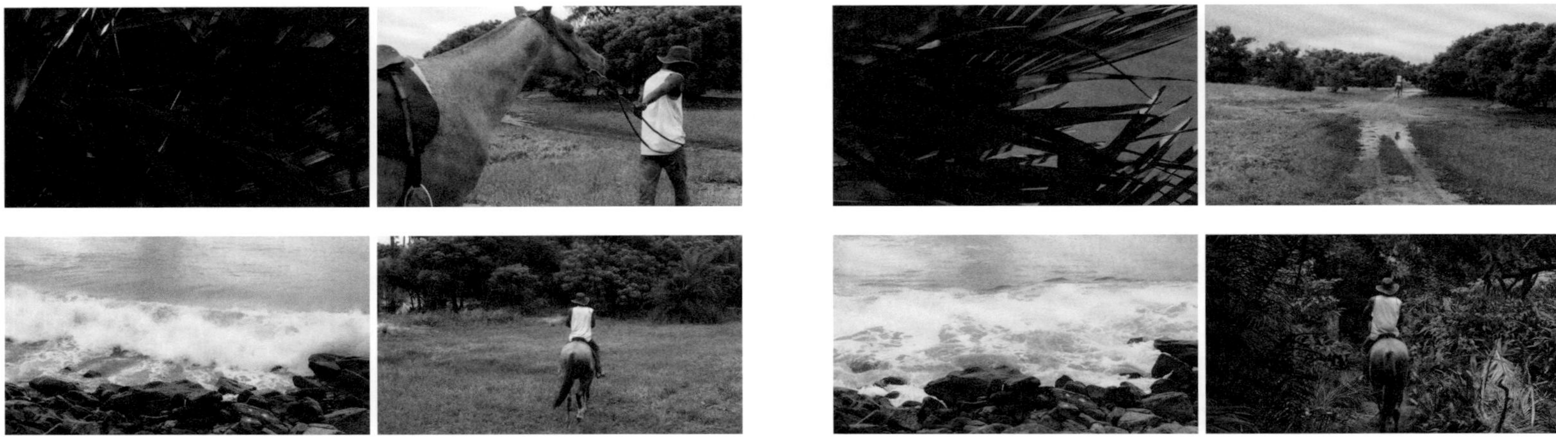

are not yet aware of how the image of ships on the horizon, with which the work closes, will become a harbinger of the all-too-many migratory routes that have turned the sea into a graveyard.

Cowboy certainly possesses a poetic quality, although the category of the 'poetic' in art literature is often overexploited, almost as if it were a shortcut to avoid confronting things as they are. I am rather inclined to believe Ashadu's work is a very crisp form of prose, structured around a few short, evocative, extremely precise sentences. It is prose with a profound formal intentionality, a sense of control that does not constrain the representation of reality but, on the contrary, frees it, allowing it to breathe even when the air feels stifling.

As a whole, *Tendered* could be interpreted as an orchestration of various forms of proximity, an exercise in saturation and distance expressed through a sequence of rooms, each with its own emotional, chromatic and formal temperature. Starting from the syncopated aesthetic that characterises *King of Boys (Abattoir of Makoko)* and which intensifies in *MUSCLE*, the exhibition concludes with a work that evokes an aesthetic of release and openness, almost a rebirth into nature, both factual and symbolic, from the throng of the urban fabric.

P. 34: Karimah Ashadu, stills from *King of Boys (Abattoir of Makoko)*, 2015. See pages 76–77.
P. 37: Karimah Ashadu, stills from *MUSCLE*, 2025. See pages 94–95.
P. 40: Karimah Ashadu, stills from *Cowboy*, 2022. See pages 89–90.

Reclaiming the Image from a History of Extraction

Bettina Steinbrügge

> The moving image possesses the capacity to gather people, in real and imagined ways, around an object of shared concern: reality itself. To care for reality is not to assert the goodness or adequacy of the world that exists; on the contrary, it is to see that the building of a new world is imperative. The common world is a future horizon, an ongoing project; as Hannah Arendt affirms, it must be continually constructed through the meeting of different perspectives.
> —Erika Balsom, 'Shoreline Movements'[1]

Film critic Erika Balsom's quote is not about the artist whose work is the subject of this text, but it could easily be a synthesis of Karimah Ashadu's work. Ashadu observes and stages social realities, particularly in a West African context, while living between very different cultures herself. As a Nigerian artist who grew up in London, resides between Hamburg and Lagos, and has made Nigeria her subject, Ashadu wields an exceptional grasp of the intricacies of the contemporary era, and a tremendous facility in taking on different and differentiated perspectives.

The second decade of the twenty-first century has witnessed an accumulation of crises – climate change, economic downturns, the mobility (or not) of populations, artificial intelligence, epidemics and growing social and economic disparities. The efficacy of capitalism is being called into question, yet no adequate alternative system has been demonstrated. Ashadu employs a multifaceted approach in her tackling of a wide range of themes pertaining to all of this, from post-capitalism to migration, labour systems, identity and relationships between people and land. The repercussions of colonialism

1 Erika Balsom, 'Shoreline Movements', *e-flux*, no. 114 (December 2020), https://www.e-flux.com/journal/114/366065/shoreline-movements/.

(especially between Africa and Europe), migratory patterns and aspirations along with their disillusionment are all exquisitely expressed in her work. Ashadu received a degree in painting first and in spatial design later, while her extensive studies in film history and the history of video art, as well as her profound knowledge of cinematic techniques and their applications, have been pursued independently. Her approach and methods blend experimental film with documentary with the painterly, especially in matters of composition, colour and texture. For Ashadu, the visual is never just a backdrop, but an unrestricted vehicle of meaning. Her artistic language is very deliberate, almost haptic. Static shots, long sequences and symbolism are everywhere.

Ashadu's way of working seems directly related to John Akomfrah's immersive installations, for instance *Purple* (2017), which deals with global migration and the climate crisis. Like Akomfrah, Ashadu breaks with the idea of linearity and the illusion of a single truth, attempting instead to dismantle the one-dimensionality of historical representations and create a structure of diverse perspectives. She generates the means to do this from the various tools of film language, such as nonlinear narrative, movement, close-ups, colour emphasis and voice-overs. Her aim is to reclaim images. She deconstructs conventional colonial narratives through a visual language characterised by proximity, dignity and self-determination. In this context, rapid cuts are also obsolete, as are any other sensationalist visual languages. Her protagonists appear as independent subjects, not objects of exoticising documentary observation.

Films such as *Destiny* (2016) and *Machine Boys* (2024) epitomise the artist's focus on mood, environment and gesture. They are not so much about constructing a plot as about depicting presence and process, and creating insight from small gestures. They merge the often-contradictory foundations of culturally diverse societies. By foregrounding her specific gaze, generated as it is by her mixed upbringing and sensibility regarding Nigerian subjects, and using self-built tools that are sometimes apparent in the final work, Ashadu reclaims authorship and critiques colonial histories – specifically that between the United Kingdom and Nigeria – embedded in the act of filming itself. Instead of merely documenting reality, she shapes the image. She reappropriates the gaze against a history in which images of Africa and its peoples were mostly made from the outside. The camera functions methodologically as a physical, political, perceptible instrument.

As early as her first film, *Lagos Island* (2012), Ashadu's distinctive and innovative manipulation of the camera was already evident. As Balsom explains, Ashadu used "what she calls a 'camera wheel mechanism' to craft a visually disorienting rendering of migrant settlements on the shore. As the rolling apparatus passes temporary dwellings that are soon to be torn down by the municipal authorities, it screeches and cracks, never ceasing to draw attention to its situated gaze, its embeddedness in a terrain subject to constant change."[2] Ever more details slowly come into view, forming a story, or at least a situation. People appear, the beach becomes more recognisable, and the film takes shape and content without giving too much away. What we are allowed to see is limited; we get only a glimpse of something bigger. This reminds me of the use of the camera in Michael Snow's films. To make *La Région Centrale* (1971), for instance, Snow developed a robotic camera system capable of moving 360 degrees on its axis, effectively turning the camera into a protagonist. Ashadu, in *Lagos Island*, dynamically portrays immigrant dwellings in the context of a government that persistently opposes such endeavours. The tension that emerges from her visual approach, juxtaposed with the sonic signature of the device as it moves along, suggests an omniscient 'I', speaking to an enduring political resistance and a perpetual historical struggle.[3]

In *Lagos Sand Merchants* (2013), the camera is again connected to a dynamic rotary device that challenges the viewer's spatial perception. It serves as a metaphor for the protagonists, who extract sand from the riverbed to sell to the construction industry. Upon its activation, the camera oscillates forward and toward the ground, then subsequently returns to its original position, as if reestablishing contact with the surface. The objective is to capture perspectives that reflect both the environment and the embodied experience of labour. Ashadu shows people who would otherwise remain invisible, but without romanticising or exoticising them. She allows them their identities, although power relations and visual regimes are always present in the space. Who is allowed to show whom, how are they shown, and to what end?

In *Makoko Sawmill* (2015), two blue sticks protrude from the camera and overlap significantly with the visible imagery. The function of the device remains unclear, but it certainly distracts from what is happening in the image, drawing attention instead to the production and construction of the film, as well as the invisible artist behind the camera. At one point there is a distraction-within-the-distraction when a fly enters the device, seemingly making a mockery of the whole endeavor. Two other observations are worth making. There is a sense of order in the film, as groups of

2 Balsom, 'Shoreline Movements'.

3 See Mónica Savirón, 'The Very Eye of Night: Karimah Ashadu', *MUBI*, January 6, 2018, https://mubi.com/en/notebook/posts/the-very-eye-of-night-karimah-ashadu.

men, also known as 'pullers', 'rollers' and 'carriers', work together to process the wood, while women and children resourcefully recycle the sawdust. The blue sticks are a constant presence of disorder within the orderly activities of these people, and at the same time they seem (however mysteriously) to be tools of order. Via the brownish landscape and workers' clothes, everything becomes a construction, an underlying structure that we follow. It makes the orderly look strange, or at least questionable. Makoko is a Lagos slum consisting mainly of stilt houses, which was scheduled for redevelopment in 2012 by razing the houses and filling in the

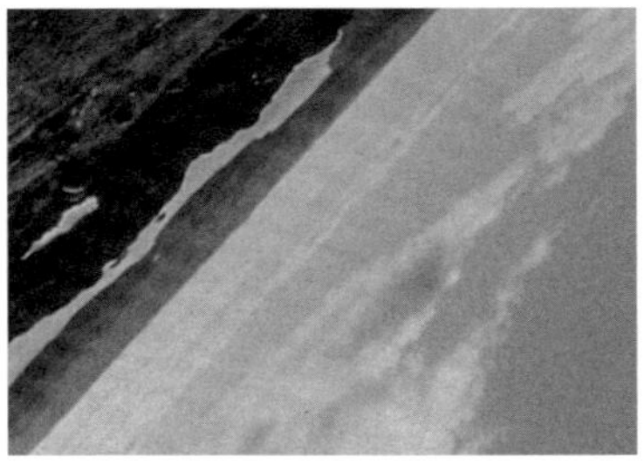

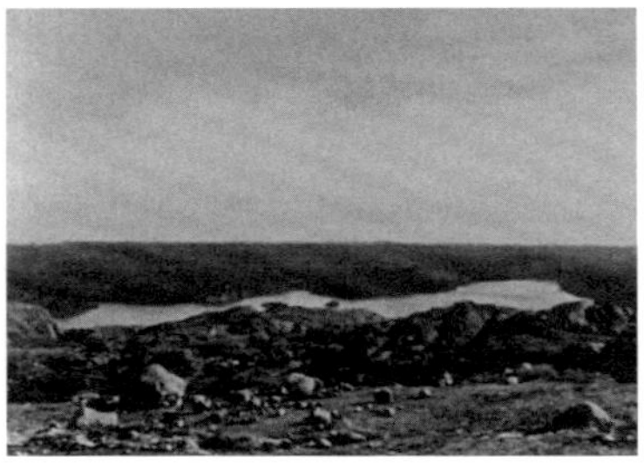

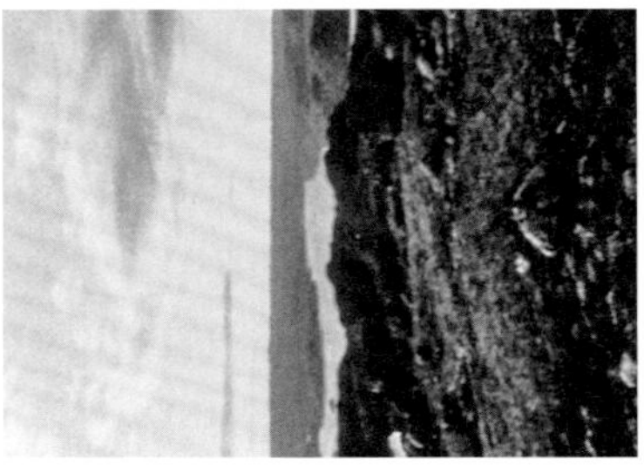

lagoon with sand. The violent eviction of the inhabitants resulted in one fatality, whereupon the operation was suspended for the time being. The trade depicted, we intuit, is founded upon the instability of the lagoon as much as on the precarity of the people's vocation and housing.

The list of camera devices utilised in Ashadu's oeuvre is extensive; beyond those already mentioned, there is the magnifier in *Apapa Amusement Park* (2013) and the oversize red plastic beer keg in *King of Boys (Abattoir of Makoko)* (2015). But after this period, Ashadu began dispensing with such devices. It appears that she developed a confidence that was not reliant on external assistance, with cinematography now deemed sufficient to achieve the desired effect. *Destiny* portrays a saw sharpener who goes by the same name. The setting is around his hut, which becomes an almost reverential motif. The camera captures its interior and exterior, as viewed through the door, the window and apertures in the wooden walls. The concept centres on the interplay of light and darkness, day and night, and the integration of exterior and interior activities through the strategic use of frames around doors and windows. The camera was moved in a deliberate and repetitive manner by a handheld dolly, creating a slow and meditative effect. In the two-channel video *Red Gold* (2016), the camera functions differently on each channel. A central perspective of one seemingly superior figure, mostly seen from behind, is juxtaposed with the twisting rotations of mostly women working in palm oil production, seen from above. In *Cowboy* (2022), the rider appears moving slowly out of frame several times in a 'following shot' until he reaches the sea, filmed in two different stages. In one shot the sea is rough, and in the other it is calm.

The water may function here as a metaphor for freedom, drawing upon the iconic image of the cowboy of the US West.

Ashadu is looking for a way to represent reality that is specific to her experience, and she uses the techniques of film not only to document, but also to construct something that leads to new insights. Perhaps it would be more accurate to call it an interruption of realism. Even in non-linear works such as *Apapa Amusement Park*, or the more seemingly conventional *Brown Goods* (2020) or *Plateau* (2021–22), she often incorporates surreal pacing, dreamlike audio or fragmented narratives. These elements disrupt immersion and remind us that this is a constructed experience. This form of breaking the fourth wall challenges the authority of realism, asking us to question what we are seeing and why. This was pioneered by Chantal Akerman, who disrupted the expectation that a documentary must explain. In works like *News from Home* (1977), Akerman's presence is both intimate and distant, using voice-over to disrupt documentary distance so that the viewer experiences time, space and mood rather than learning a lesson or absorbing facts. The gaze in Ashadu's films centres issues of perspective, power and representation. The visual storytelling functions as a medium for interrogating, examining the presentation of diverse perspectives, with a particular focus on identity, especially in relation to male behaviour.

In *Machine Boys*, cinematic devices such as voice-overs and close-ups create distance and intimacy simultaneously. The protagonists are male motorcycle riders involved in Okada, a now illicit taxi enterprise in Lagos. They are observed performing manoeuvres that resemble the circular 'donut' stunts. It feels like a ritual scenario, but the motivation behind it remains unexplained. The boys' facial expressions suggest strength and determination. A close-up may isolate a detail – a face, hands, eyes, or an object – that leads the viewer to form an intense emotional or tactile relationship with what they see. At the same time, the voice-over conveys a certain vulnerability that contrasts with the prevailing expression of masculinity. The boys are workers who are not normally 'seen' as individuals. Accordingly, Ashadu captures their presence through diversions, for instance through their reflections in the bike side mirrors, while the motorcycles themselves are in turn reflected in the rain-soaked streets of the city. Ashadu imbues the whole gaze with a certain poetry, creating the impression that the set is floating in a psychological space where image and thought blur. The double subjectiv-

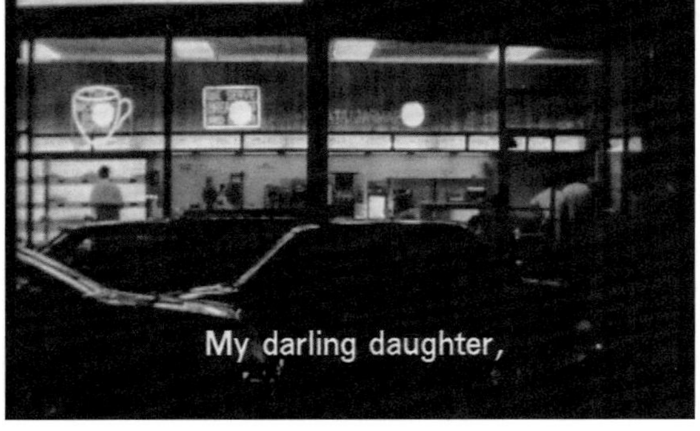

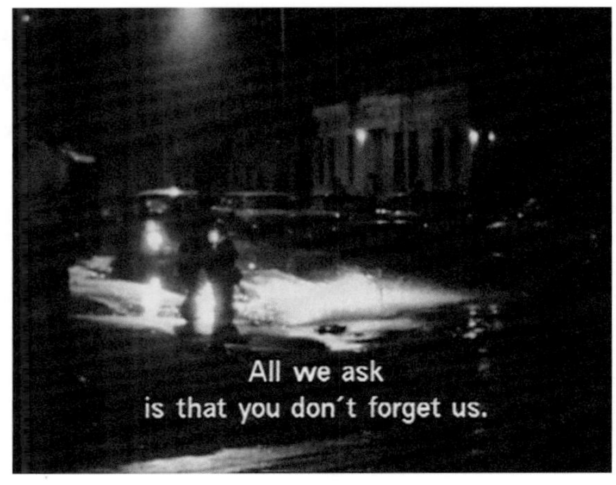

ity in her approach – in this case, her own and that of the boys – points to an inner conflict that is irresolvable, and thus also deeply human. Feminism plays a subtle but deeply structural role in Ashadu's films – not always overtly declared, but embedded in how she frames labour, subjectivity and agency, especially through the lenses of gender and class. Her feminism is partly a critique of the colonial and patriarchal gaze that objectifies, exoticises or flattens Black African subjects. Her protagonists are ordinary people, including workers, migrants and marginalised groups. In *Makoko Sawmill* and *Brown Goods* the depicted workers are approached through the prism of gender, Black identity and postcolonial geographies. Ashadu draws attention to the way space is traversed – whether controlled, claimed or resisted. This is pertinent to feminist geographies, namely the question of who is permitted to move freely and who is not. It is an important point to consider, as it concerns the relationships between bodies, especially those that are racialised and gendered, and their environment.

In *Machine Boys*, Ashadu explores the dynamics of hypermasculinity and precarious economic conditions. Rather than glorifying or romanticising these, she presents them in a deliberate and unhurried manner, stressing moments of pause, contemplation and spatial navigation. This concept of finding vulnerability in masculinity is further reinforced in *Power Man* (2018) and *MUSCLE* (2025). In Ashadu's world, masculinity is not heroic; it is laborious, fragile and tied to economic pressures. She examines how it is exhibited, constructed and negotiated in space, for instance the intimate setting of an outdoor gym in the slums of Lagos, offering a feminist perspective that interrogates how men are themselves shaped by the male gaze, especially within capitalist and postcolonial frameworks. As opposed to simply replacing that gaze with a reversal, Ashadu proposes a more radical approach: a gaze that is both ambiguous and destabilised. Her framing negates voyeuristic and patriarchal camera traditions, and rather challenges the conventional practices inherent in both Western art history and documentary filmmaking. Ashadu actively reclaims the gaze – both as a female artist and as a Nigerian British filmmaker. This is, in other words, a very personal matter.

As noted before, Ashadu has a particular focus on labouring bodies, such as those engaged in sand mining, cattle herding or migrant labour. In *Plateau*, for example, the cinematic perspective is corporealised, accentuating the physical demands and repetitive strain of labour. The artist's camera movements frequently emulate these rhythms, thereby establishing a somatic connection between viewer and subject. This embodied perspective in *King of Boys (Abattoir of Makoko)* posits a late capitalist society, contending that bodily lives are shaped by a complex of daily and ongoing practices, including work and consumption. The commodification of these and other social practices in the late twentieth century, often understood to refer to the needs of the body, is in fact a means of capital accumulation. Ashadu's research examines how the body is constructed under postcolonial economic conditions to illustrate its transformation into a nexus of exchange value.

Work and the worker are often treated in experimental film in such a way that labour is no longer action oriented, heroic or even background noise. Rather, its material, emotional and political aspects are emphasised, often through the medium itself. By focusing on marginalised subjects and granting them space, dignity and complexity, Ashadu inverts the traditional subject-viewer power dynamic. The subjects occasionally look directly at the camera and acknowledge its presence, breaking the fourth wall through the gaze rather than via dialogue. And as the gaze is necessarily reciprocated, we viewers transform from passive recipients into active participants. In *Plateau*, the approach is lyrical, drawing us in. Once we are settled, however, it becomes apparent that the film deals with some uncomfortable topics.

Ashadu's compositions offer space for the subjects to breathe and be complex. The camera doesn't dominate, and never adopts the speed of our capitalist times, but rather listens carefully and attentively. Another look back into film history feels appropriate here. Harun Farocki's *Workers Leaving the Factory* (1995), for example, highlights the problem of cinema's limited engagement with the interiors of workspaces, an observation that serves to critique the invisibility of labour and the politics of representation. Ashadu's approach in *Destiny* offers a counterargument. It employs a range of manual labourers in different sequences and, as previously mentioned, a central motif involves differentiating between external and internal scenarios. In *Red Gold*, the artist employs a two-screen installation, with the workers depicted on the left side of the composition and a Prince – who is not working but sitting and walking, and the sole individual who is speaking and looking directly into the camera – on the right. There is clearly a discrepancy in the sequence of events depicted, and the workers are shown from an overhead perspective, implying control, whereas the Prince is shown frontally, implying equality. Yet ultimately, Ashadu allows the workers to be present on their own terms, thereby disrupting the usual extractive visual economy.

Also interesting is how Ashadu highlights Black skin. She doesn't just use blackness as a token; she thinks about it, especially when it comes to texture, work, land and light. Unlike in the early days of colonialism, it is now about how blackness is experienced, worked, seen and sometimes made invisible. It is also about how the camera can be part of that notion – and resist it. A Black man is shadow boxing in *Power Man*, and she films him in low light, so only sweat and movement are perceptible. In *Brown Goods*, the title itself is suggestive of the commodification of brown skin, in terms of both race and labour. Ashadu's visual language aligns skin tones with goods, tools and the environment, thereby interrogating the production and consumption of blackness. By addressing the viewer and the construction of the image, she constantly questions ethnographic authority.

Ultimately, Ashadu's filmmaking is not only an artistic practice but also a profoundly social act. The artist creates visual spaces where marginalised voices and informal economies are granted visibility and agency. Her camera does more than observe or document – it participates. It listens, lingers and reveals, becoming an engaging, and engaged, witness.

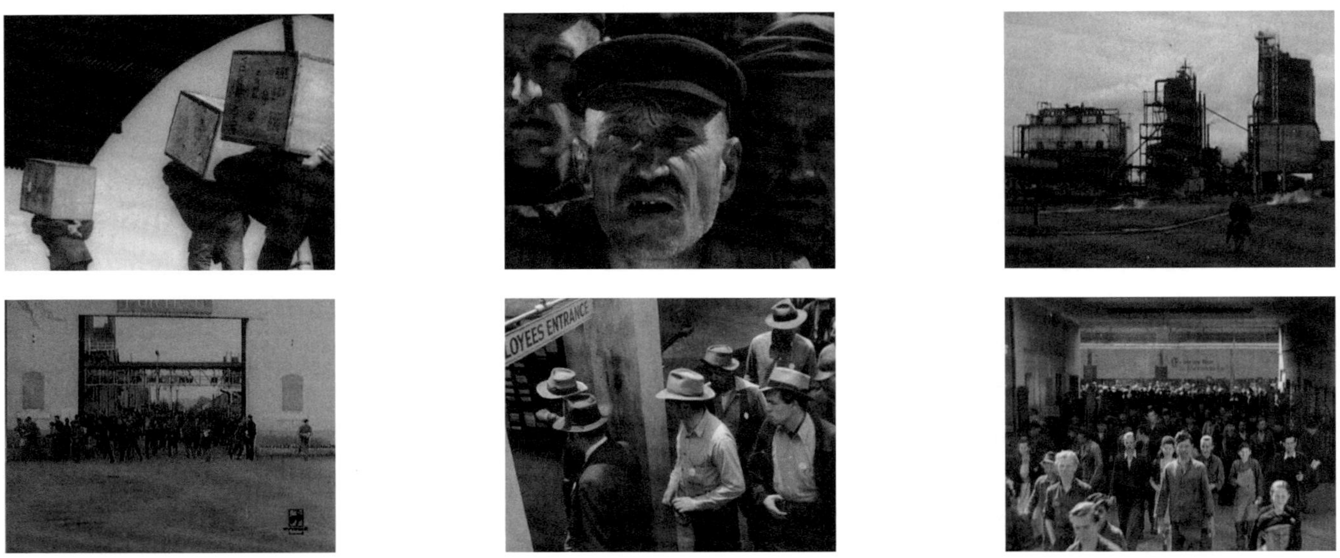

P. 44: Michael Snow, stills from *La Région Centrale*, 1971
P. 45: Chantal Akerman, stills from *News from Home*, 1977
P. 48: Harun Farocki, stills from *Workers Leaving the Factory*, 1995

Bodies and Labour

Karimah Ashadu

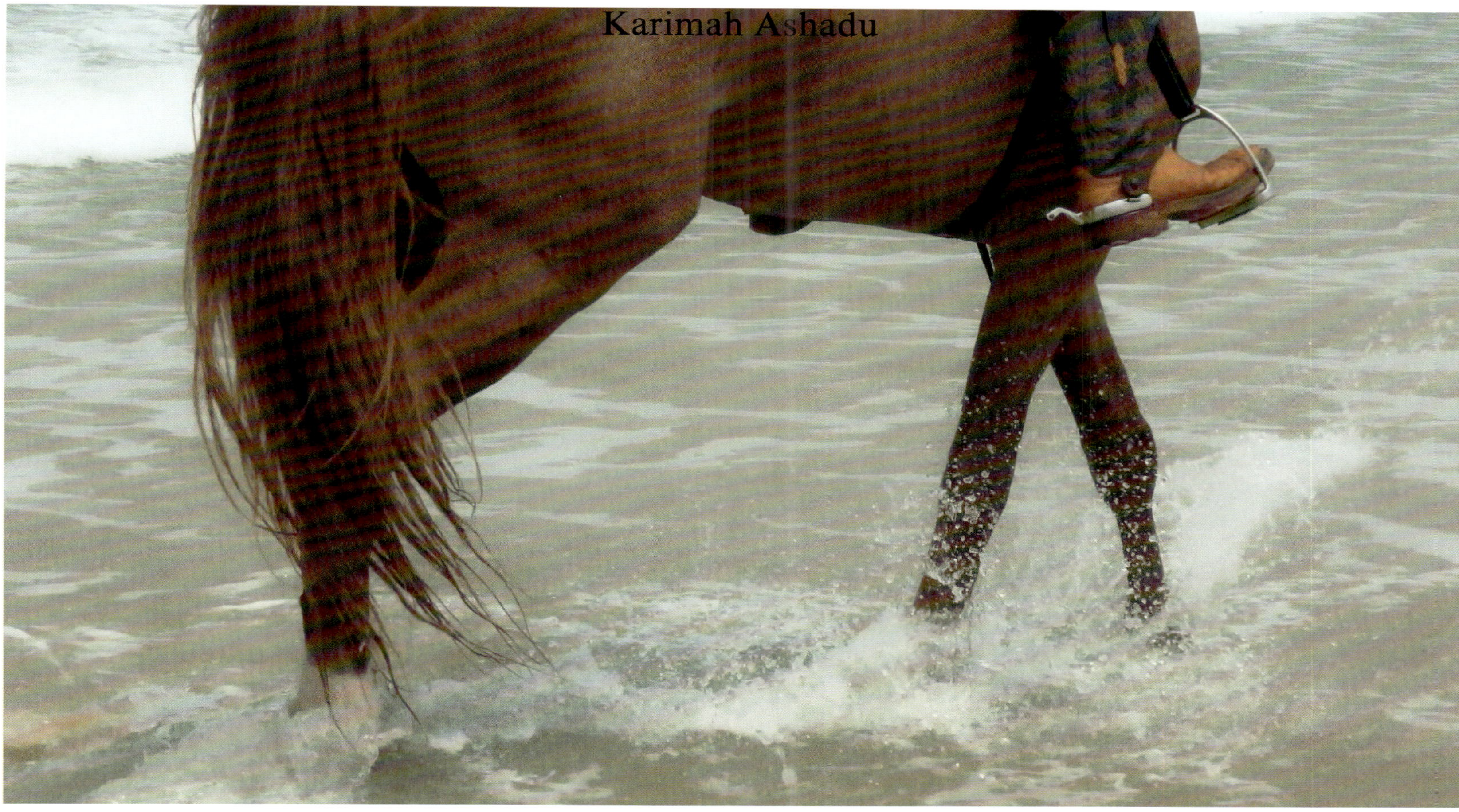

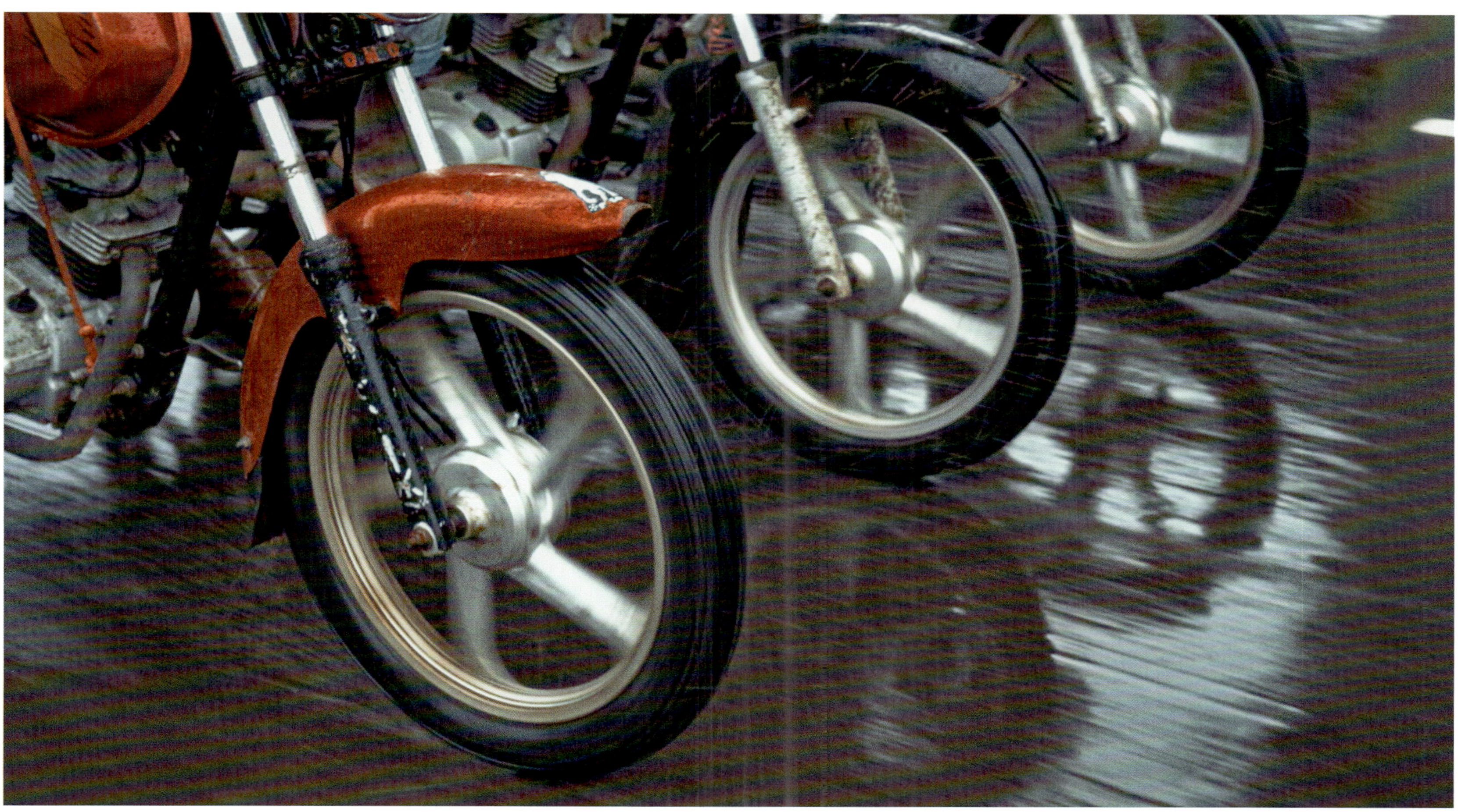

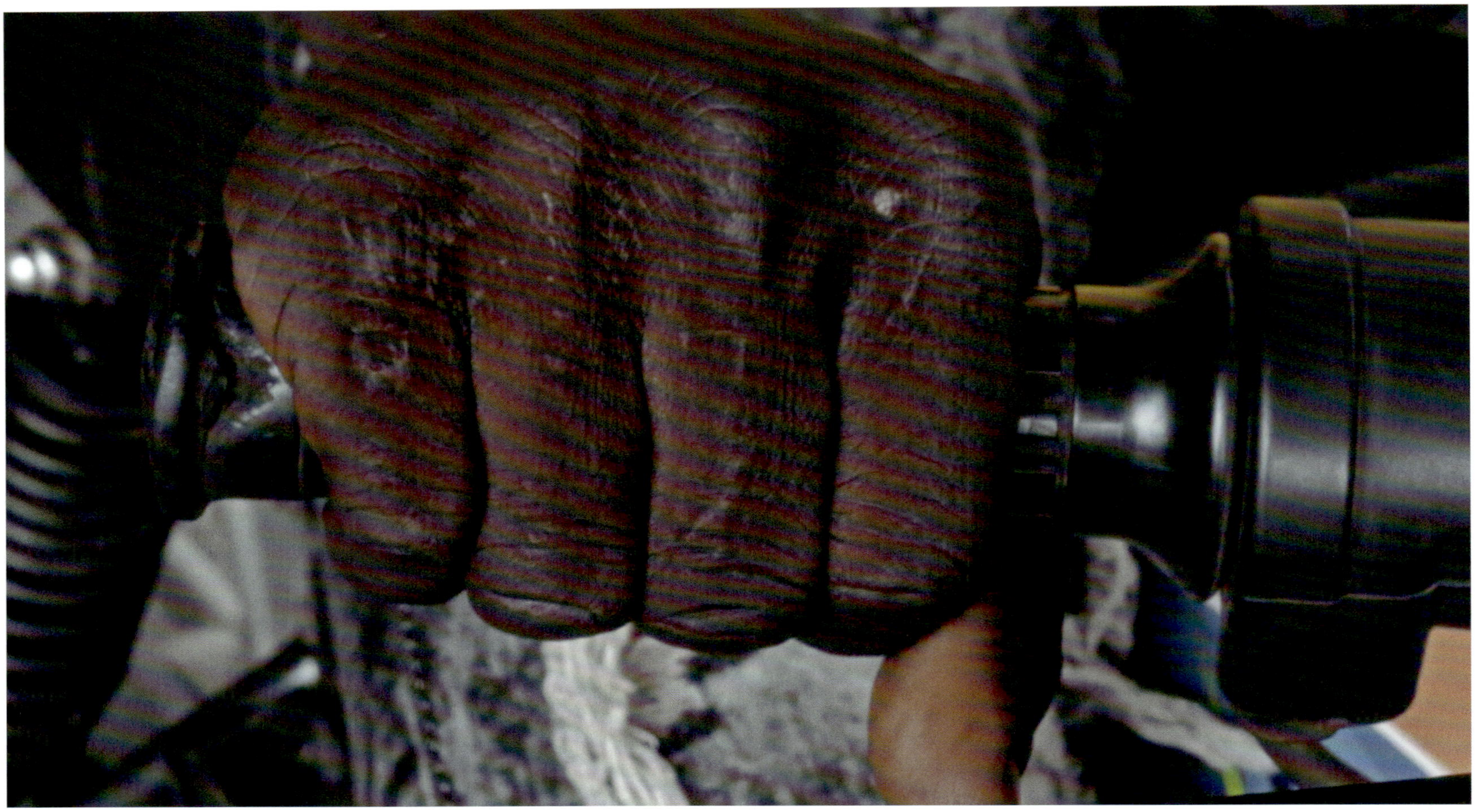

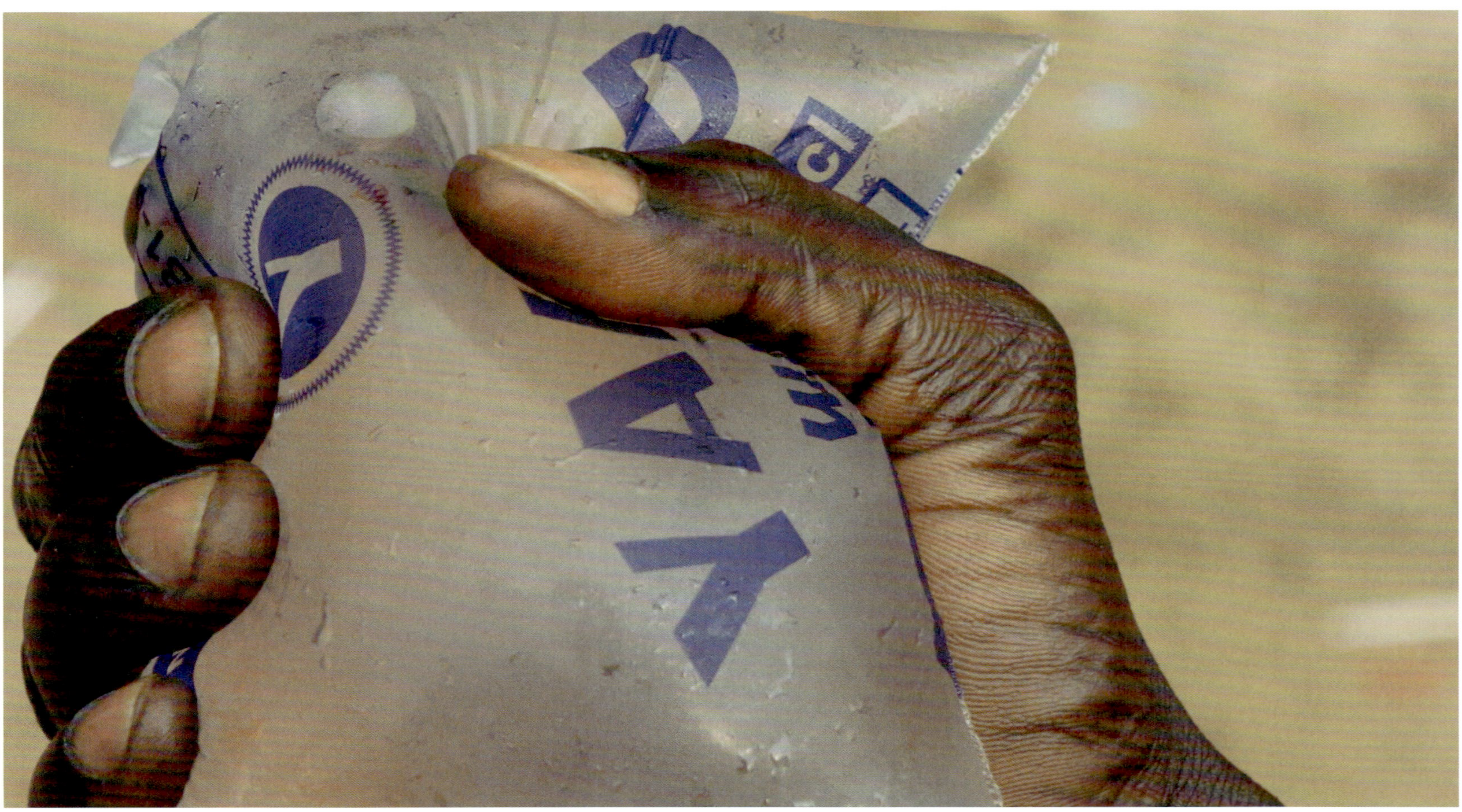

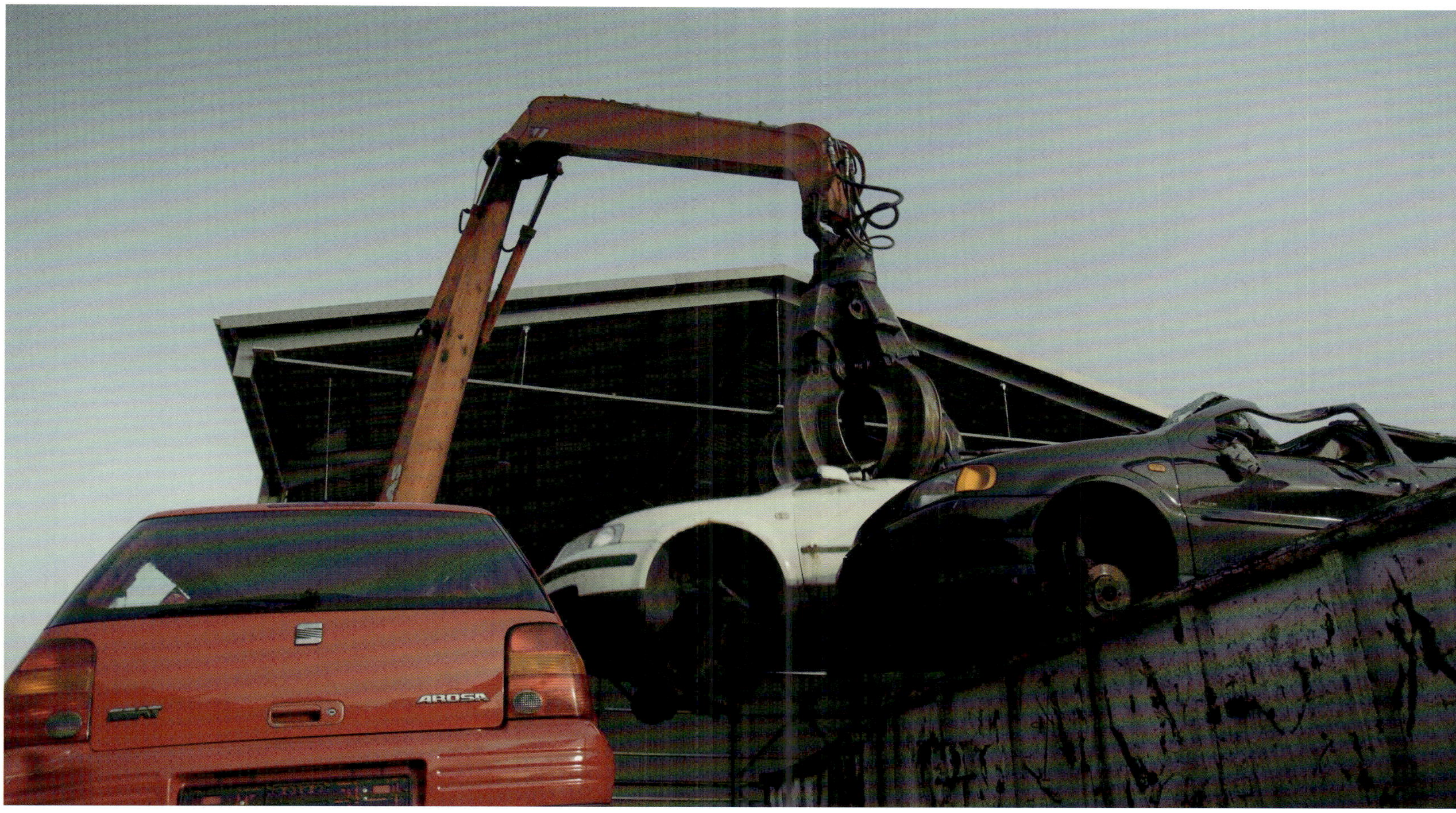
AROSA

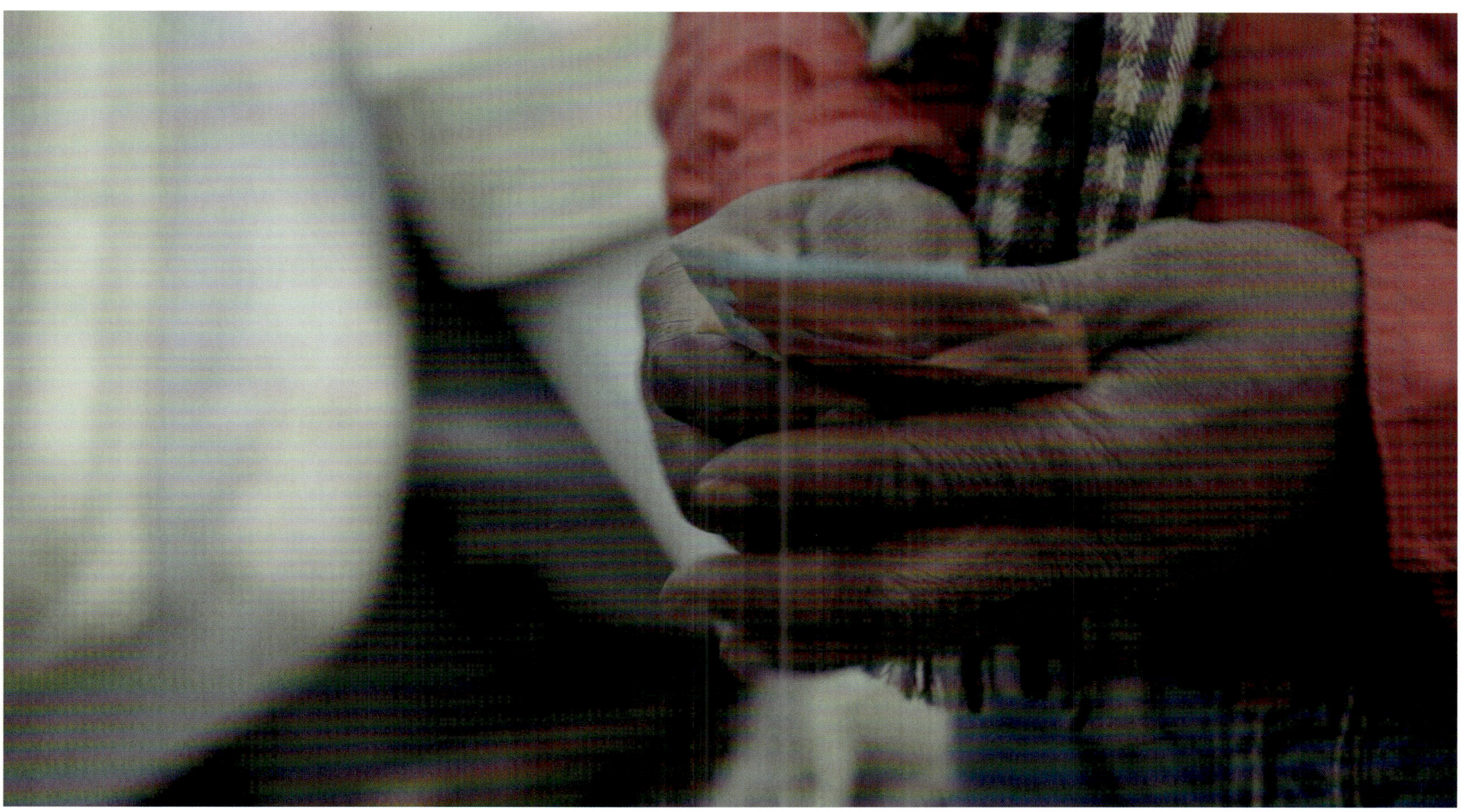

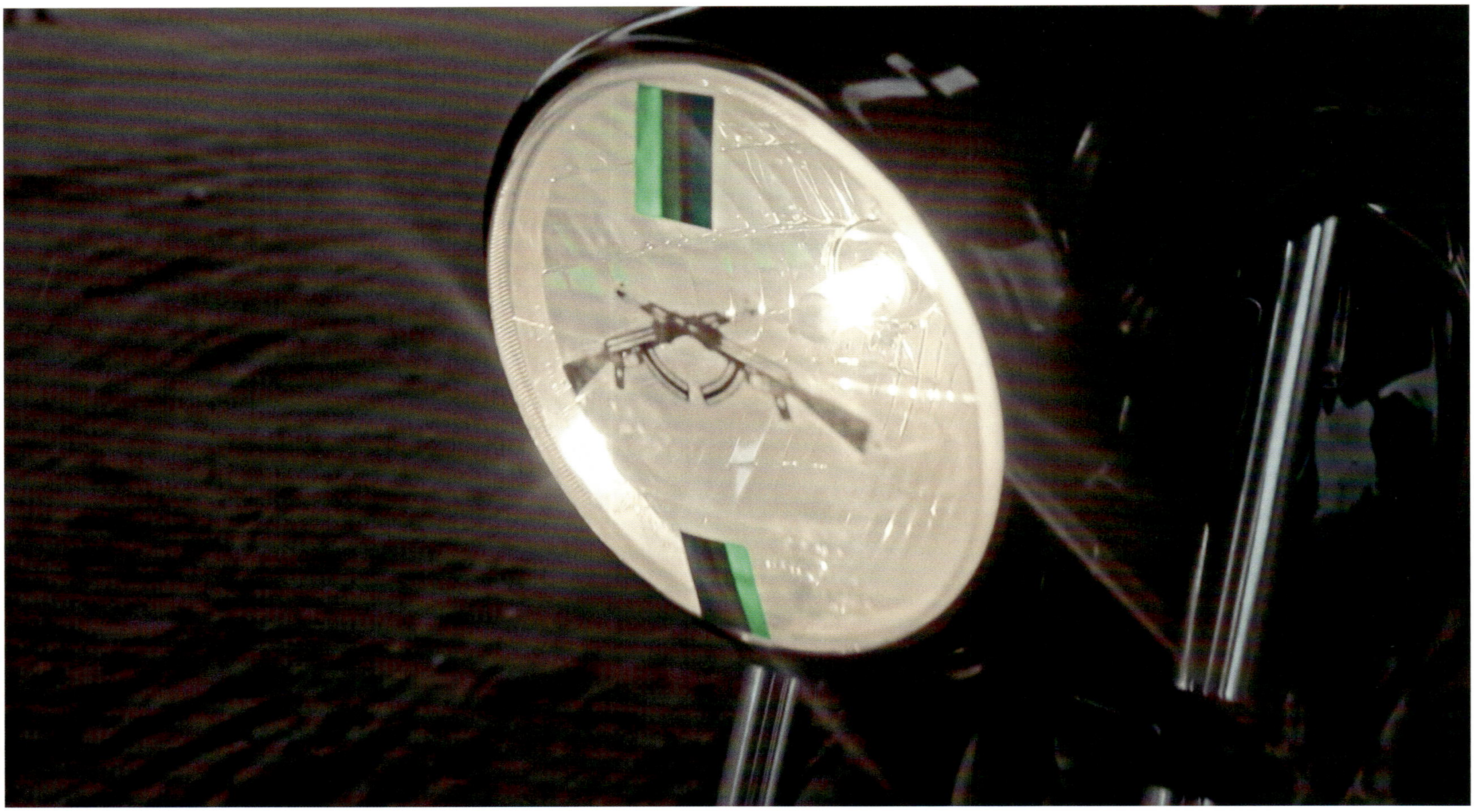

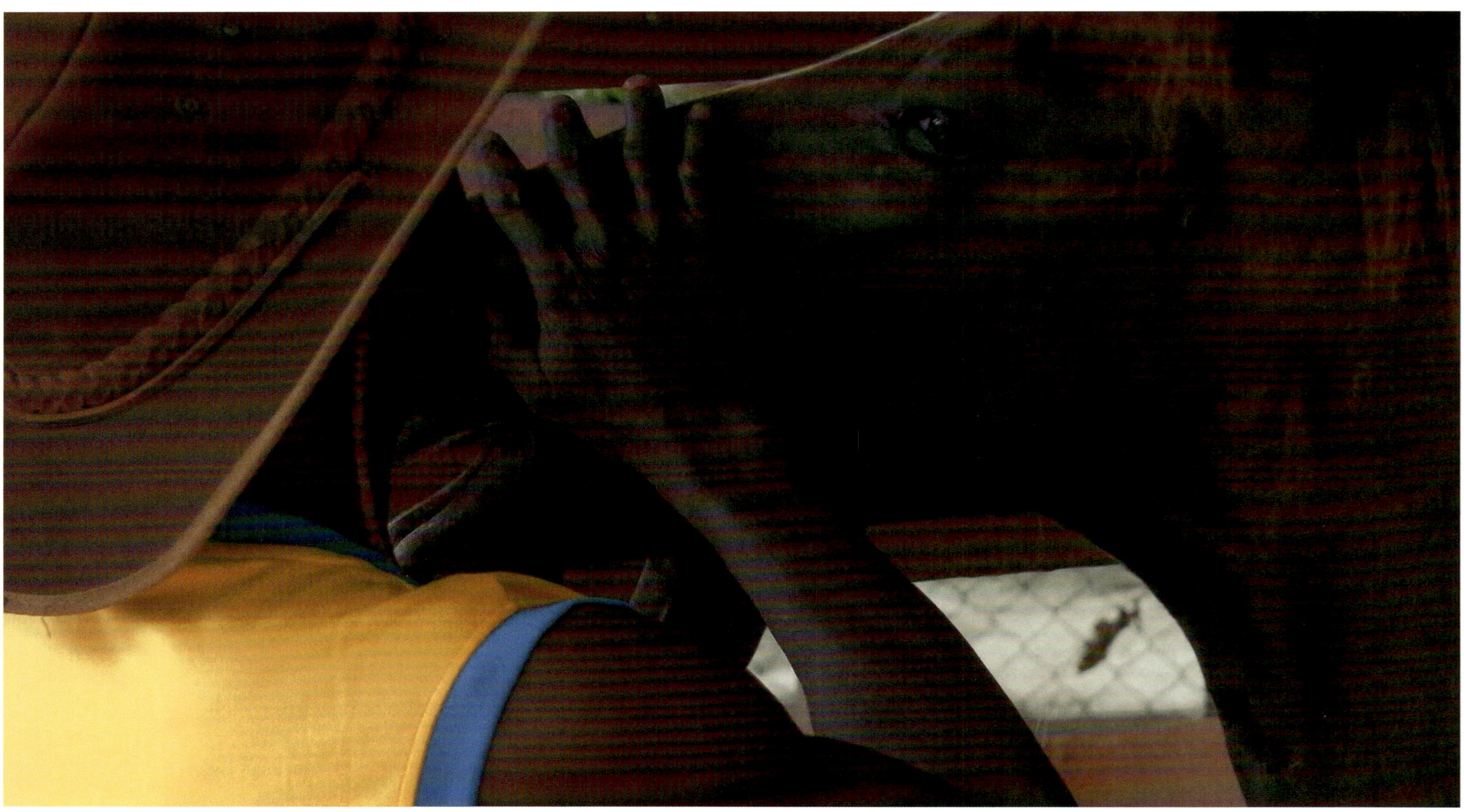

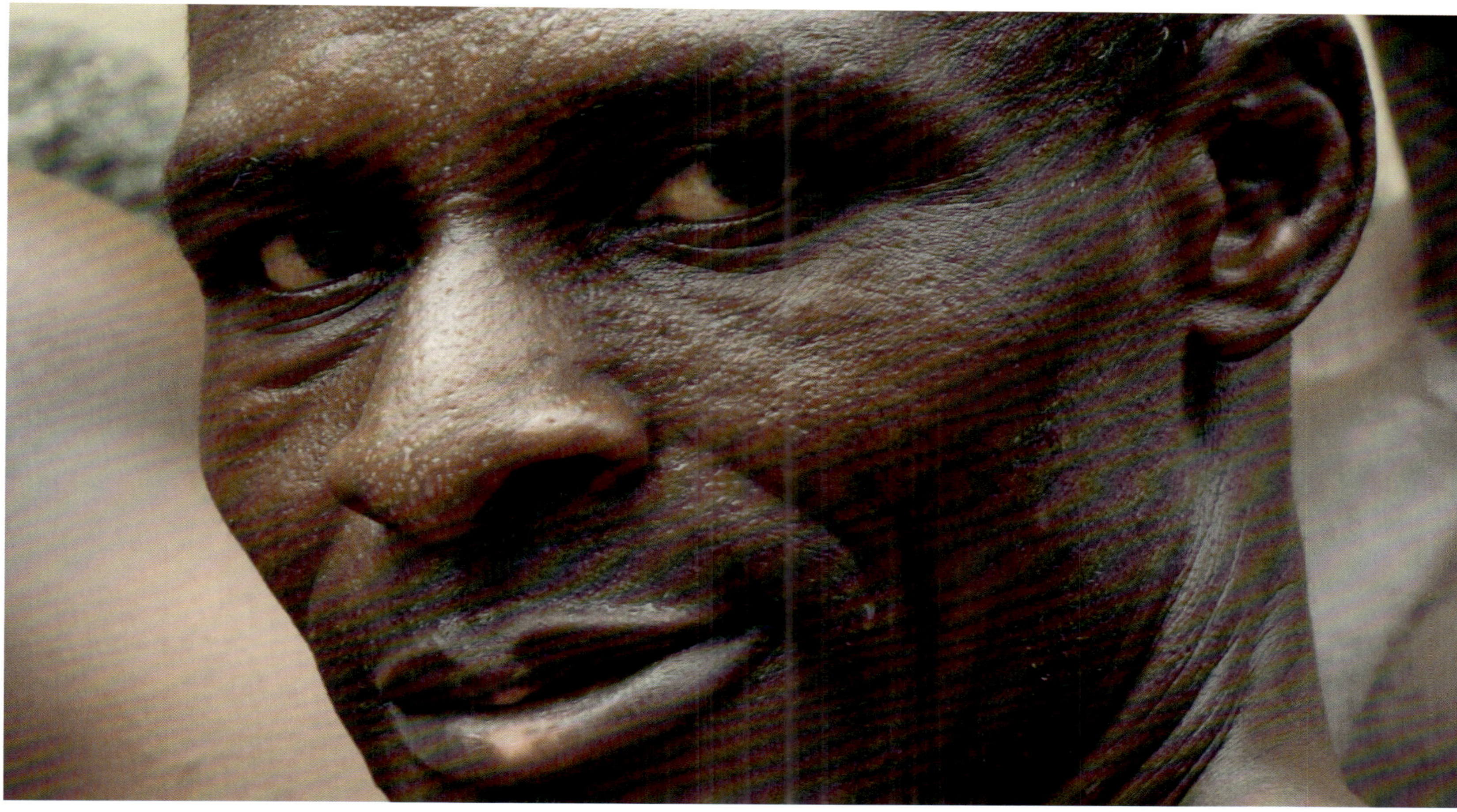

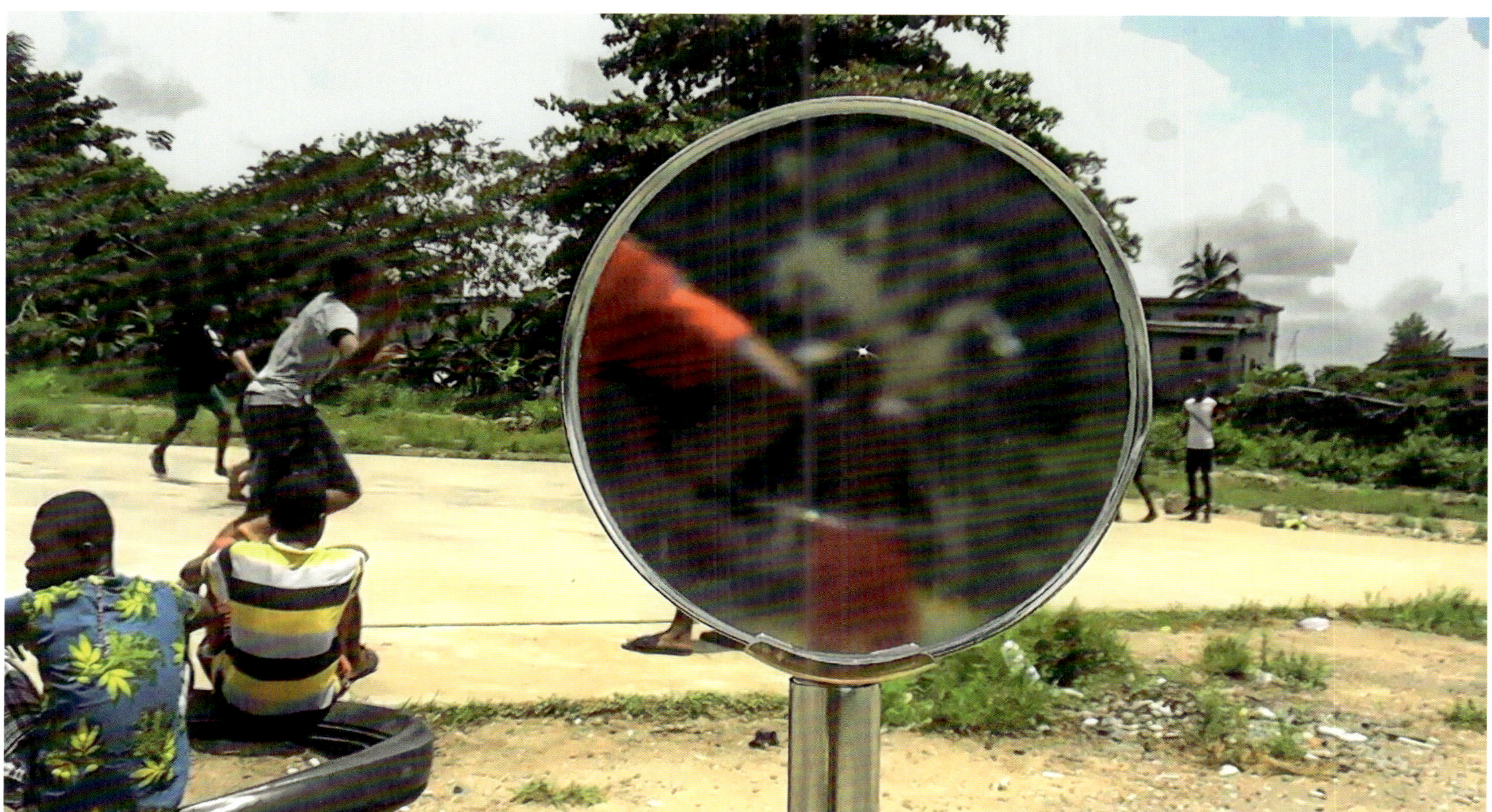

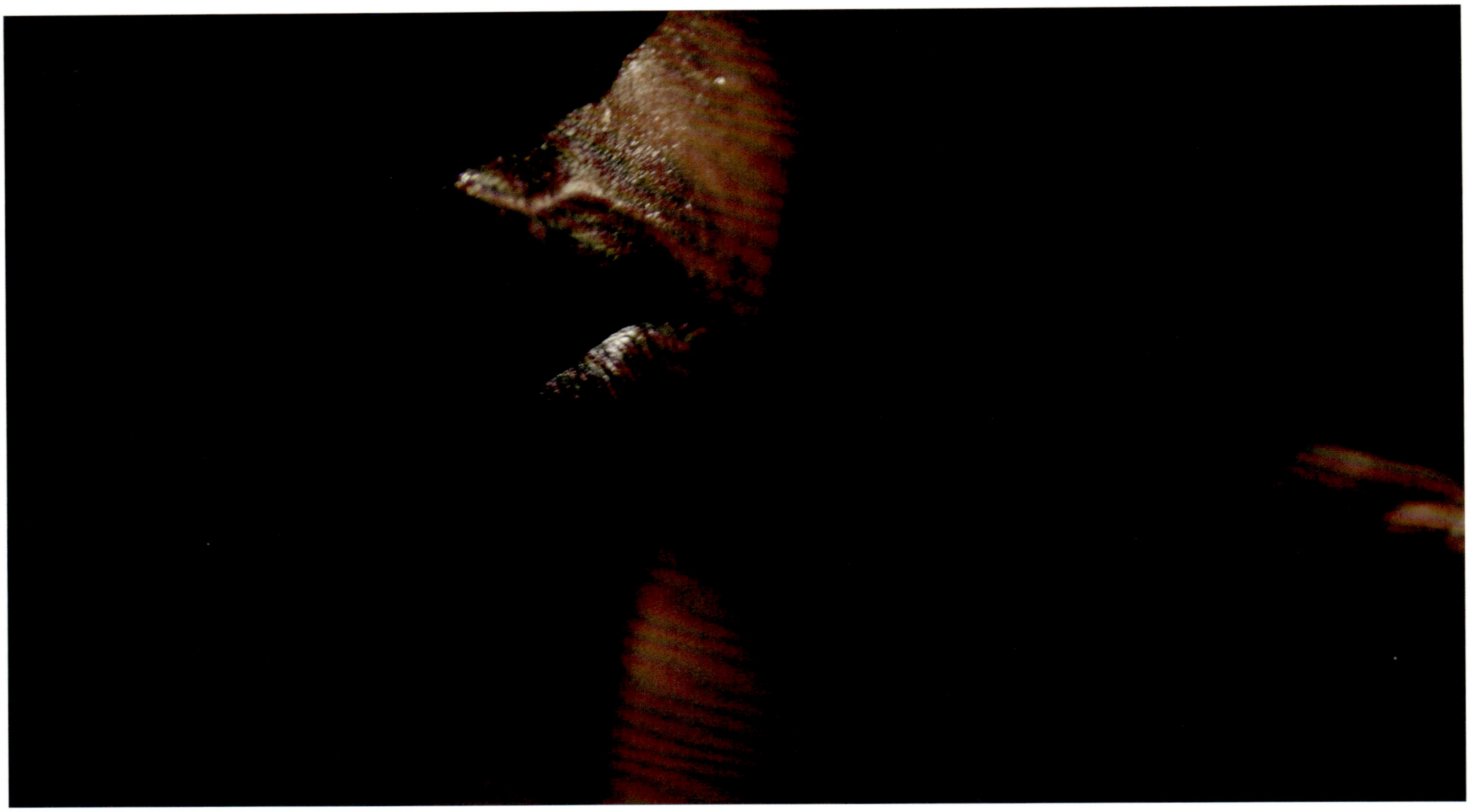

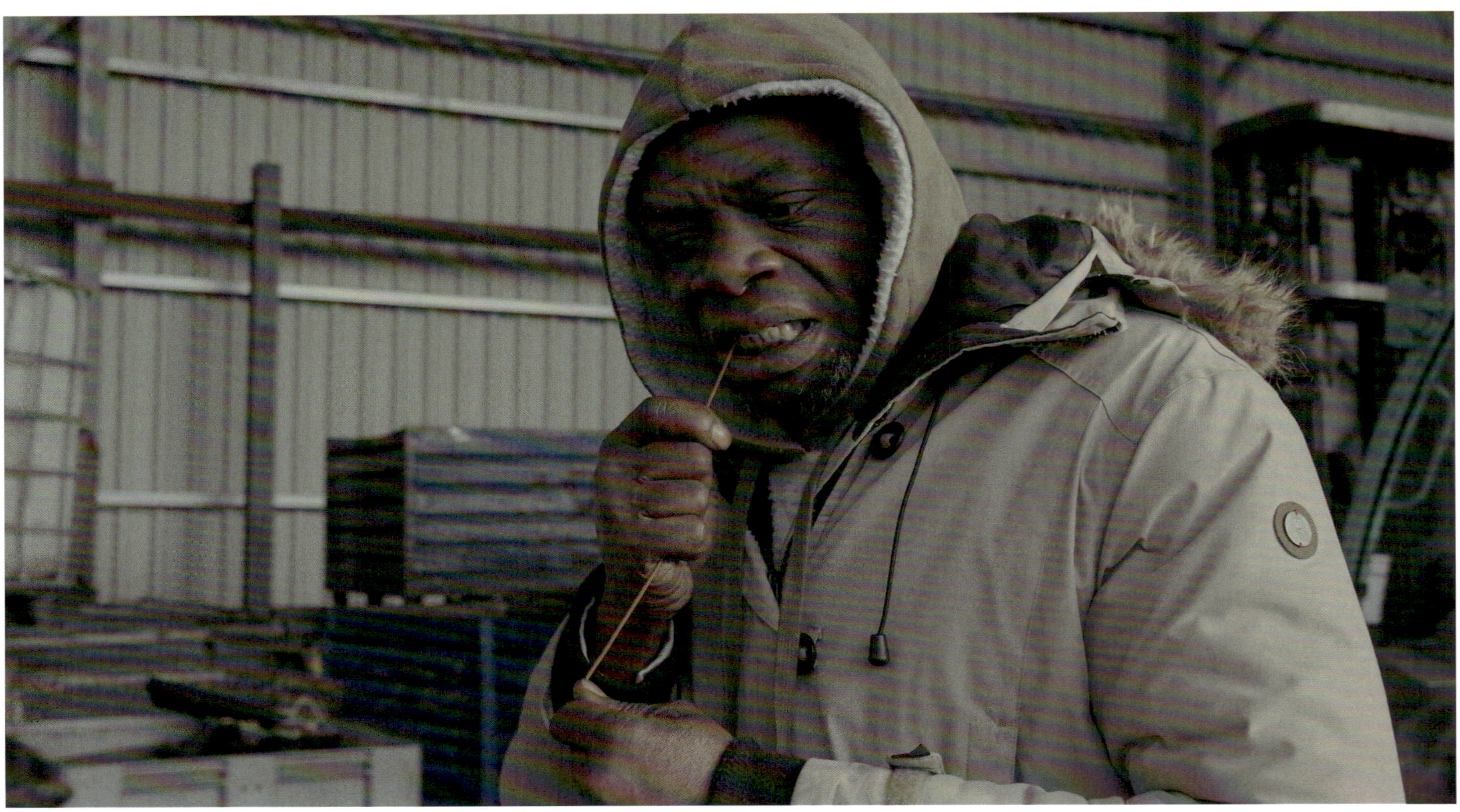

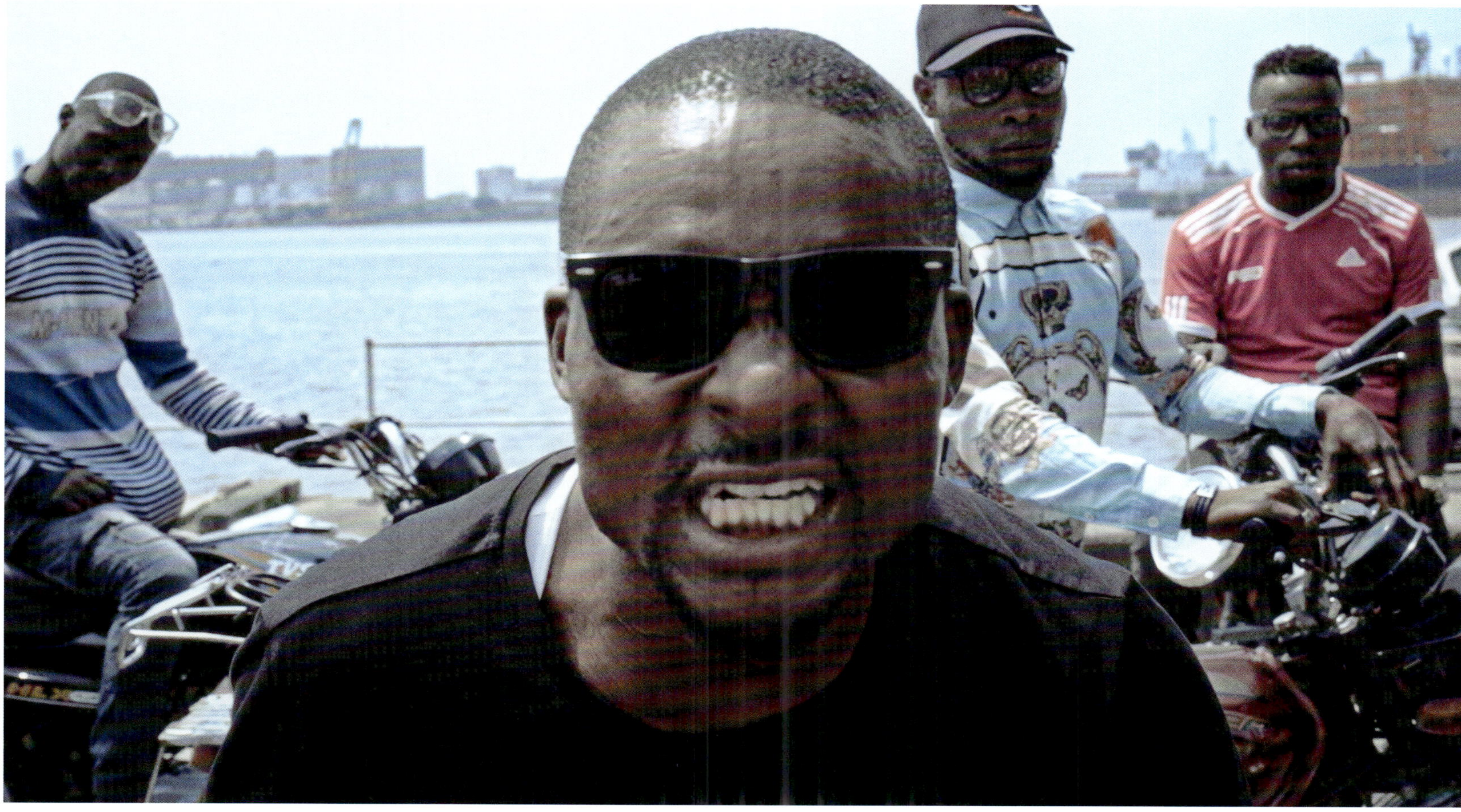

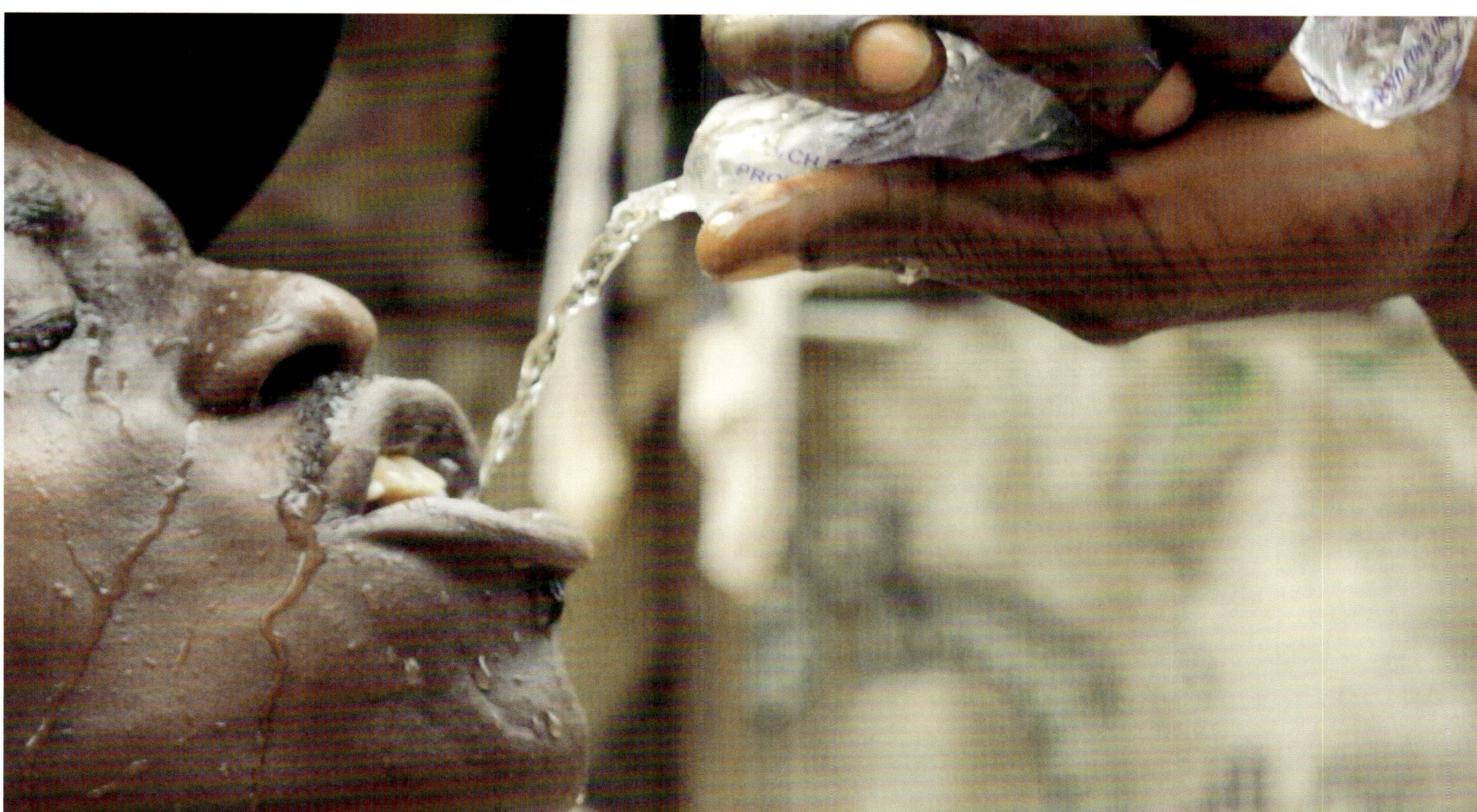

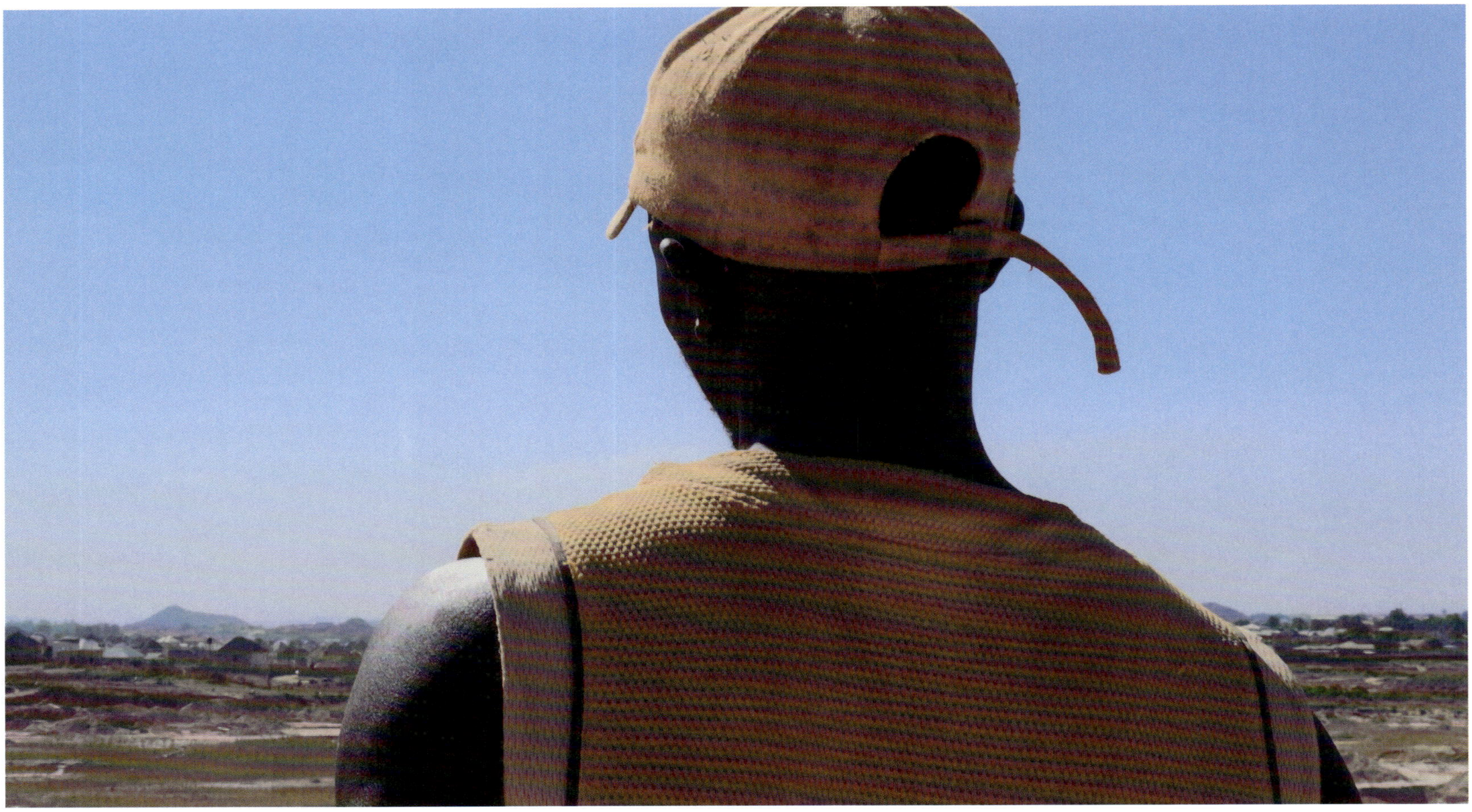

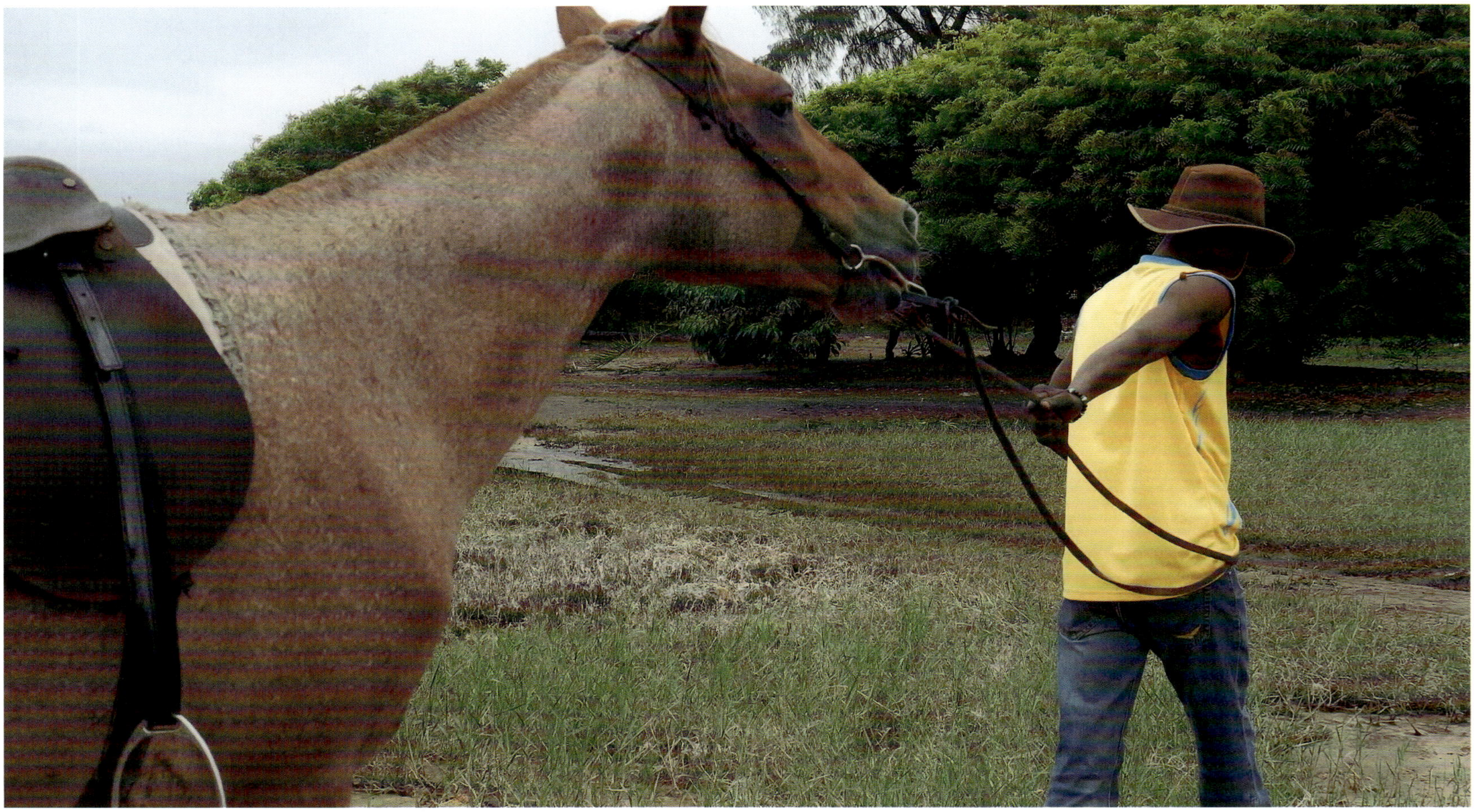

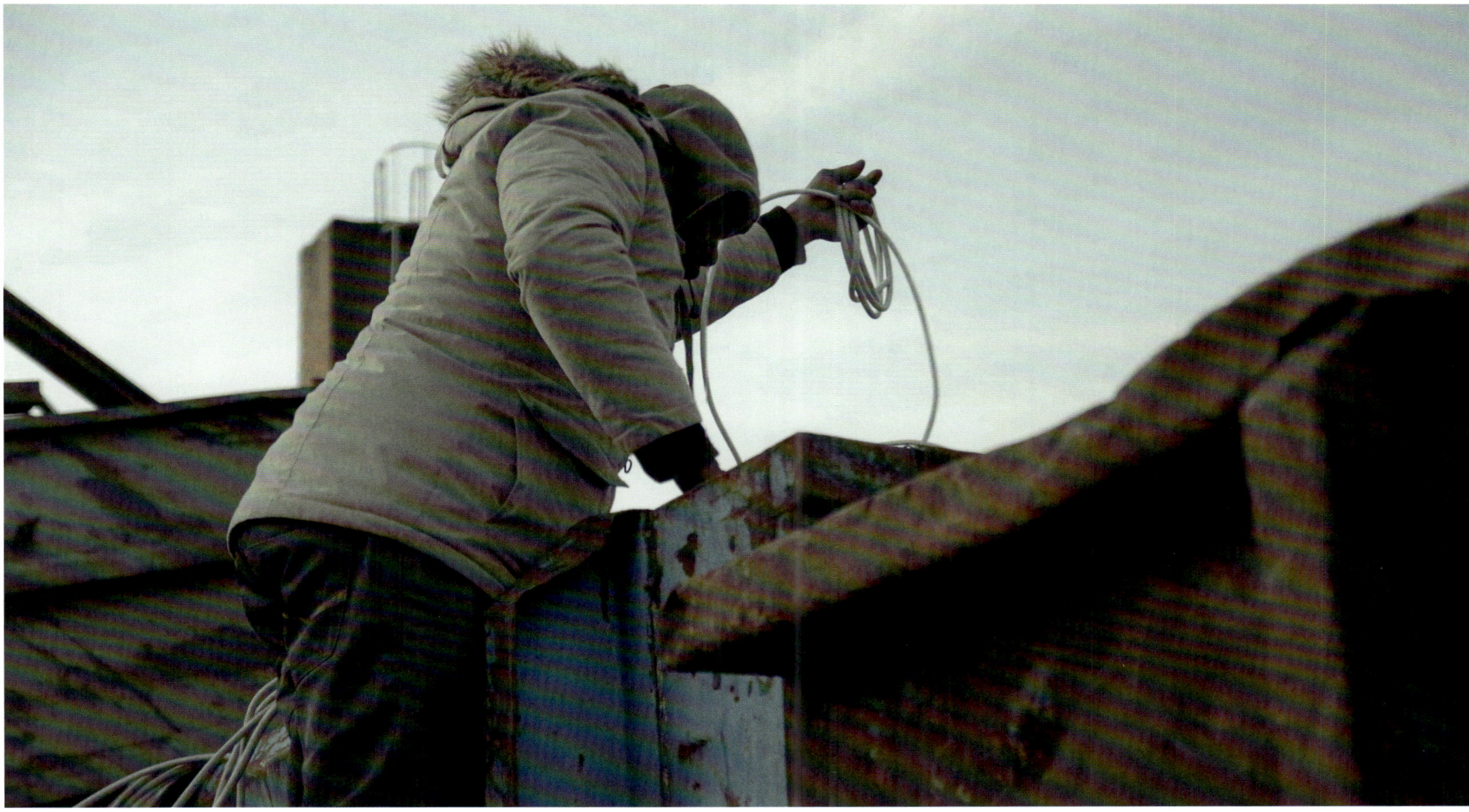

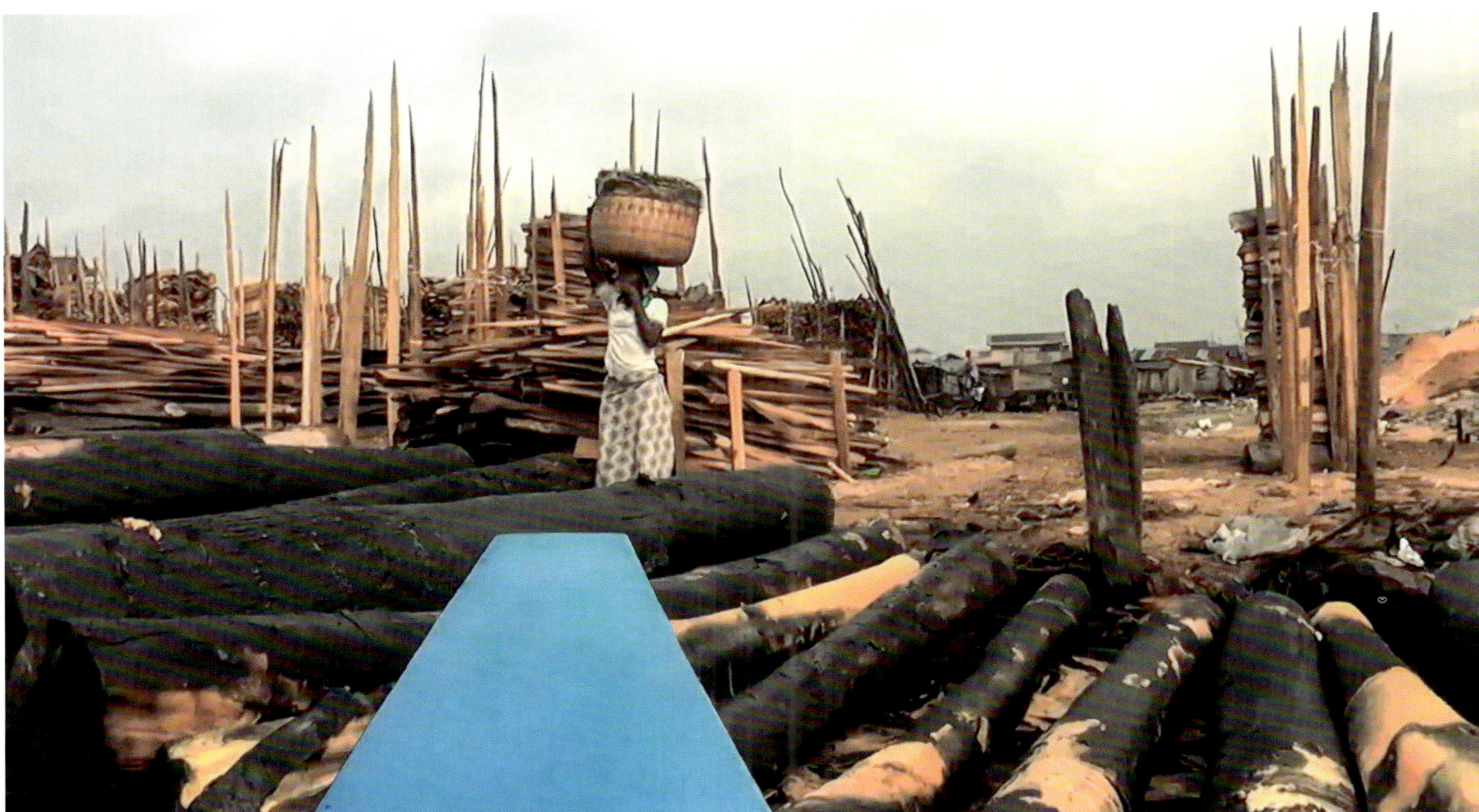

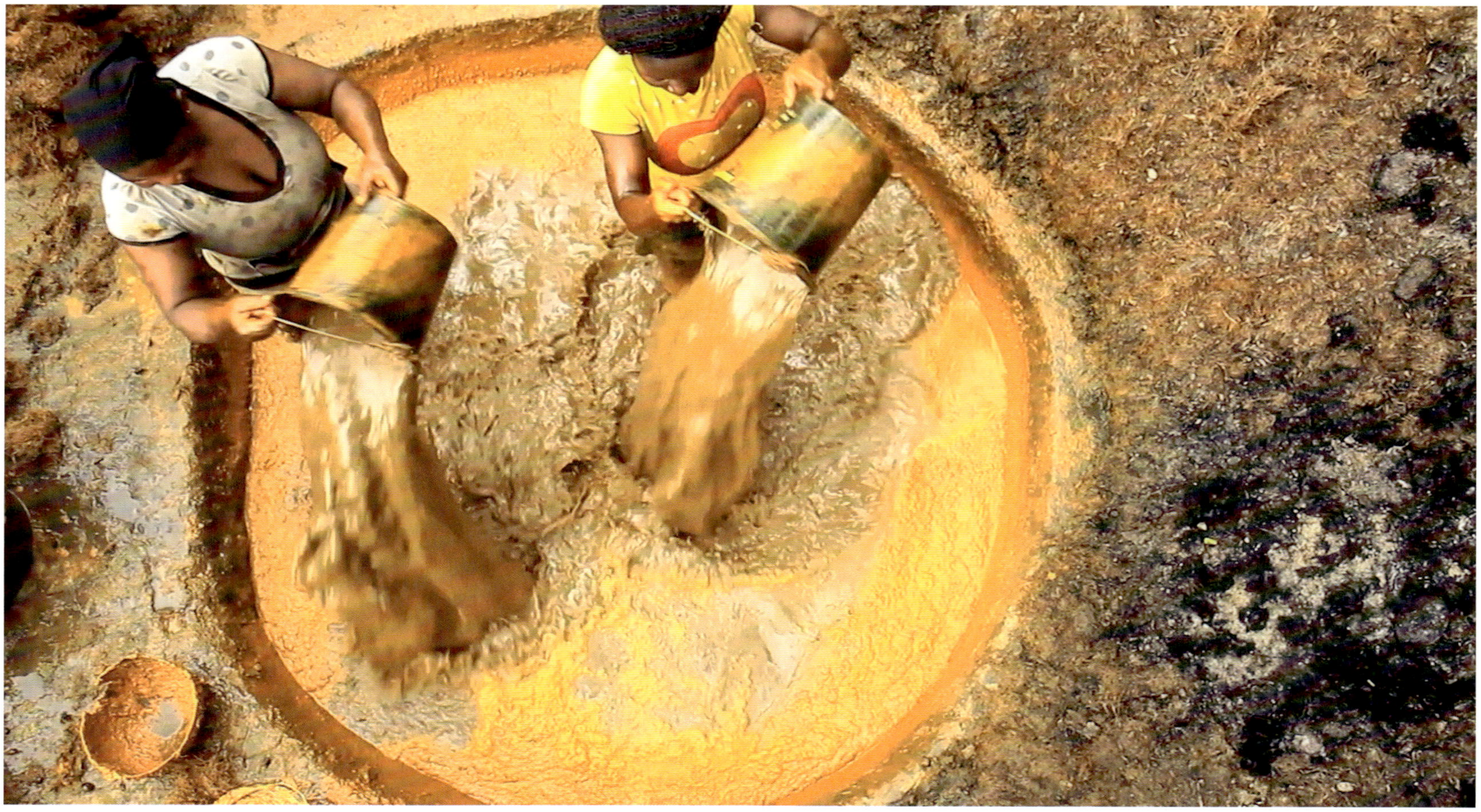

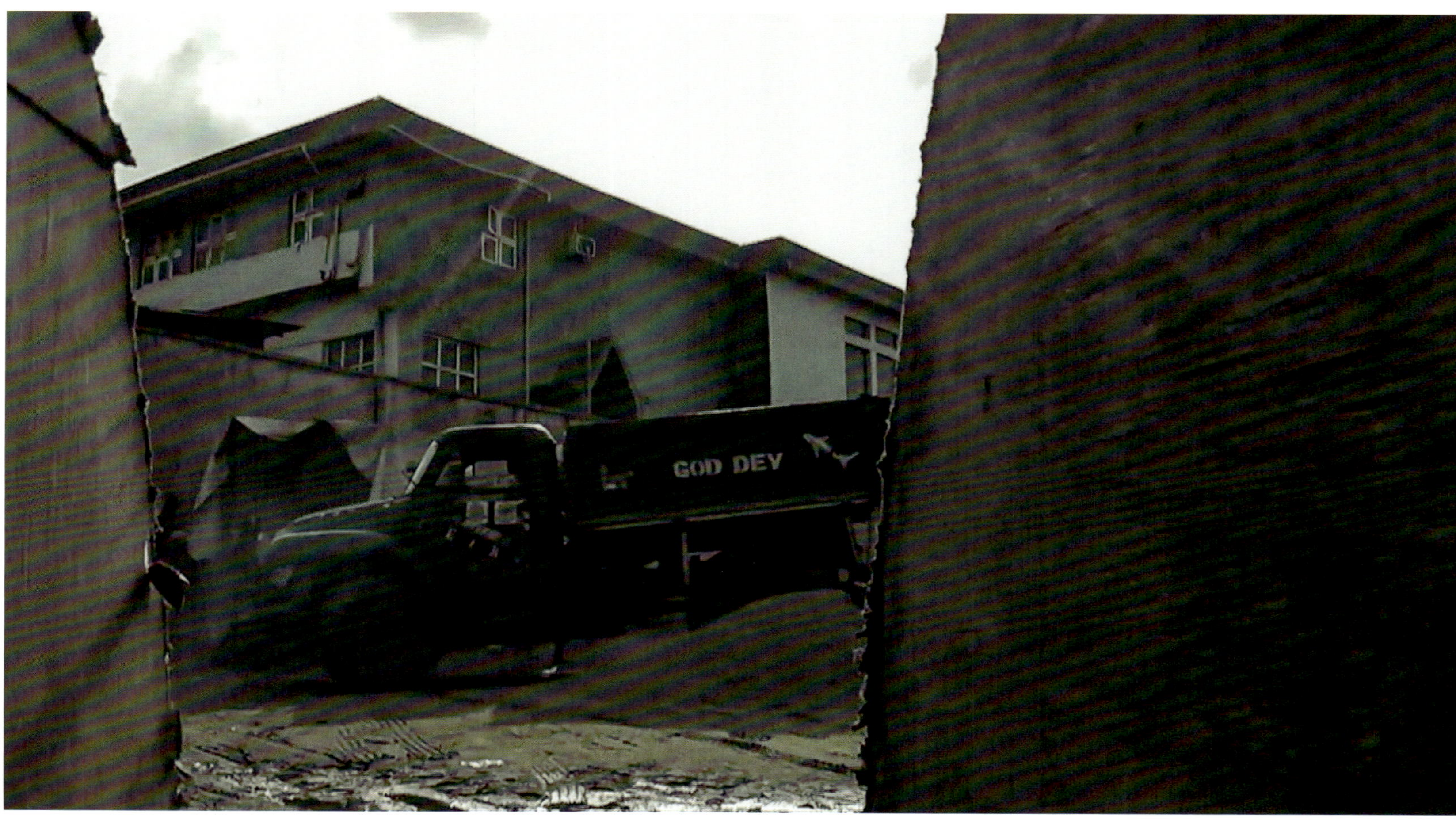
GOD DEY

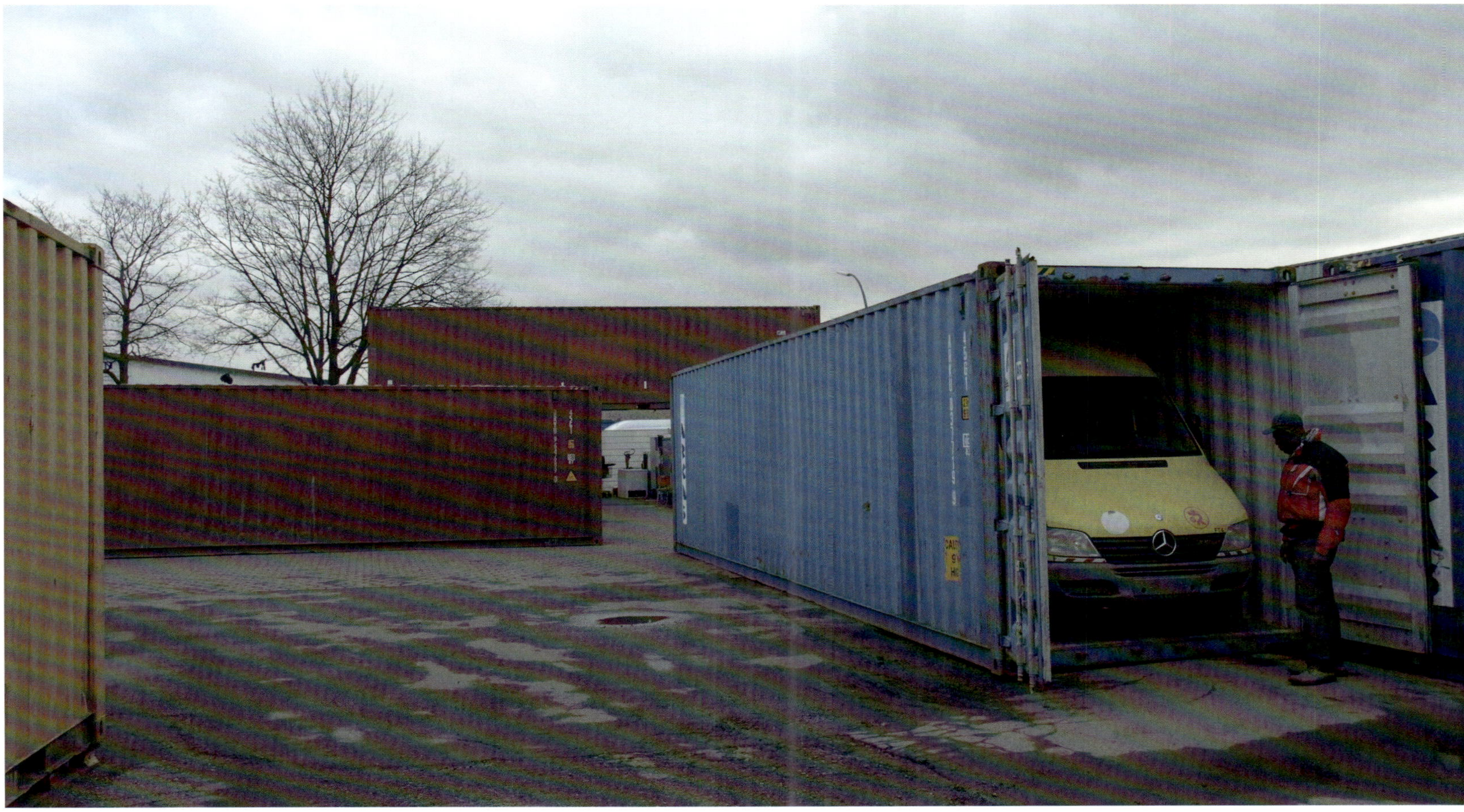

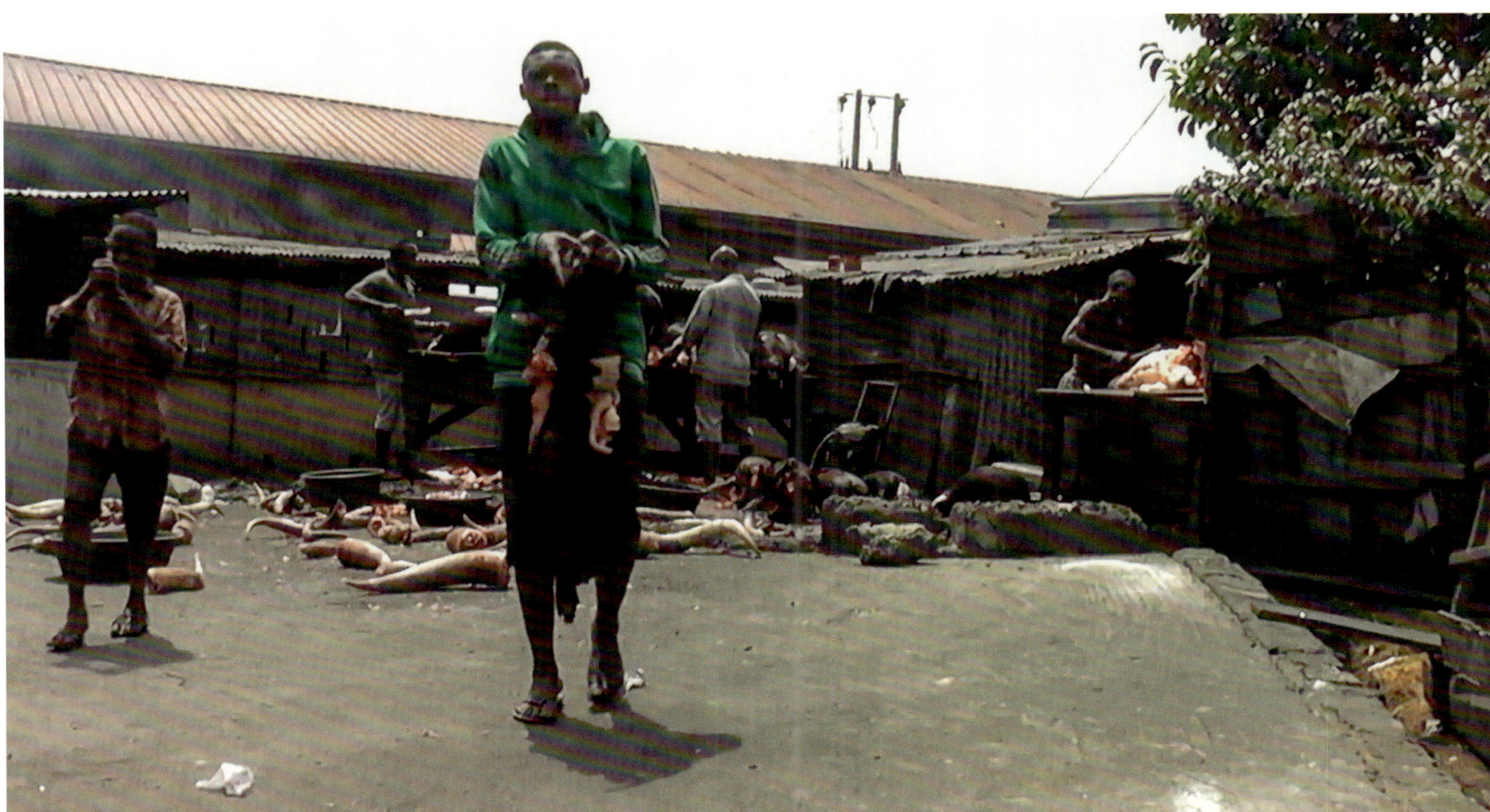

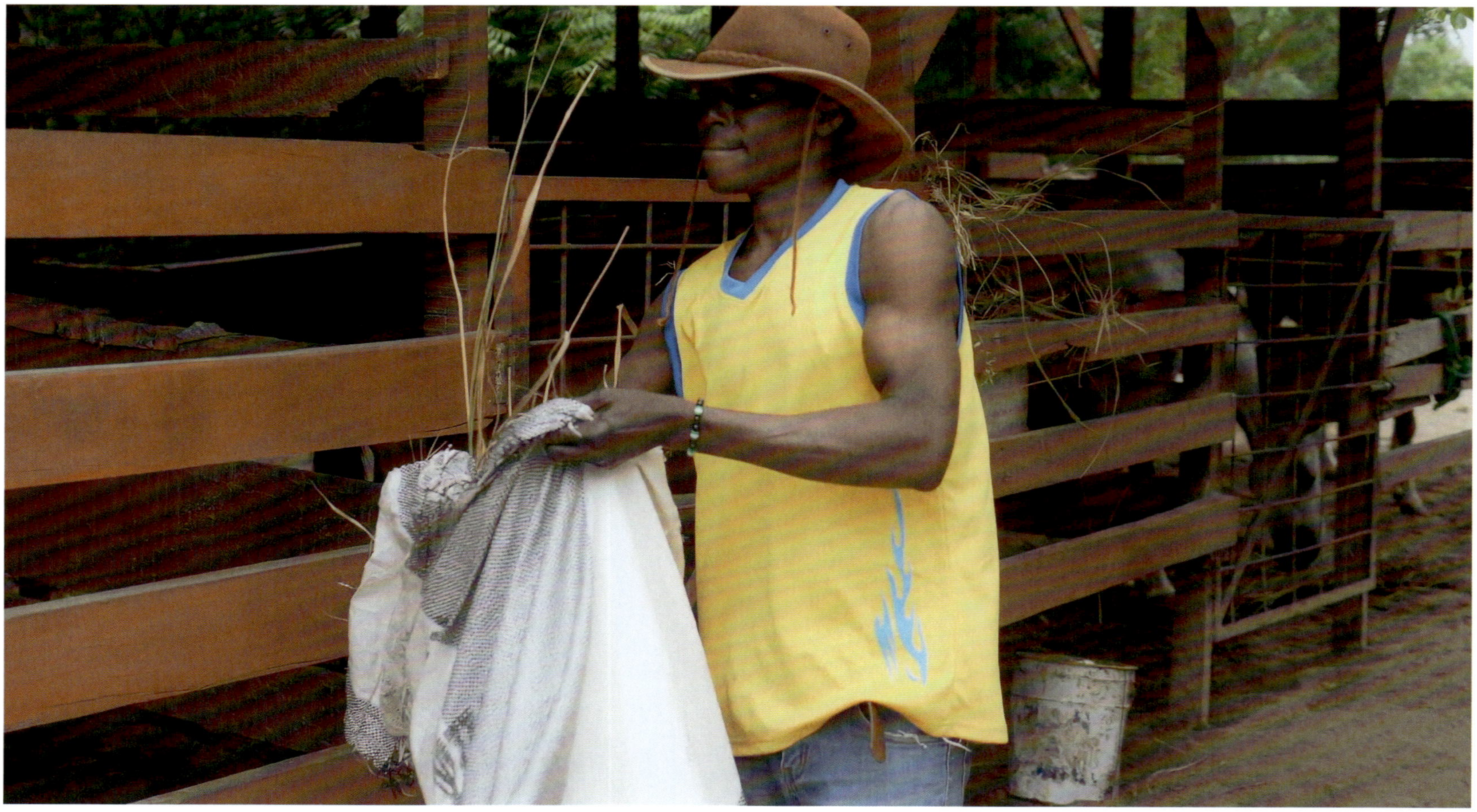

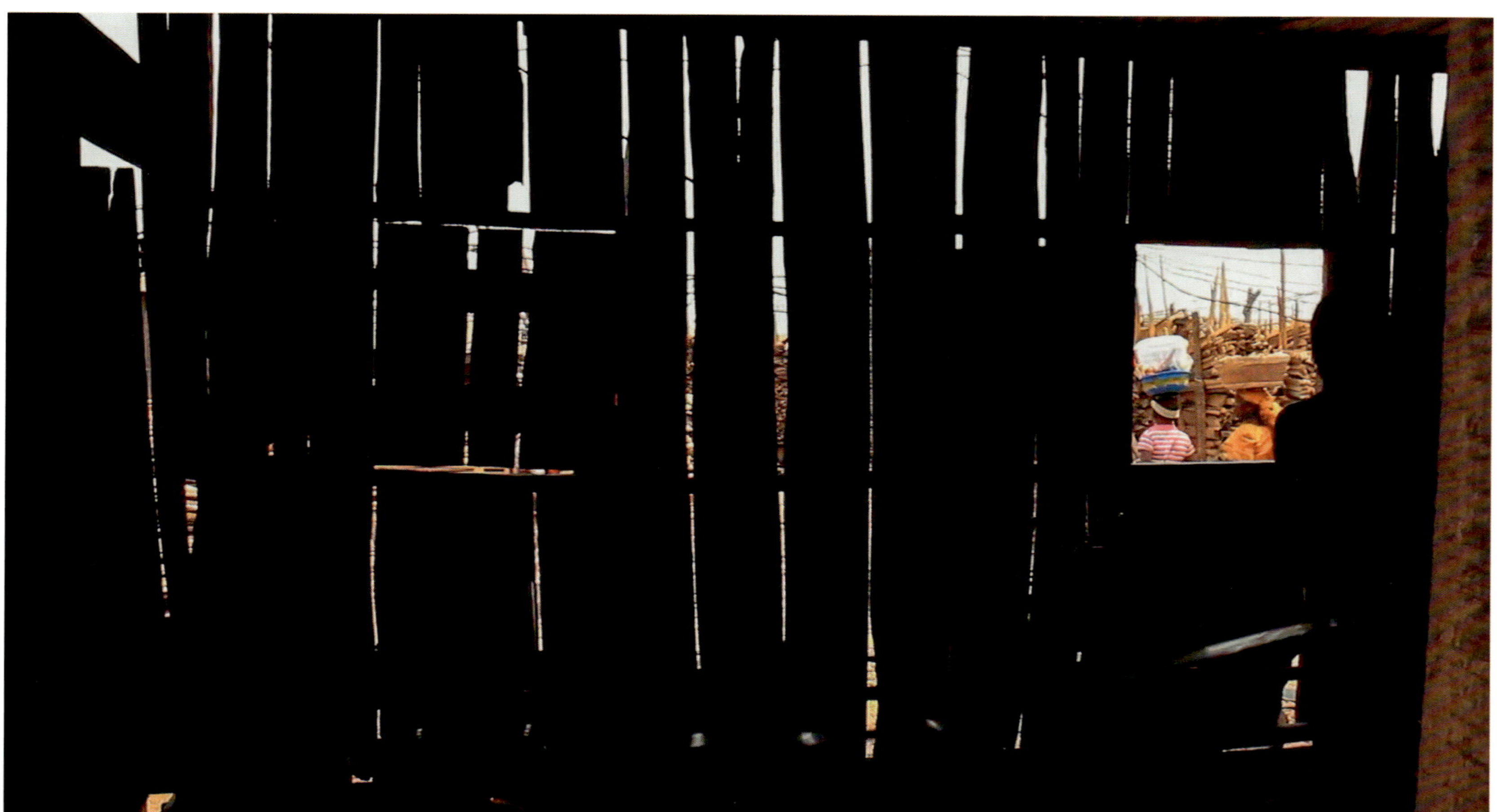

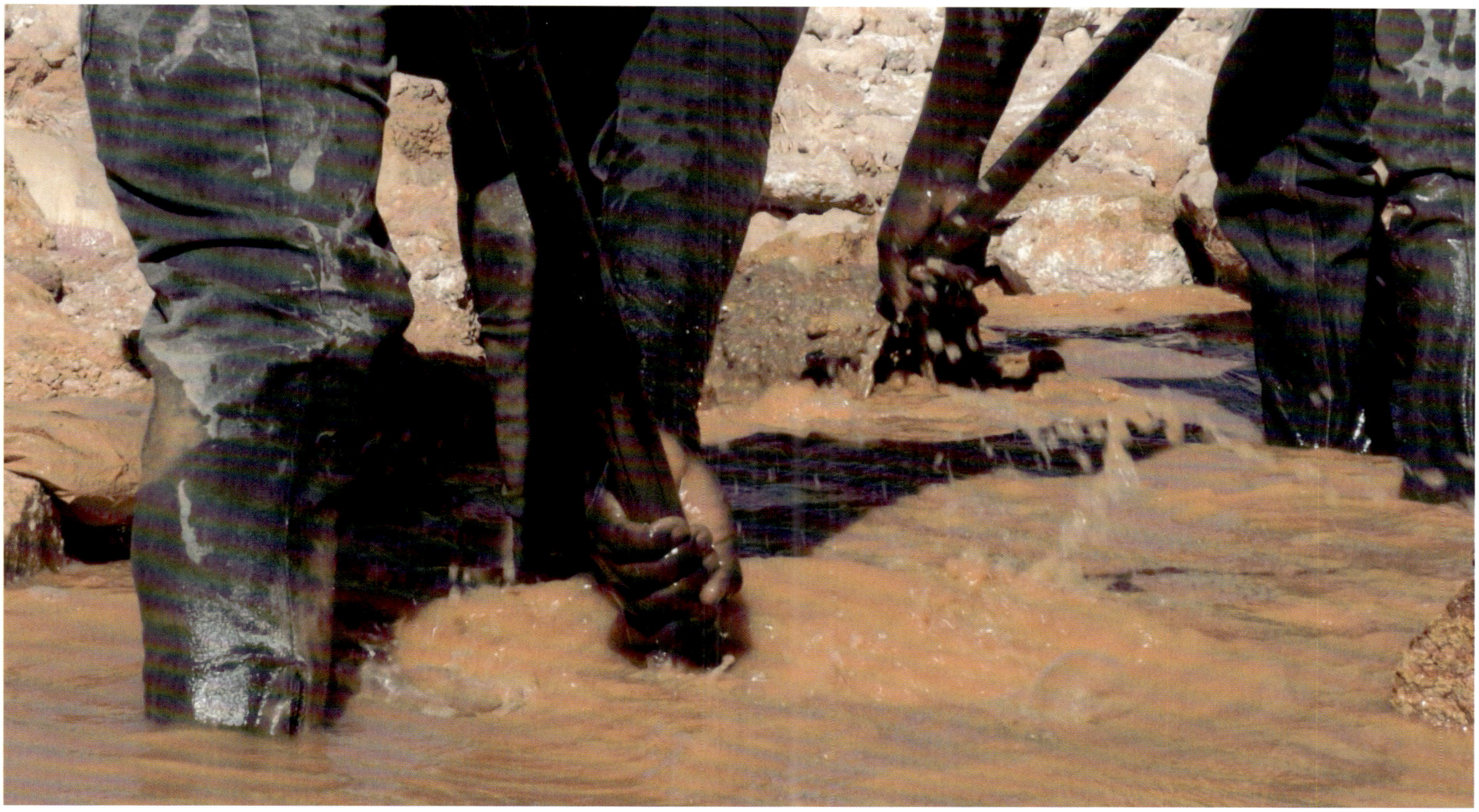

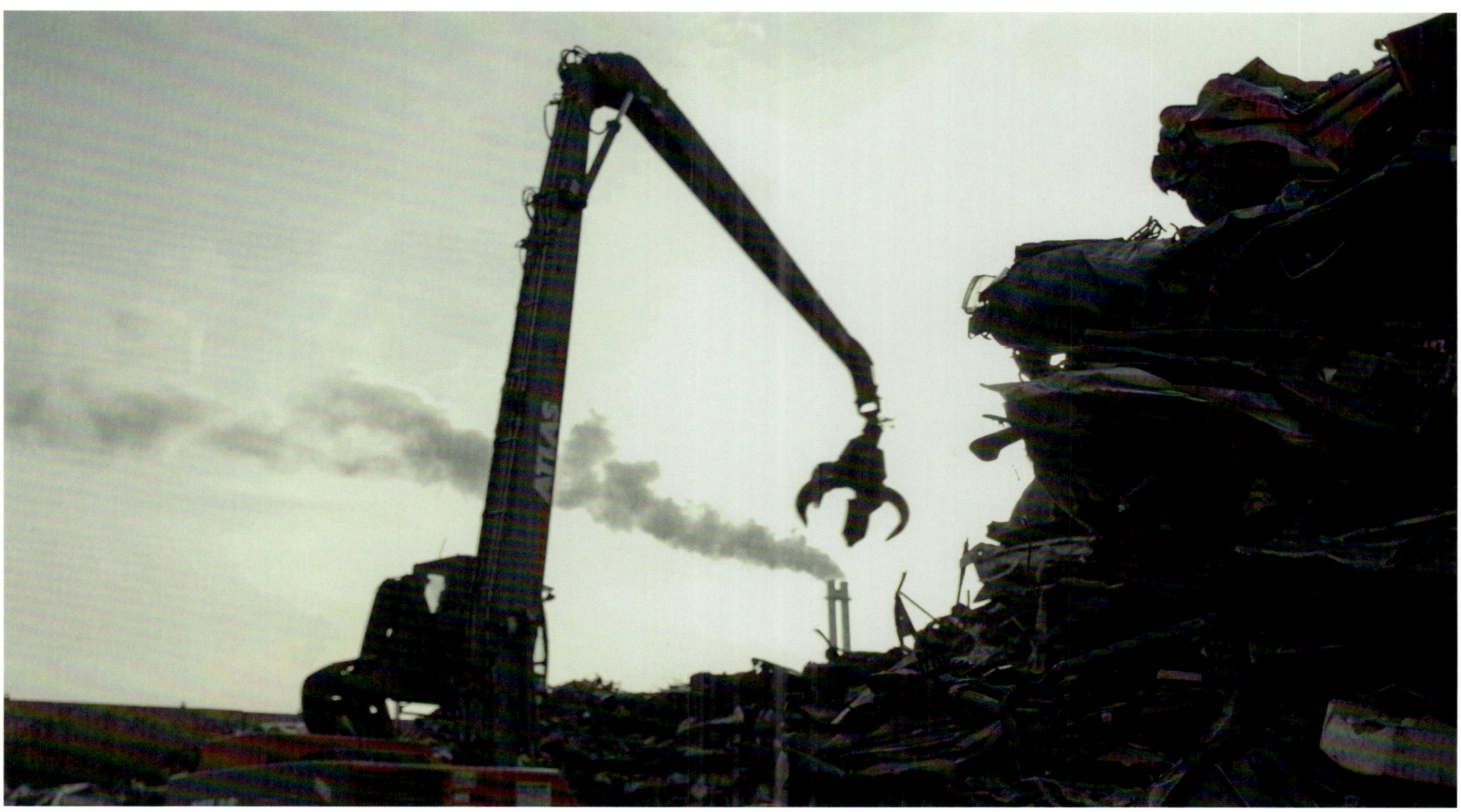
ATLAS

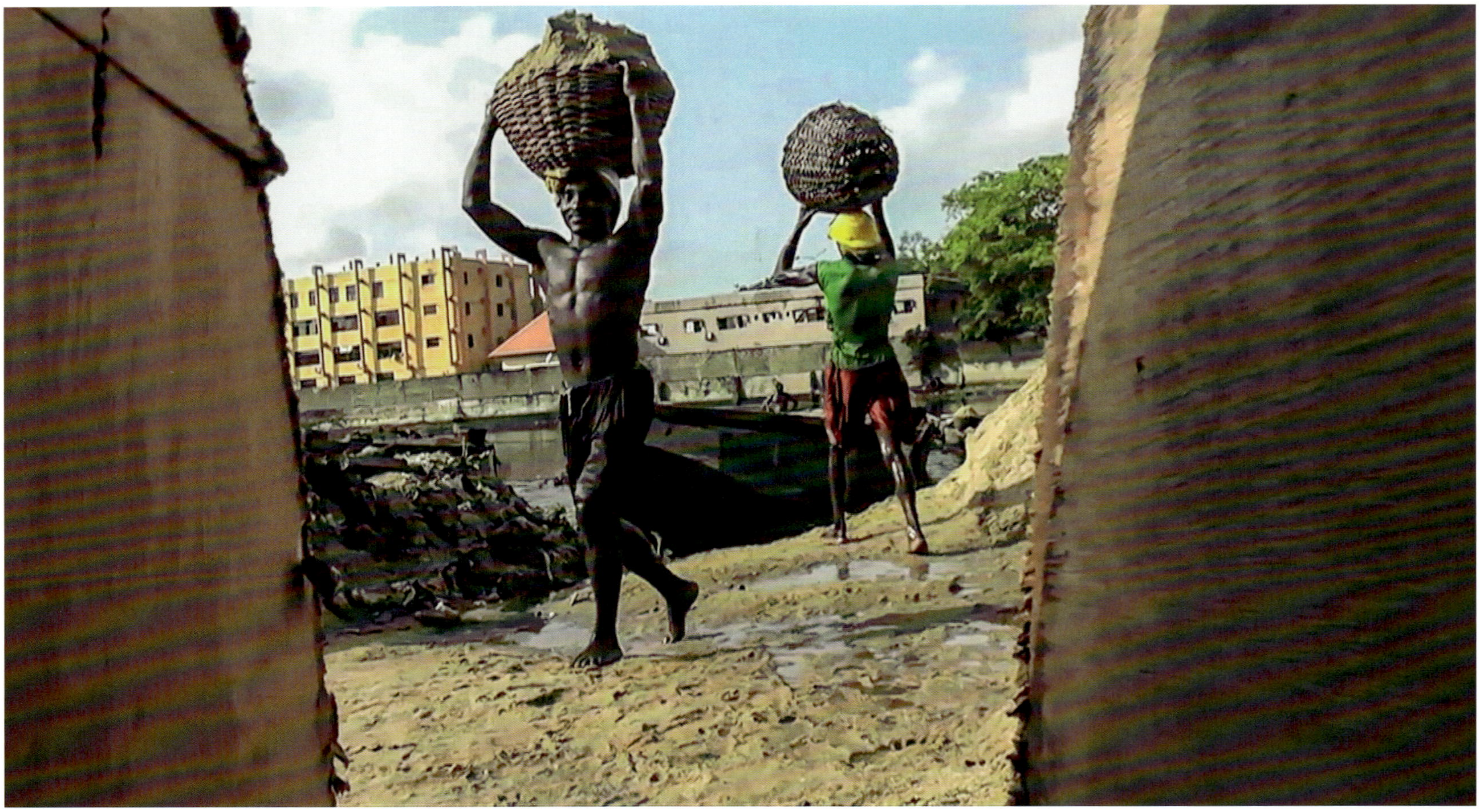

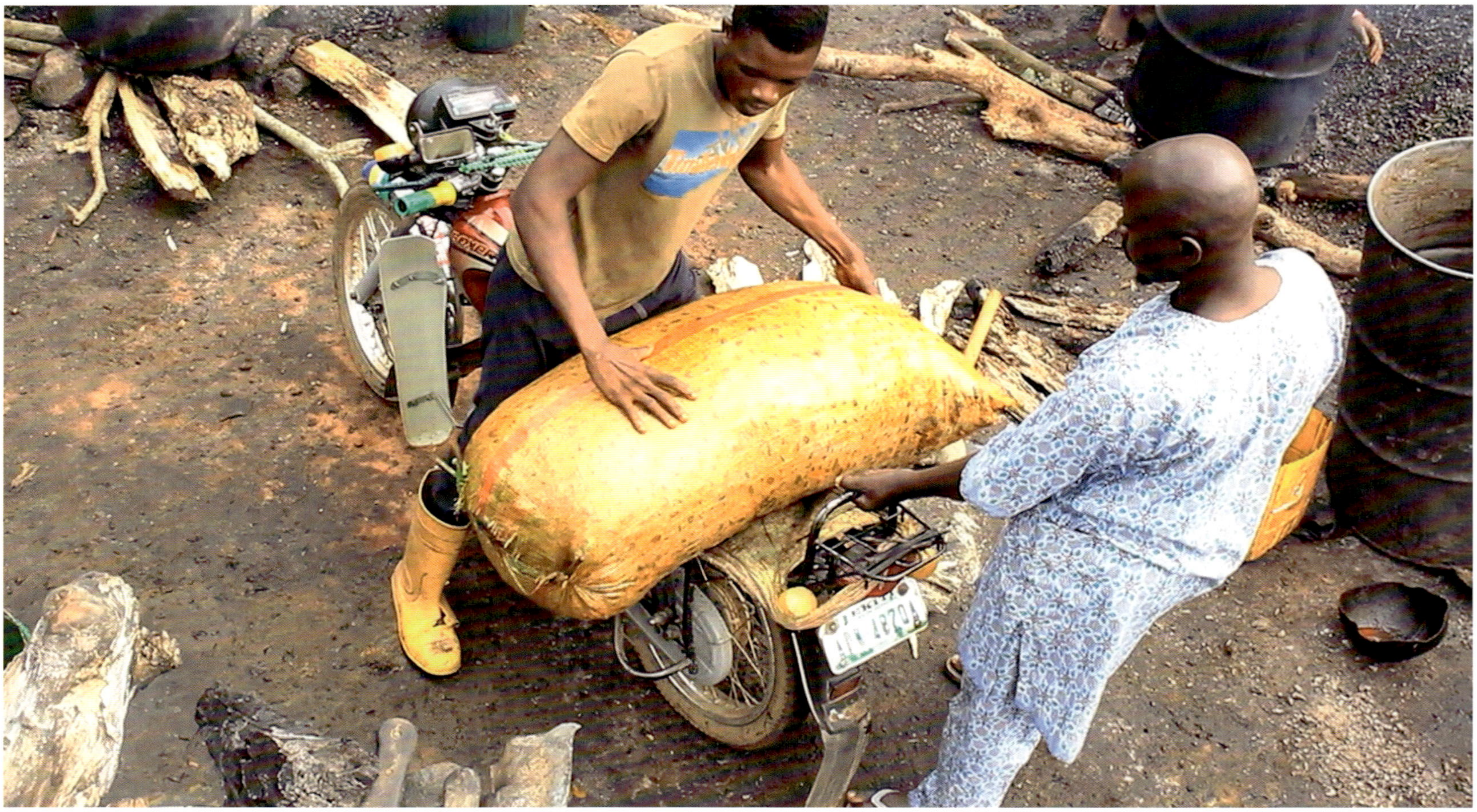

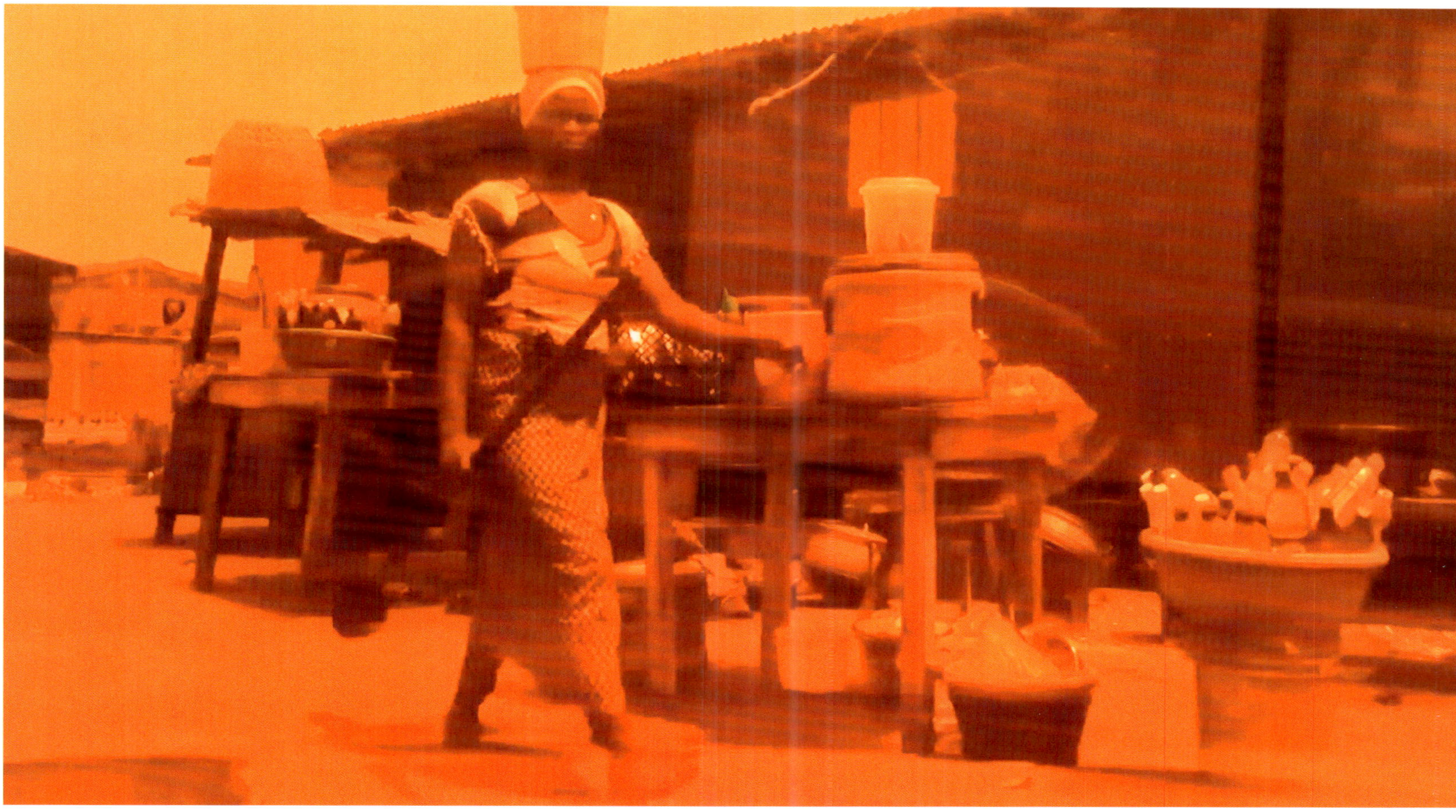

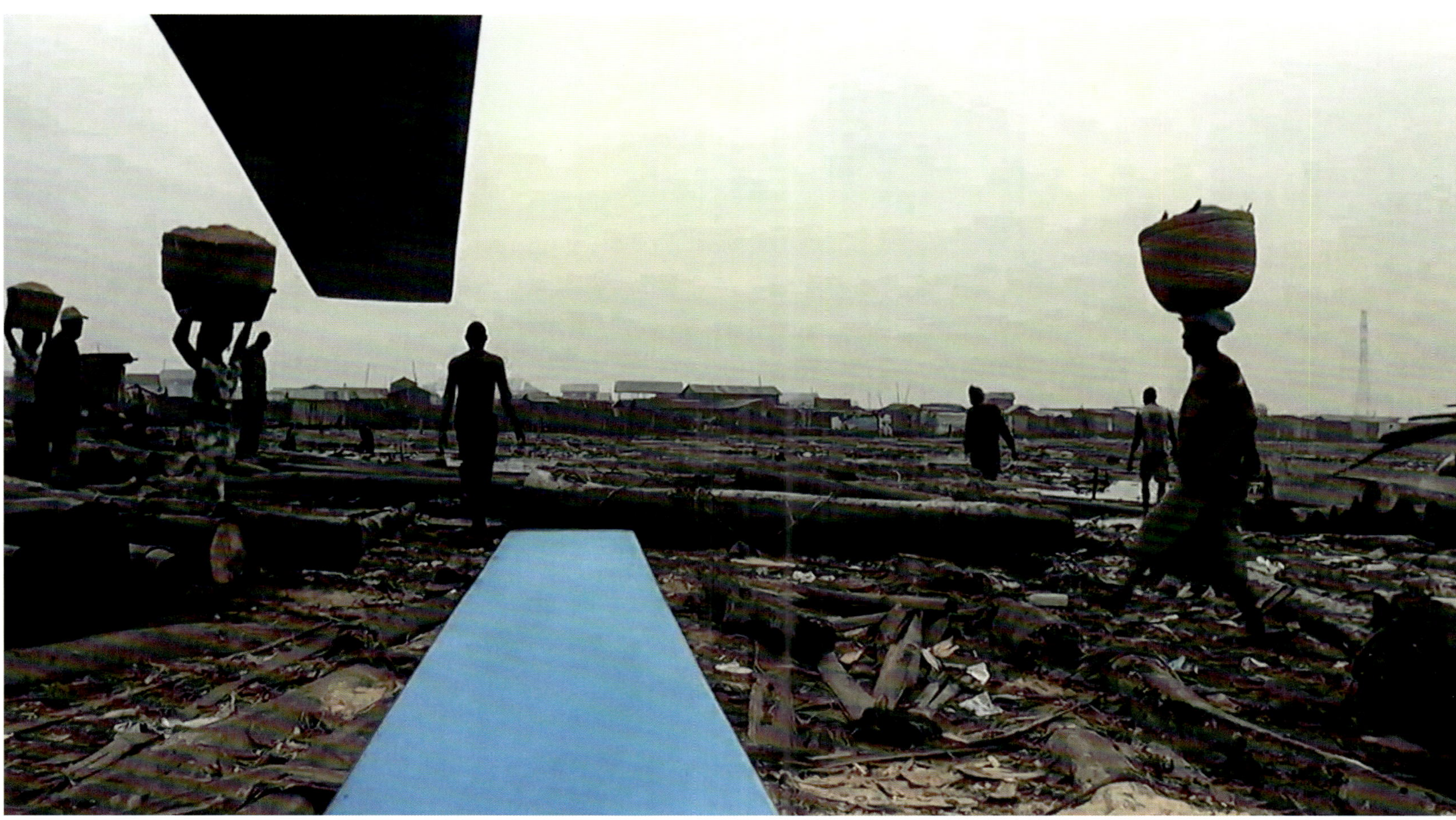

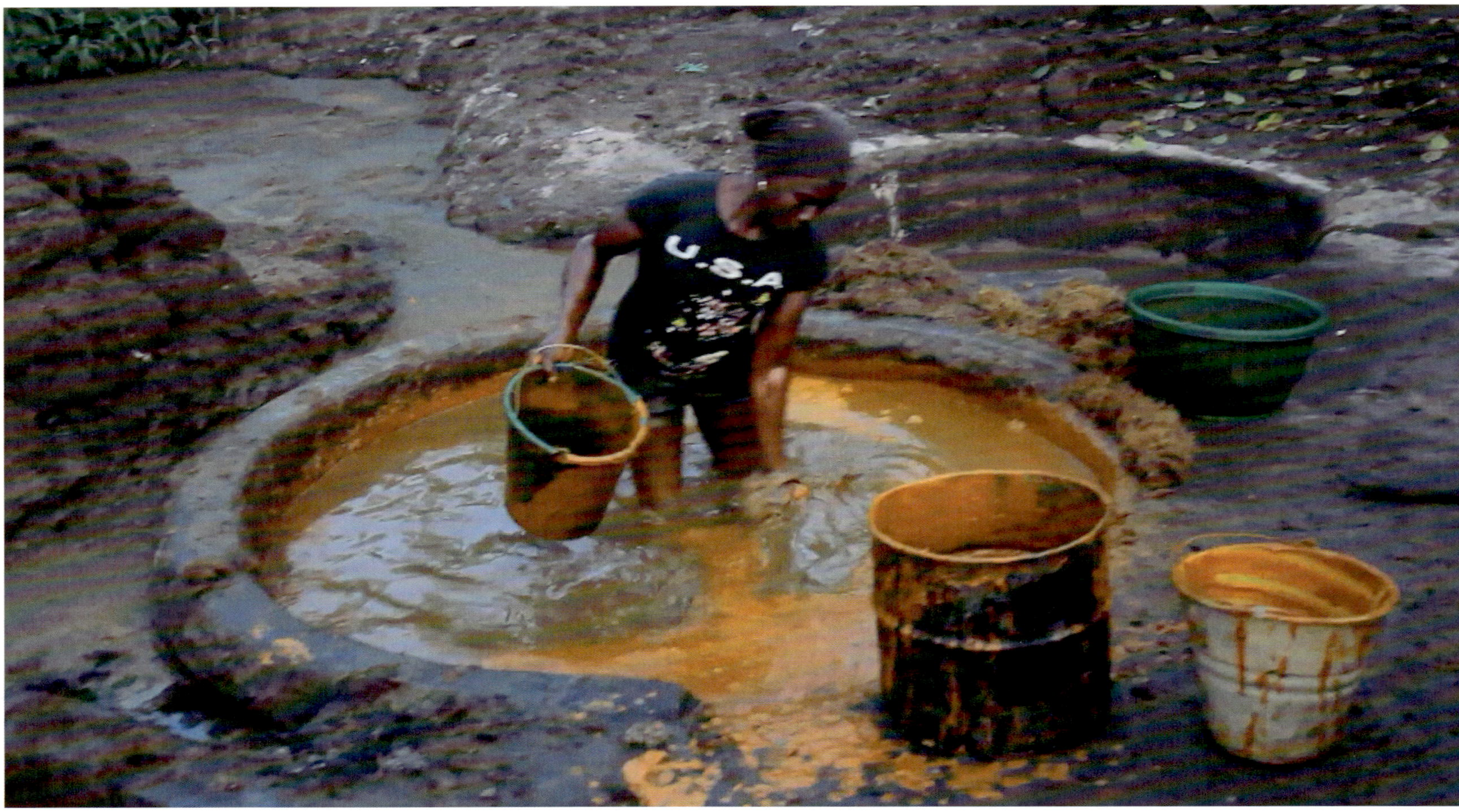
U.S.A

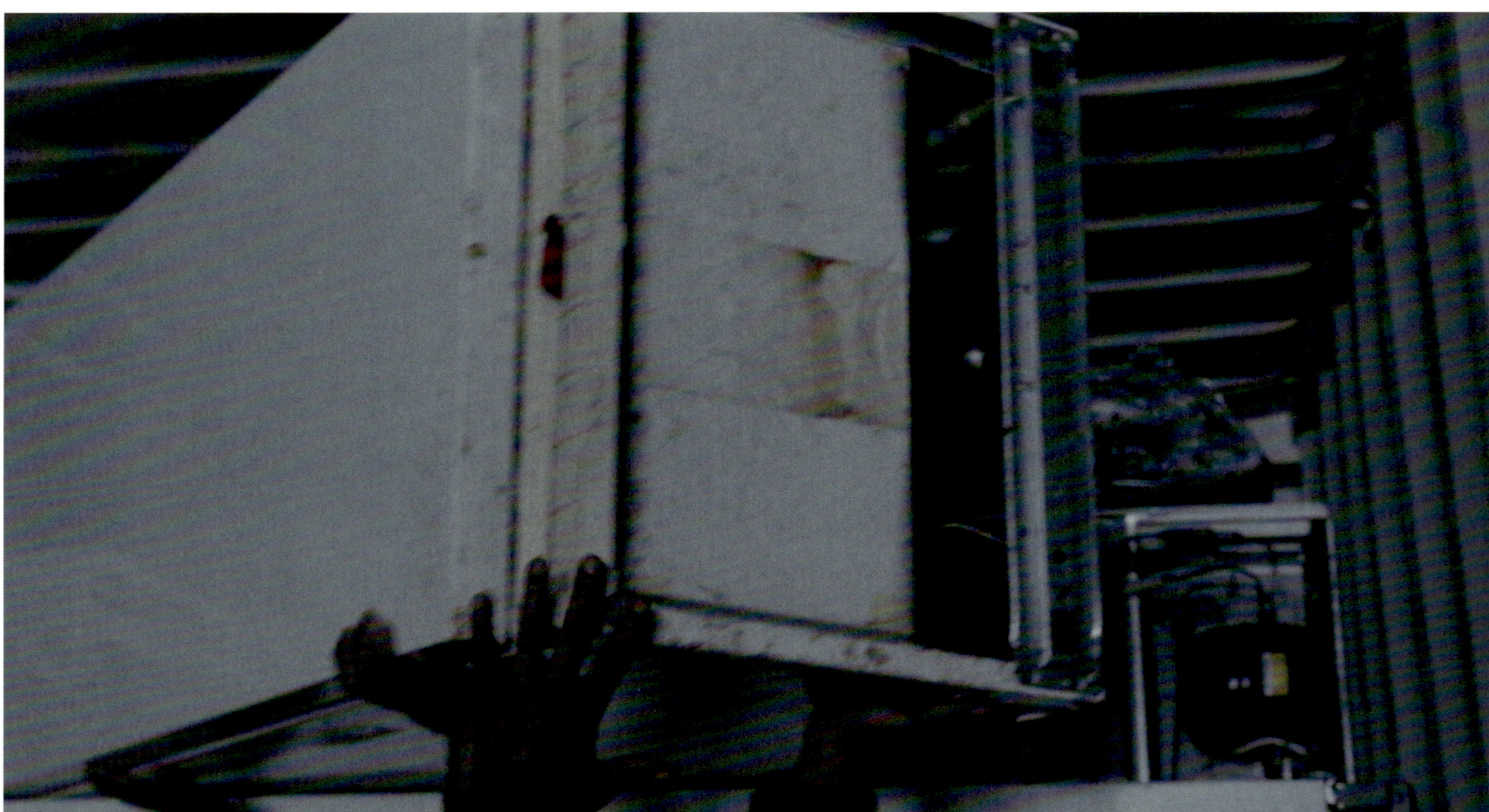

Films' Synopses (2014–25)

Arese Uwuoruya

Lagos Island, 2012
Single-channel video, colour, sound, 4'44"

What distinguishes the camera from the one who wields it? At what point does it take on a sentience of its own, imbue itself with agency, either inherited or conjured, and embark upon a journey across landscapes and communities? In Karimah Ashadu's first film, the camera is fixed to a tyre-wheel mechanism the artist constructed out of found objects and observes

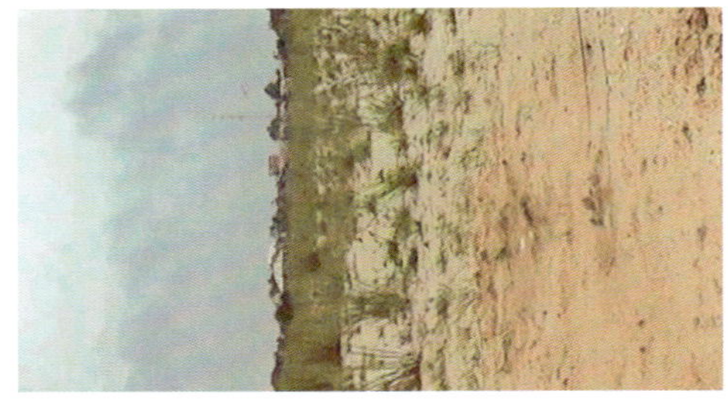

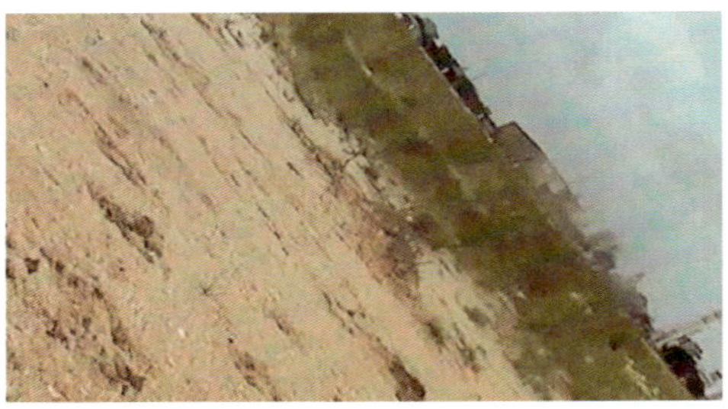

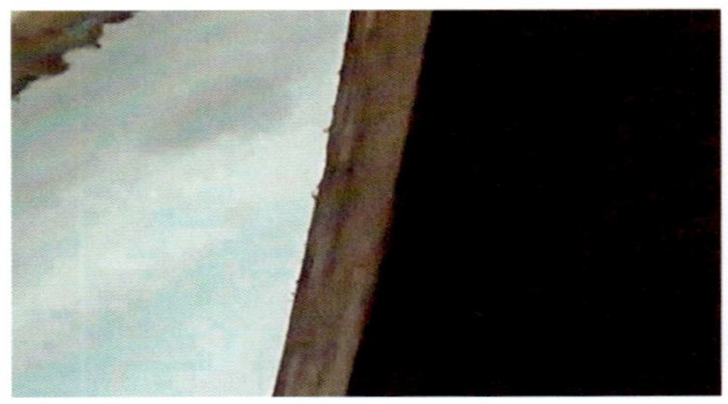

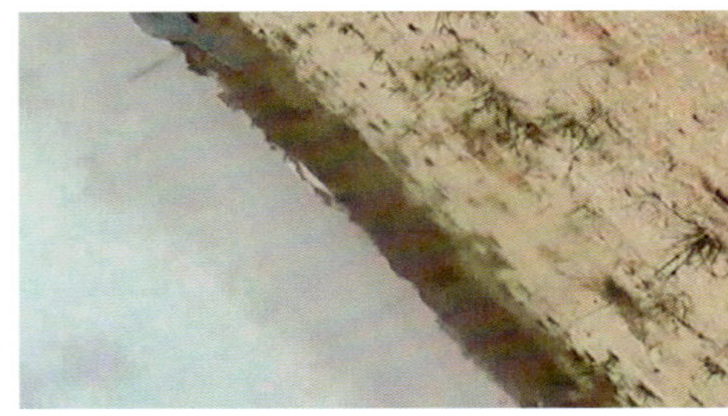

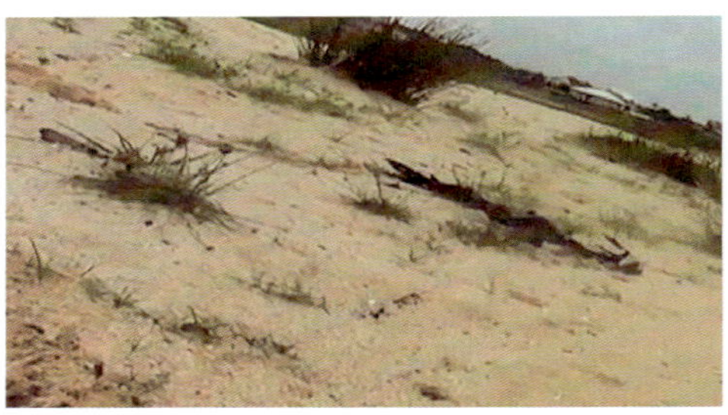

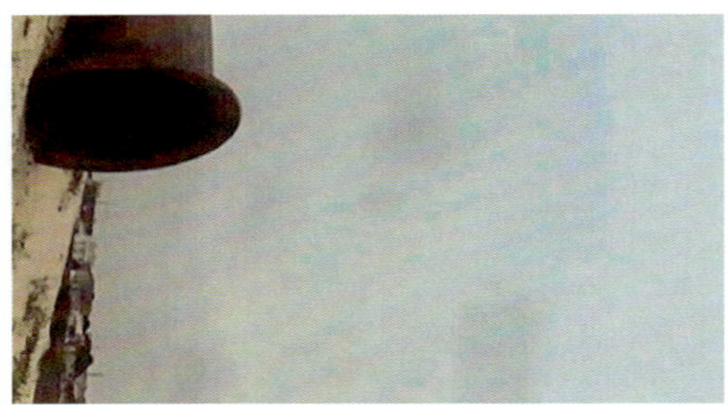

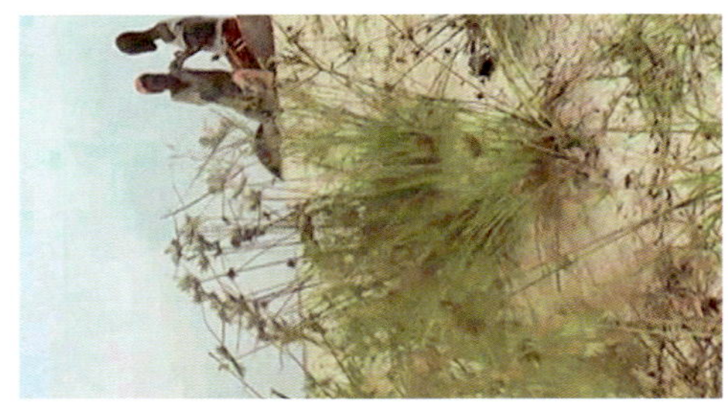

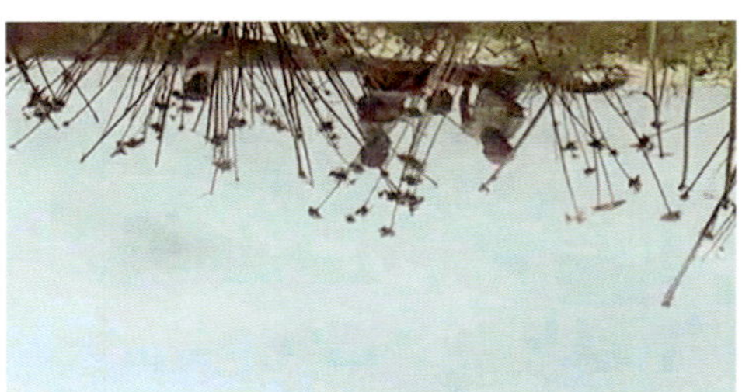

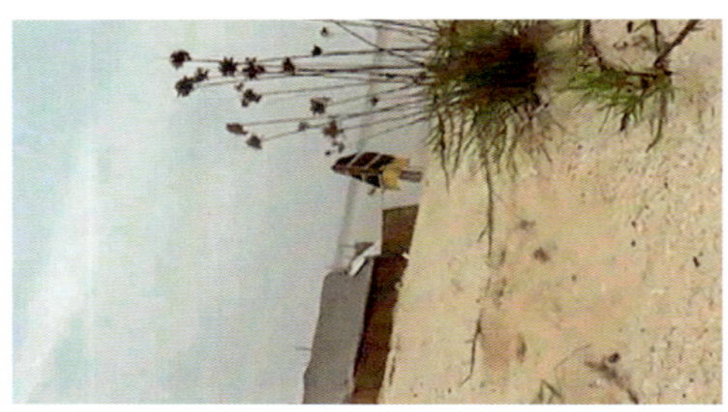

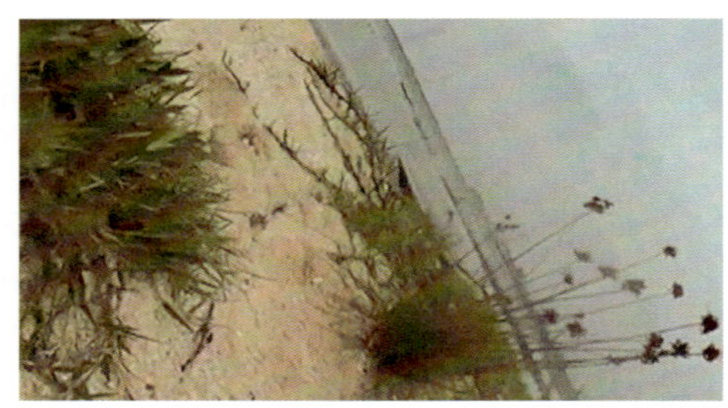

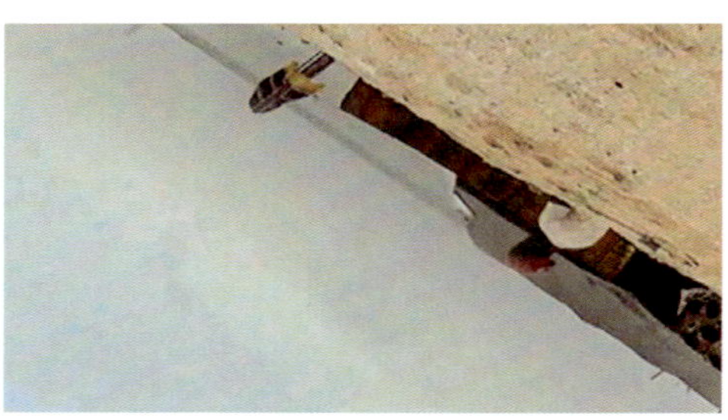

Togolese migrants who live along the coast. The film opens horizontally, immediately disorienting the viewer, and the dizzying rotations are accompanied by the whining, writhing sounds of the mechanism, as if it itself bemoans the exertion demanded to navigate the landscape. A sudden jolt of wind or irregularity in the terrain causes the rotations to quicken,

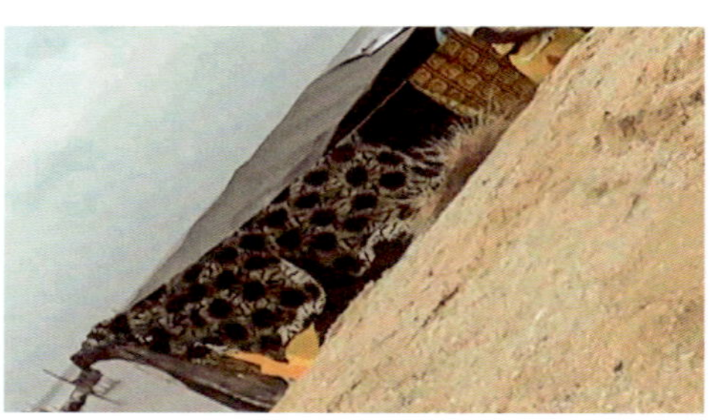

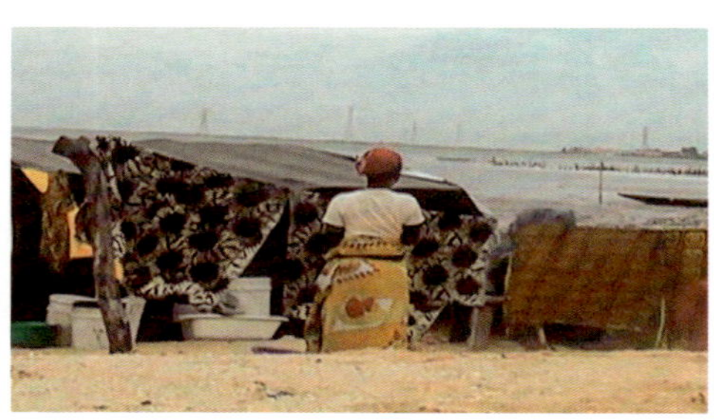

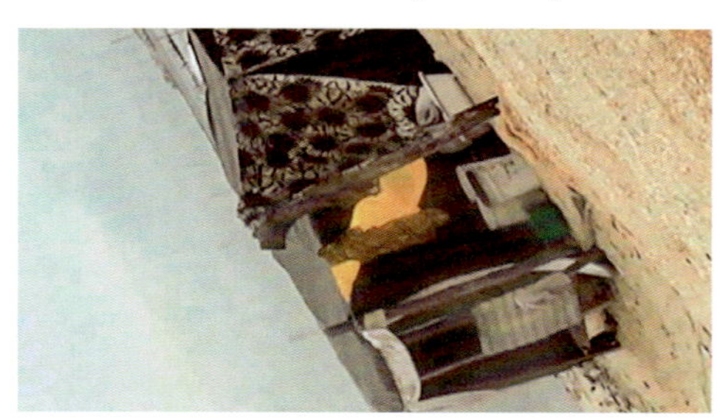

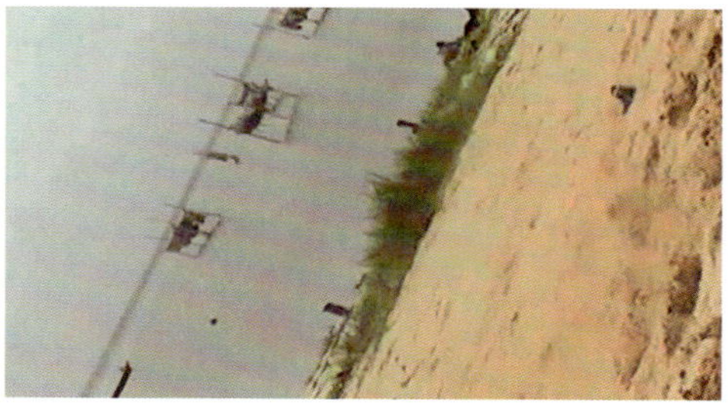
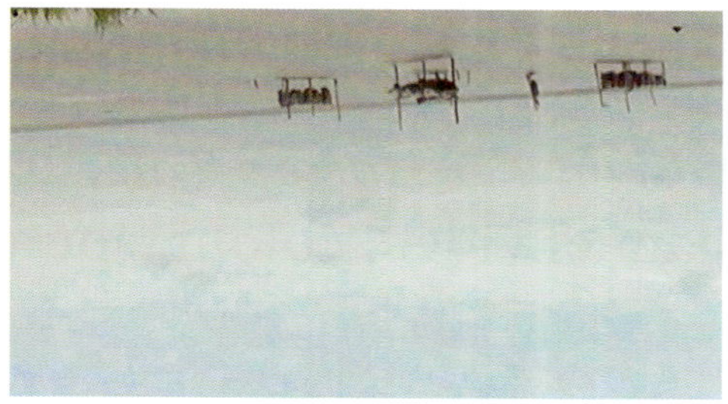
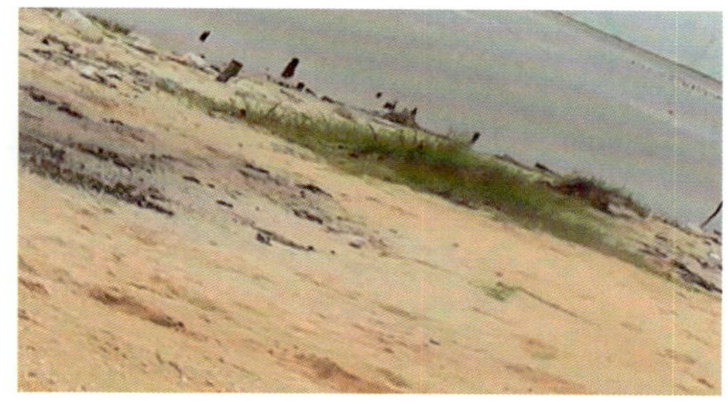
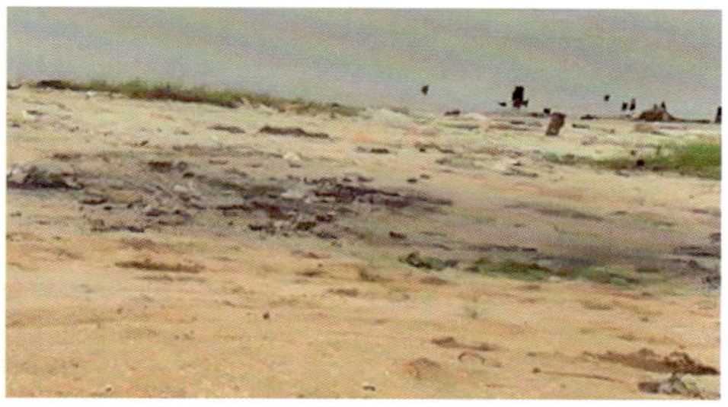

exacerbating the disequilibrium. We see groups and individuals going about their everyday lives. In a moment about halfway through the film, the rotations pause and the camera fixes on a woman hanging her laundry. As the camera holds, we wonder if this subject's appeal lies in the simplicity of her task. The desire to

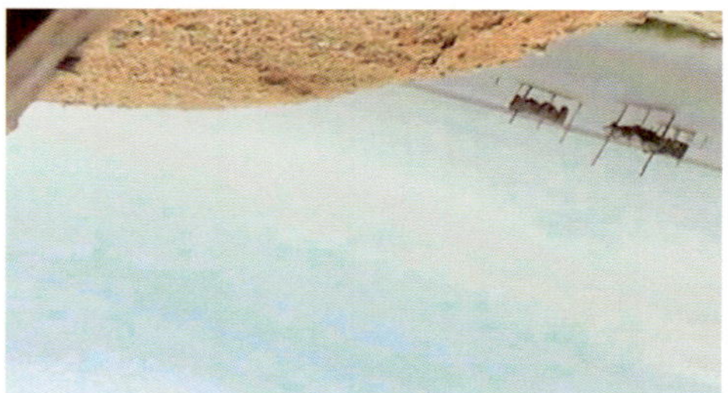
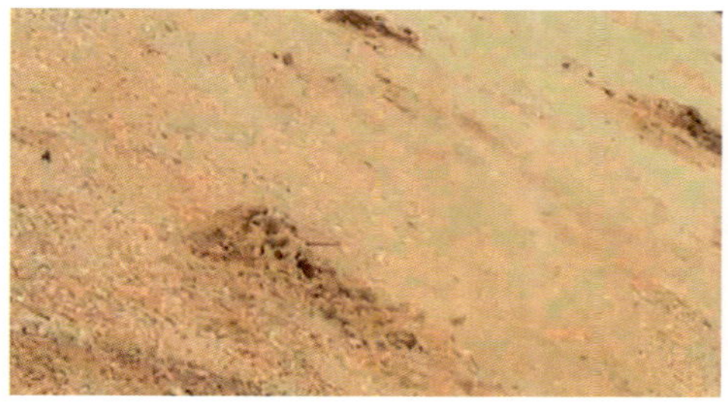
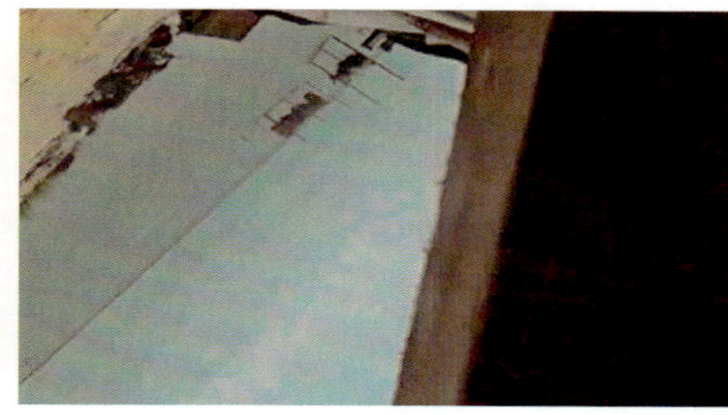
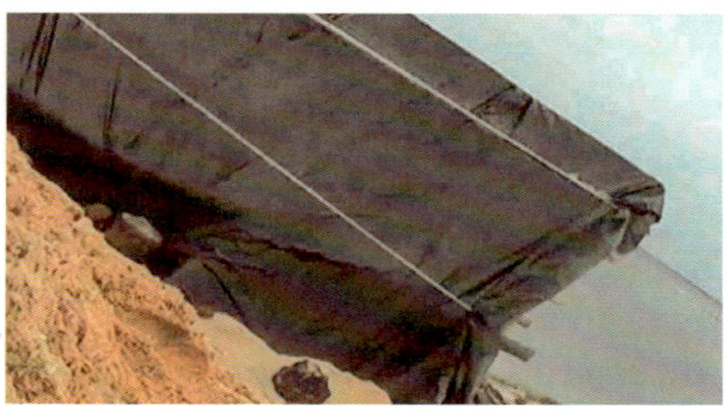

enter the mind of this autonomous camera and understand its attraction, as if it were a sentient being, comes not without surprise. In this film, the camera is encased in the landscape and the people who provisionally occupy it. Their physical and economic precarity is mirrored by the constantly rotating image.

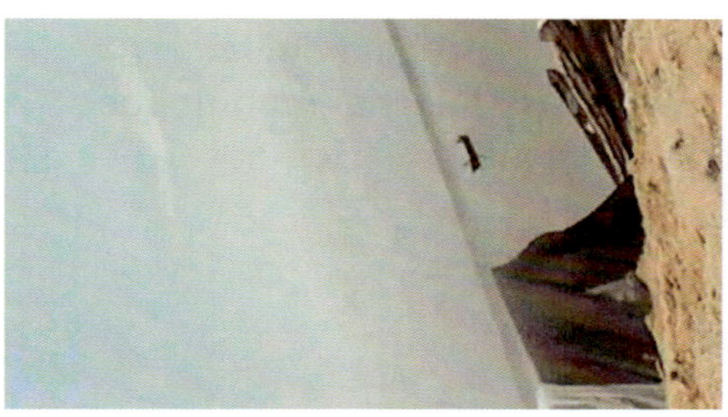
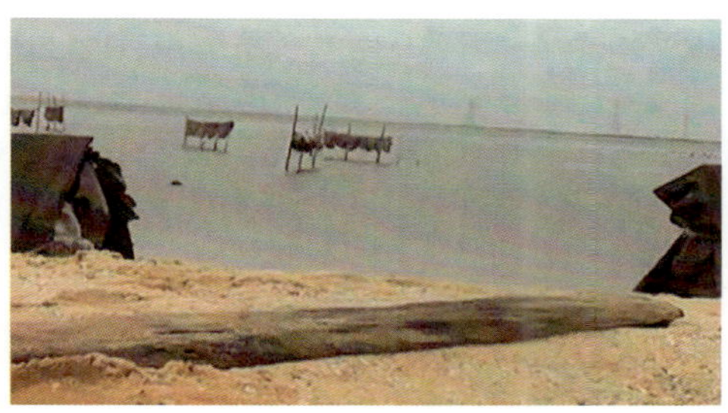
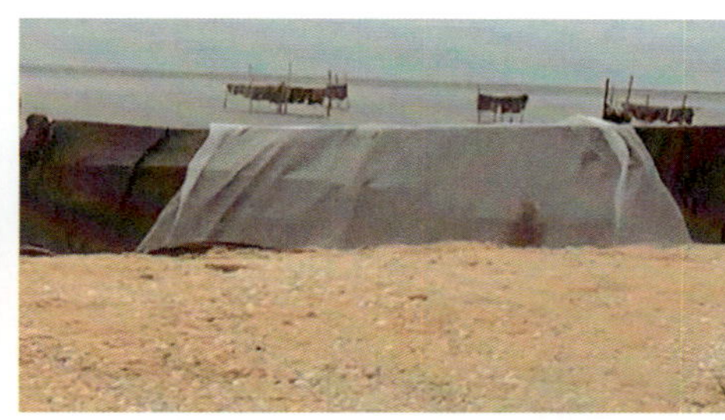
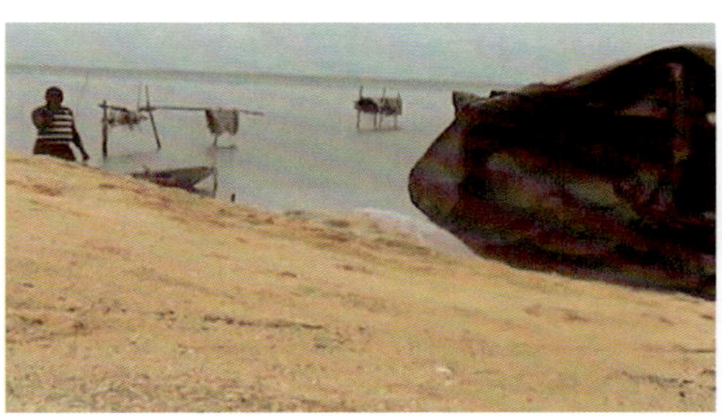
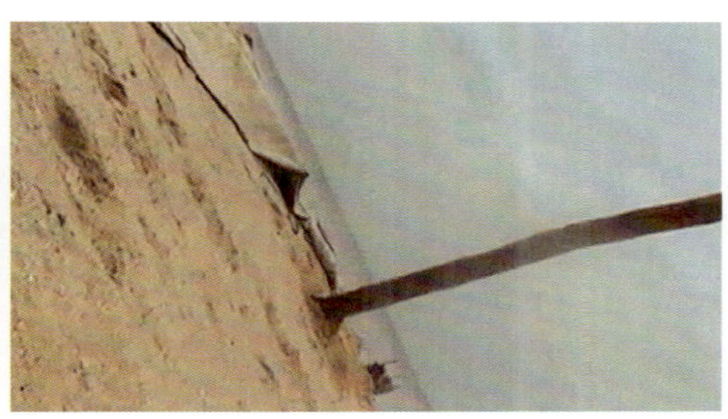
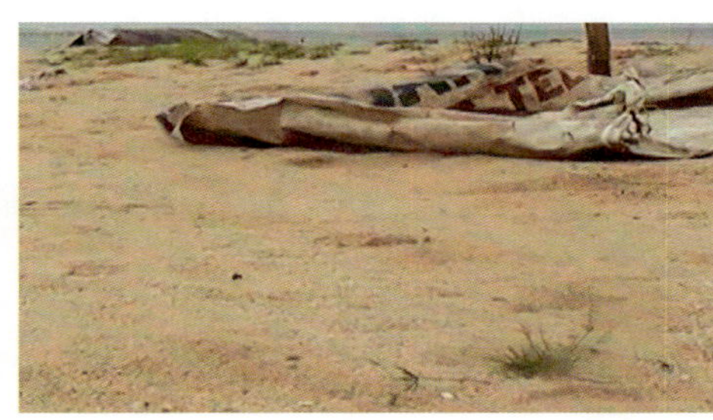
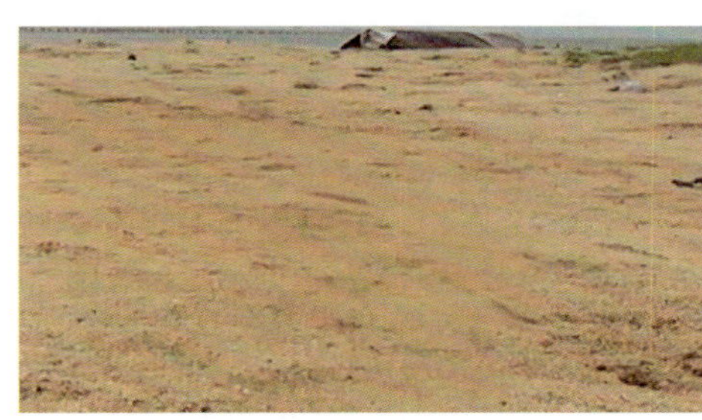

Director and Editor
Karimah Ashadu

Camera
Karimah Ashadu

Produced by
Karimah Ashadu

Hindsight – A Horse's Tale, 2012
Single-channel video, colour, sound, 3'44"

Fixed to a polo-mallet-like mechanism of the artist's devising, the camera is guided by the movements of a horse as it jaunts on its morning walk. It trots, gallops and prances along a brief journey from the polo bar where the northern

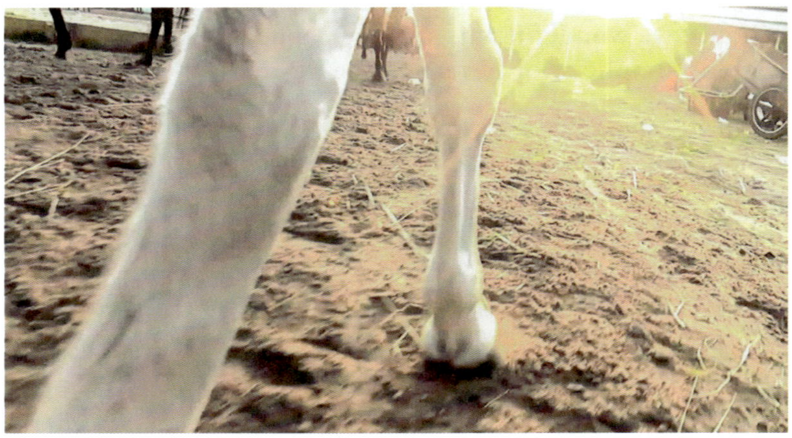

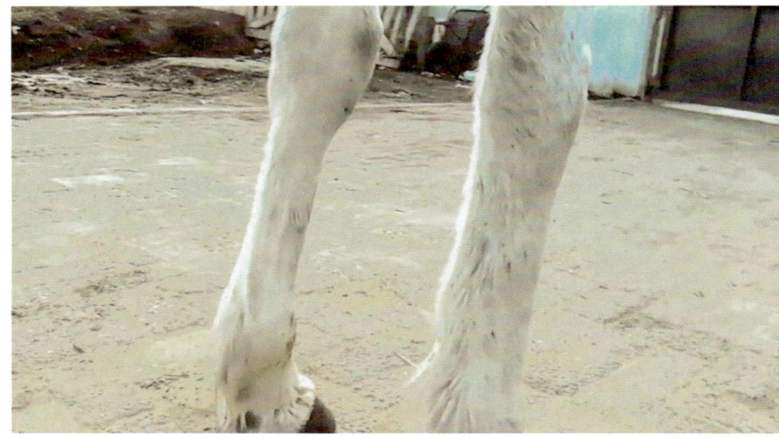

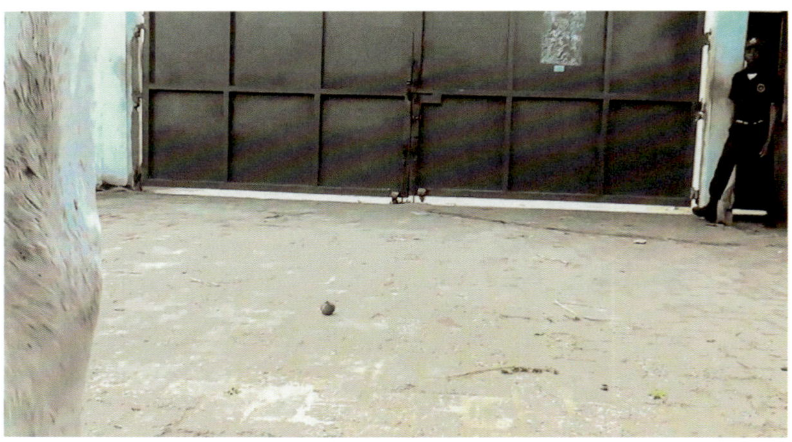

Nigerian Hausa tribe engages in polo matches to a nearby beach, moving from thick mud to gravel to sand. The horse is not entirely unconstrained. Someone opens a gate to allow its trek to begin across the noisy urban landscape of Lagos' streets, and the presence of a rider is never really confirmed or denied. However, the included subtitles relaying the horse's internal monologue suggest that any environmental restrictions are of little consequence.

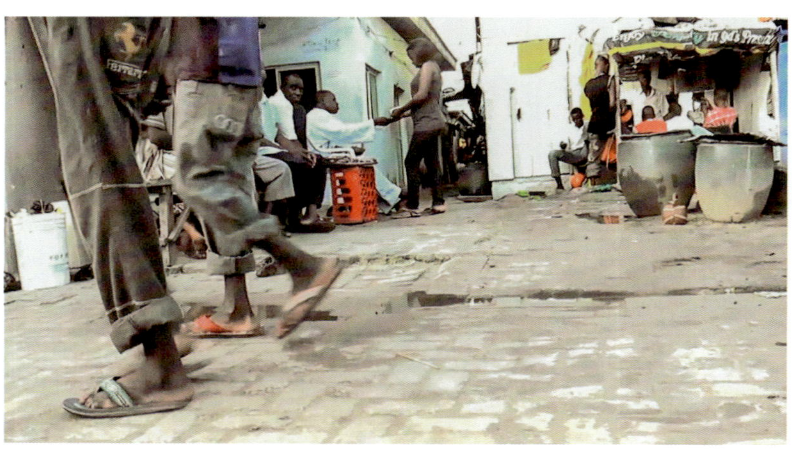

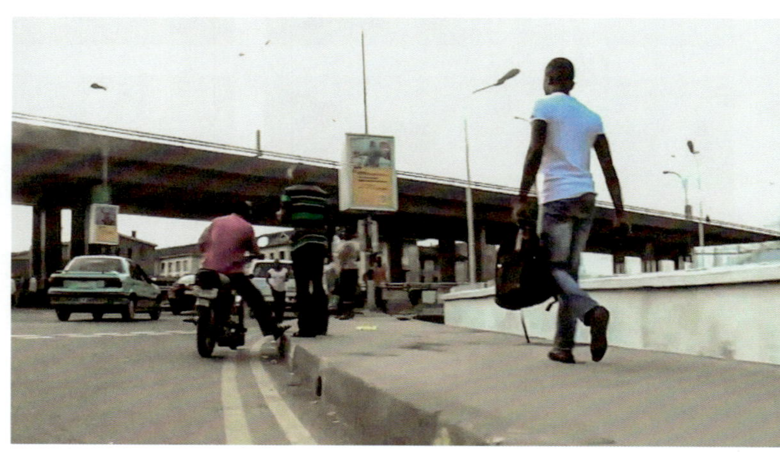

Elements of humour in the text convey Ashadu's understanding of the playfulness and subversion inherent in the film via the camera mechanism she has constructed. "I compete in a match once or twice a year, then I spend the rest of my time just horsing around", muses the animal. Of course, these glimpses into the horse's mind are just that, small

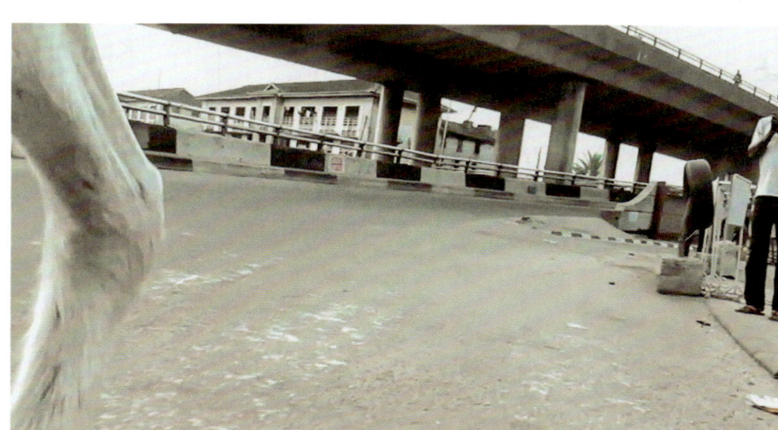

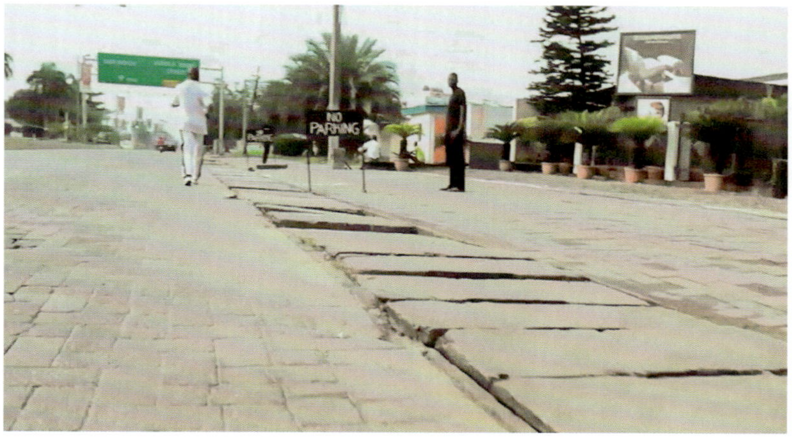

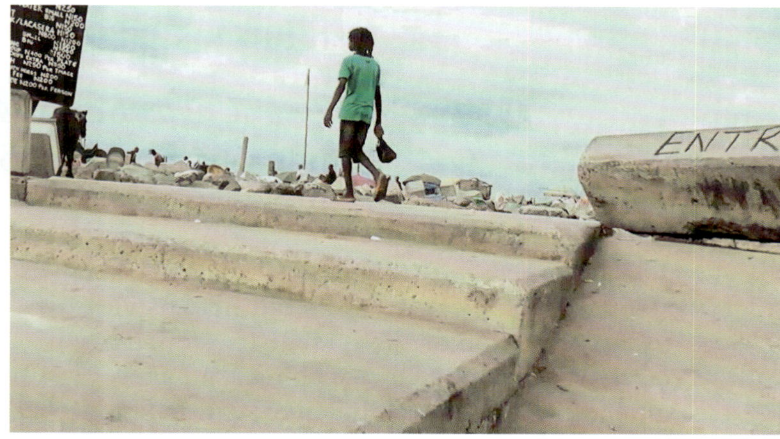

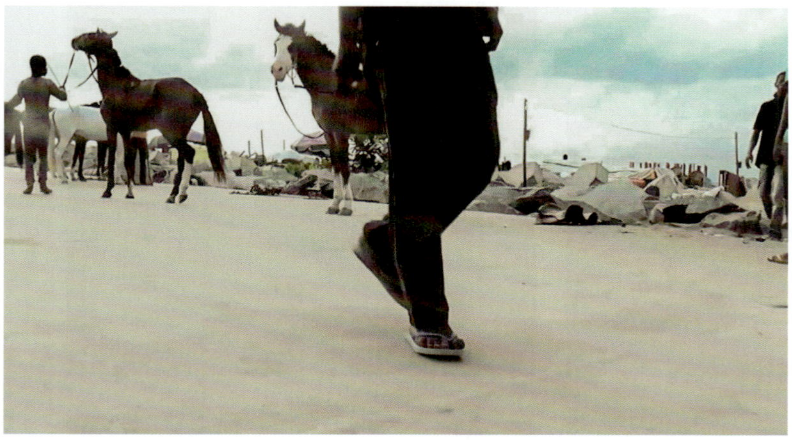

peeks into a perspective that we can come into proximity with, but never fully inhabit. Once the expanse of the beach is in sight, the horse's pace quickens, and whatever has not been communicated through interspecies translation – "I'm plotting my escape", the animal continues – is articulated through movement and presence. The waves grow louder, and the horse scans the beach before setting off down the coast.

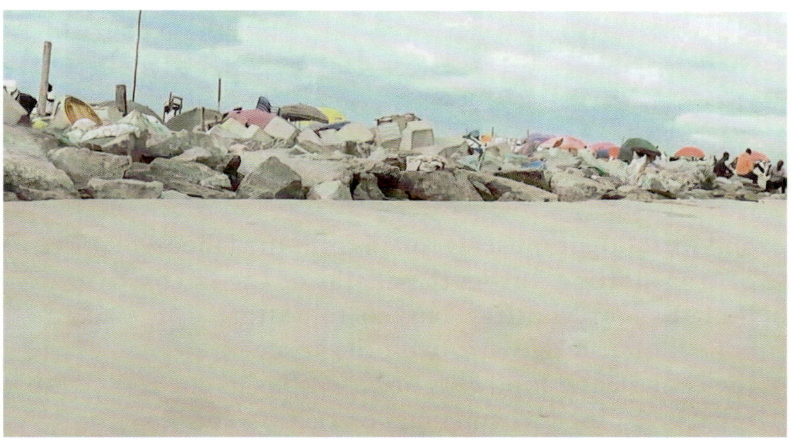

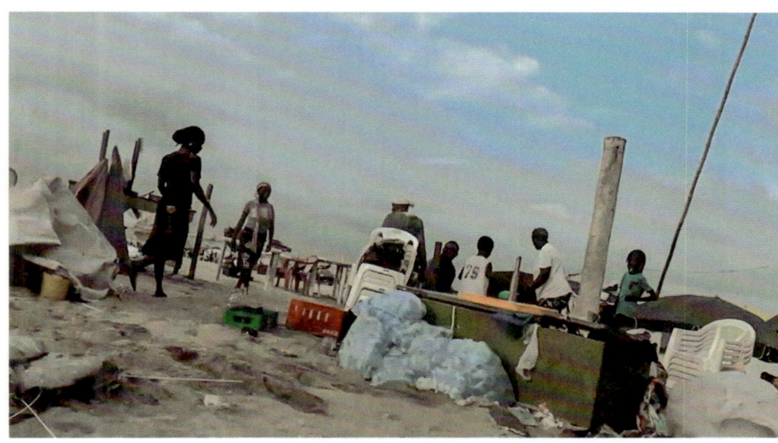

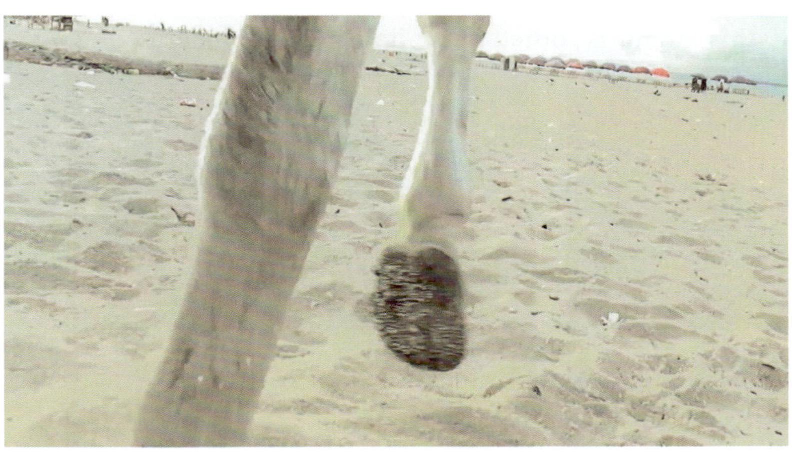

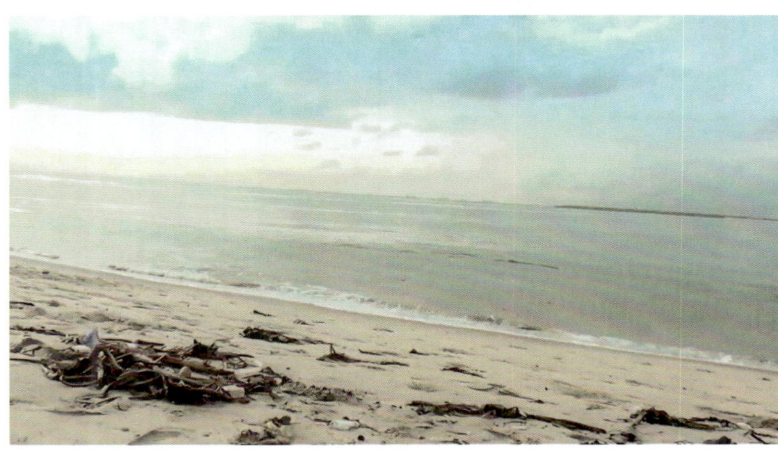

Director and Editor
Karimah Ashadu

Camera
Karimah Ashadu

Produced by
Karimah Ashadu

Lagos Sand Merchants, 2013
Single-channel video, colour, sound, 9'21"

The film opens with wooden wheels on either side of the frame, narrowing our field of view to just a fraction of the screen. The sounds of creaking wood and crunching sand are immediate, and the rudimentary construction suggests that we are within another of Karimah Ashadu's self-fashioned camera mechanisms. Mounds of sand abound, and men walk back and forth, their muscles toned from the labour of transporting it from the depths of the Lagos State Lagoon via straw baskets to waiting collection trucks. We inhabit the space of the camera and follow its observations of the repetitive process of manual extraction and conveyance. As the title implies, the impulse for this labour is rooted in capitalism. The camera

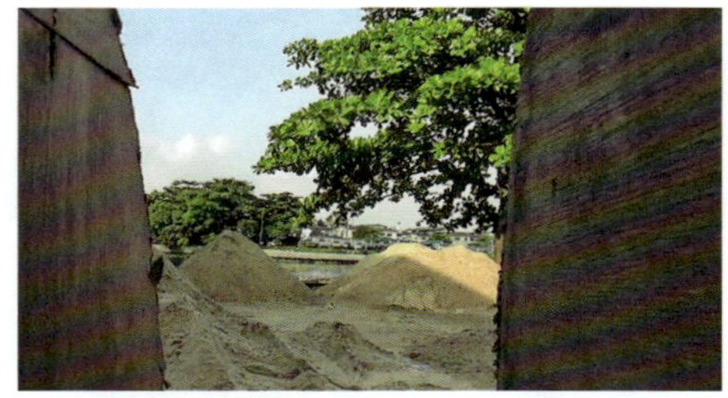

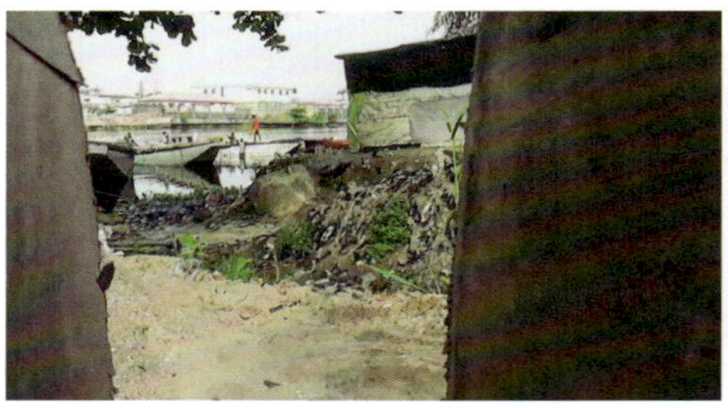

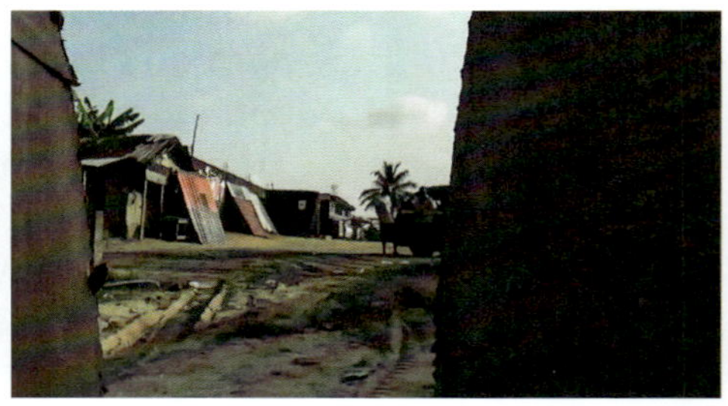

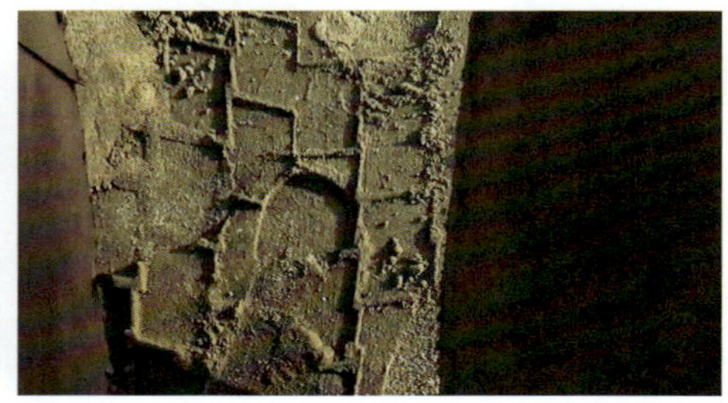

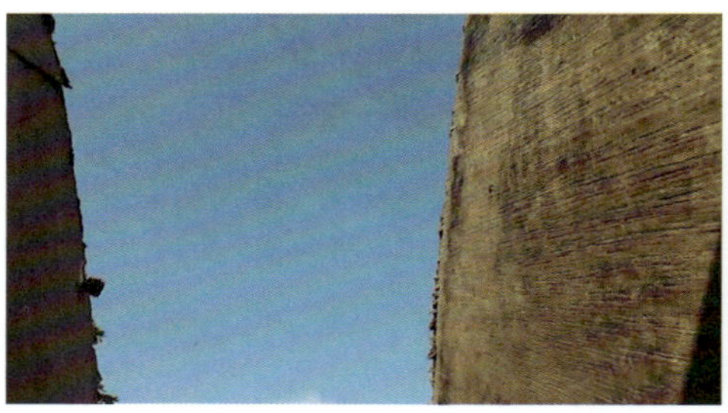

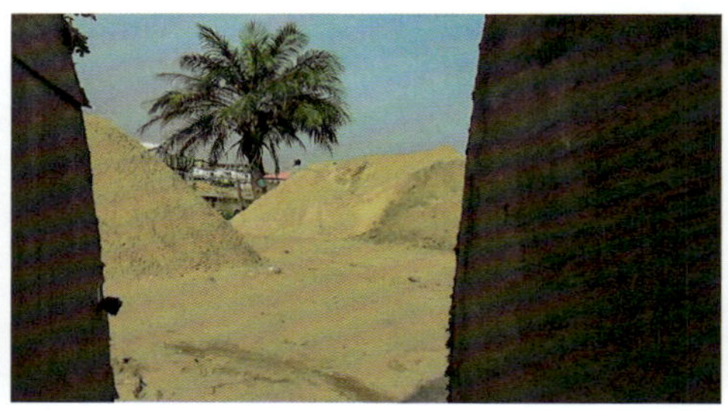

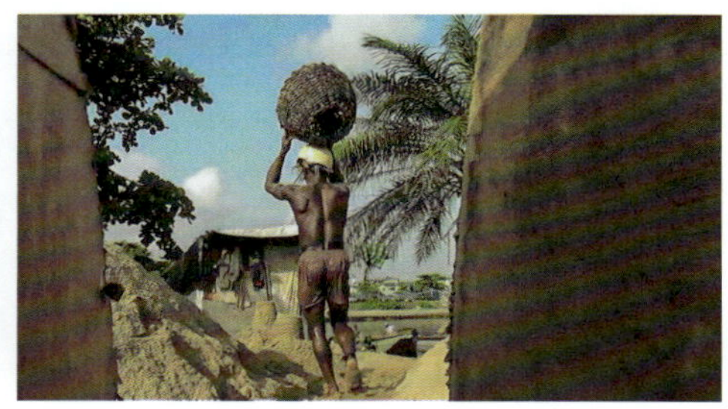

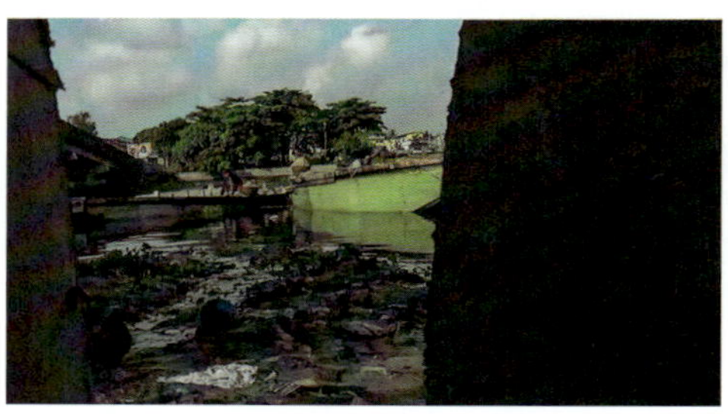

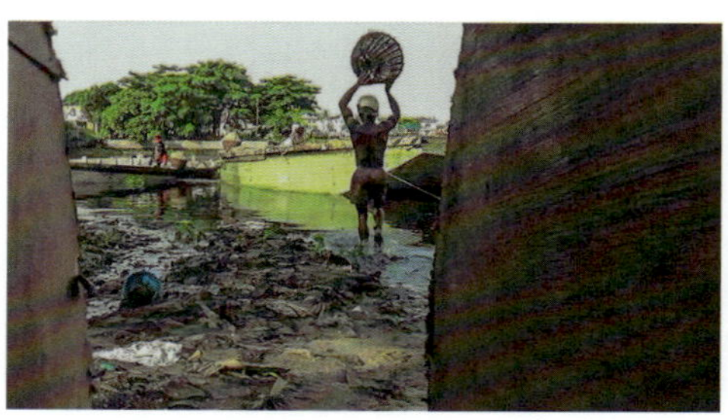

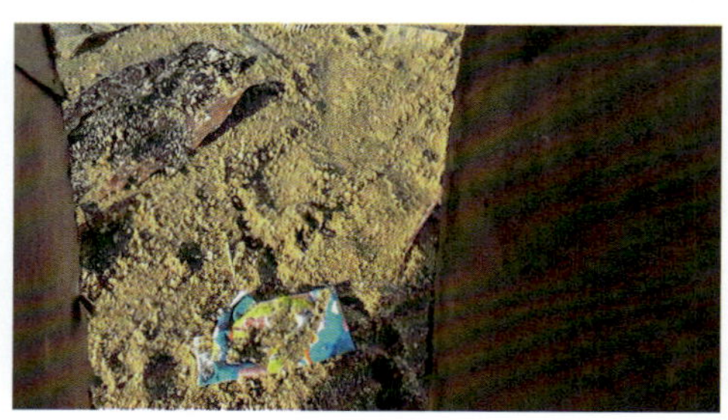

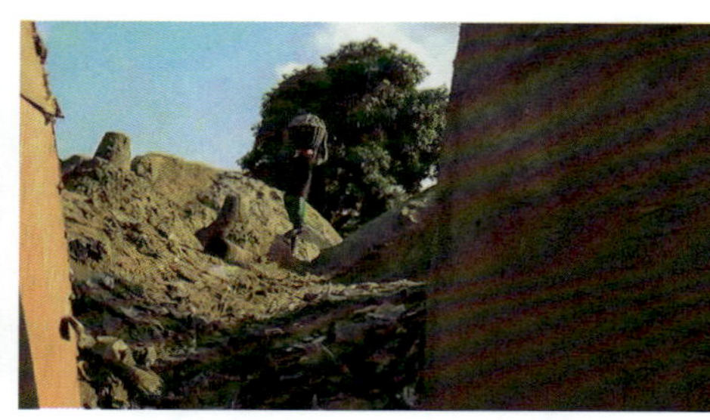

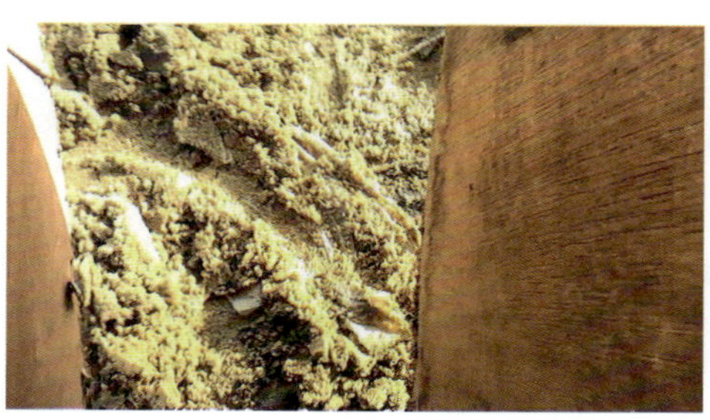

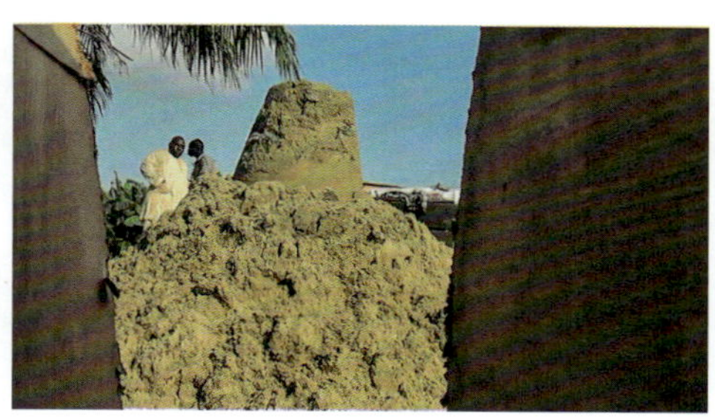

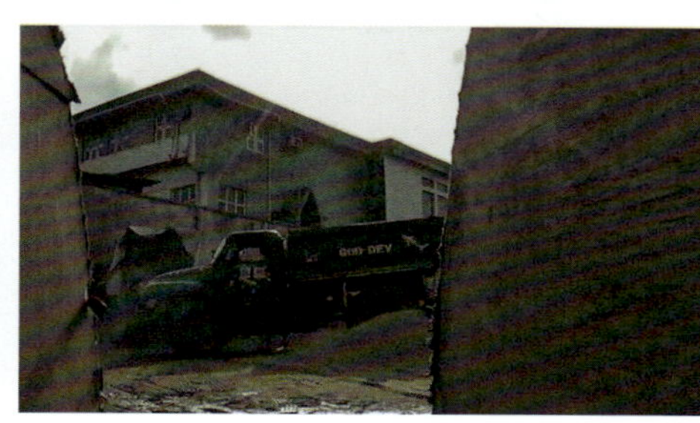

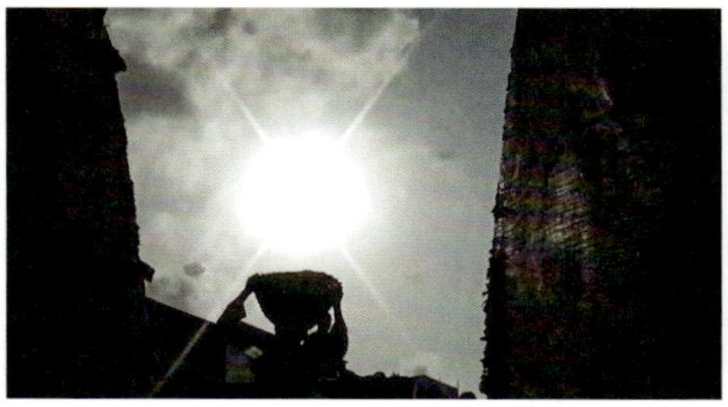
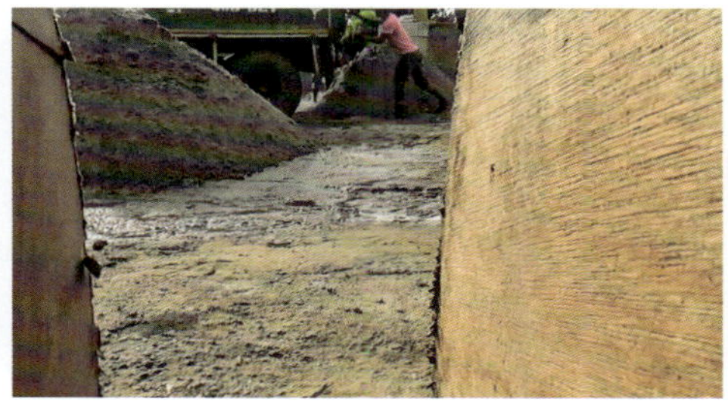
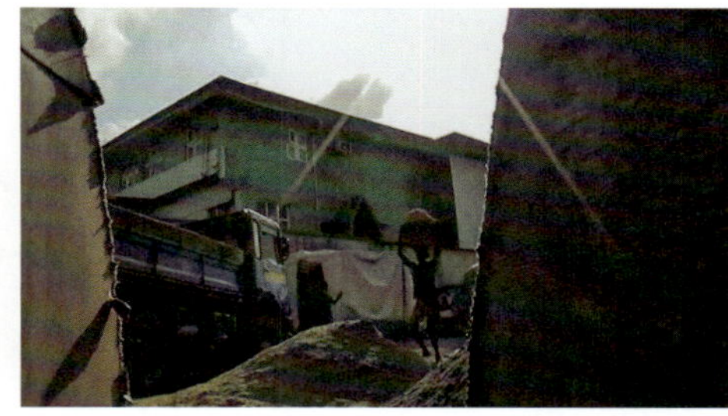

mirrors the gaze we might wield in the space, for instance following the paths of individuals and machines by trailing their prints in the sand, scanning the horizon and determining its next move. Fast-paced edits from shot to shot are interspersed with long, lingering takes. About midway through, we see the camera picked up and moved; at one point, it offers an inverted perspective, and jolts us from somewhat passive observation into the knowledge that elements of choreography may be present. Toward the end of the film, a man directs his gaze to the camera, then quickly moves on, focused on the task ahead. An external lens is of little significance, we are made to understand, compared to the need for productivity and survival.

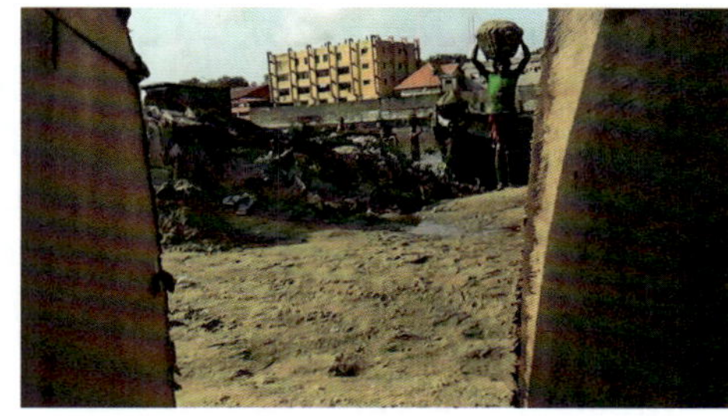
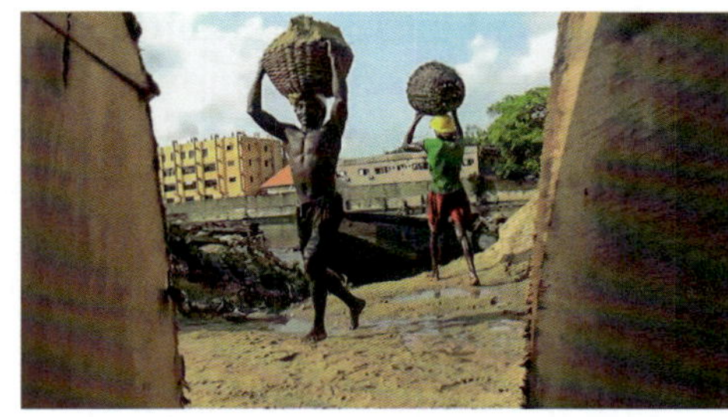
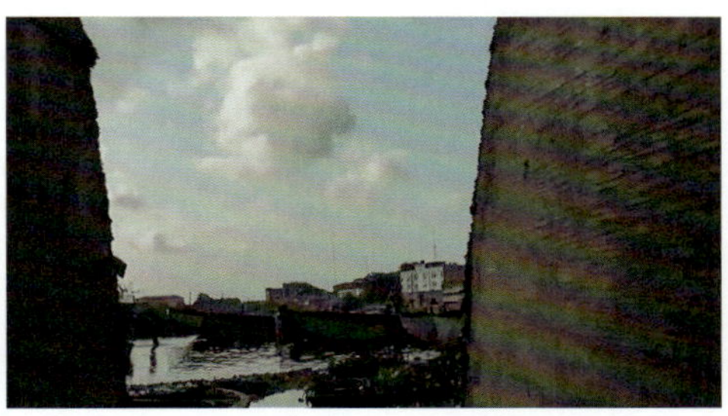
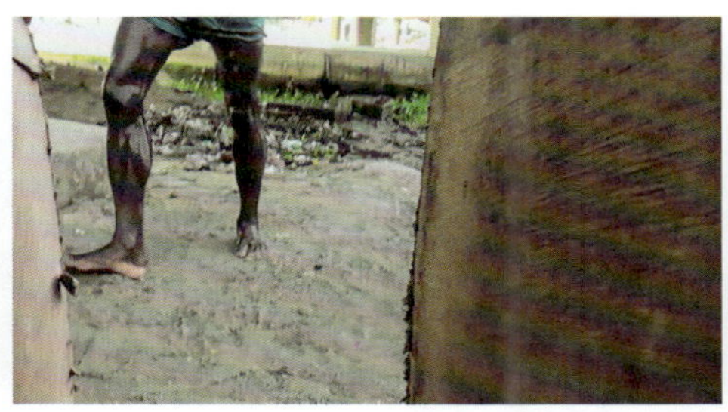
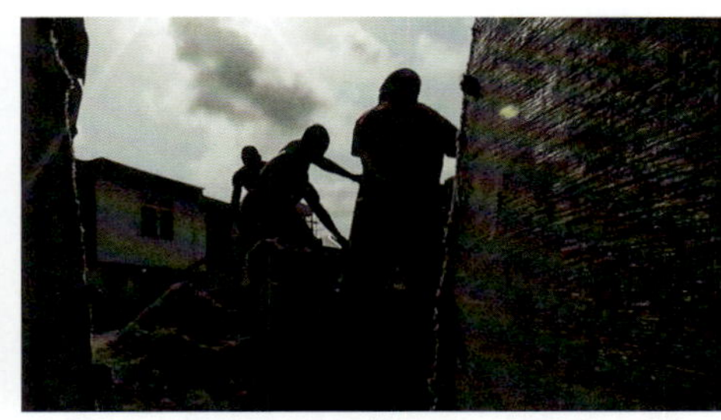
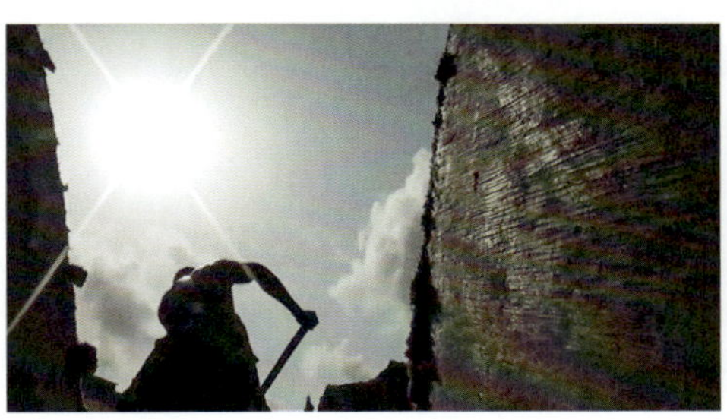
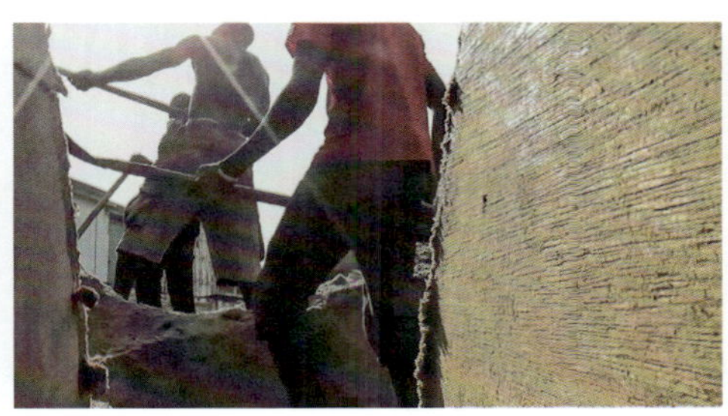
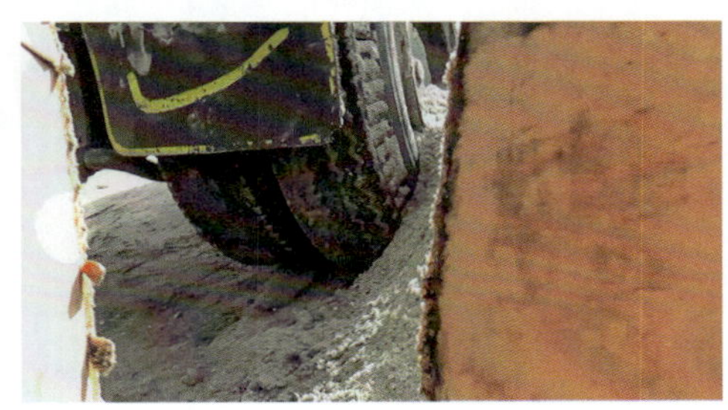
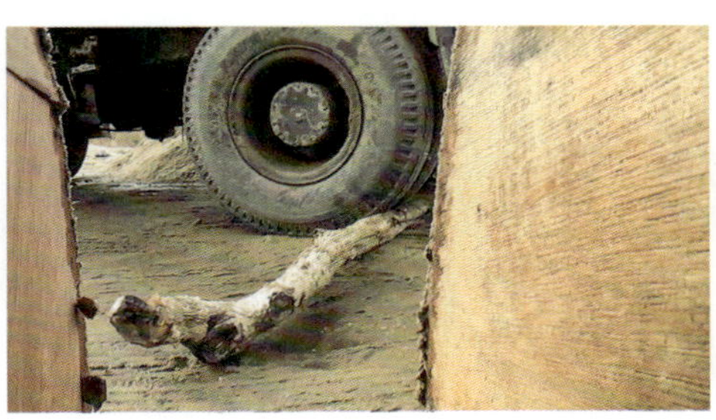
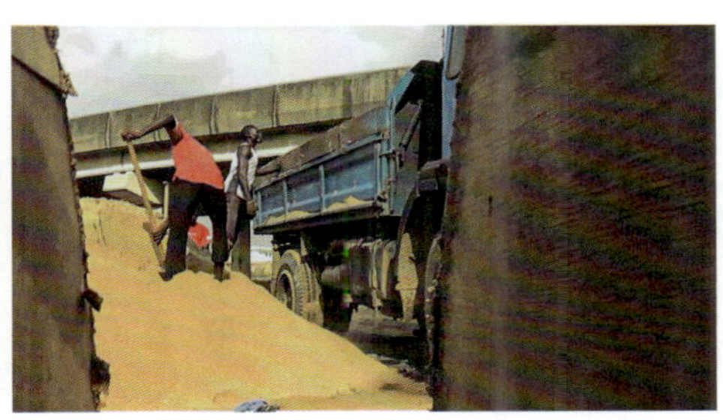
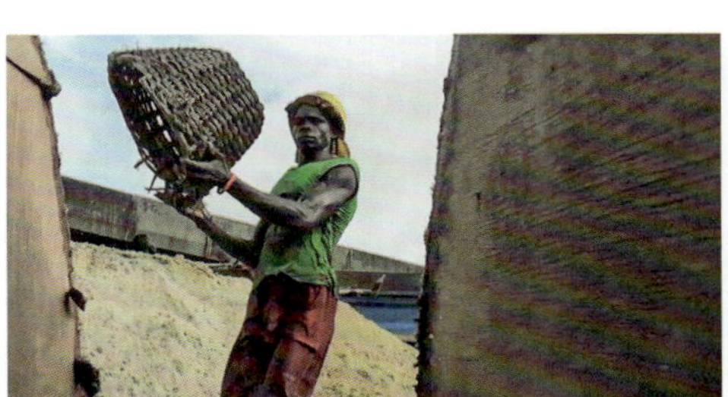
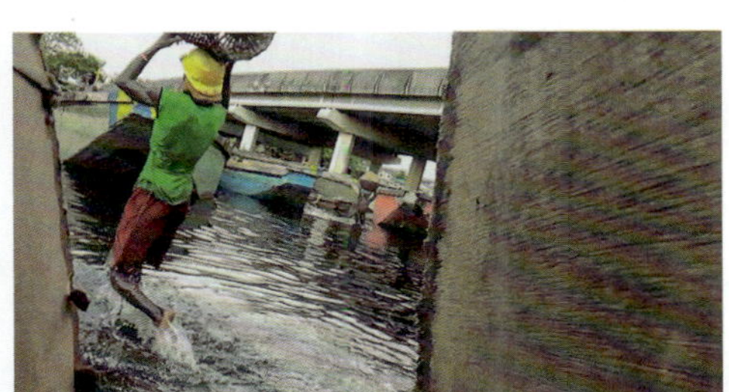
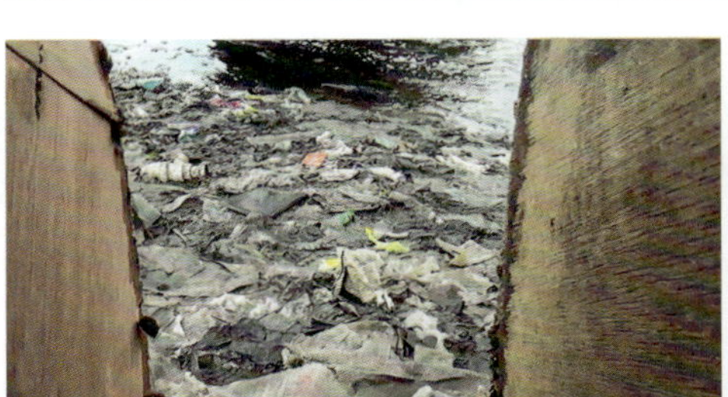
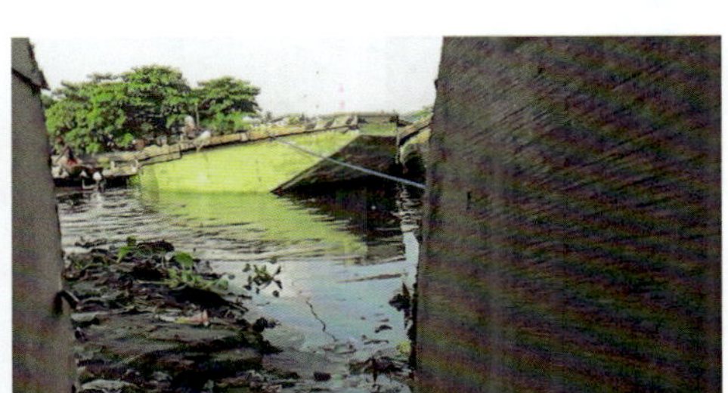

Director and Editor
Karimah Ashadu

Camera
Karimah Ashadu

Commissioned by
Arte Creative, France

Produced by
Karimah Ashadu

Apapa Amusement Park, 2013
Single-channel video, colour, sound, 2'38"

The film captures the titular Lagosian park after its demolition in 2012, as well as abandoned shops and buildings in the vicinity. In a clearing, young boys play a lively game of football, and the only sounds heard are the jeers, cheers and commentary from those sitting on the sidelines. Their action remains in the background, never approaching the camera in focus. Lush green foliage spreads in and around black and barren buildings, and an unsettling, haunting presence announces itself, however subtly. The smooth, panning movements of the camera are interrupted by the presence of a convex glass Ashadu configured as part of a mechanism that she manually operates, through which one boy at a time is brought into amplified focus. But as quickly as the glass shows up, it vanishes again.

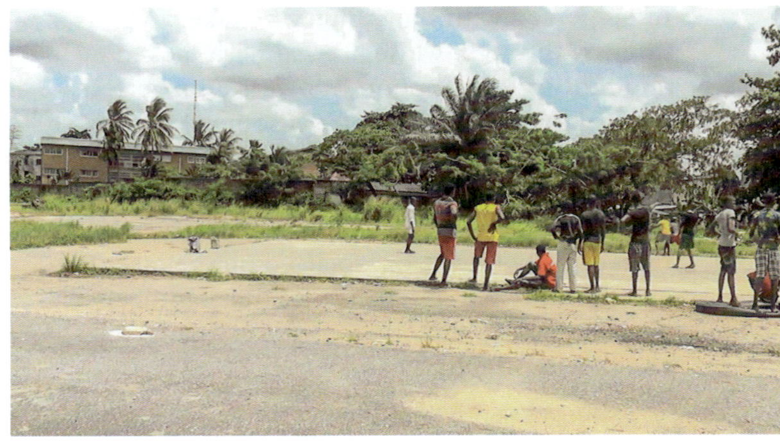

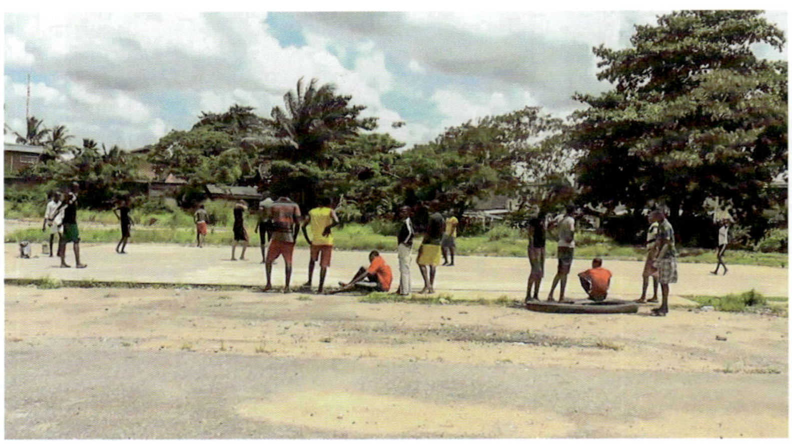

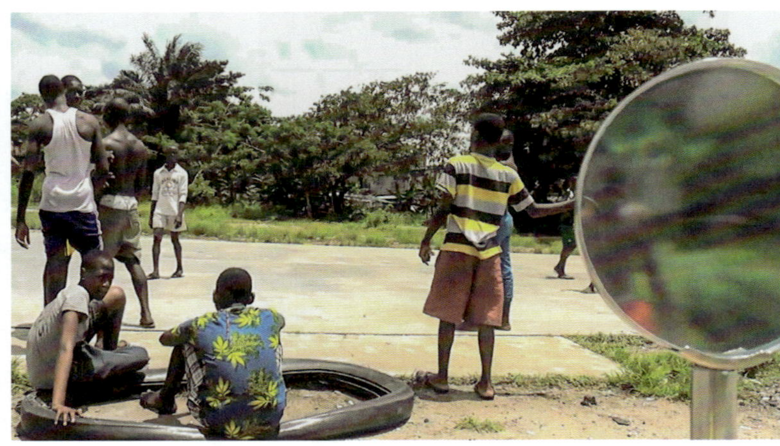

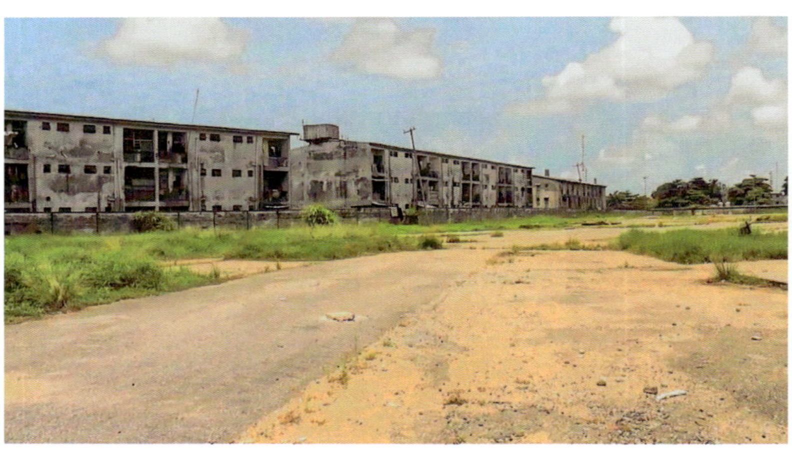

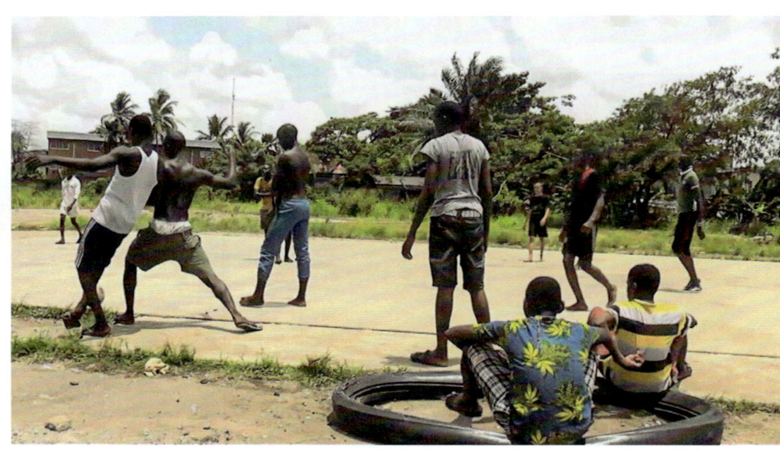

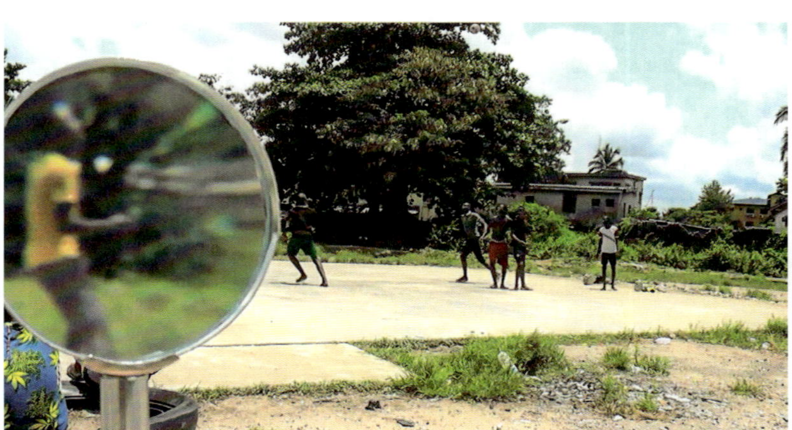

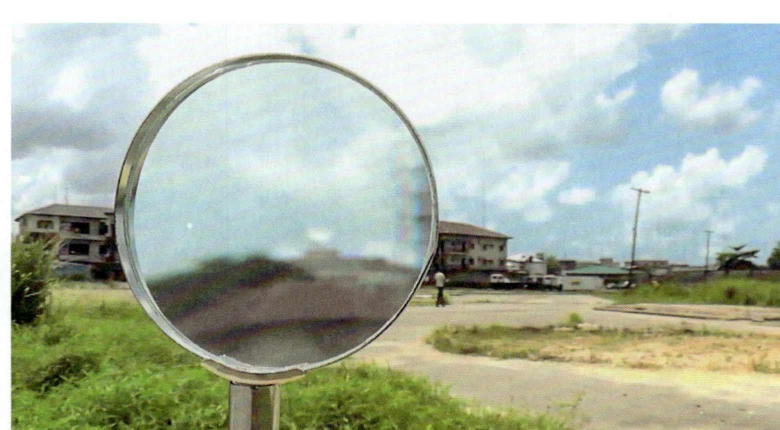

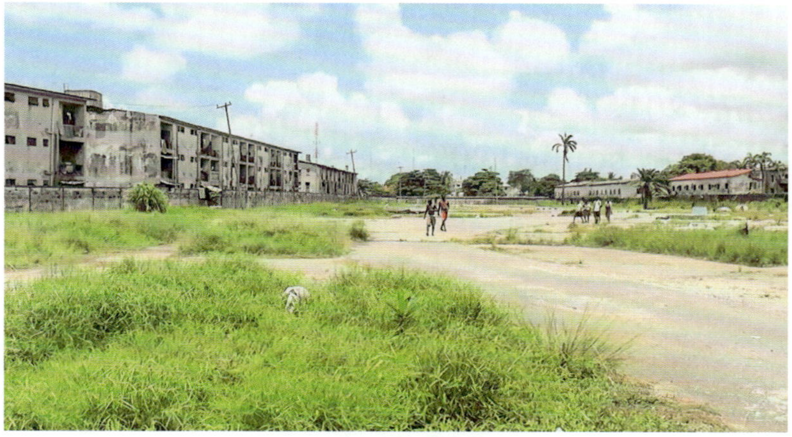

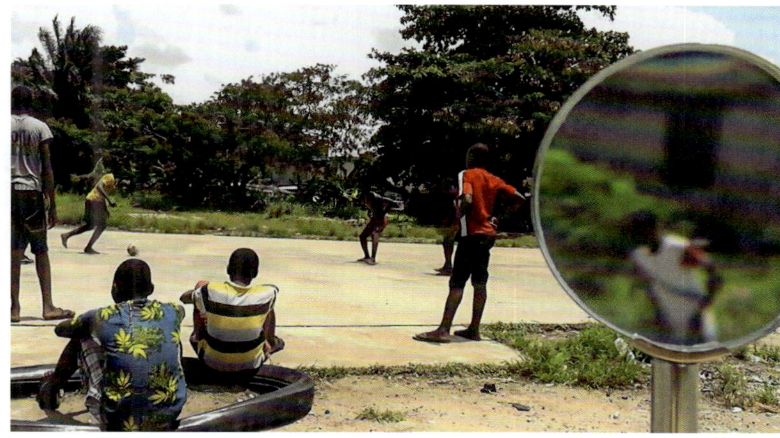

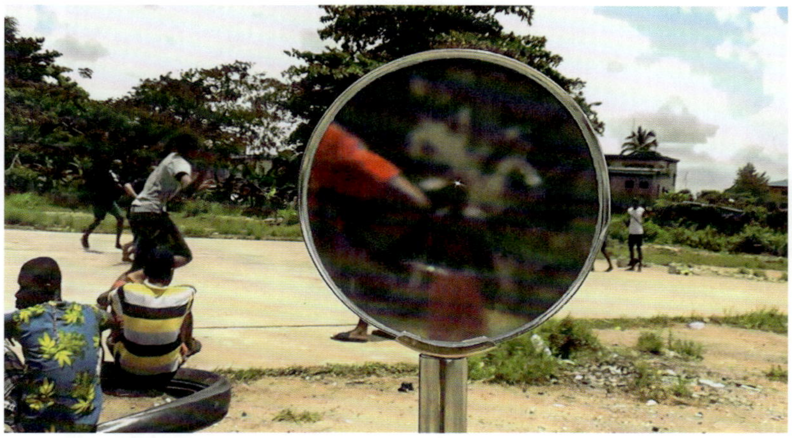

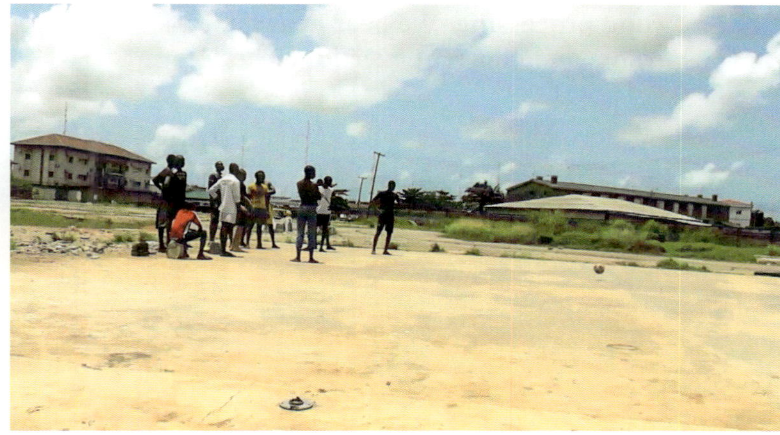

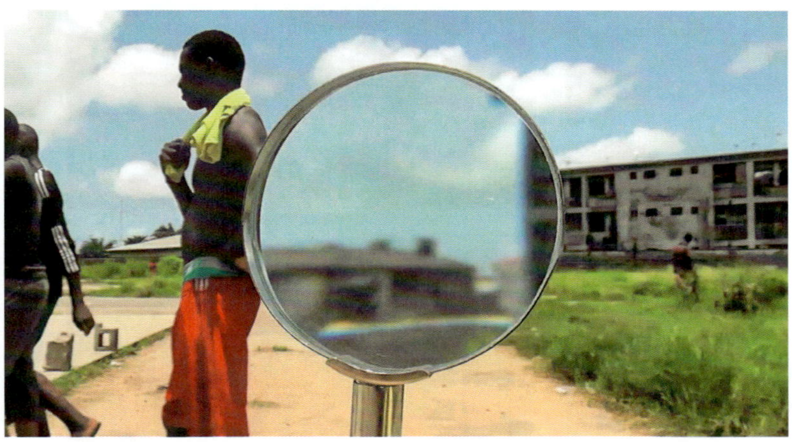

Ashadu edits the film in quick jump cuts that never allow us to linger on a single element for too long, mirroring the camera mechanism's flux. In moments where the glass appears, it conjures a vortex-like portal where its subject, for just a few seconds, exists in a world unto himself. The fragmented editing, quick-paced game and intermittent presence of the glass coalesce into a disquieting effect, made all the more so given the sullen atmosphere and environment.

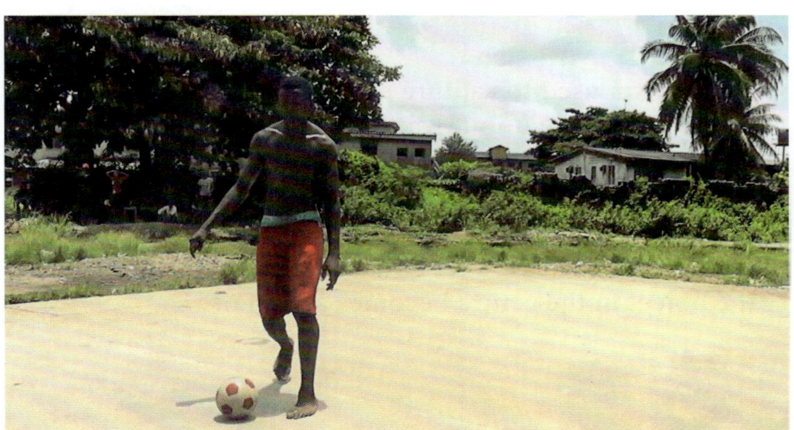

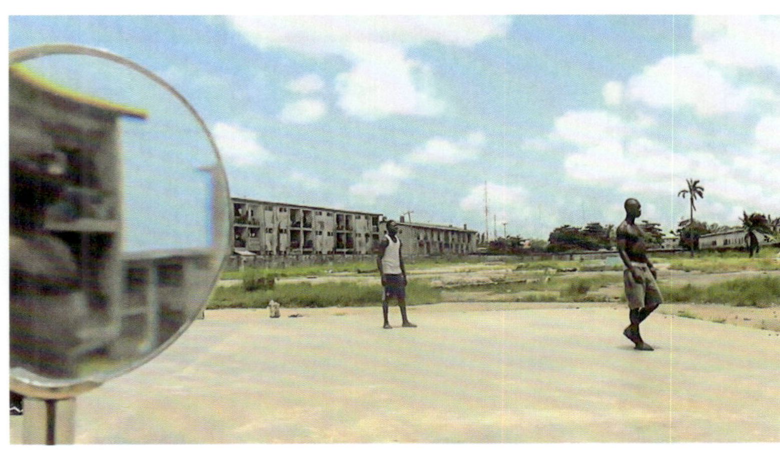

Director and Editor
Karimah Ashadu

Camera
Karimah Ashadu

Produced by
Karimah Ashadu

Makoko Sawmill, 2015
Single-channel video, colour, sound, 20'

The Makoko sawmill, jutting out from the shoreline of Lagos Lagoon, is a landscape hazy and diffused with smoke, sawdust and sunlight. The sound of chopping accompanies low-level conversation, and smooth tracking shots take us back and forth across the different stages of wood processing. We hear heavy axes, strained grunts and constant exertion. The rotating

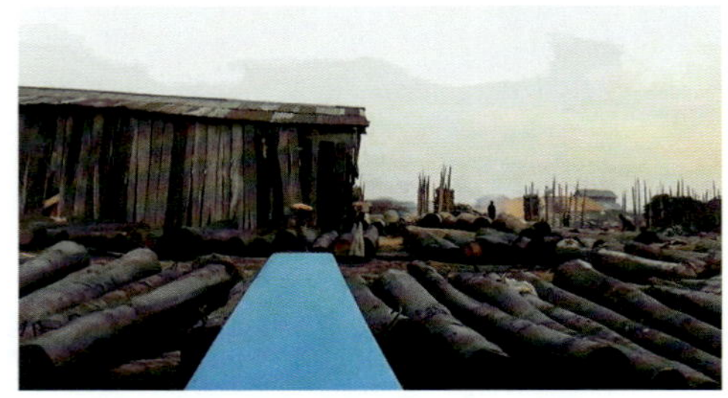

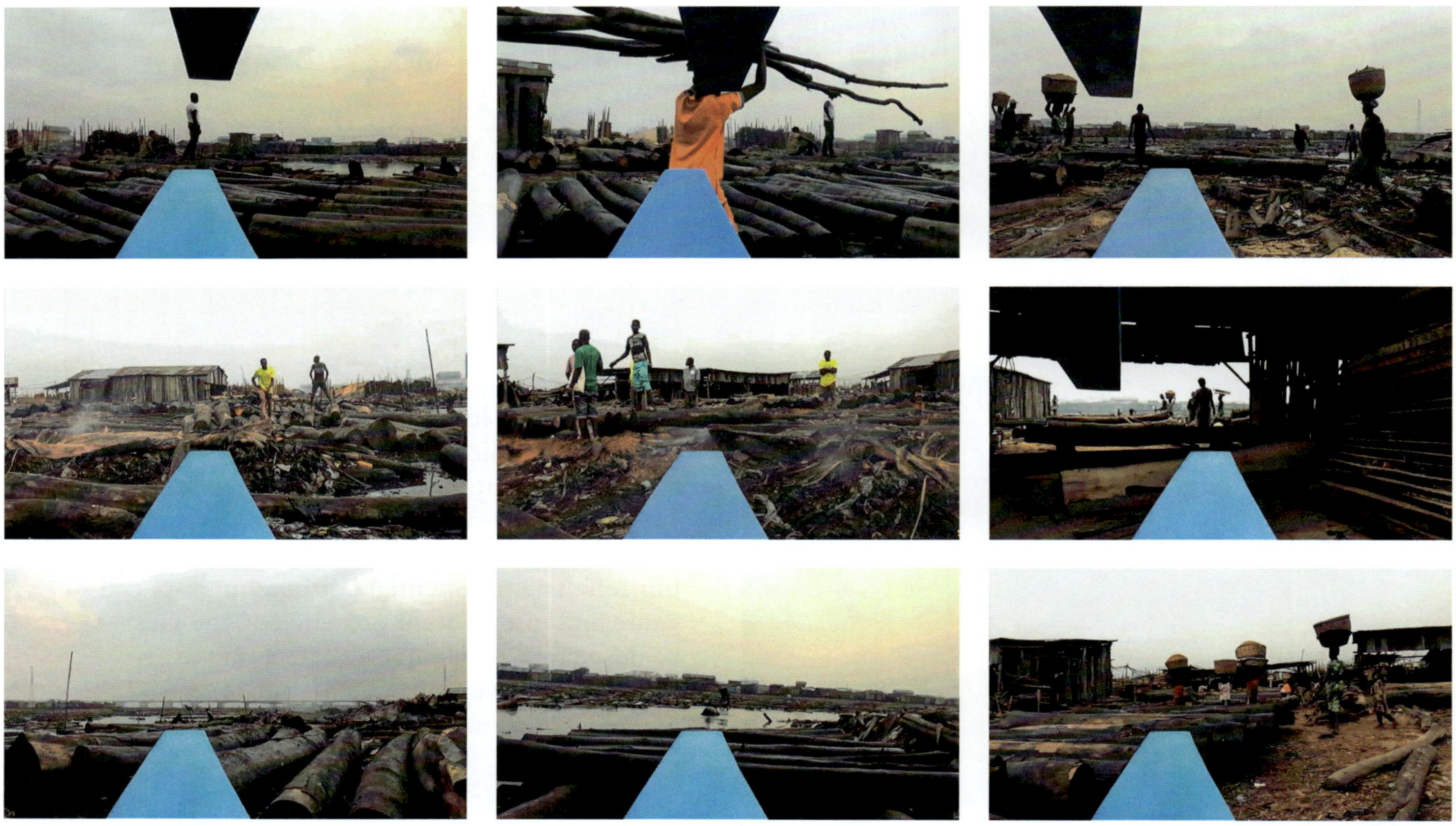

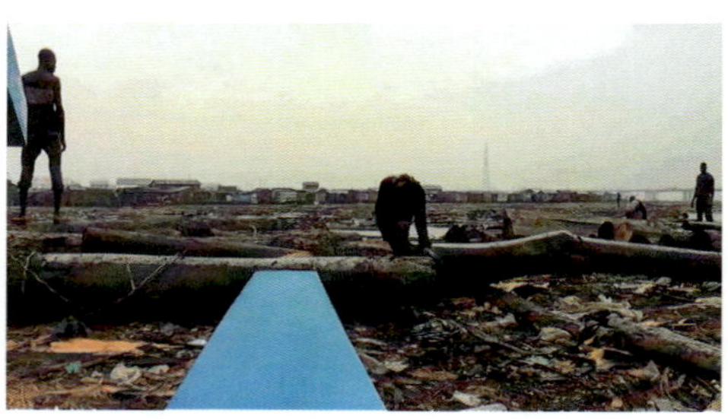

mechanism used to capture these images, however, is not without Karimah Ashadu's intervention. A bright cyan-coloured stick sits at the bottom of the image, while a second stick atop the frame periodically moves in and out of view. When held parallel for several moments, the object in the centre becomes a kind of

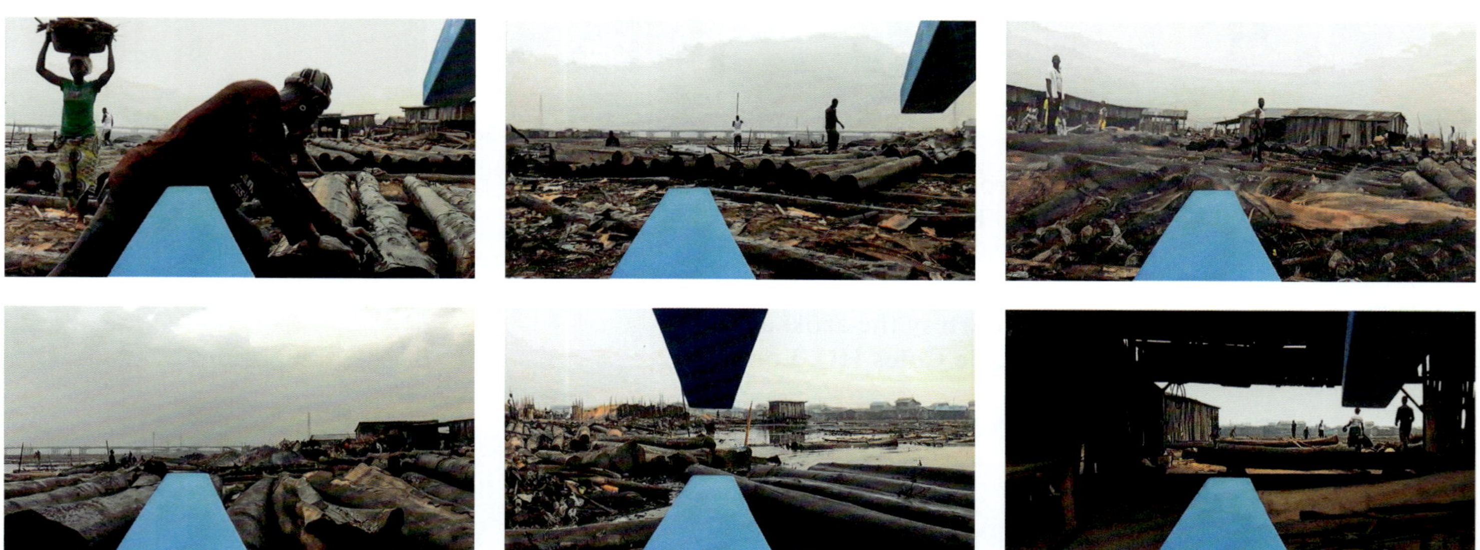

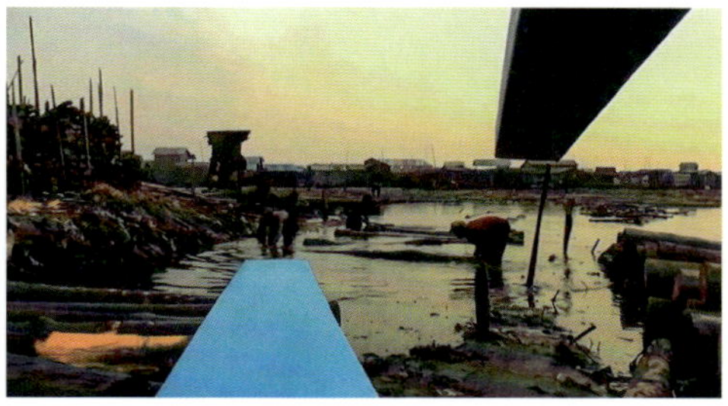

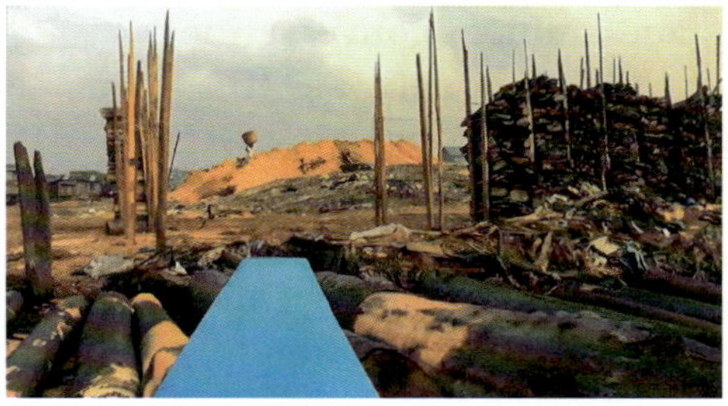

vanishing point, and our gaze is guided to that subject or action. The sticks imbue the activity in the foreground with a sense of order, among the brisk activity of men processing wood and women and children carrying baskets of sawdust. The film's non-linear sequence heightens our reliance on these idiosyncratic blue sticks as a grounding yet dynamic force placing us within and amid the work.

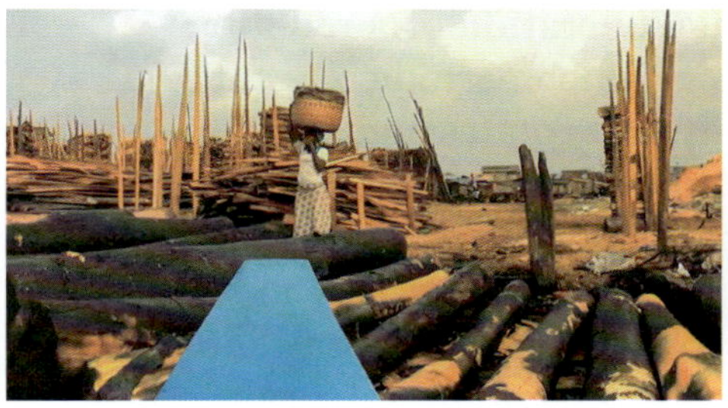

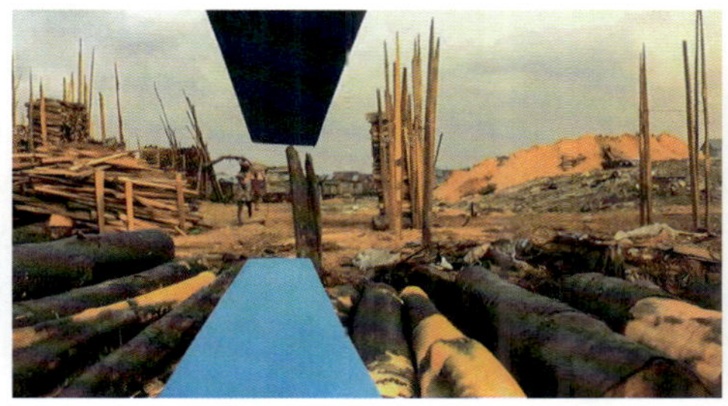

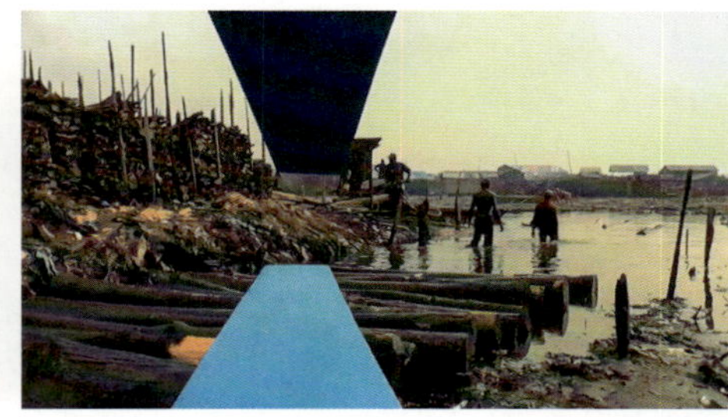

In moments where the camera is close to the subjects and we expect them to meet our gaze, they turn away instead, denying us acknowledgement. Even when their eyes meet the camera, they remain undeterred from the task at hand, their focus perhaps more attuned to the 'area boys' who loom and surveil their work.

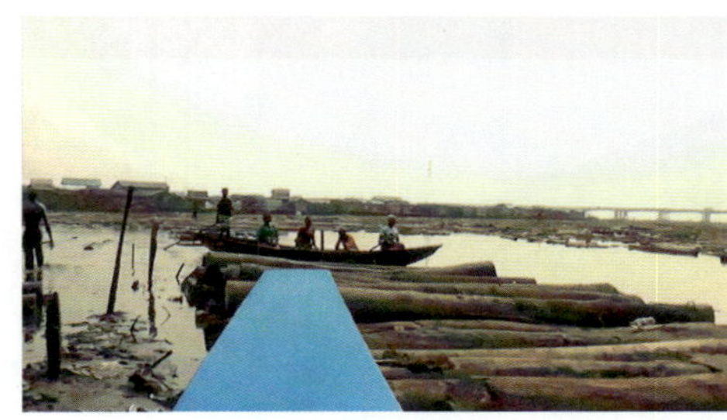

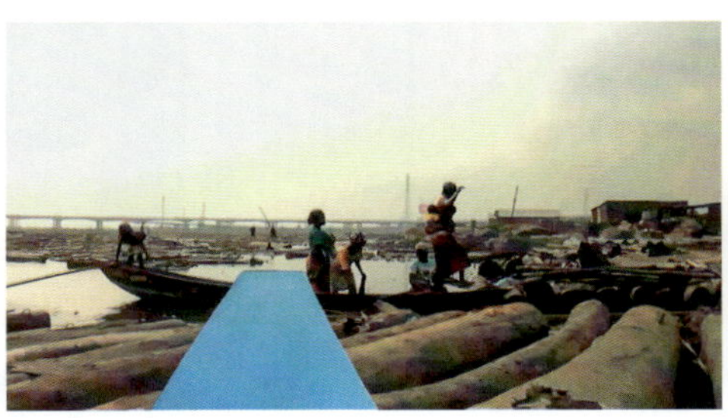

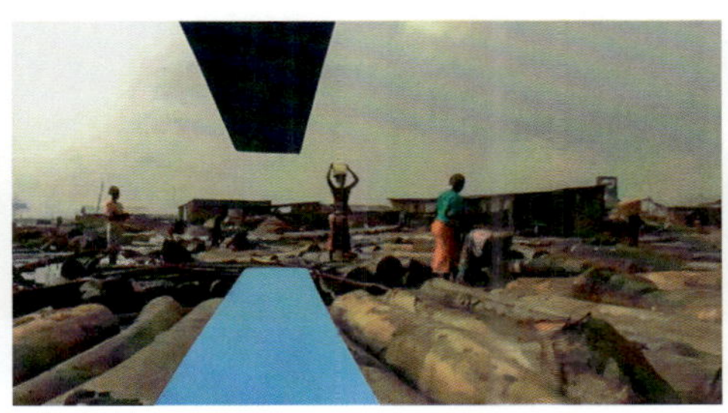

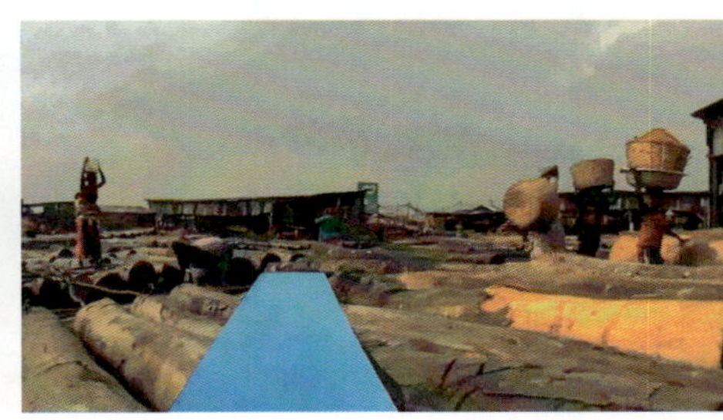

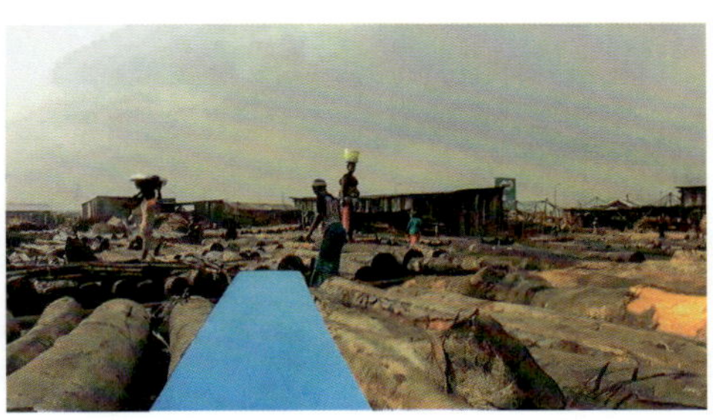

Director and Editor
Karimah Ashadu

Camera
Karimah Ashadu

Produced by
Karimah Ashadu

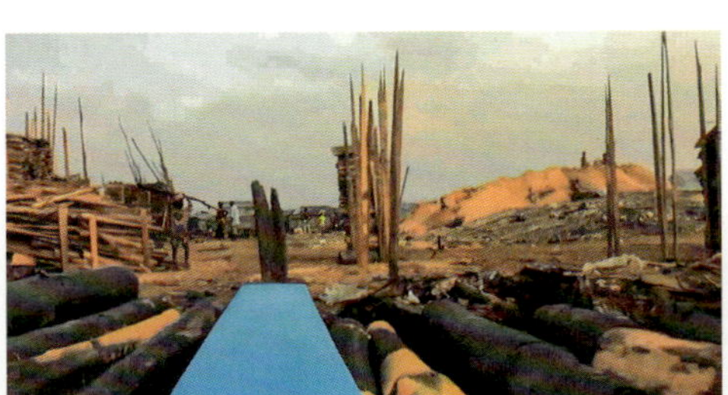

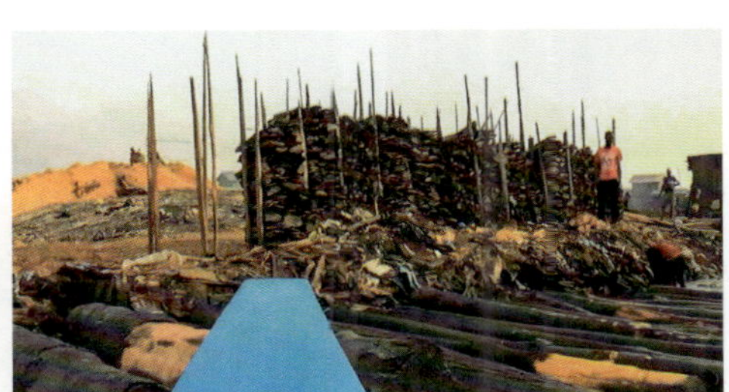

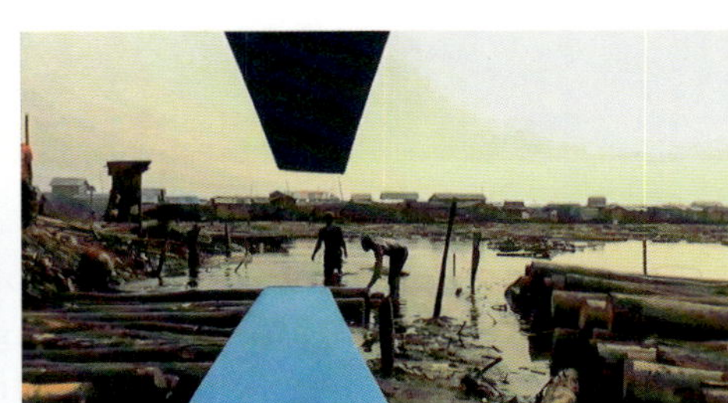

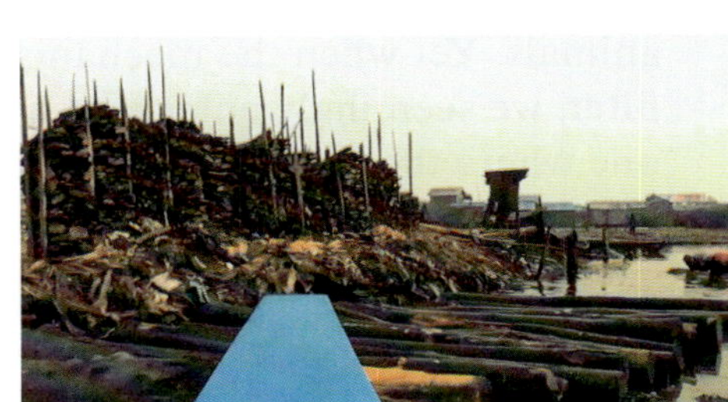

King of Boys (Abattoir of Makoko), 2015
Single-channel video, colour, sound, 5'

If considered apart from the image, the sound of hacking blades and ambient conversation takes on an almost rhythmic quality, as if we were listening to musicians warming up moments before taking the stage. For Karimah Ashadu, however, the visual and the auditory are entangled beyond the possibility of distinction. In the film, we understand the artist is further exploring this connection through her manual operation of a red filter made of a beer keg, which periodically appears in front of the lens as it rotates and scans the environment. Men, women and children all watch or participate in the slaughter of bulls and rams. A boy wields a knife nearly the size of his own body to slice cuts, and elsewhere a man skins a carcass. Given the subject,

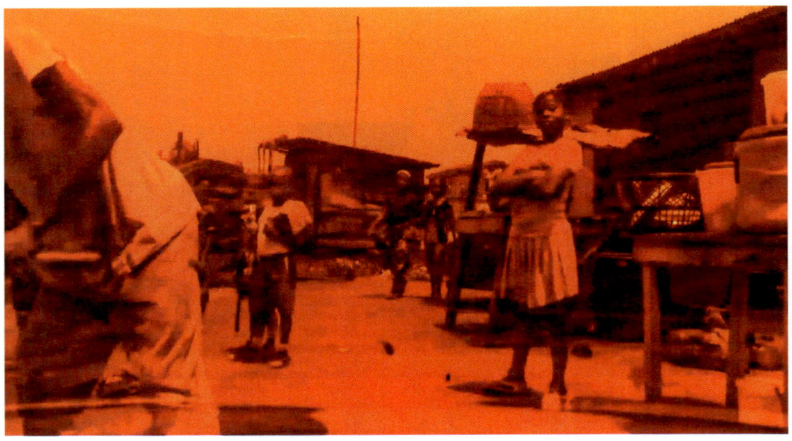

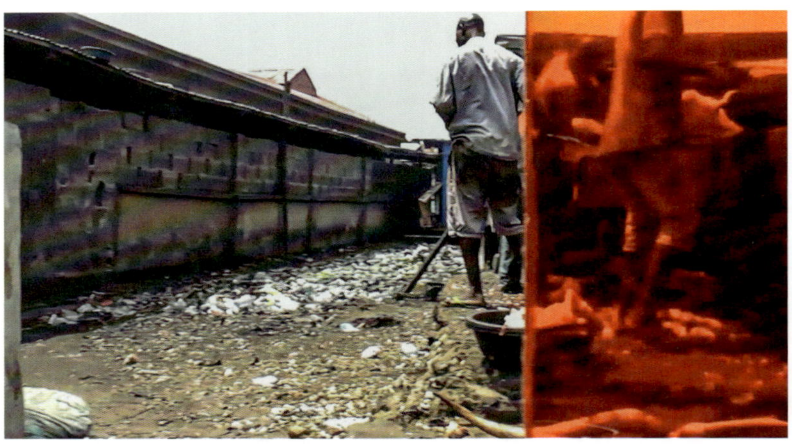

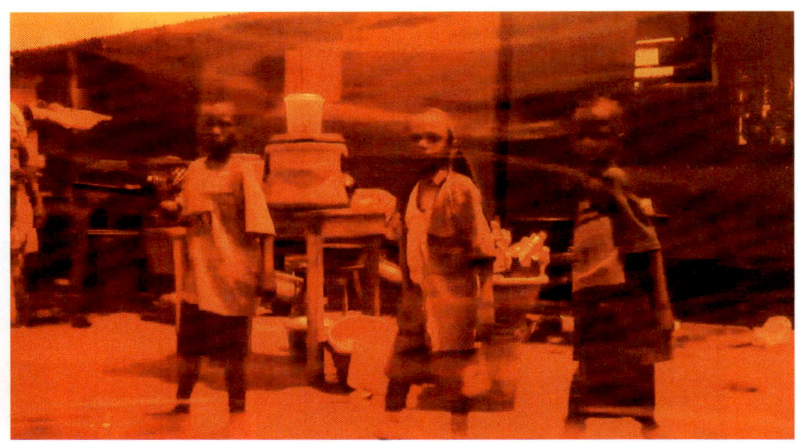

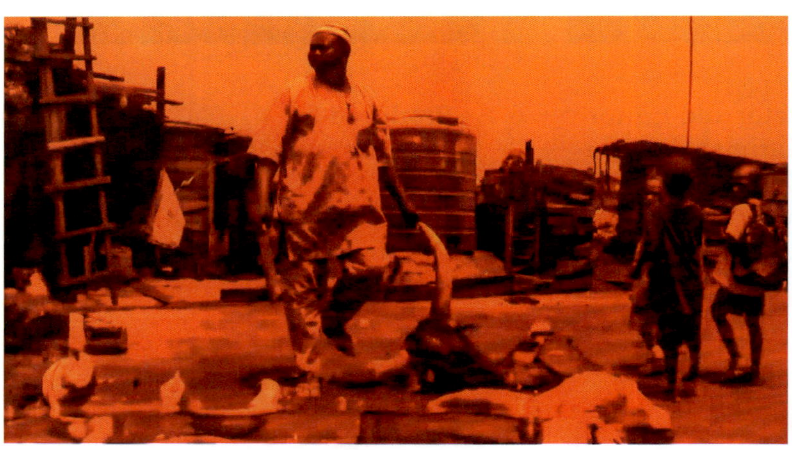

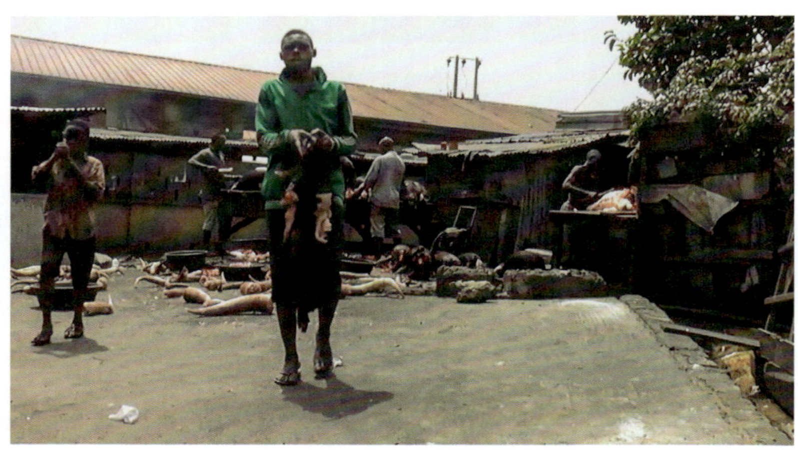

an open-air abattoir in the Makoko slums of Lagos, one might imagine finding relief that the filter creates a degree of separation from the jarring viscerality of raw flesh and decapitated animals. Yet when the mechanism shifts to the filter, we seemingly enter into another world, one where the hues are unnaturally vibrant, the sound of scraping knives uncannily close

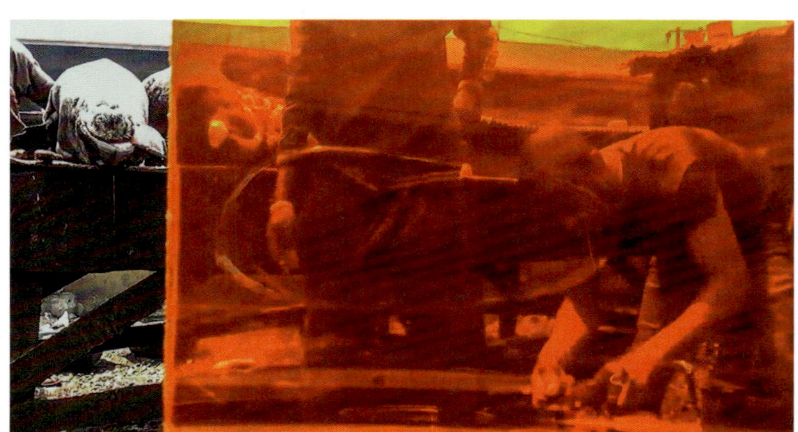

and the movements from one scene to the next increasingly piercing. The baleful score and crescendo of a Nollywood movie playing nearby contribute to the impression of a visceral, violent space. Then, when the filter disappears and the music stops, we return to what for many is just another part of daily life.

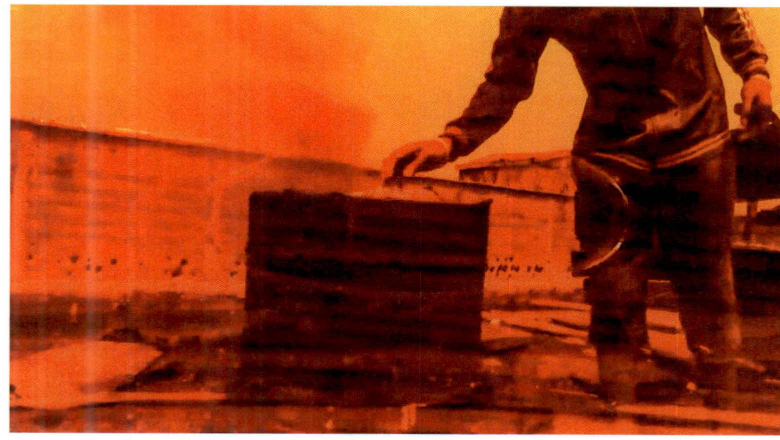

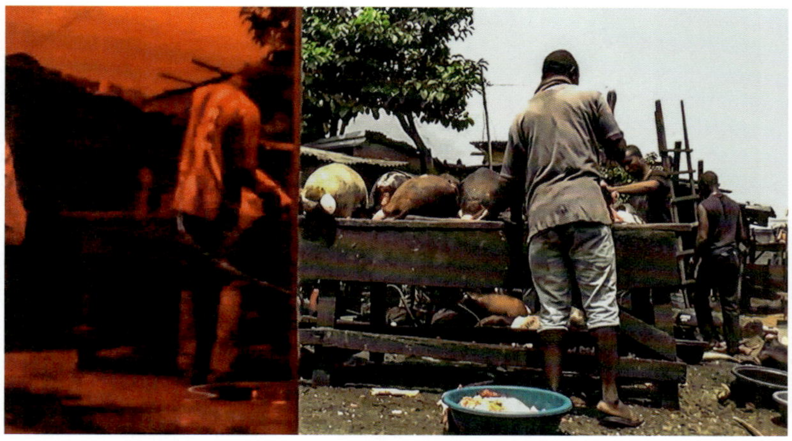

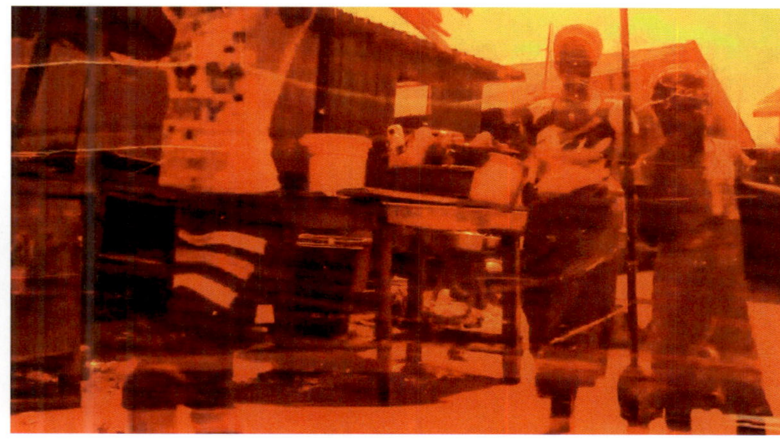

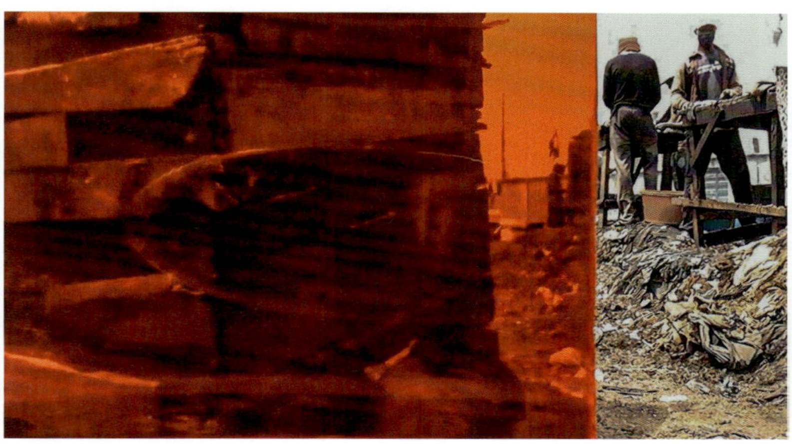

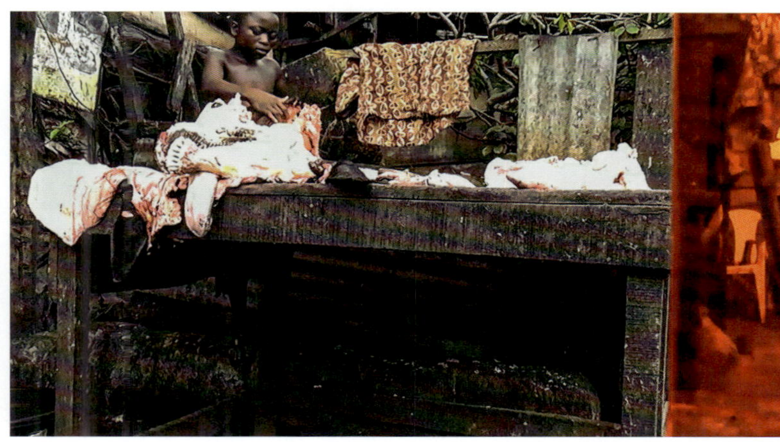

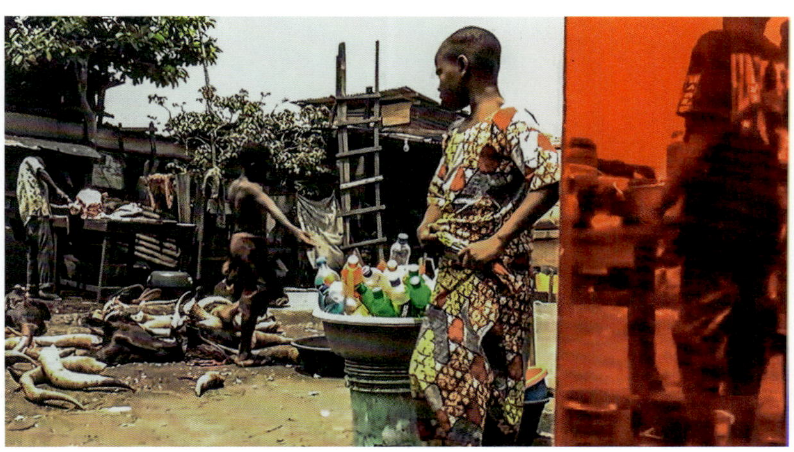

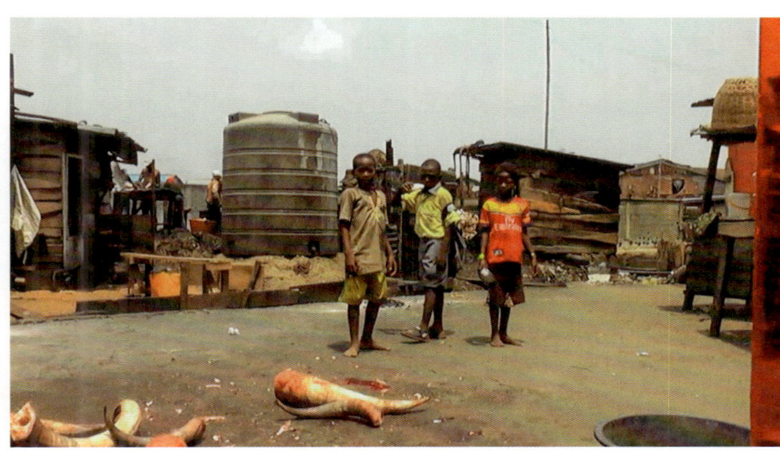

Director and Editor
Karimah Ashadu

Camera
Karimah Ashadu

Produced by
Karimah Ashadu

Red Gold, 2016
Two-channel video, colour, sound, 18'

For the first time with a two-channel screen, a direct narrative approach and multiple perspectives, Karimah Ashadu introduces the trade between palm oil farmers in the Ekiti state of southwestern Nigeria and the Ikoyi royal family, from whom they lease land. Two women stand knee-deep in a pool of unrefined palm oil and fruit kernels, and the bright yellow mixture stains their arms and legs with a golden hue that reflects light with each vigorous movement

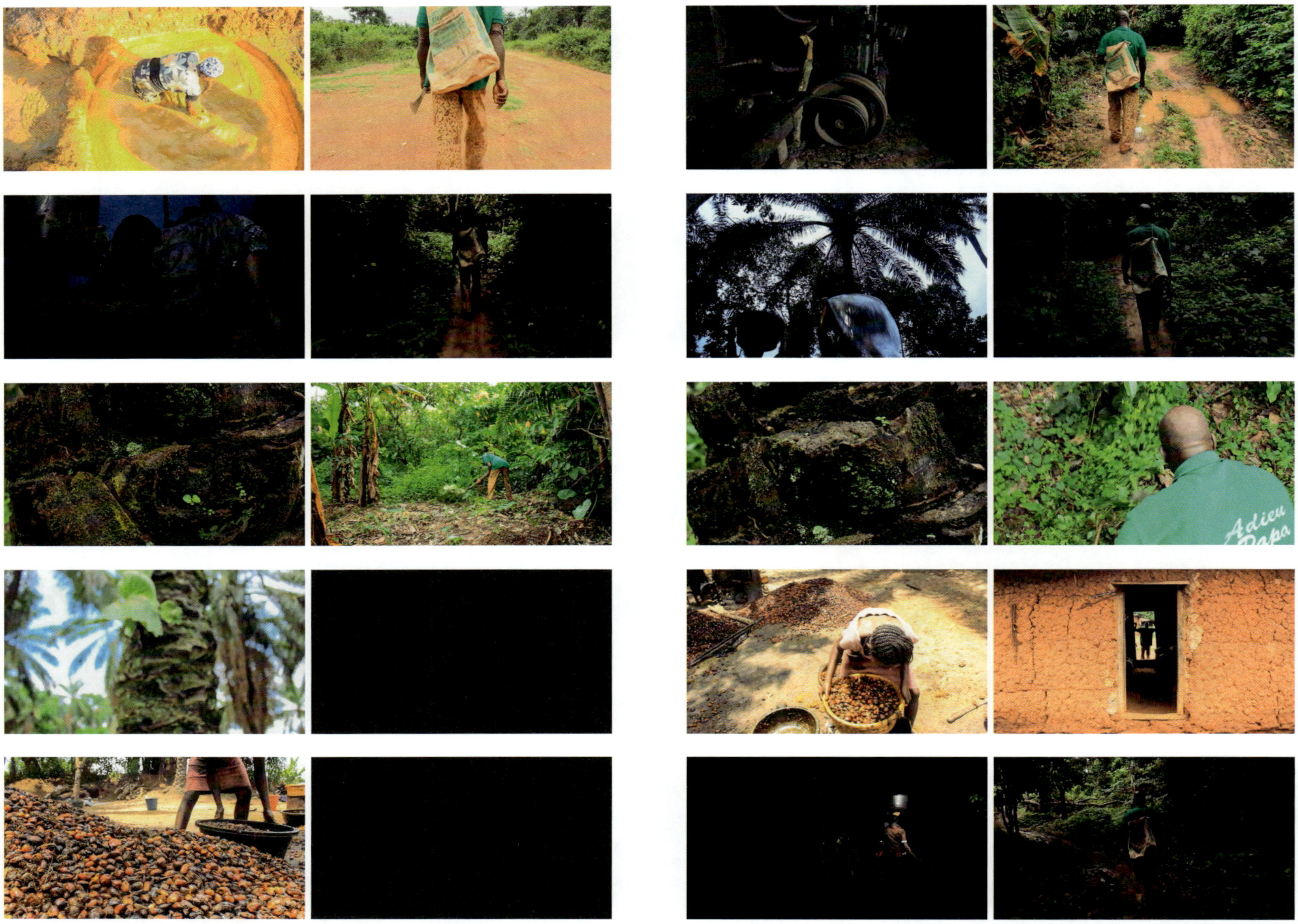

of sieving through the liquid. We are shown the multiple stages of extraction and refinement, all of which demand the labour of many people, aided by only a few machines. Their pace, like a quickened heartbeat, punctuates both day and night. Ashadu positions the camera far above the subjects, as if we were perched atop a palm tree looking down at their repetitive undertaking. In subsequent moments, the camera mimics their sightline as they look up into the trees, so tall they seem a blurred mass of leaves and dappled light.

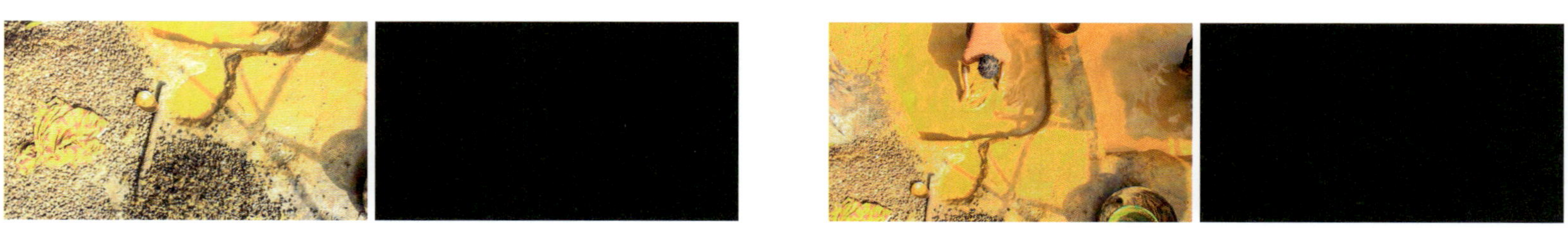

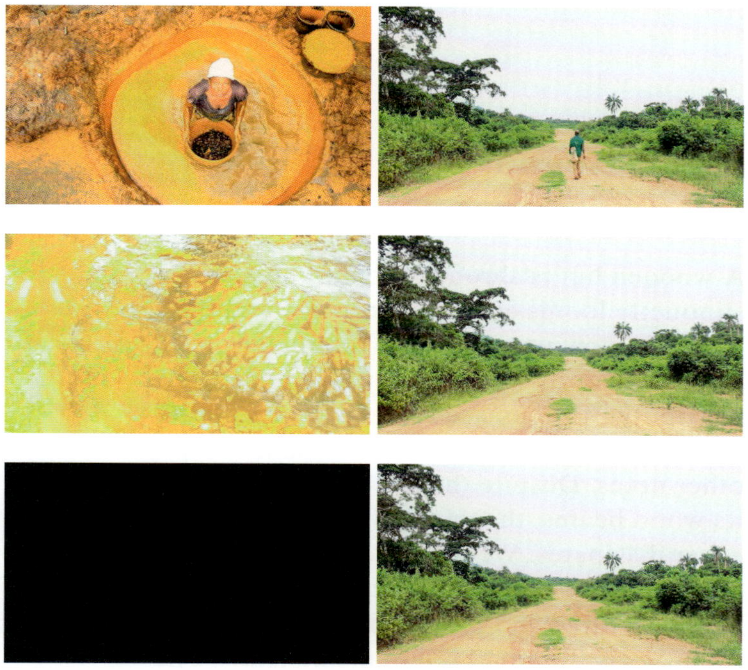

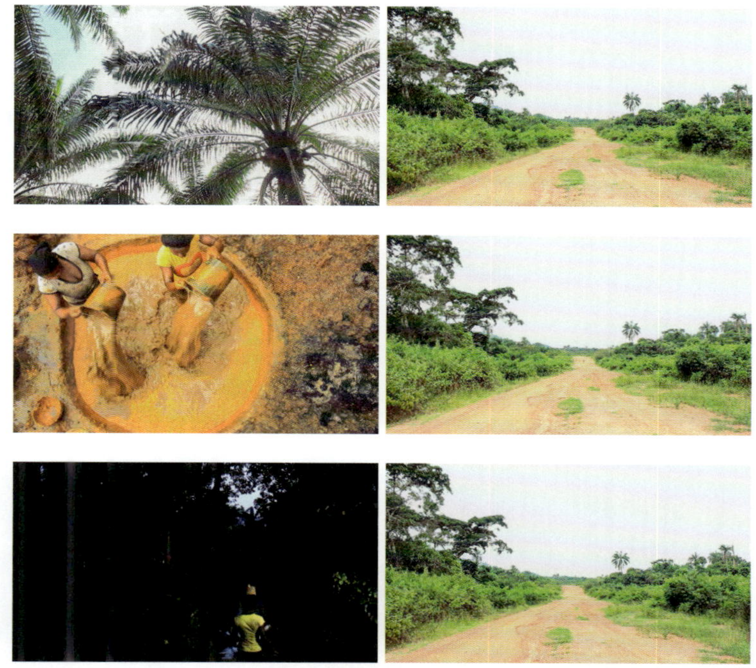

On the opposite channel we follow a Prince's venture into a forest as he describes how his father, once a warrior king, bequeathed him a land indescribably vast and rich. His figure is dwarfed by the expanse; the lush vegetation appears endless. Speaking in Yoruba, he describes himself and his family as 'fathers to strangers', since they have taken on the post left vacant after the departure of colonial powers and the government's ensuing abandonment of the farmers.

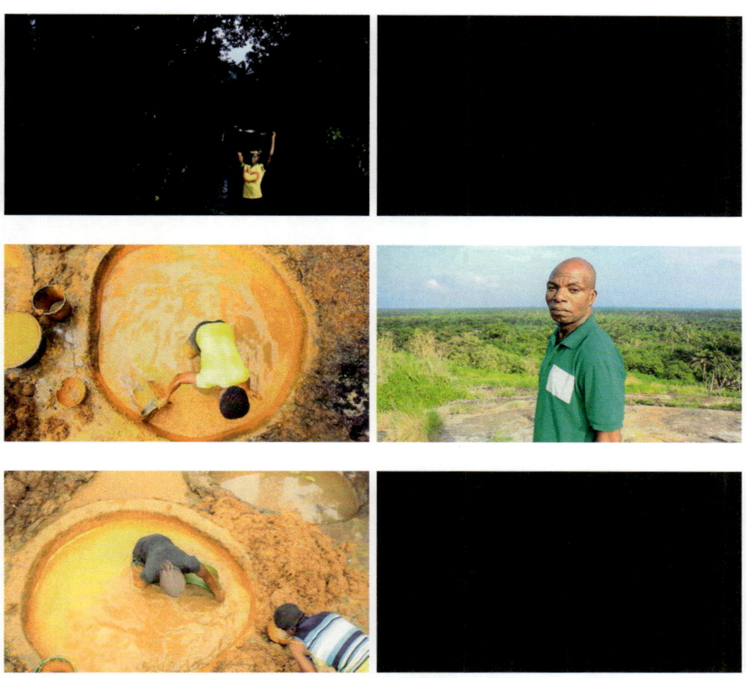

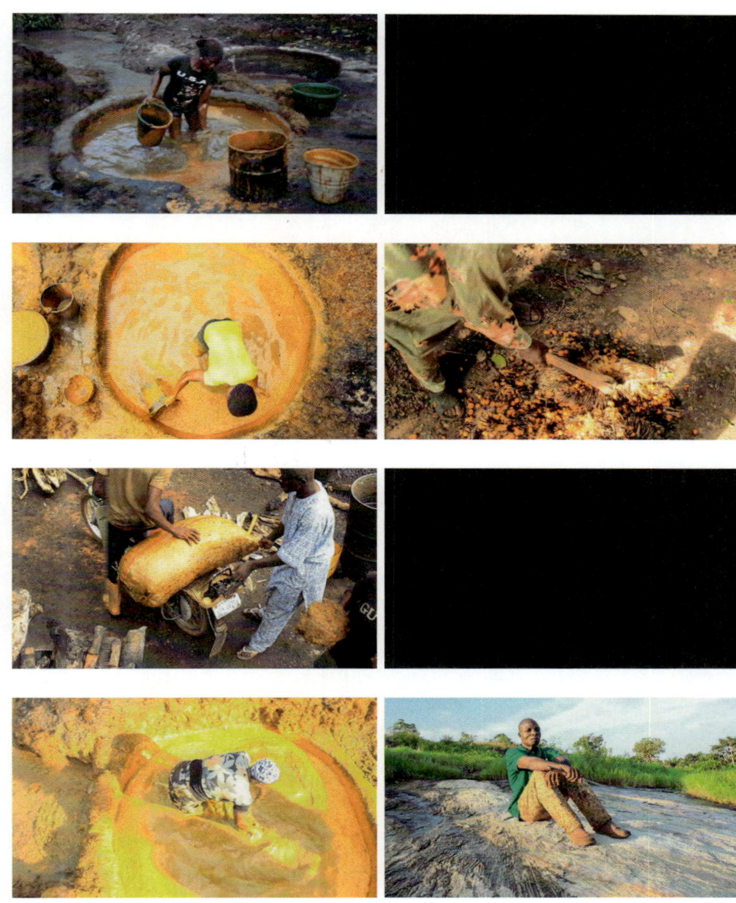

Director and Editor
Karimah Ashadu

Camera
Olatunde Raphael

Commissioned by
Centre d'Art Contemporain Genève

Destiny, 2016
Single-channel video, colour, sound, 9'

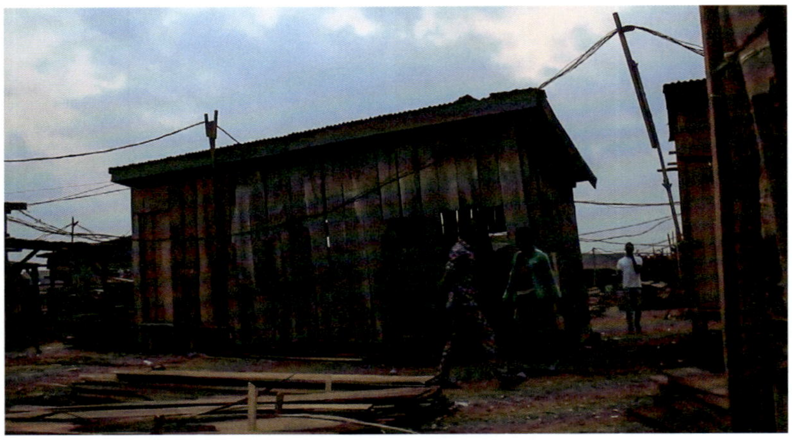

A wooden hut is shrouded in darkness. Its silhouette looms against a grey sky, and the camera's slow pan across its perimeter on a handmade dolly imbues it with an unsettling proximity. We then see it in daylight, and the word 'Destiny' written in white chalk amid other notes. Despite the sun pouring through its wood beams, the darkness inside the hut never dissipates. We never get a clear look at the man inside, the titular subject. Only his arms, torso and profile are caught in the frame, as is the small red flame he tends. The camera itself appears apprehensive, peeking around corners and behind walls, allowing us glimpses of parts, but never the whole.

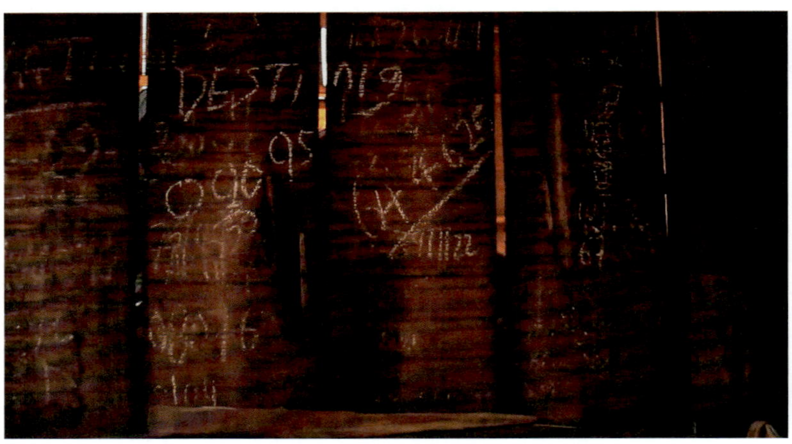

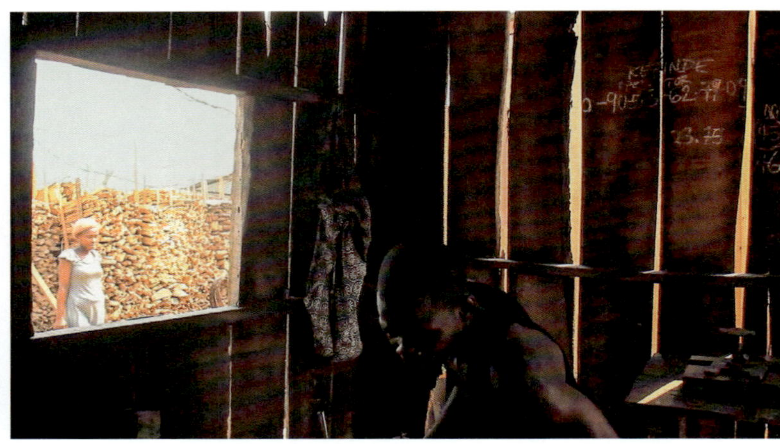

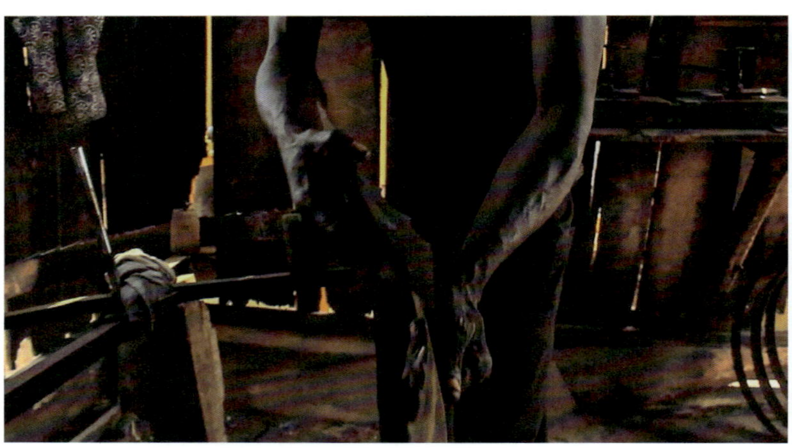

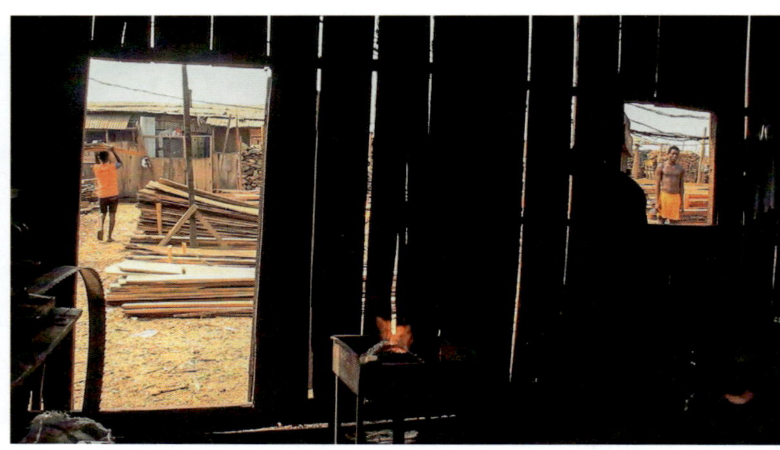

As the scenes alternate from day to night, the sounds in the film similarly shift between active, bustling conversation and quiet stillness. When we are with Destiny in the hut, it is as if we occupy a space unto itself, a kind of reverential separation, only merging with the world once again when the sun sets and the darkness of the exterior reflects the interior.

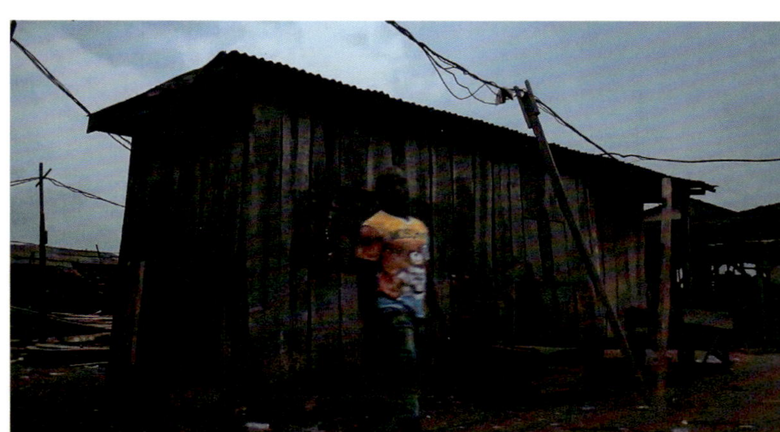

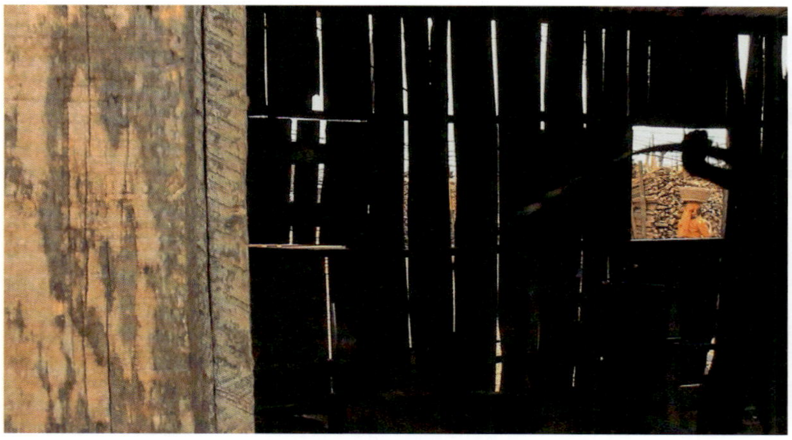

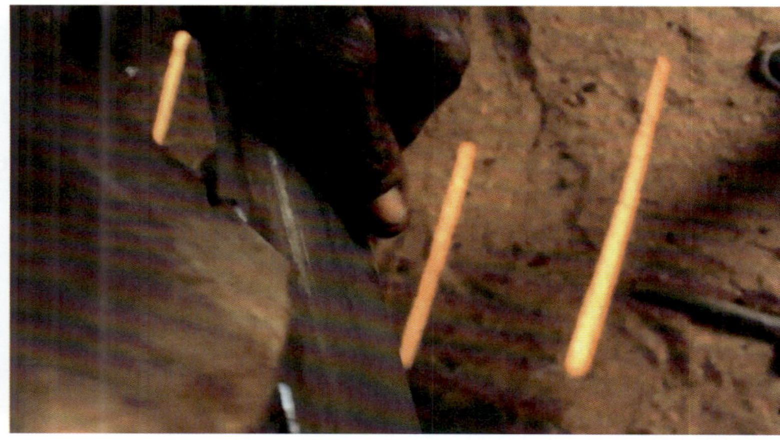

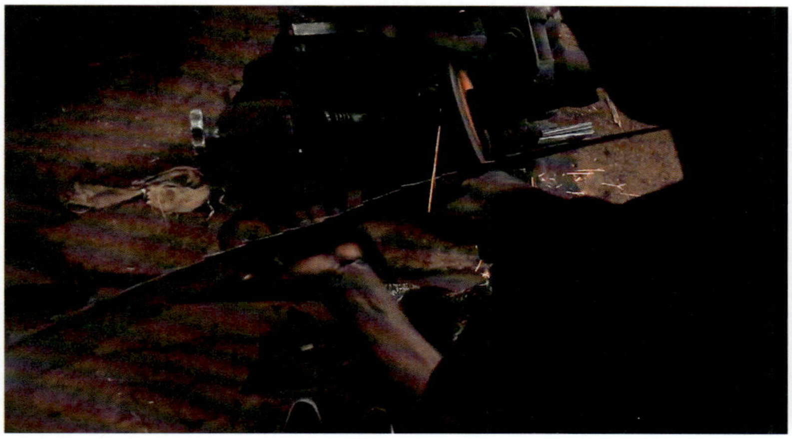

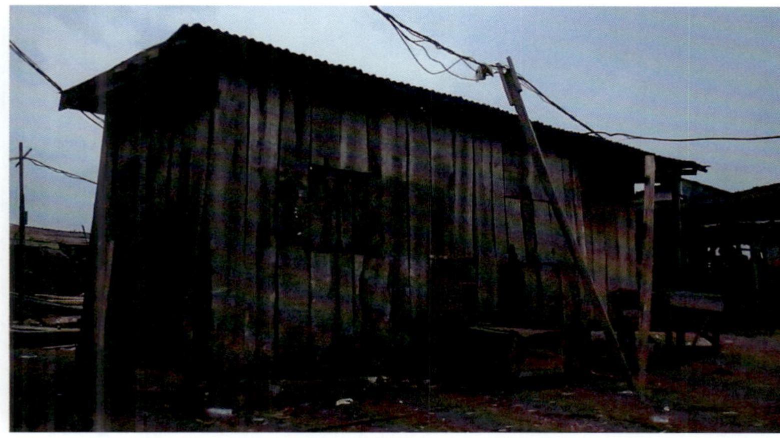

When ‘area boys’ are present, they at times assist Destiny in his work, but more often they watch, as we do. The sounds that populate the film, from sharpening metal blades to the stoking embers of a small fire, originate in Destiny’s labour and self-sufficient practice, namely providing the needed tools for the nearby Makoko sawmill.

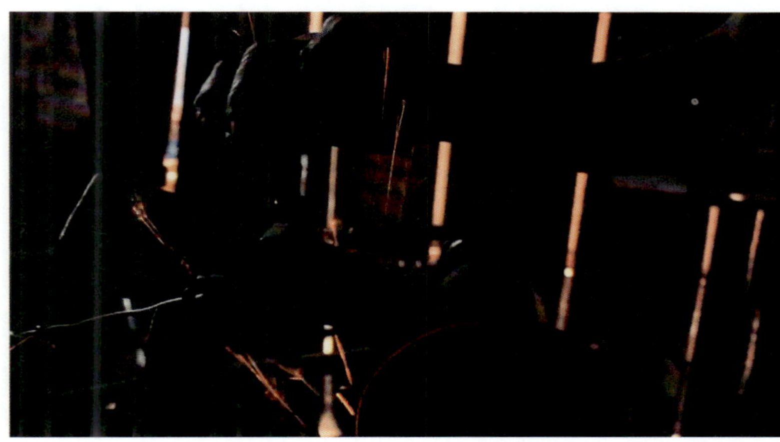

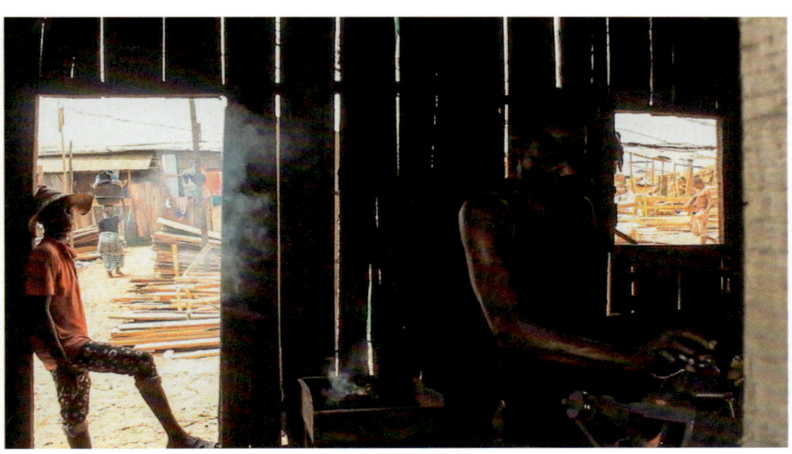

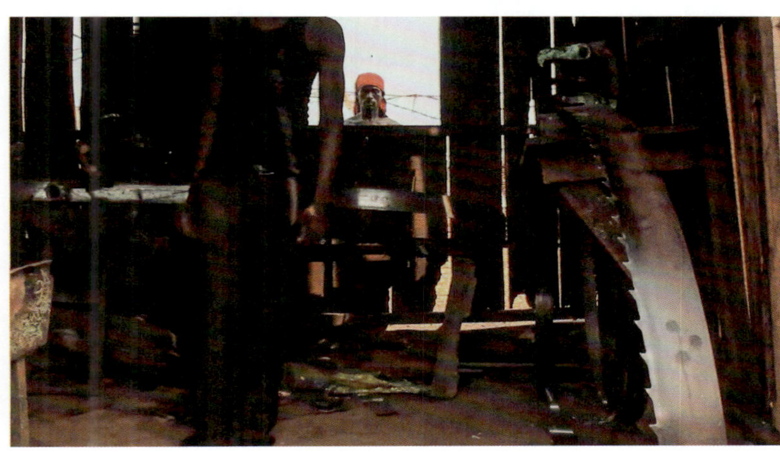

Director and Editor
Karimah Ashadu

Camera
Olatunde Raphael

Produced by
Karimah Ashadu

Power Man, 2018
Two-channel video, colour, sound, 5'

Cast in near-total darkness, the subject of this film, an 'area boy' from the slums of Lagos who goes by Sodoko (meaning 'power man'), carries a propulsive force. A dim overhead light provides just enough illumination to distinguish his presence. Defined muscles glisten with sweat before receding from view again. Heavy breathing on one channel and the sharp thud of an axe hitting its target on the other are the only sounds we hear throughout.

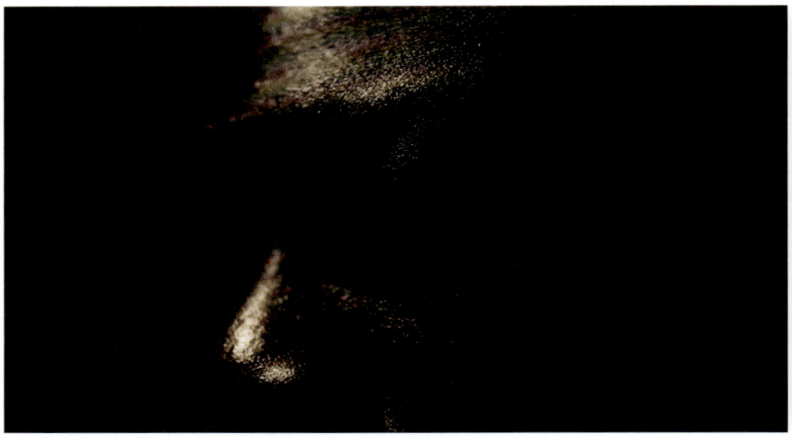

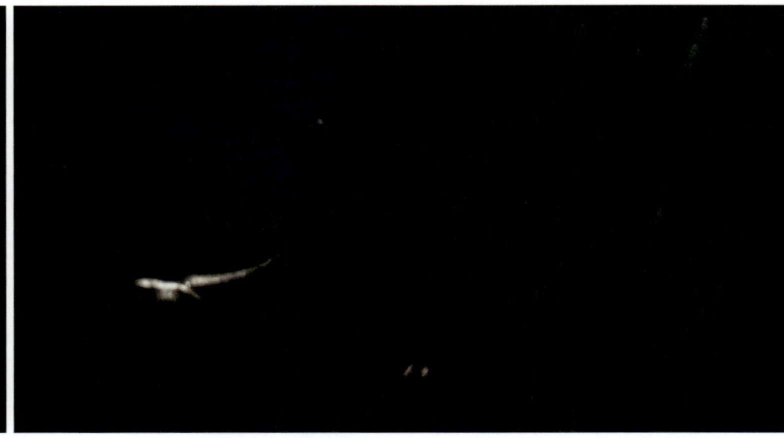

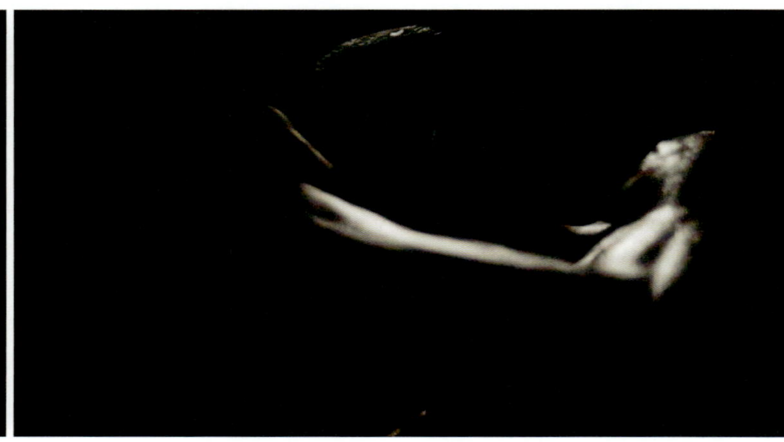

As time progresses, Sodoko's breathing becomes strained, his grunts become more guttural, and it is clear he is pushing his body to its limit. But any signifiers of exhaustion are met with further exertion – as his training intensifies on one channel, so too does his axing on the second, with the weight behind each swing growing. Karimah Ashadu never reveals Sodoko's face, just as she never shows what he is chopping or who his opponent is.

The disquieting nature this concealment engenders, however, is counterbalanced by the apparently reverential nature of his activity. The rhythmic nature of his breath and the definition of his torso imply a long-practiced routine of engaging the physical, to an even ascetic degree. As the jabs slow and his breath steadies, we see a glimpse of a makeshift home gym cast in golden light from above, then returned to darkness once more.

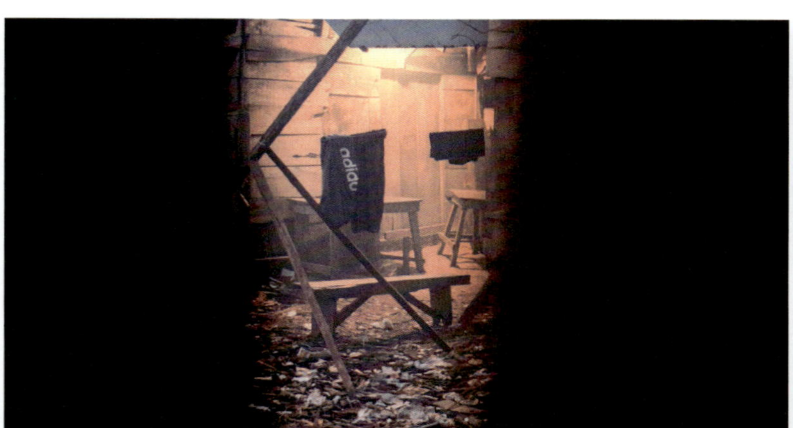

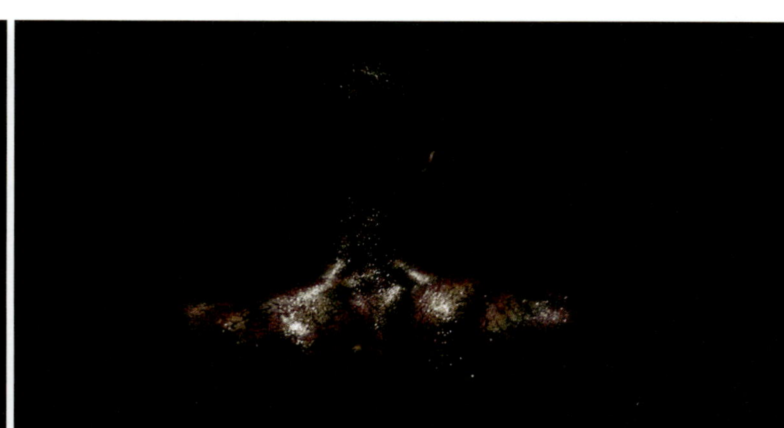

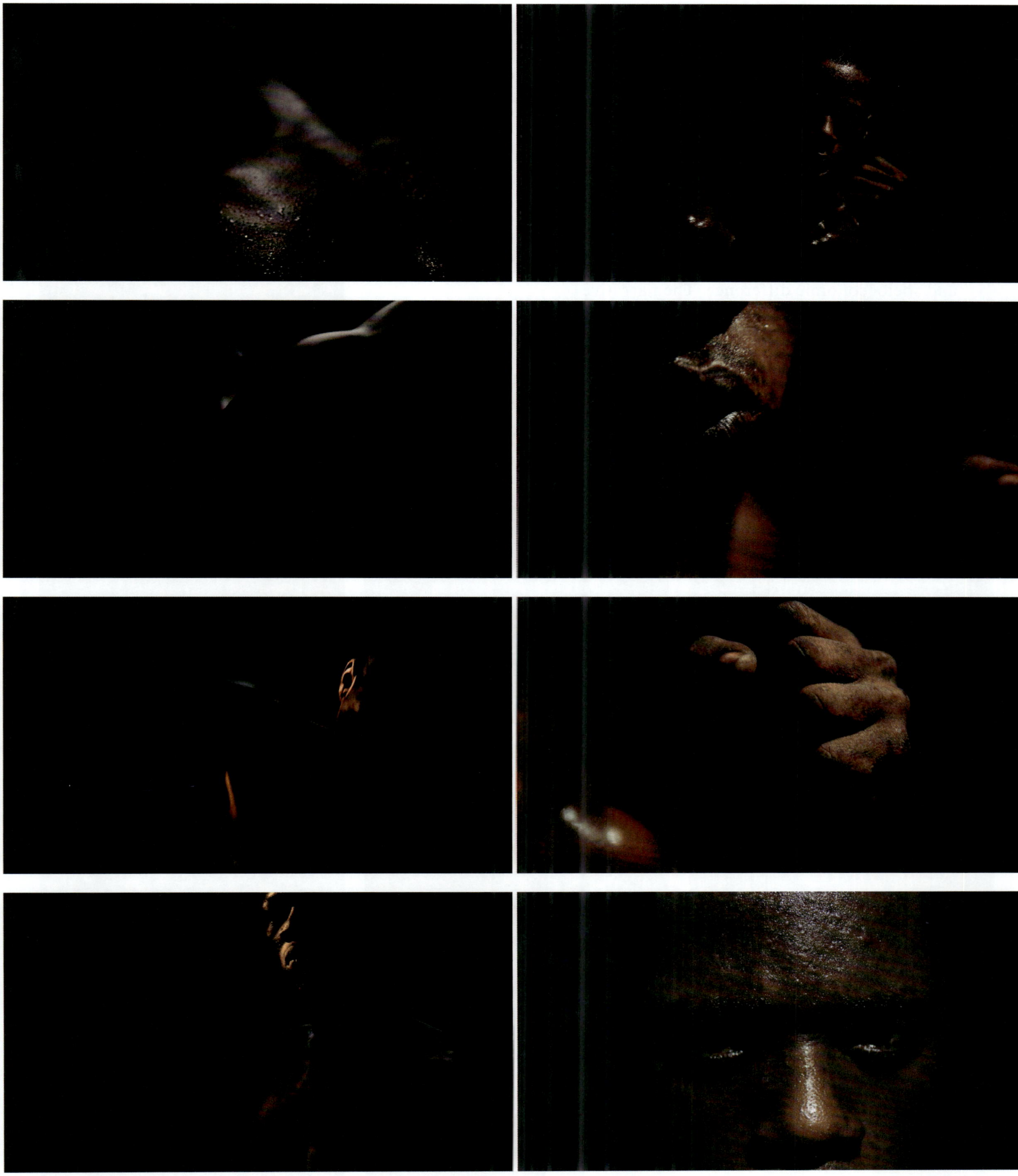

Director and Editor
Karimah Ashadu

Camera
Olatunde Raphael

Sound Recordist
Anthony Monday

Brown Goods, 2020
Single-channel video, colour, sound, 12'

In this film, the camera is a means of self-exploration and self-articulation. In opening oneself up to receiving the complexities of another's story, one can achieve an intimacy and proximity otherwise obstructed by cultural and socioeconomic difference. The narrative concerns Emeka, a Nigerian migrant who has spent the last seven years in Germany

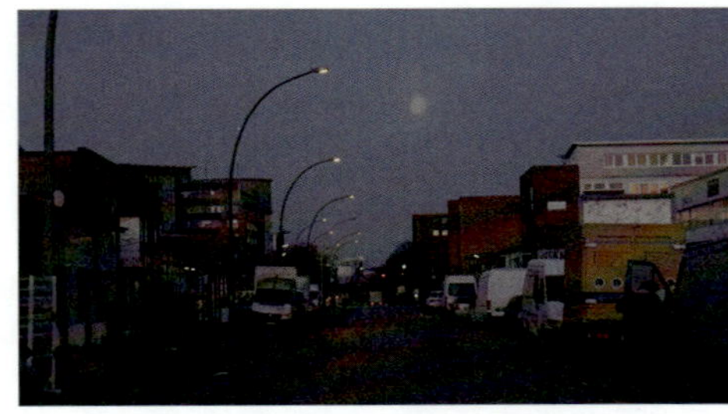

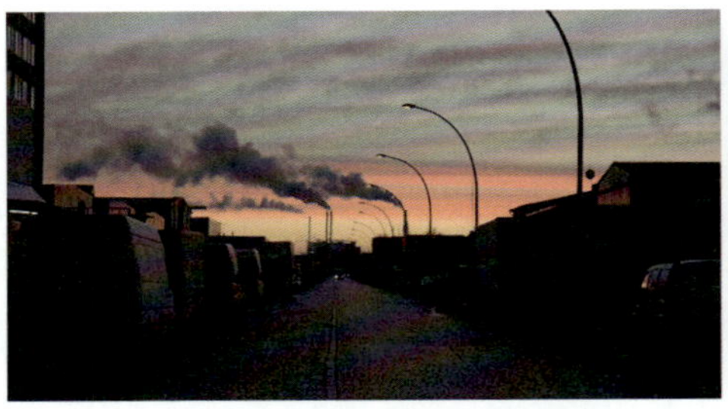

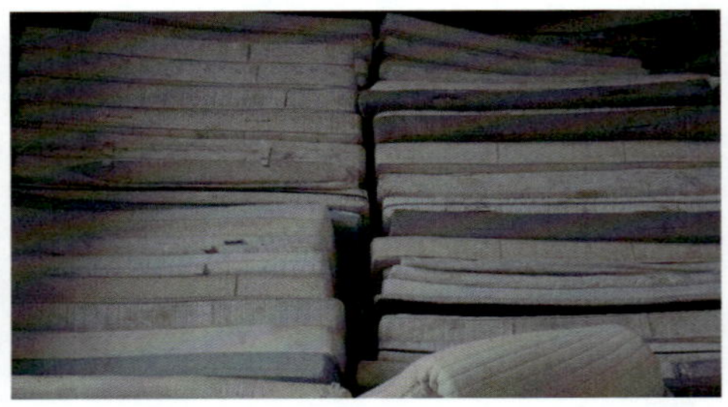

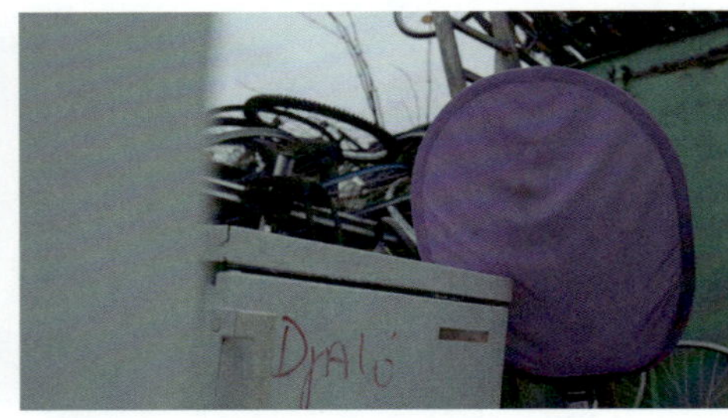

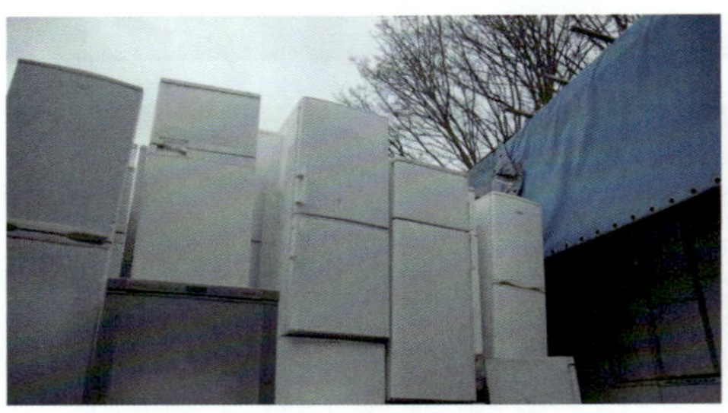

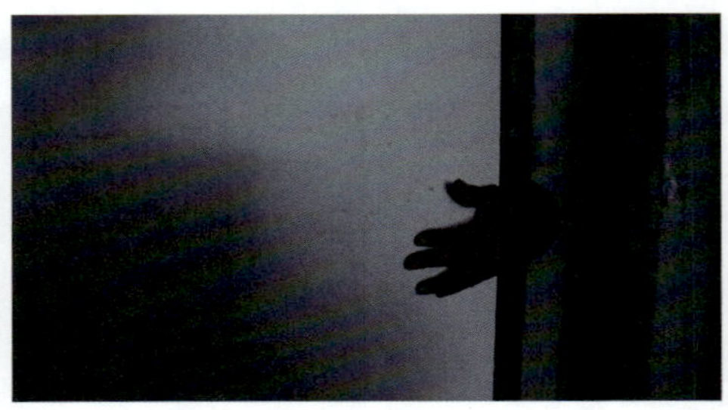

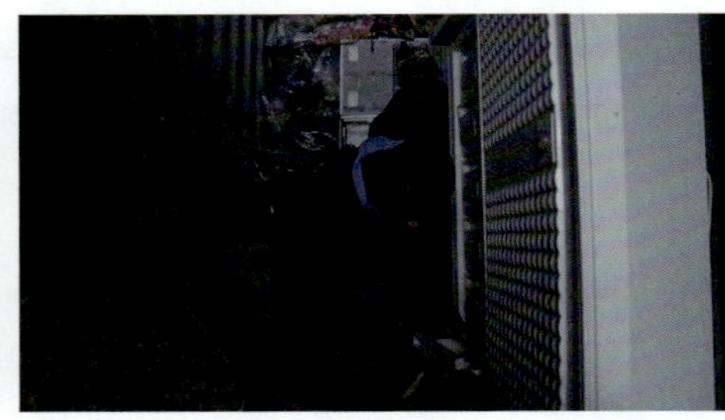

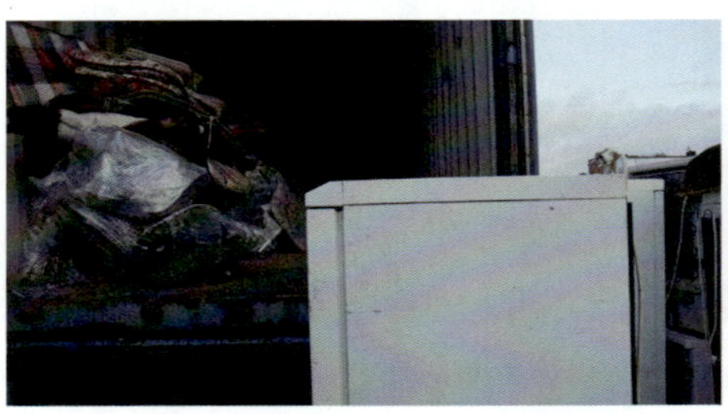

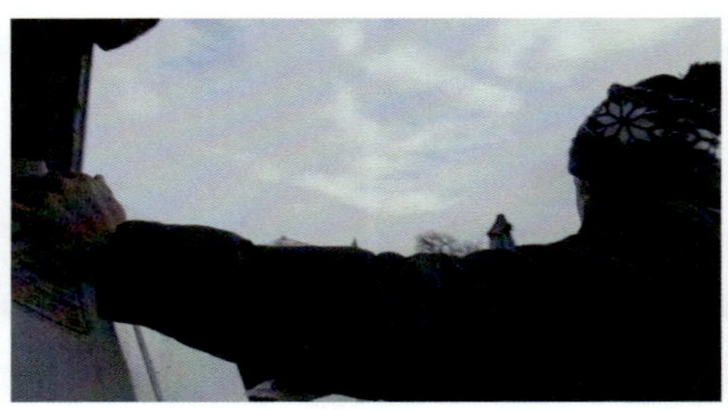

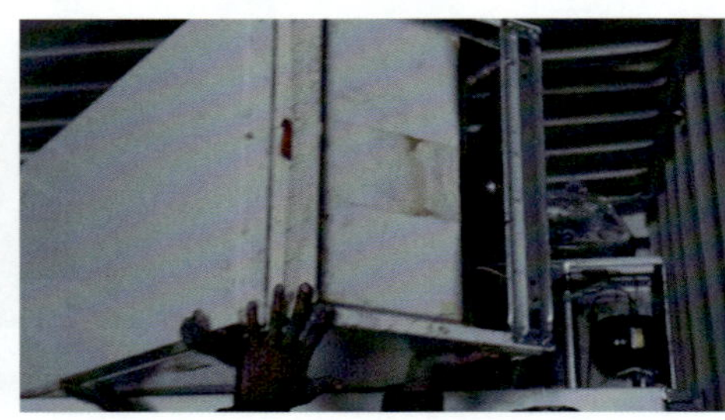

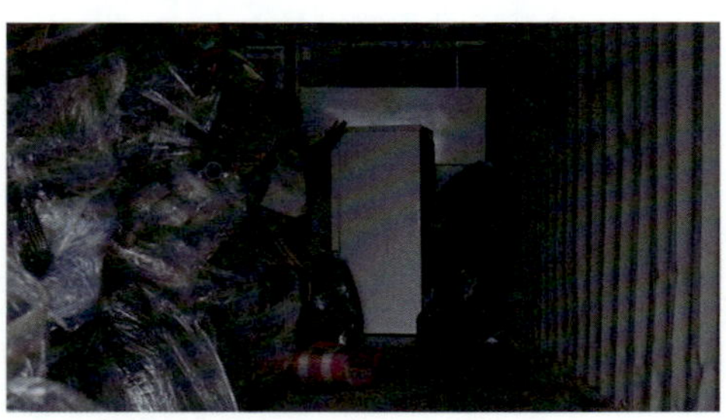

by way of Libya and Lampedusa. He makes a living buying discarded European electrical appliances, often referred to as 'brown goods', on Hamburg's infamous Billstraße and resells them in Lagos, which still weathers the colonial depletion of local manufacturing industries. As he speaks, we are shown masses of tires,

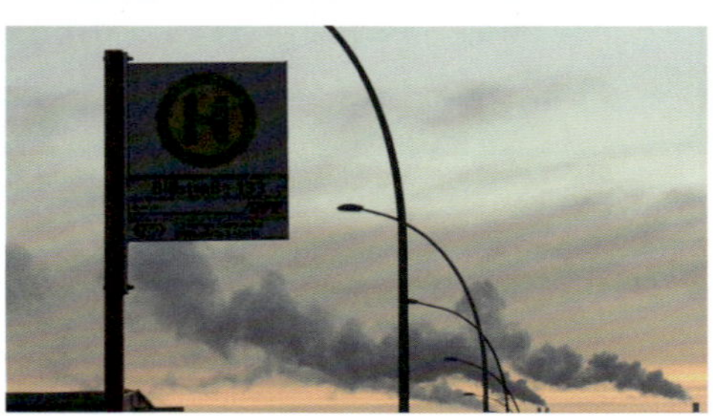

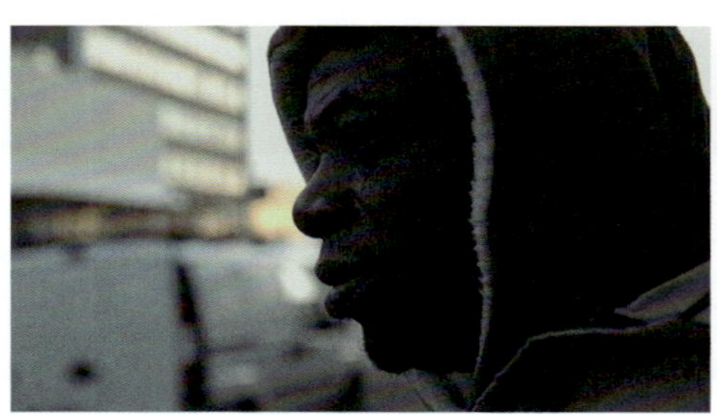

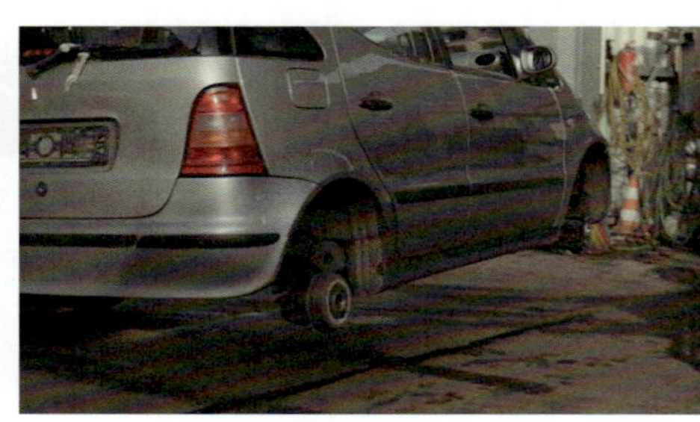

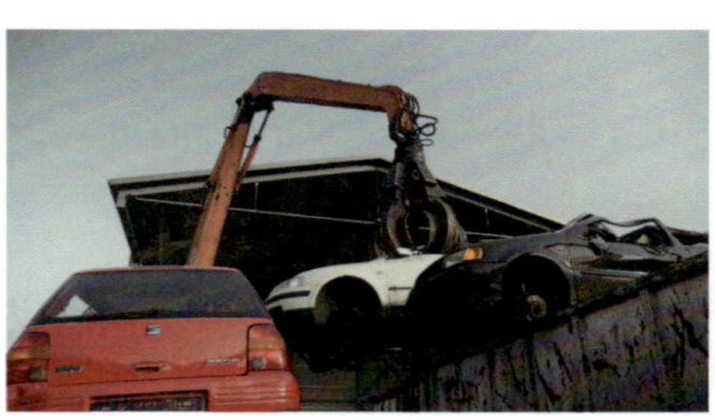

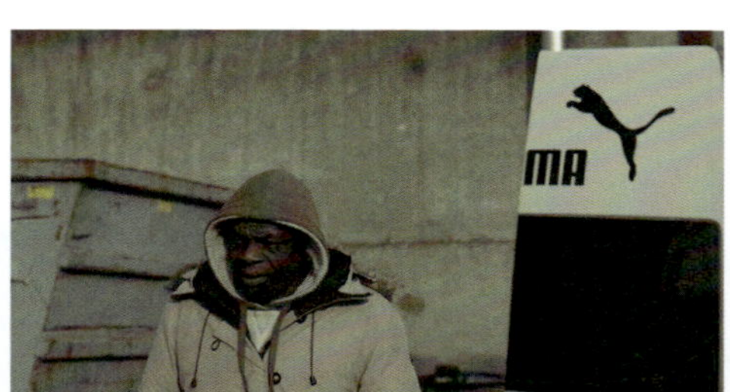

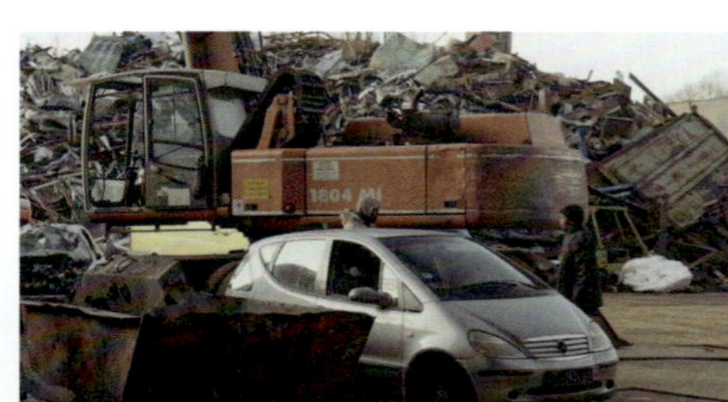

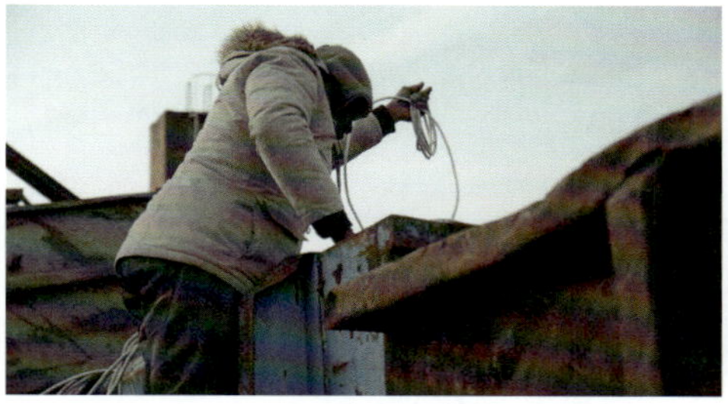
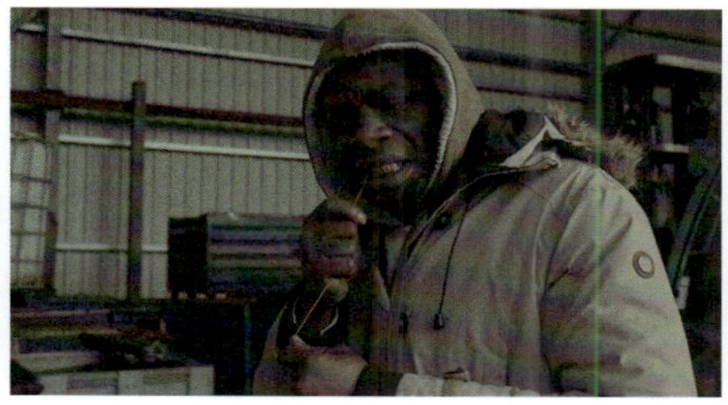
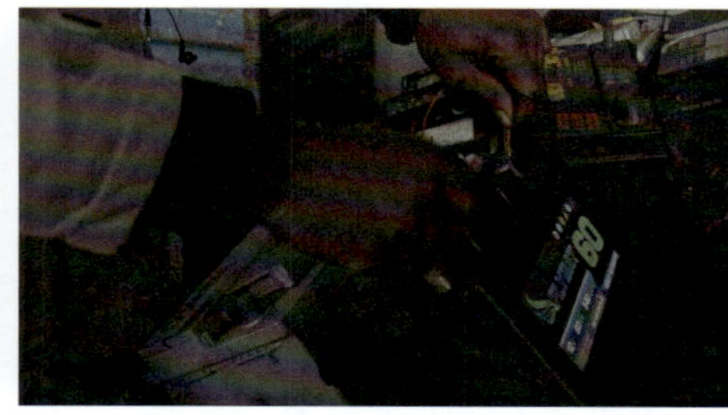
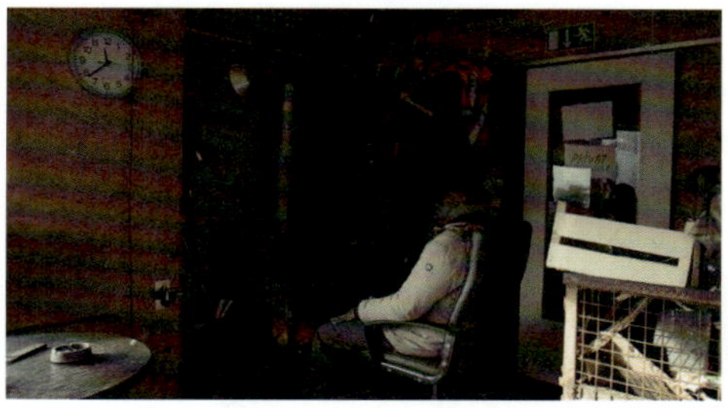

refrigerators, batteries – each item a tool toward Emeka's economic security, predicated on African money. The objects in the film seemingly guide the movements of the camera as they are loaded into shipping containers. We are presented with a formal depiction of the space as it exists for those who inhabit it, and this restraint allows room for Emeka's narrative

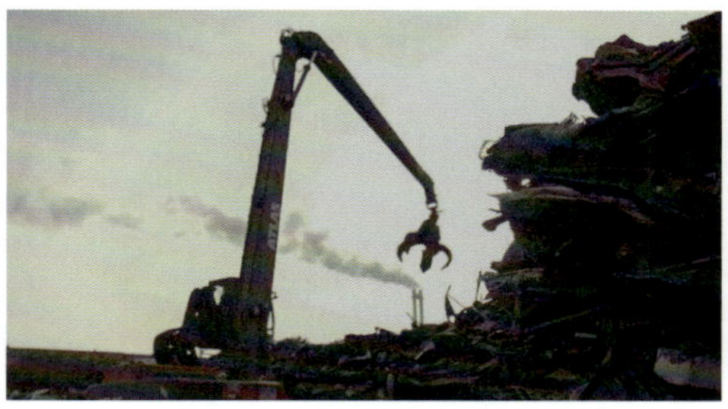
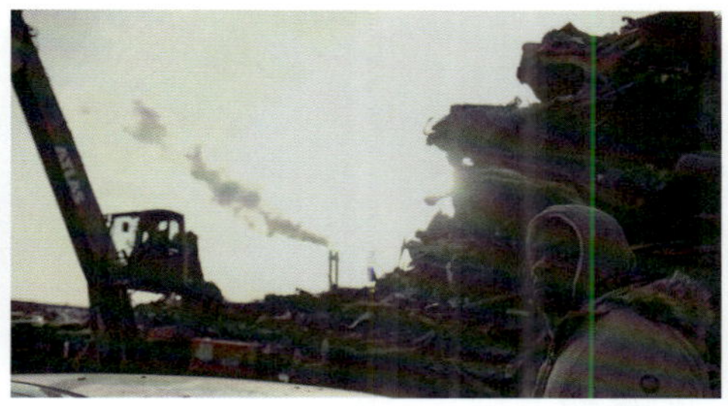
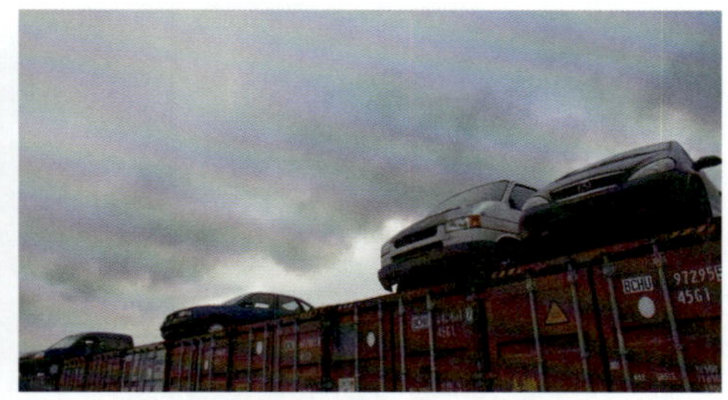

to take hold. We feel his bemusement as he tells of the advanced degrees he holds in Nigeria – of little consideration in Germany – and his somber tone when he remembers his daughters back home. Nevertheless, when we are confronted with his gaze, we see his endurance and self-determination, necessitated by an unwillingness to accept the circumstances he is given.

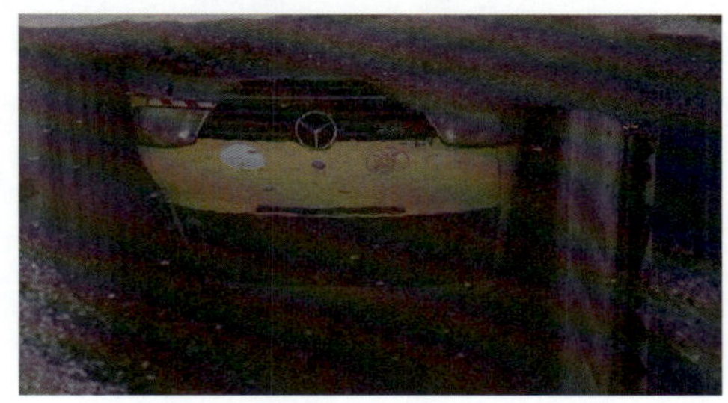
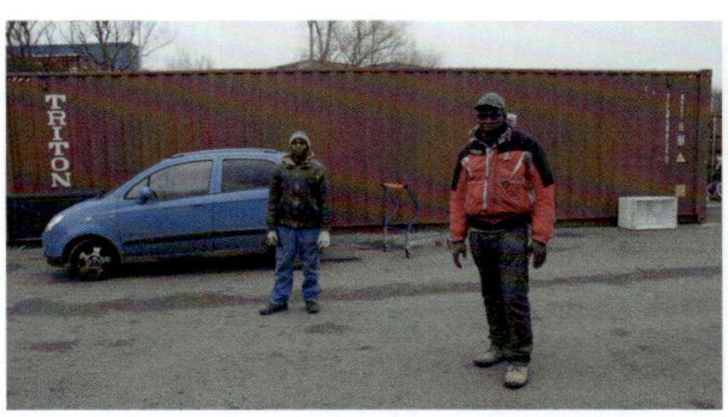

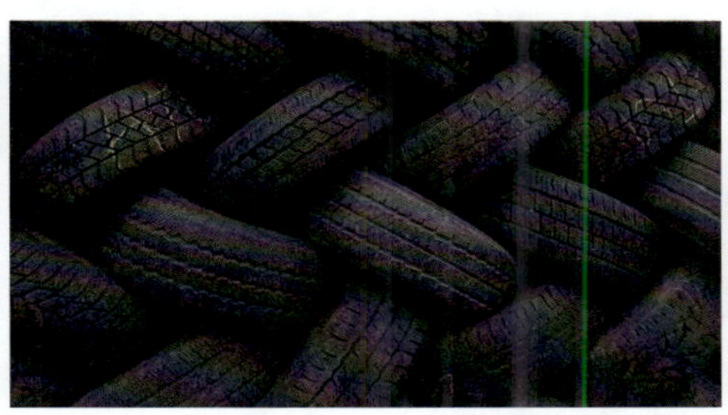
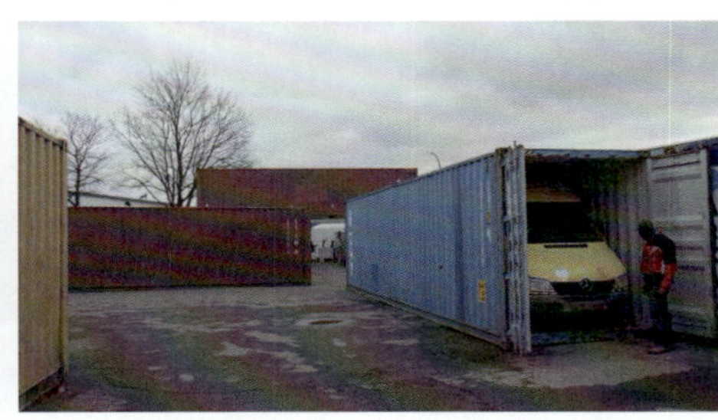
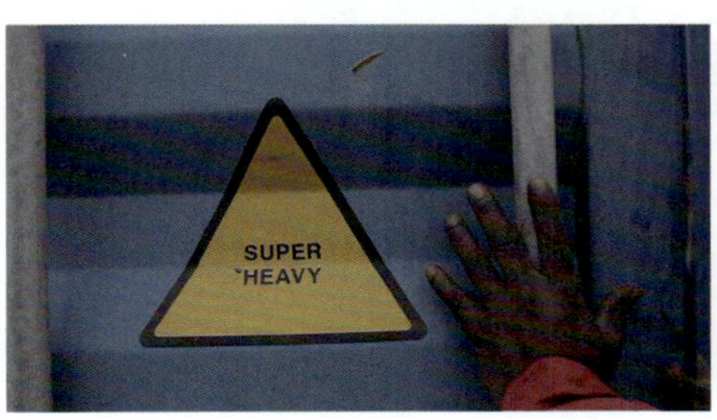

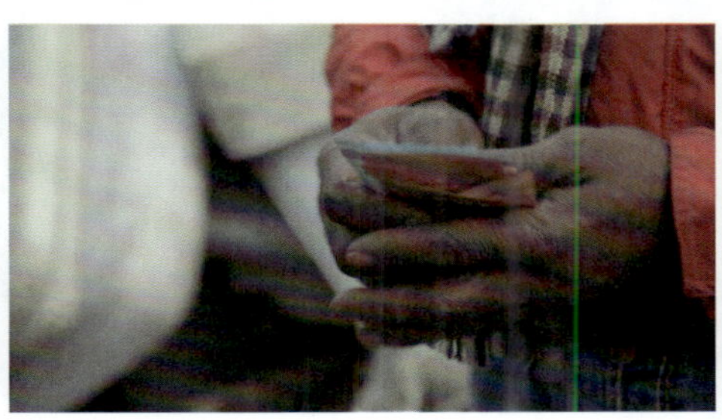
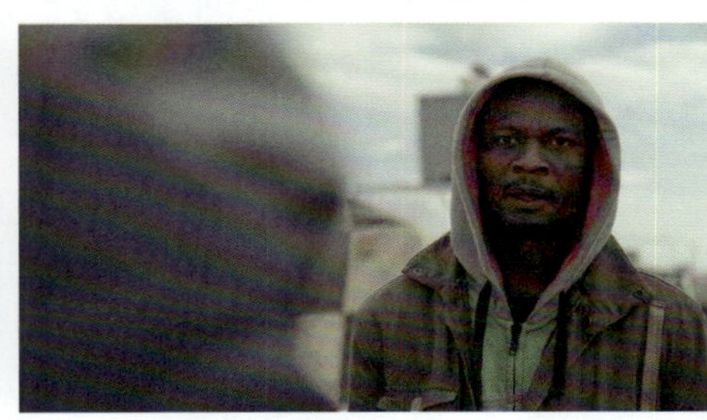
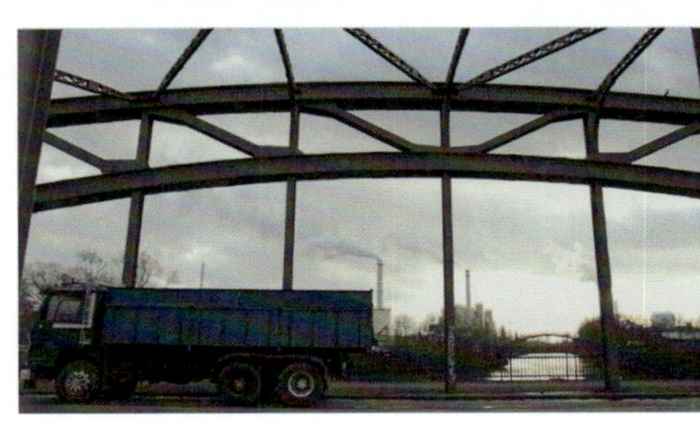

Director and Editor
Karimah Ashadu

Camera and Colour Grader
Sebastian Bock

Produced by
Golddust by Ashadu

Supported by
Filmförderung
Schleswig-Holstein

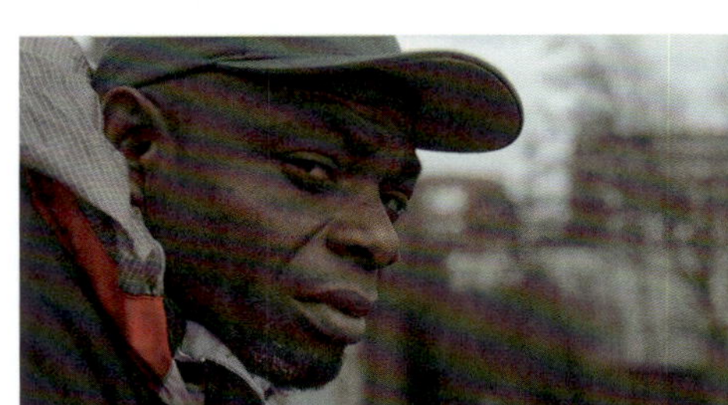

Plateau, 2021–22
Two-channel video, colour, sound, 27'
Single-channel video, colour, sound, 30'

What remains in the wake of imperialism, when the afterlives of colonisation stretch from the twentieth century into the present? Complex networks of extraction, labour, pollution and (inter)dependence, all predicated on the initial colonial encounter, are the subject of this film, and the answer is sought via a logic that is both visual and auditory. In both its single- and double-channel formats, Karimah Ashadu follows the dangerous work of undocumented

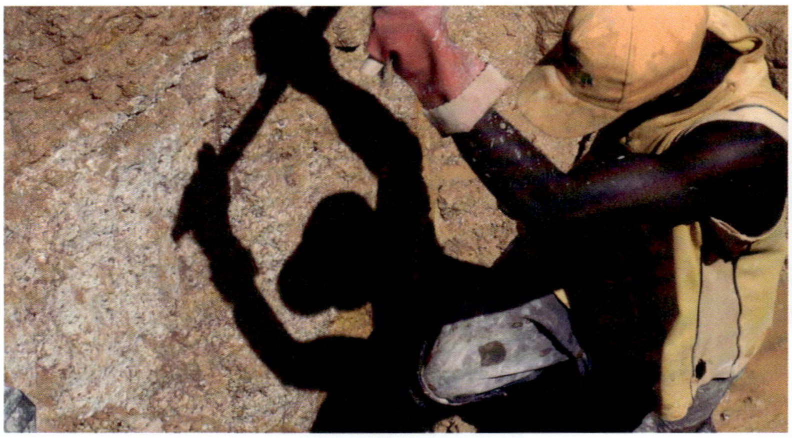

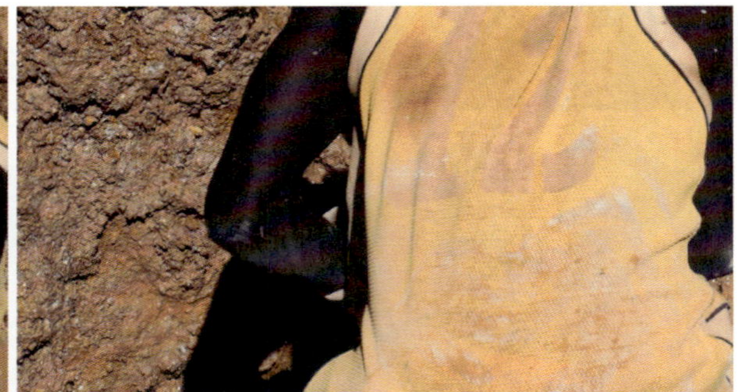

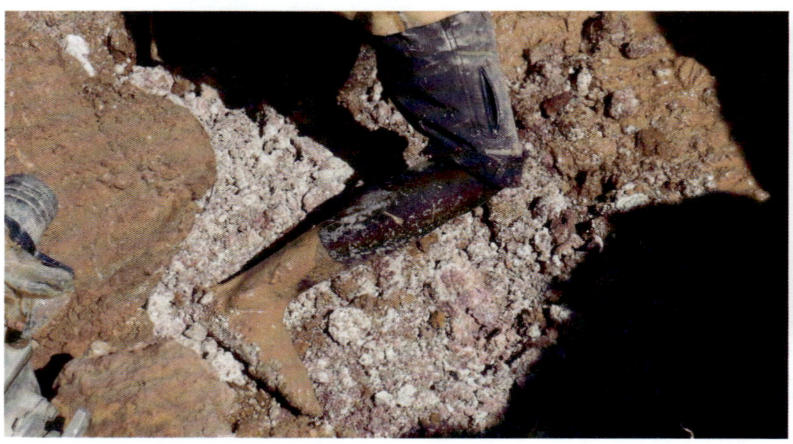

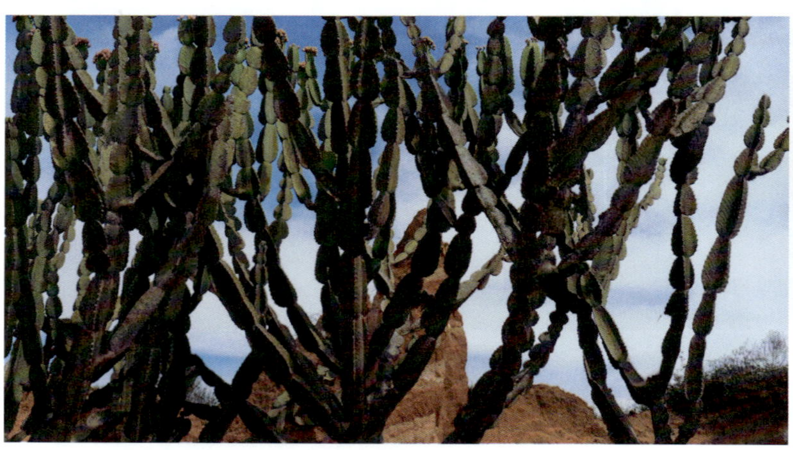

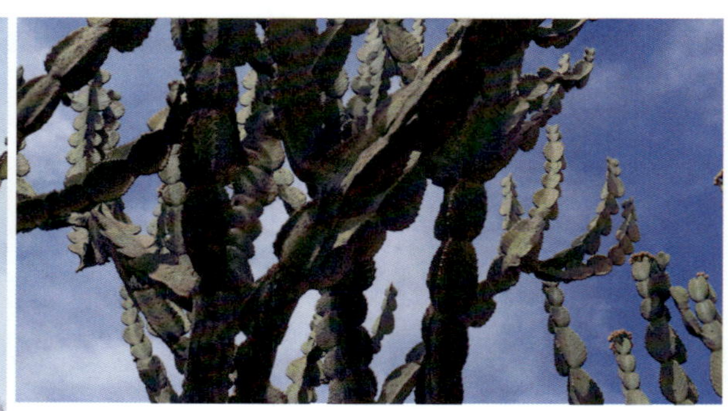

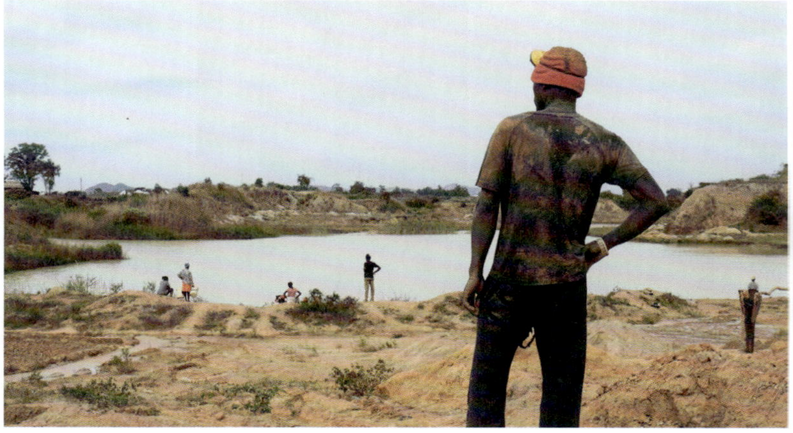
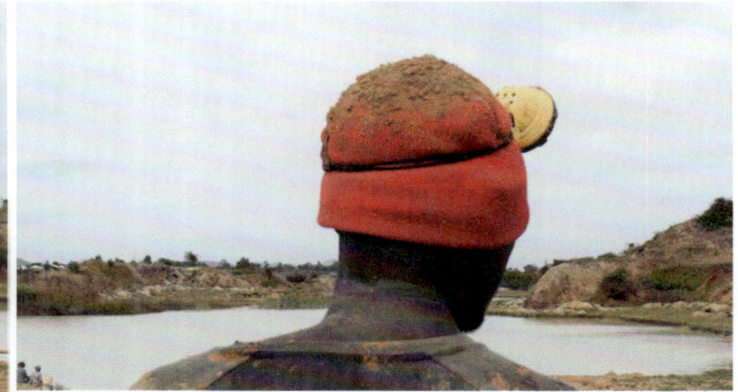
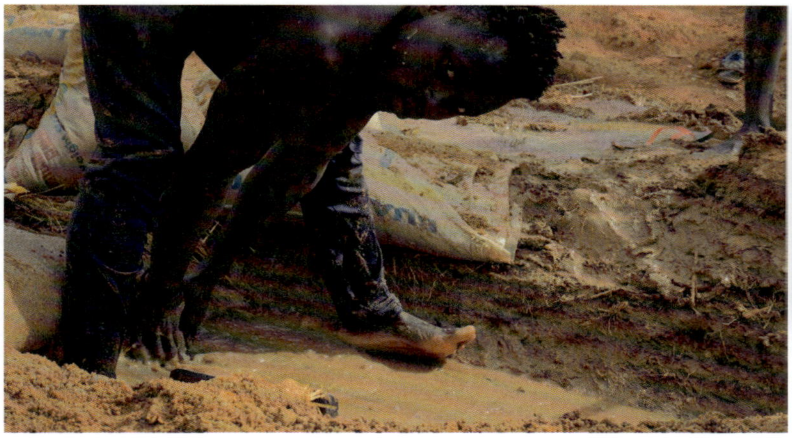

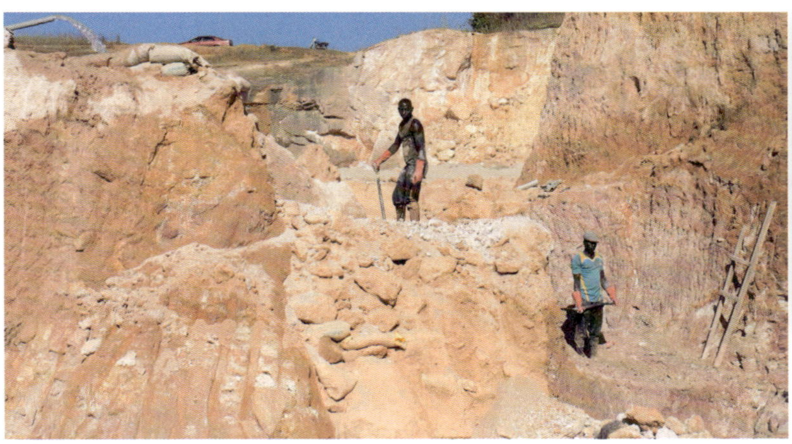
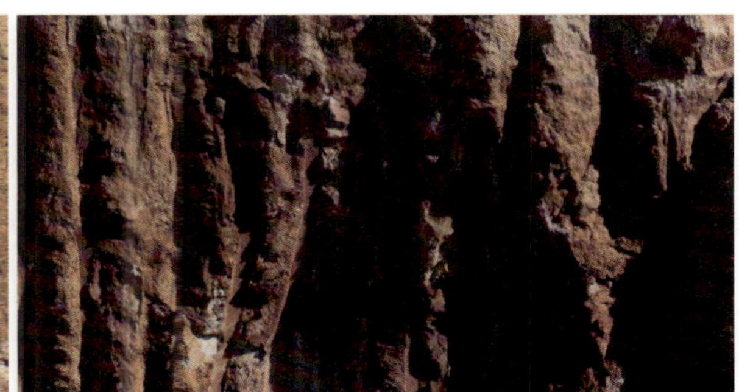

tin miners in Nigeria's Jos Plateau; her camera takes us directly to the rudimentary and gruelling drudgery by which they make a living. We hear them drill, dig and tunnel into the environment. Dirt cakes their bodies, and water from artificial ponds, coloured orange from the rock and sediment, sloshes around their legs. Throughout, we hear narration directly from the subjects as they explain how damage to the land is inevitable given the material conditions they've inherited. The cactus, which the men compare their resilience to, is framed in grandeur and expanse, with its arms appearing to reach the sky. As a young miner sifts through water with his hands, his gaze meets the camera, and our external perspective is released from isolation, acknowledged and challenged. The power balance of the interaction shifts in an instant, and the nature of the exchange is made clear: the men tell their stories, we see their labour, and we have little to provide in return except for our attention.

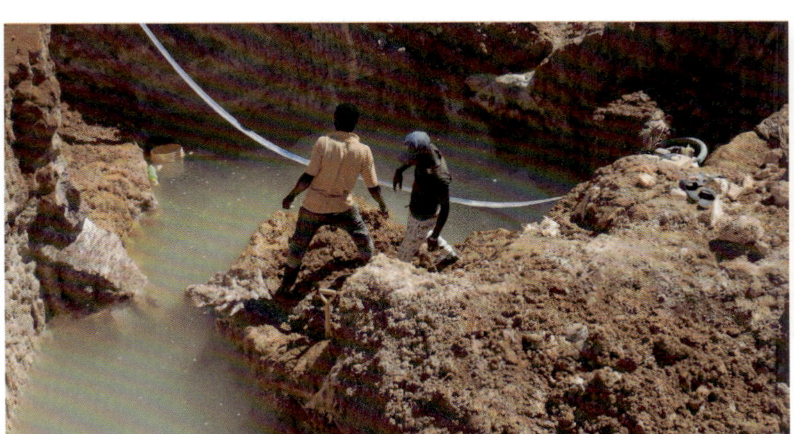
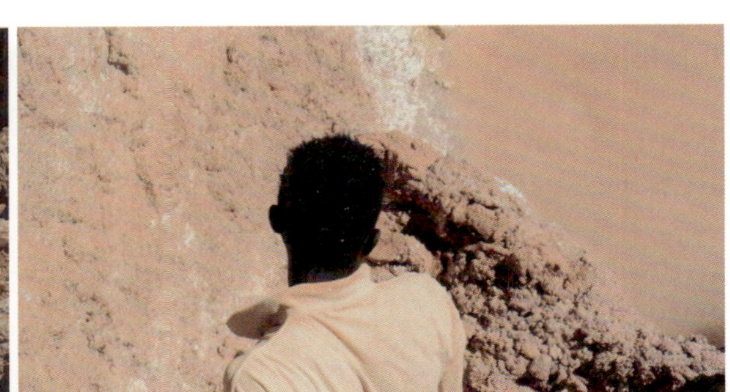

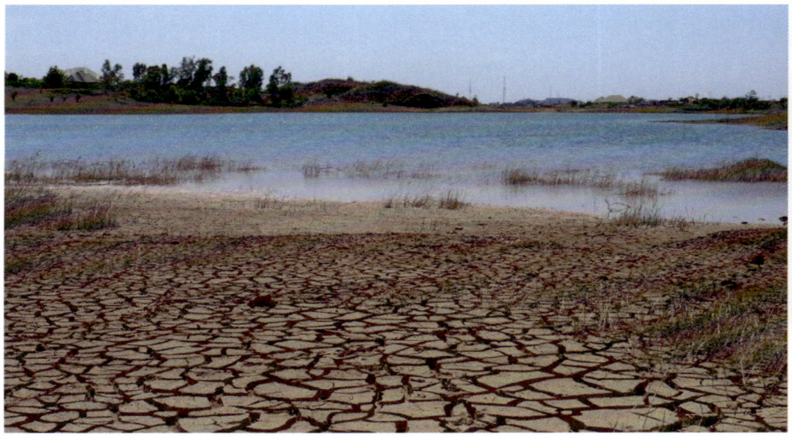

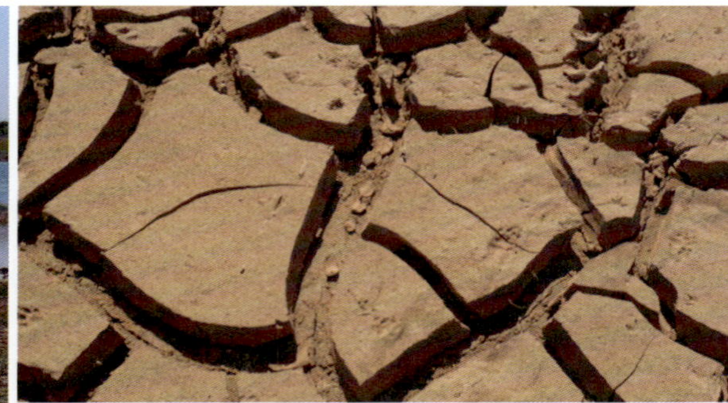

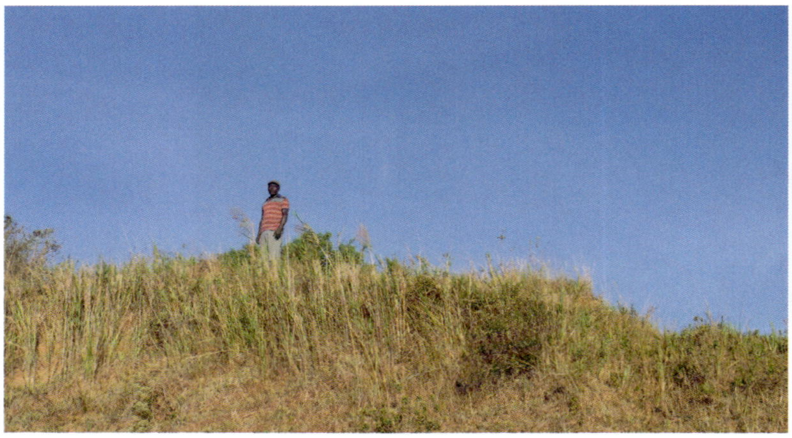

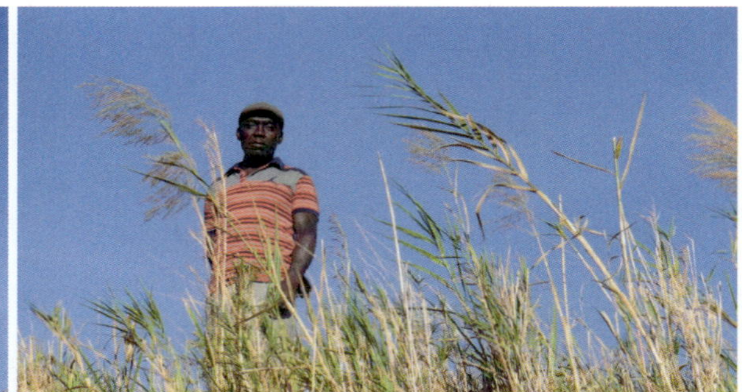

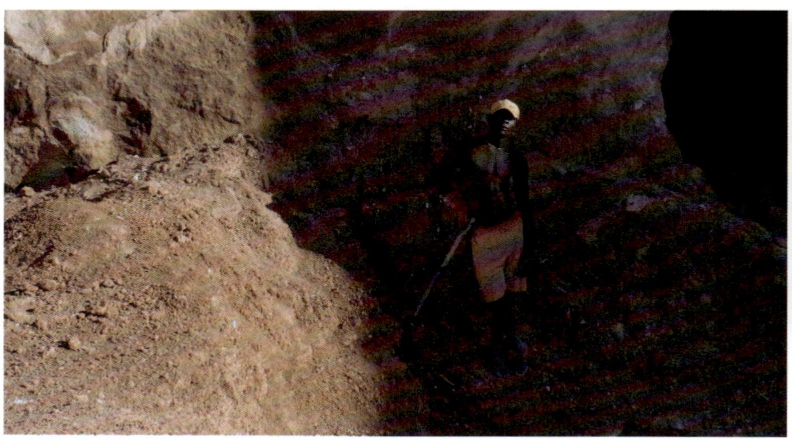

Director and Editor
Karimah Ashadu

Camera
Aigberadion Israel Ikhazuangbe

Sound Recordist
Anthony Monday

Colour Correction and Sound Adjustments
Cristian Manzutto

Credit Designer
Abdulmonim Twebti

Commissioned and Produced by
Fondazione In Between Art Film

Creative Producer
Leonardo Bigazzi

Co-produced by
Golddust by Ashadu

Supported by
African Culture Fund, Mali

With special thanks to
The miners and crew; Fondazione In Between Art Film: Beatrice Bulgari, Leonardo Bigazzi, Alessia Carlino, Alessandro Rabottini, Bianca Stoppani, Paola Ugolini; and Columbia Institute for Ideas and Imagination, Paris

Cowboy, 2022
Two-channel video, colour, sound, 10'40"

Across a two-channel screen, Karimah Ashadu combines voice, image and sound into a meditative exploration of a man named Cowboy, his background marked by migration and a love of horses. On one channel, we see palm tree leaves rustling against a blue sky, alternating with images of the ocean, grey and churning, its tides advancing and receding against black rock. On the other channel, the protagonist recounts the past thirty-five years he has spent

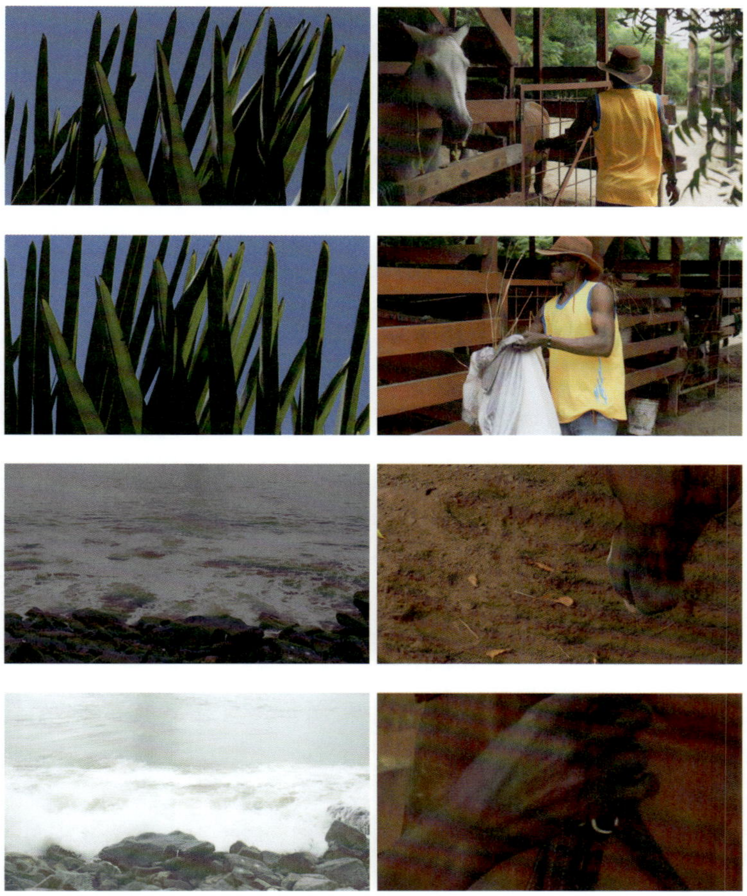

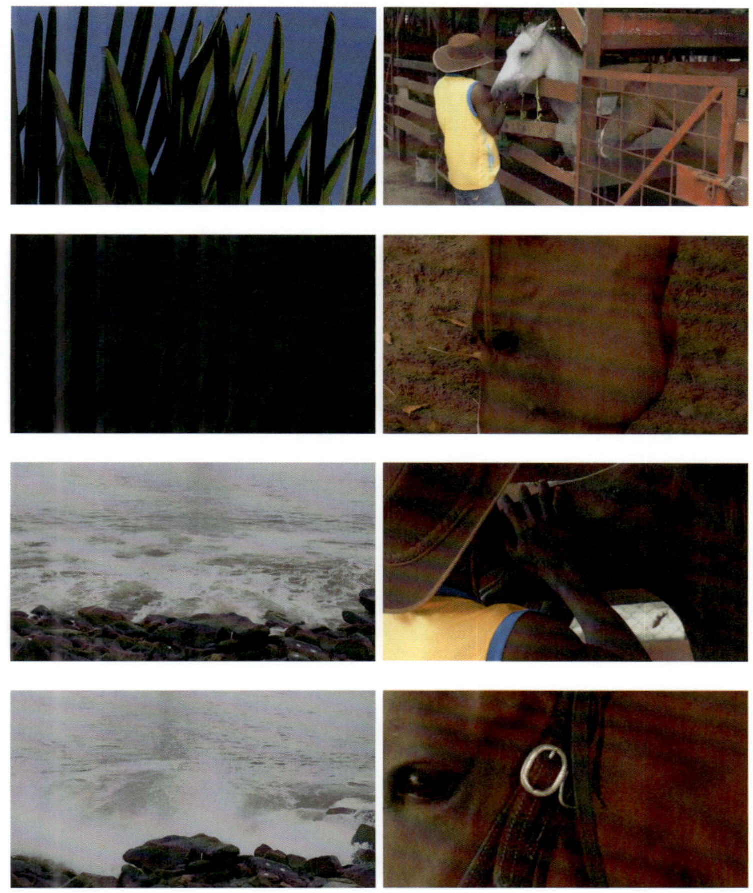

in service to horses. By his own admission, he has given his life to equestrianism, and in return has received the experience and lessons of a lifetime. The tender hand with which he strokes and feeds the horses in their stables becomes the confident grip used to mount an animal and ride through the Lagosian beach to the shoreline. We hear the steady sounds of waves crashing as Cowboy recounts the moments of peril inevitable when positioning

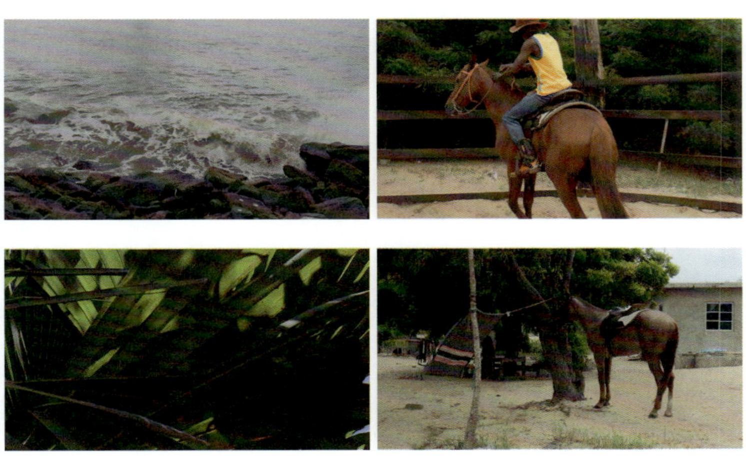

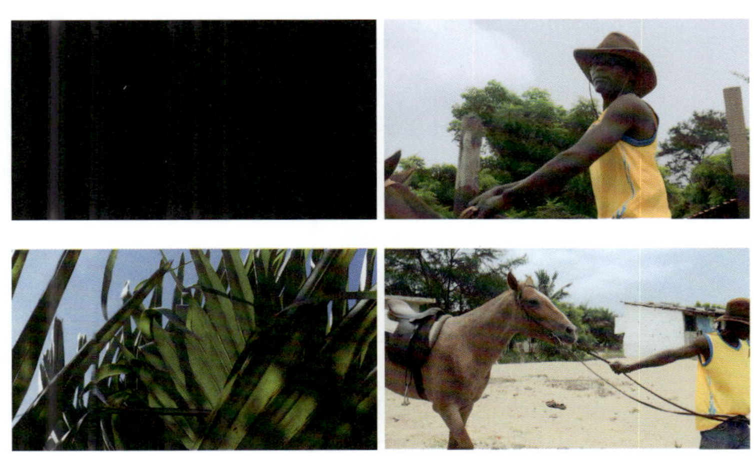

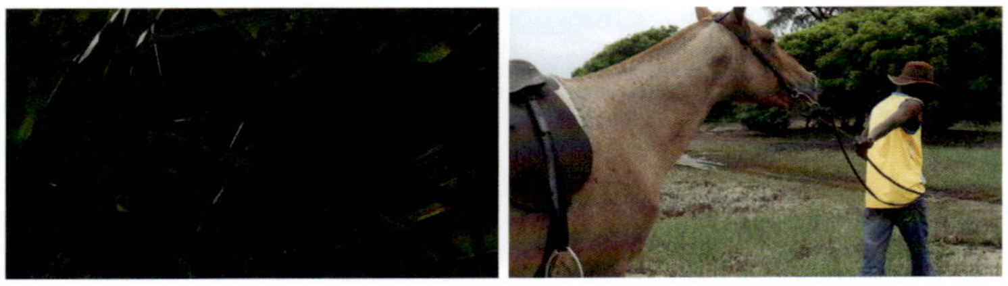

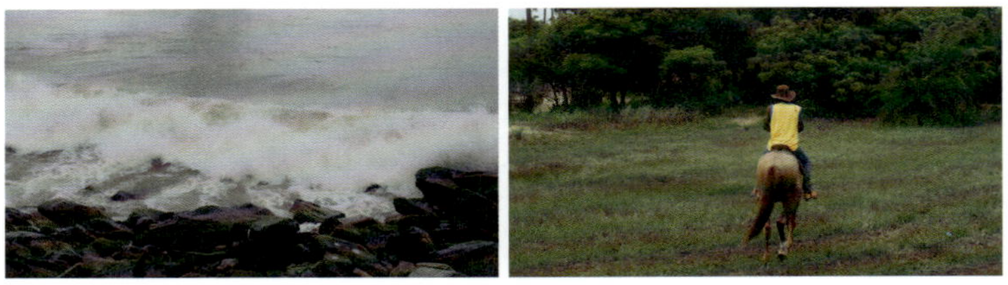

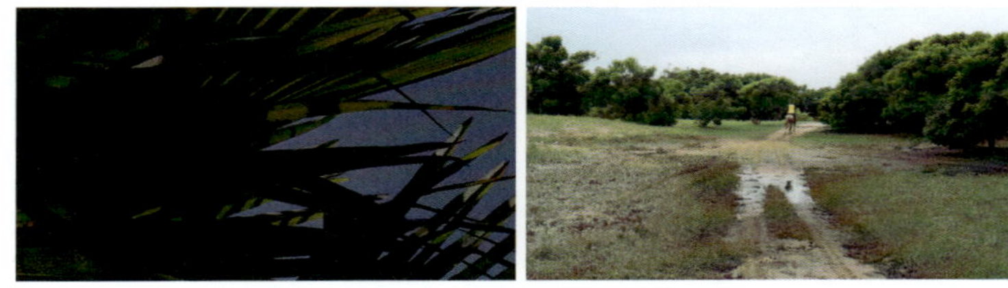

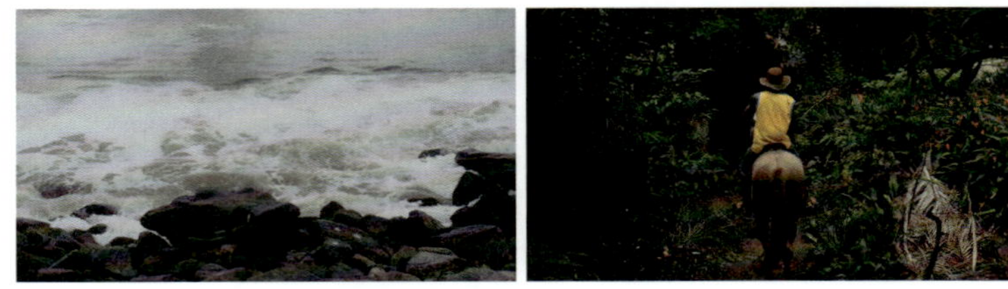

oneself close to another creature. The strength and autonomy of the horse finds its complement in the rider – they take care of each other, and each grows to intuit the other's movements. As the protagonist reaches the sea, the two screens sonically coalesce. The cargo ships in the far distance evoke notions of economic trade, slavery and the connective threads between the two. Removed from its typical US cultural associations, the cowboy in Ashadu's film appears unified with the halcyon movements of the seas and his own internal tenderness.

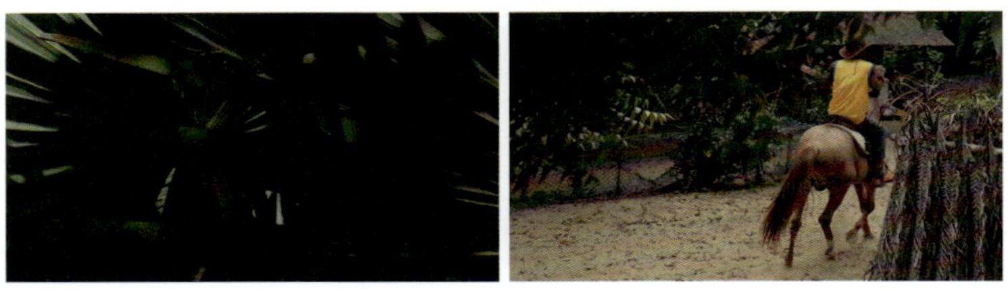

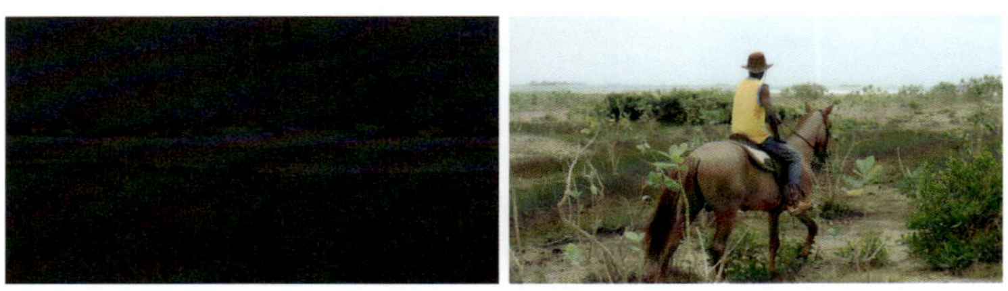

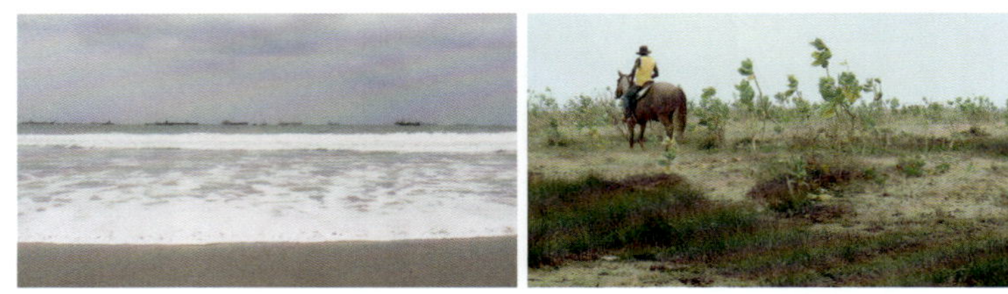

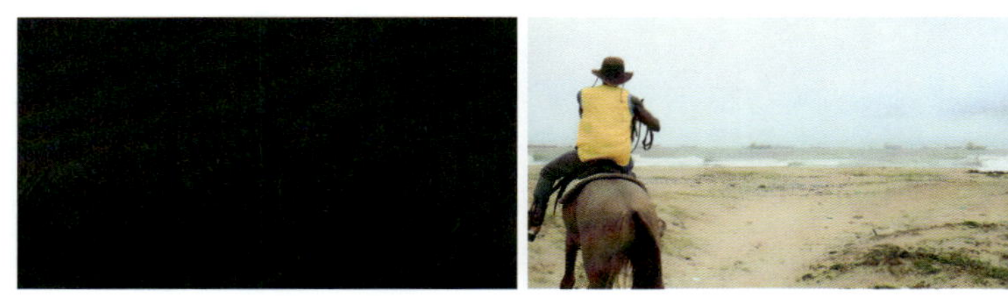

Director and Editor
Karimah Ashadu

Camera
Aigberadion Israel Ikhazuangbe

Sound Recordist
Anthony Monday

Sound Adjustments
Jochen Jezussek

Colour Grading
Abdulmonim Twebti

Produced by
Golddust by Ashadu

With special thanks to
Cowboy and crew;
Bettina Steinbrügge and Behörde für Kultur und Medien, Hamburg

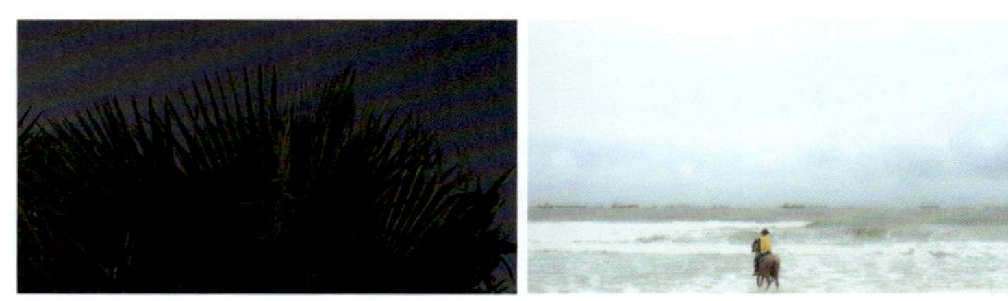

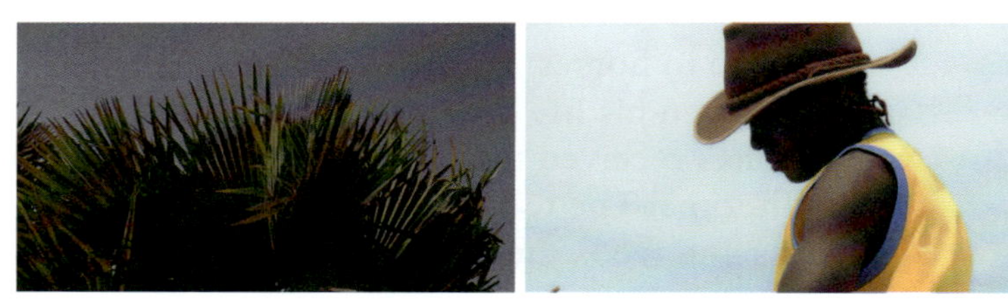

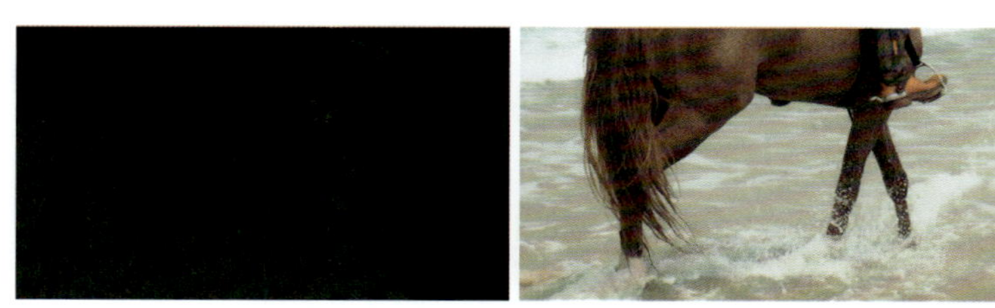

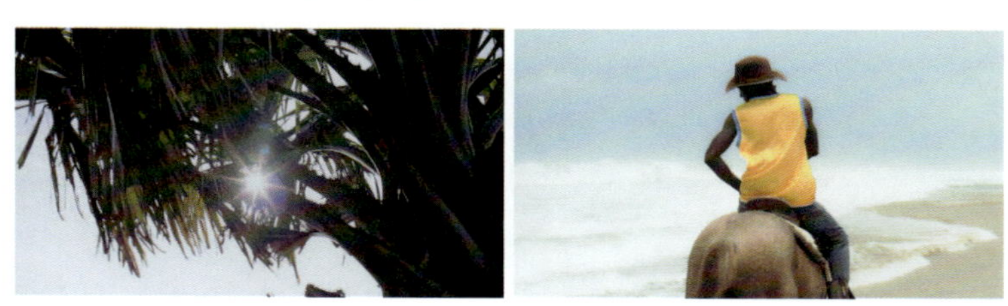

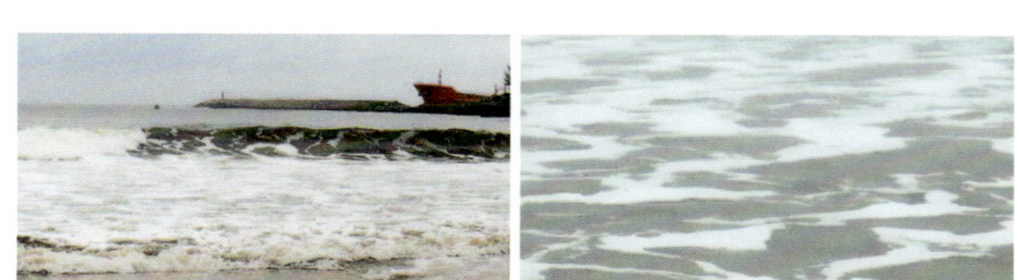

Machine Boys, 2024
Single-channel video, colour, sound, 8'50"

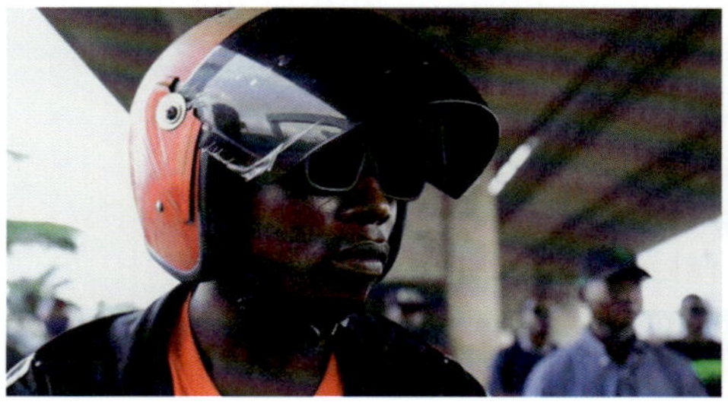
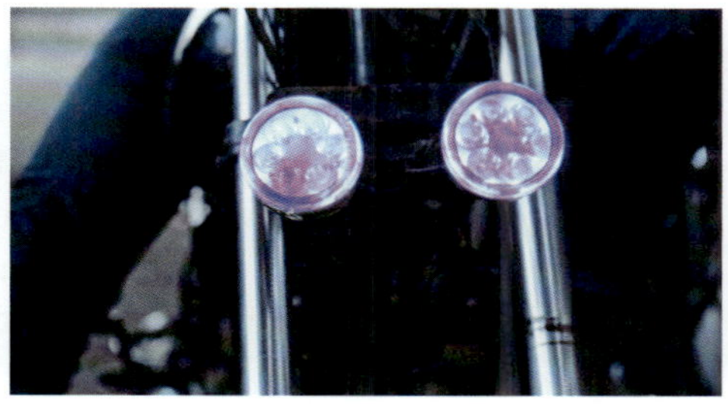
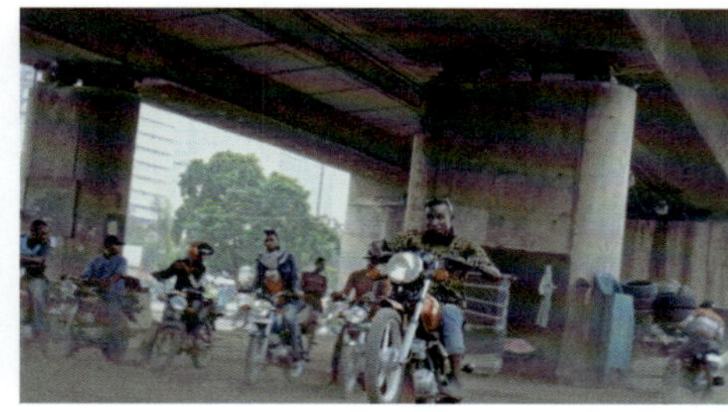

Before we see any image, we hear the revving of a motorcycle, an indication of the forthcoming intensity and momentum. Known in Lagos as *okada*, the informal economy of motorcycle taxis was banned in 2020 due to ineffective government regulation. Yet it persists. In the film, Karimah Ashadu captures the subsequent

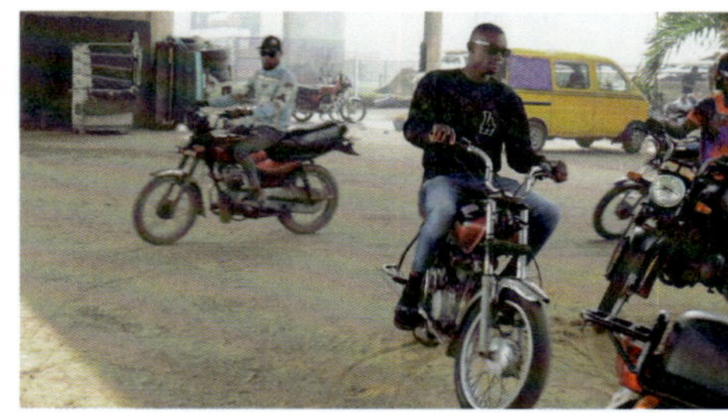
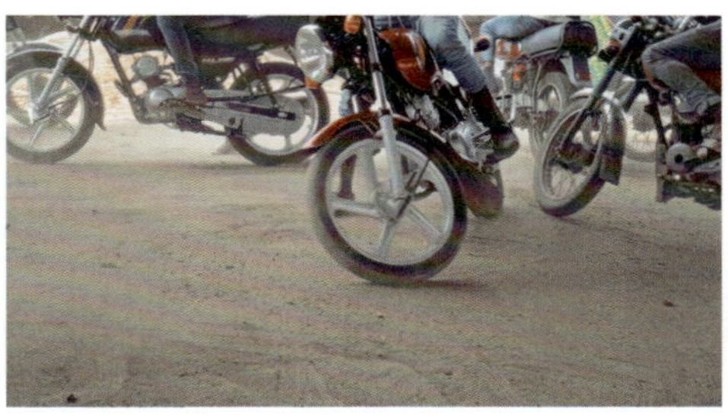
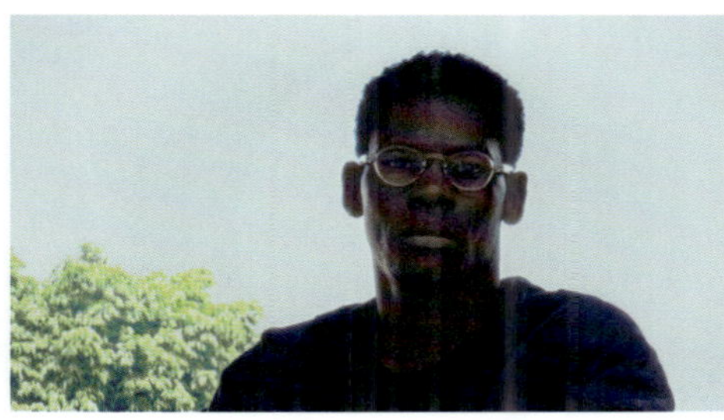
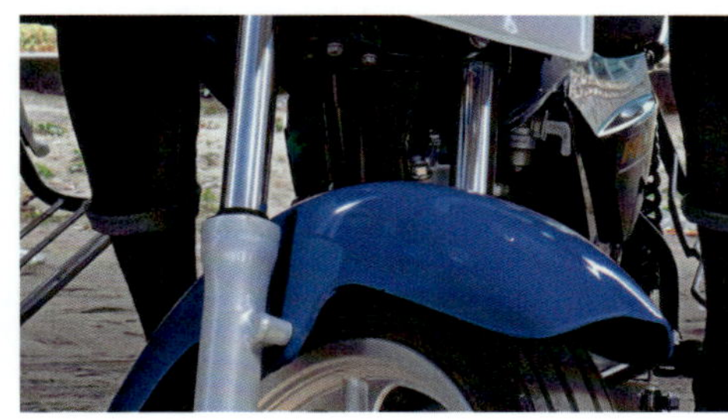
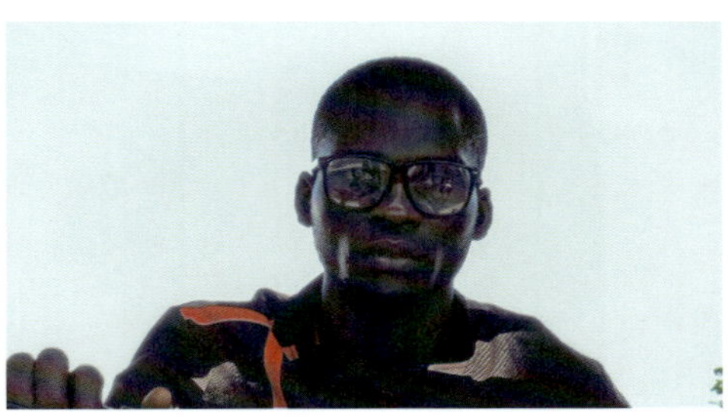
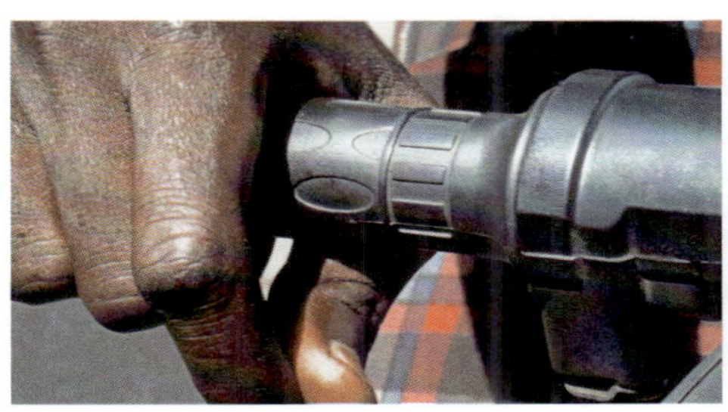
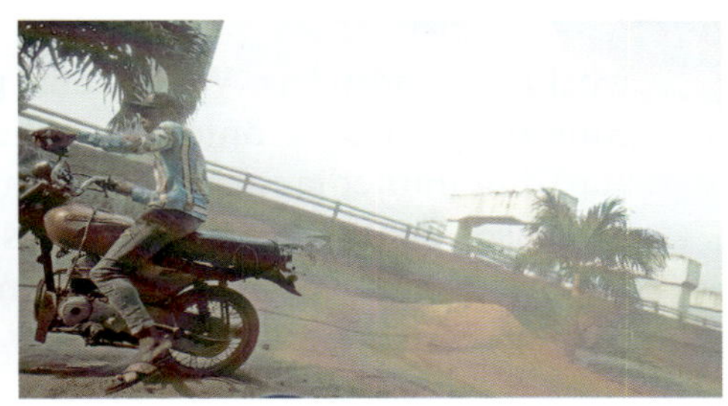
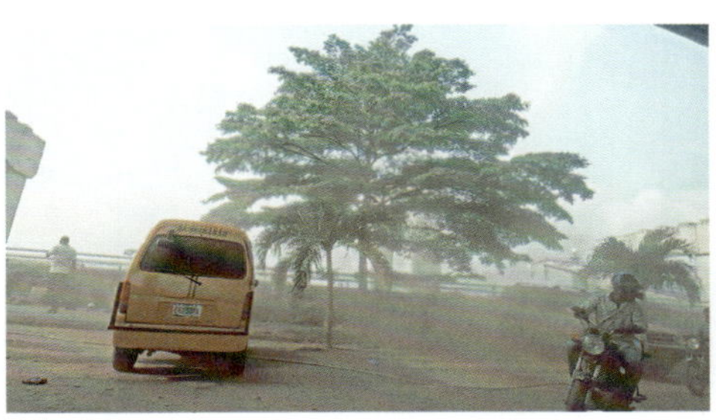
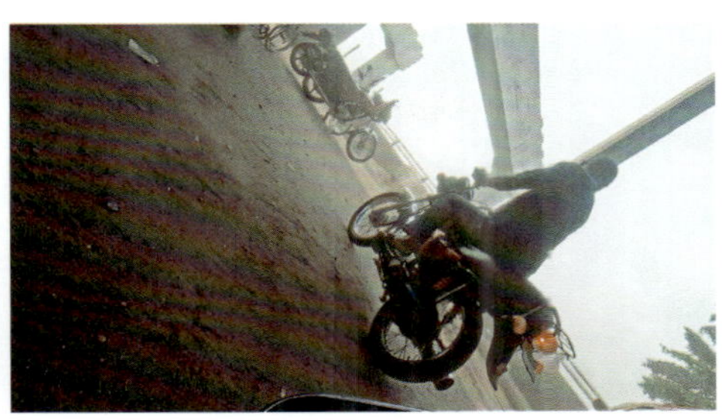
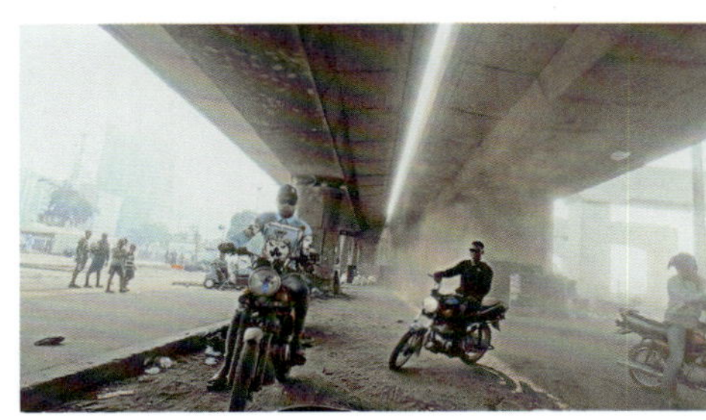
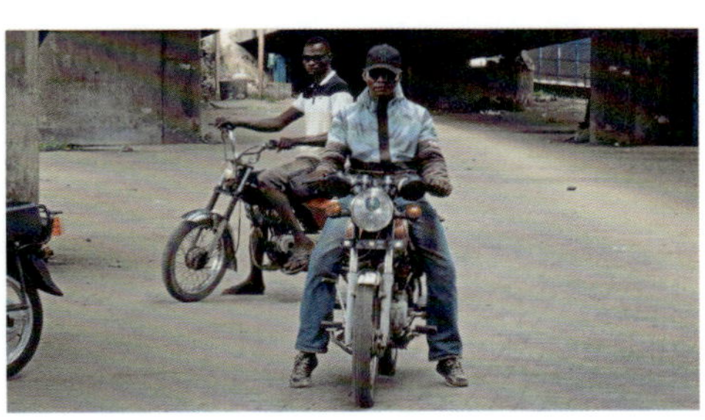

evolution of the group into a subculture grounded in machines, muscle and bravado. We hear remarks from several young men, some of whom have spent decades with the *okada* and have used the income to sustain themselves or fund their educations; others, somewhat paradoxically, seem to be driven

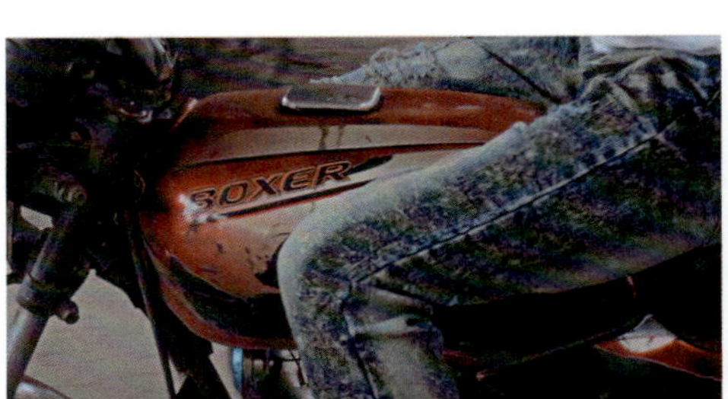

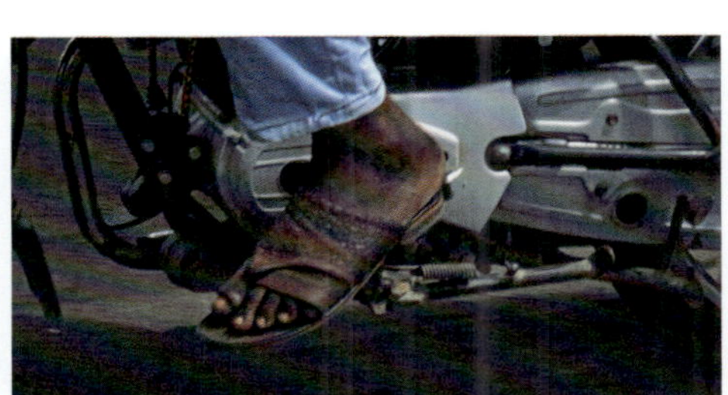
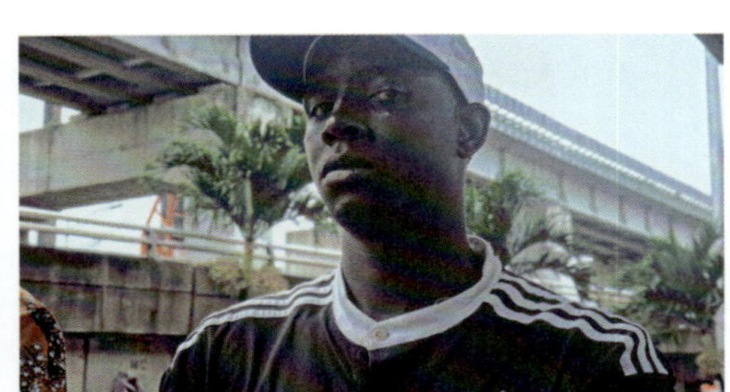

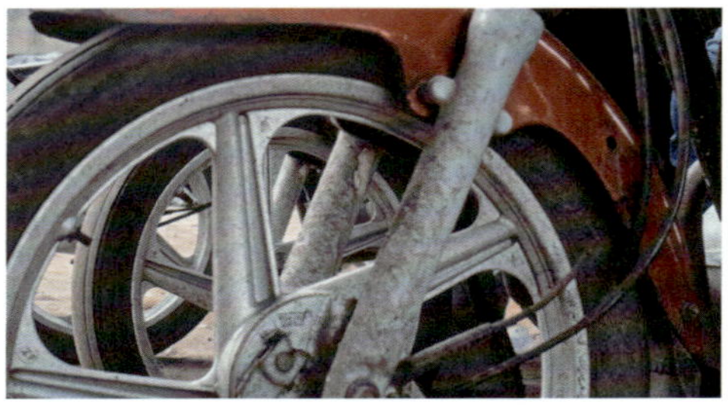

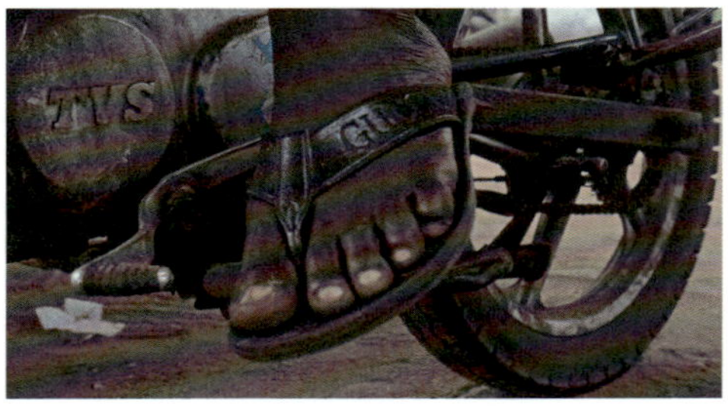

by the constant evasion of police and 'area boys'. The dull hum we hear as the men speak is periodically overtaken by the roar of engines as they ride through the city. At times we see clouds of dust, luminous chrome and tangled webs of legs and wheels in granular detail. The men place themselves in formation and ride in loops, demonstrating a mastery of their bikes, a willingness to perform. Their clothes, most of them bearing fake designer logos, reflect desire for capital success even within precarious

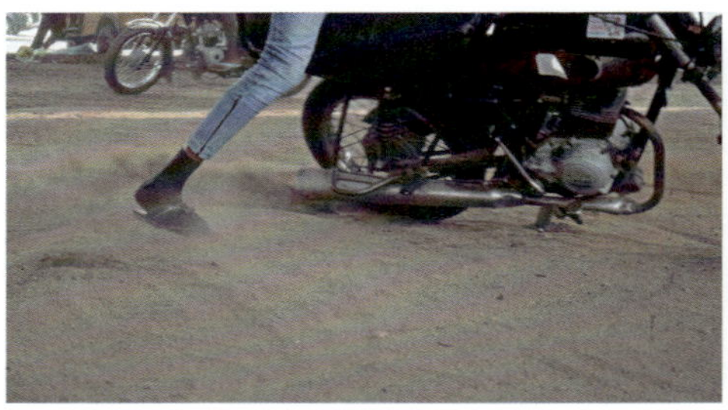

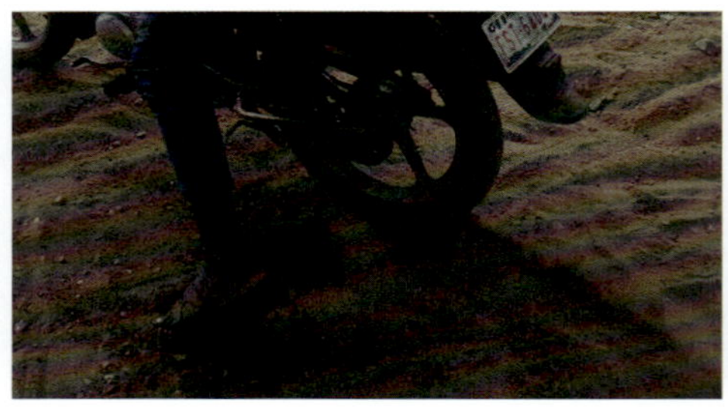

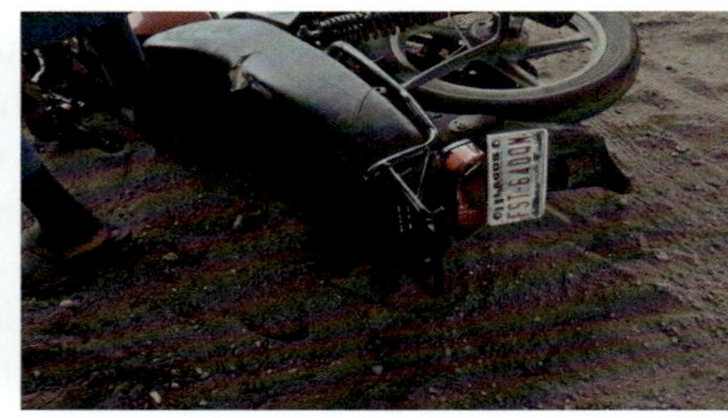

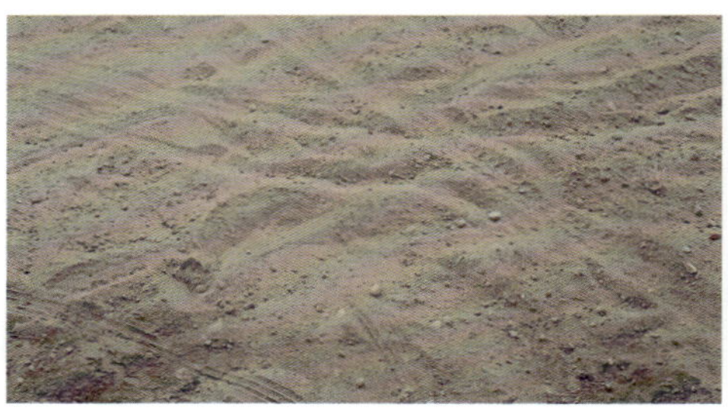

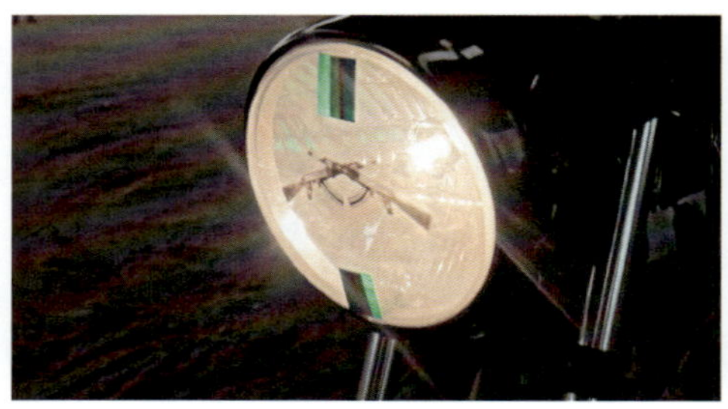

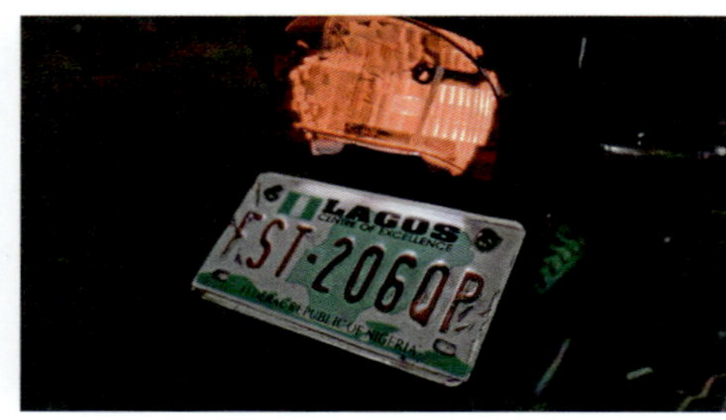

working conditions. When their gaze meets the camera, their confrontation comes through with startling immediacy. As one man offhandedly discusses death, referring to it as an unavoidable fate, we are left wondering how much they are willing to risk.

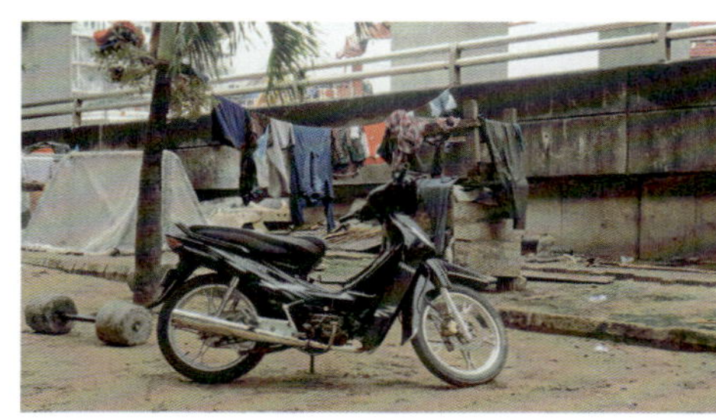

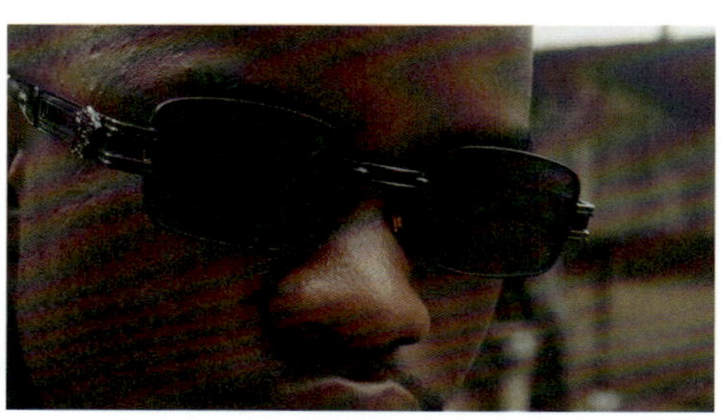

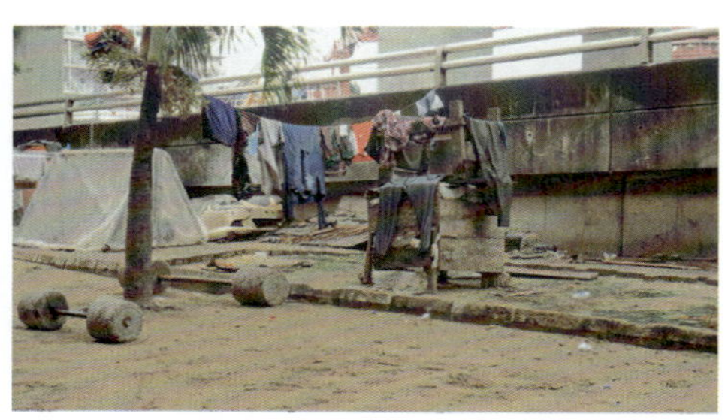

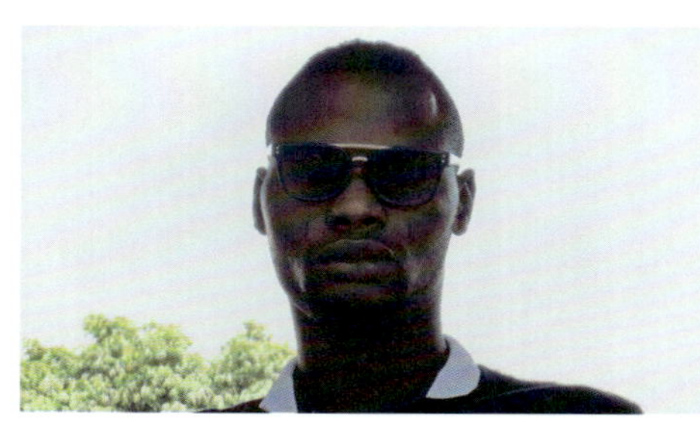

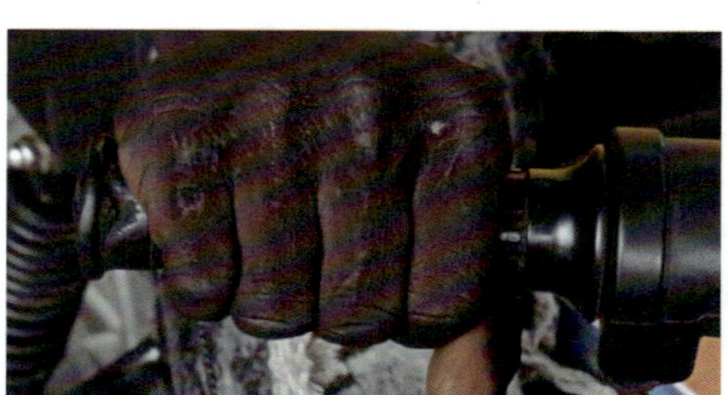

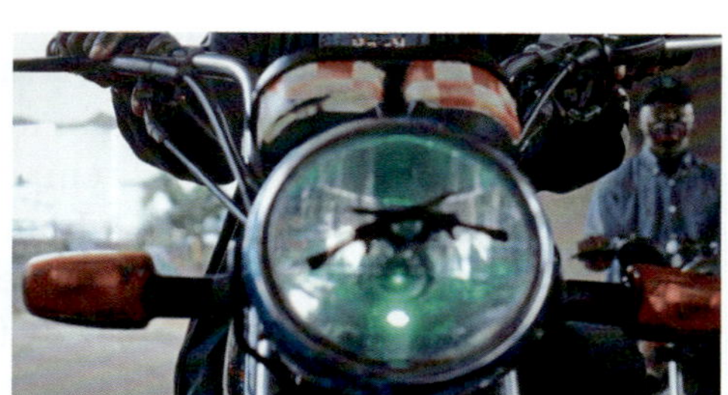

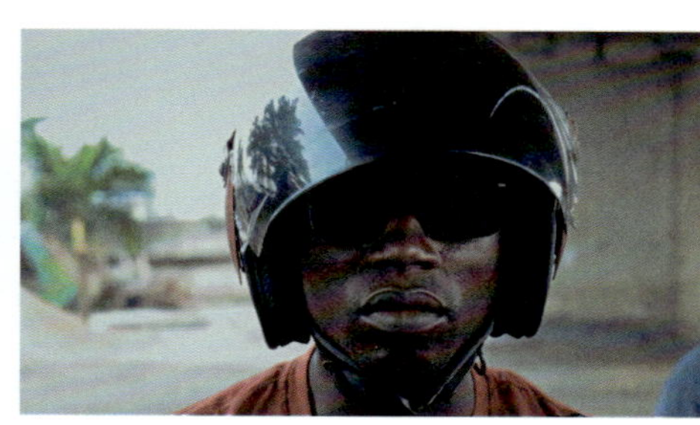

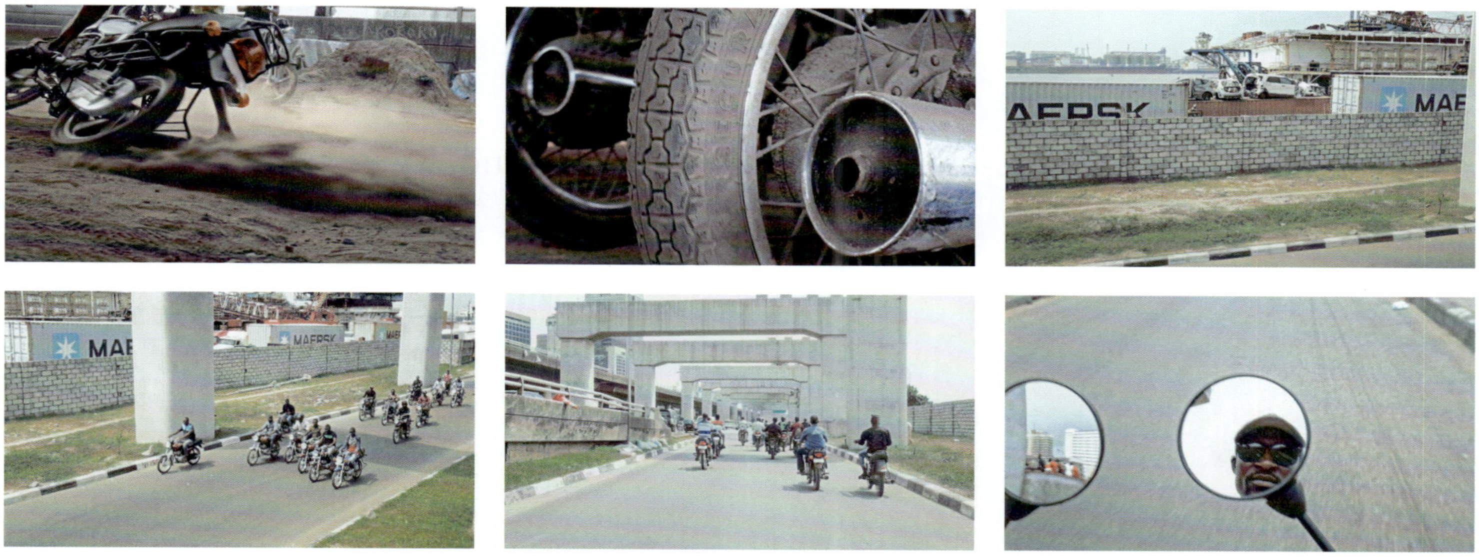

Director and Editor
Karimah Ashadu

Camera
Aigberadion Israel Ikhazuangbe

Sound Recordist
Joseph Eyo Edem

Colour Grader and Graphic Designer
Abdulmonim Twebti

Audio Post-production
Jochen Jezussek

Production Coordinator
Japhet Philibus

Production Assistants
Ibrahim Babatunde Adebayo and Anthony Monday

Produced by
Fondazione In Between Art Film

Creative Producer
Leonardo Bigazzi

Co-produced by
Golddust by Ashadu

Supported by
MOIN Filmförderung Hamburg Schleswig-Holstein, Fondazione In Between Art Film, Golddust by Ashadu

With special thanks to
The bikers and crew, Beatrice Bulgari, Leonardo Bigazzi, Alessandro Rabottini and Zainab Ashadu

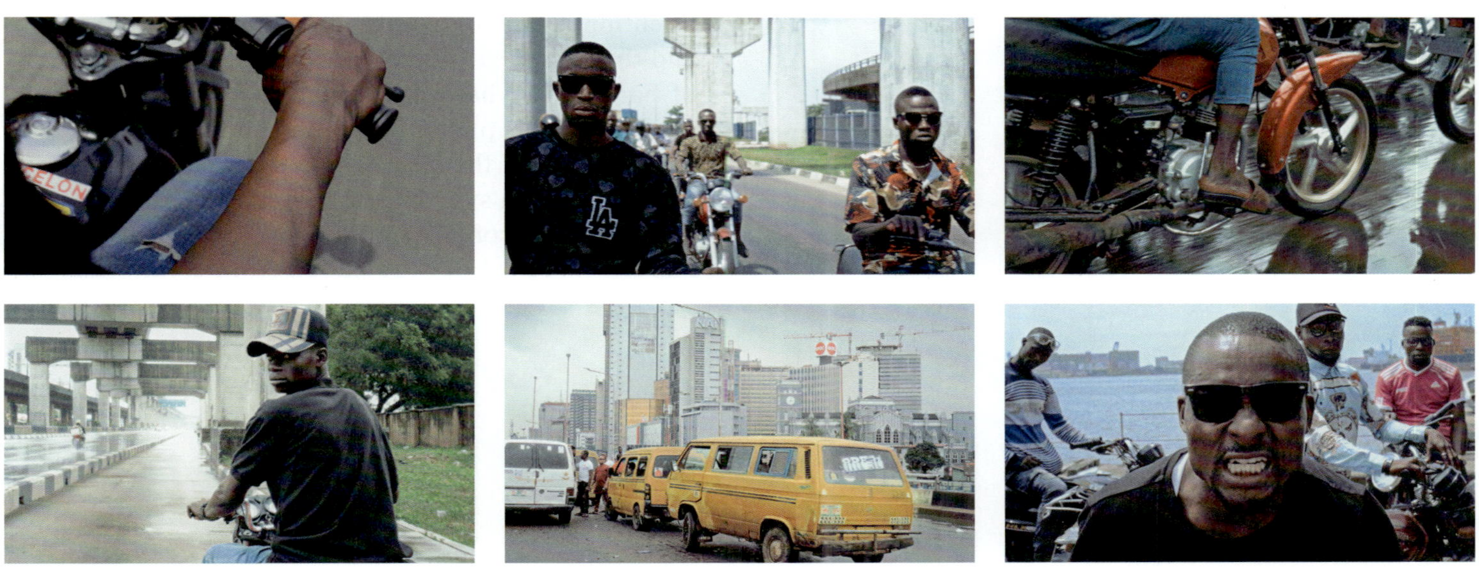

MUSCLE, 2025
Single-channel video, colour, sound, 22'

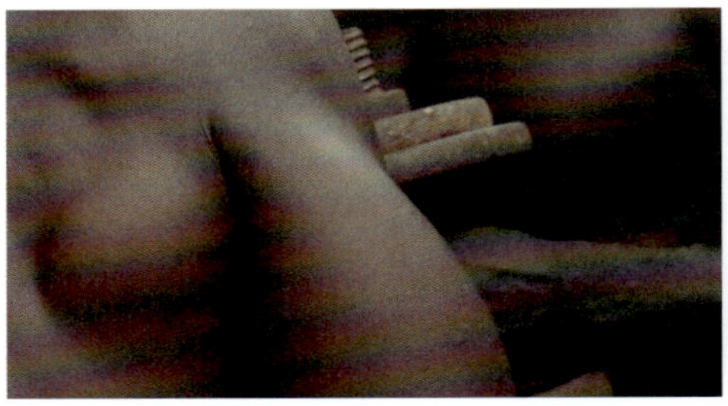
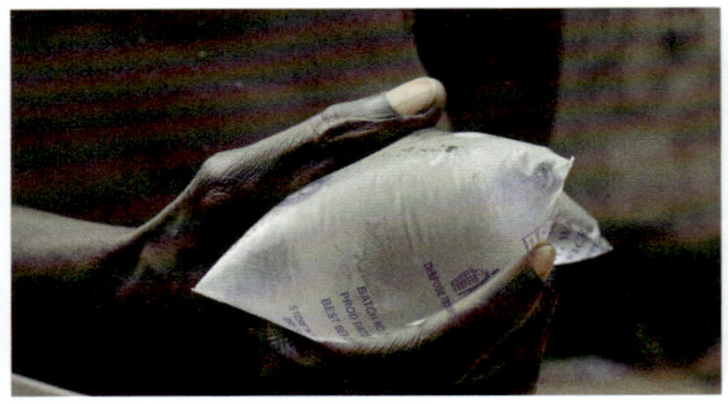
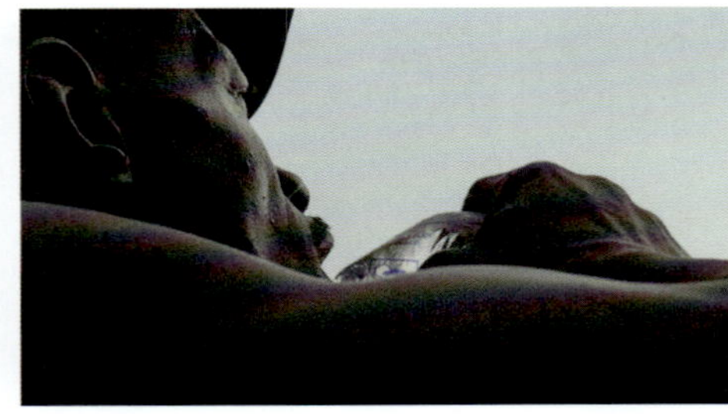

With no single protagonist or linear narrative, the film immerses us in a spectacle of strength through an intimate, amplified portrait of bodybuilders in the slums of Lagos. Inflated muscles, bulging veins and skin glistening with sweat fill the screen. Shot almost entirely in close-ups, the camera hovers near its subjects

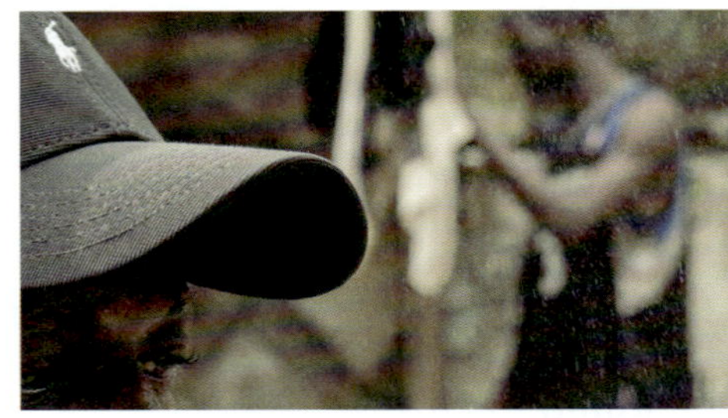
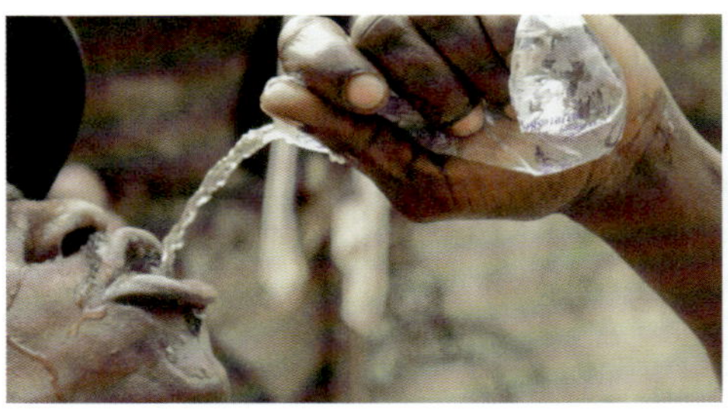
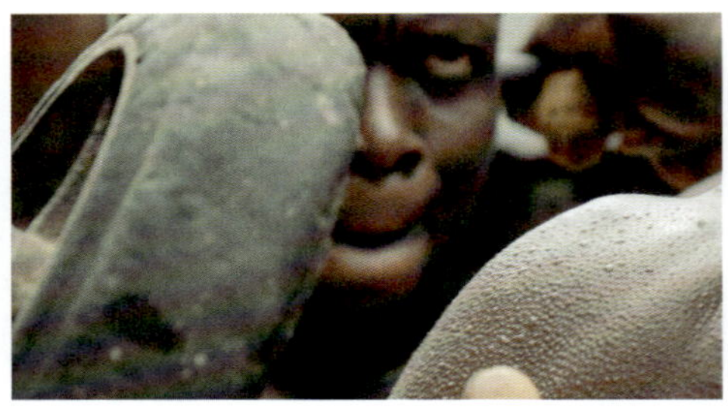
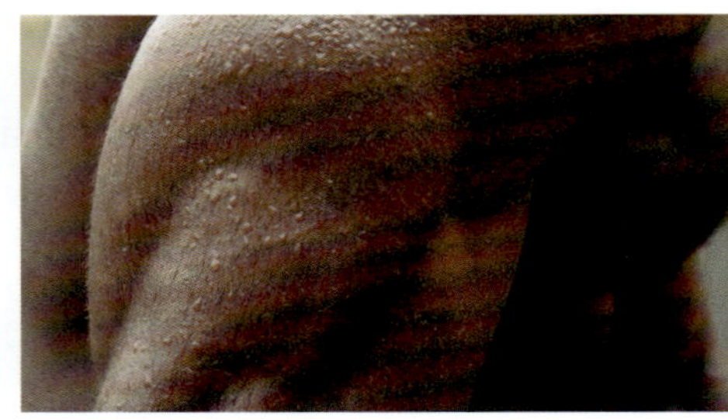
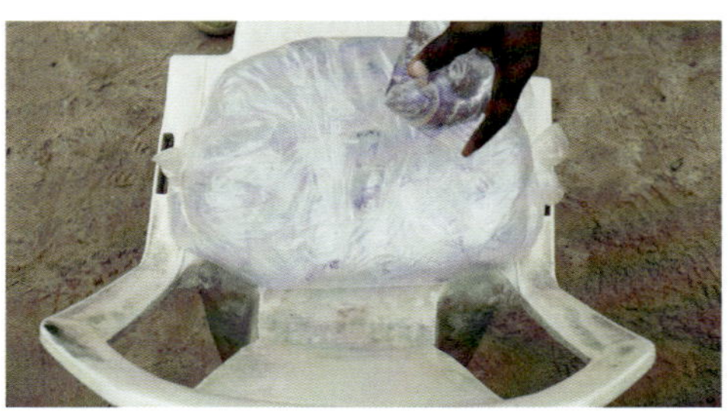
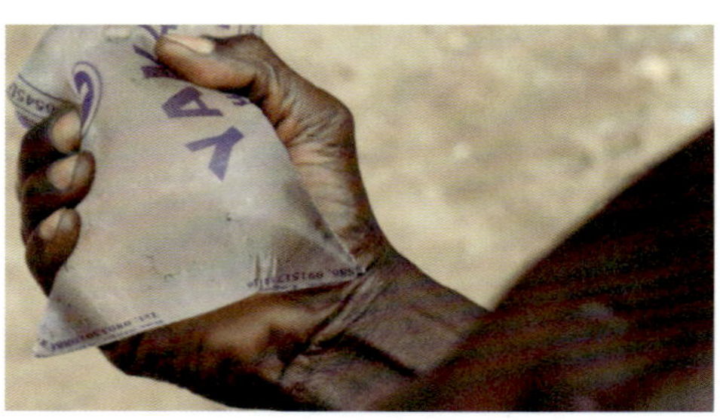

with a weightlessness that intimates the feeling of soft breath on skin. Absent of a depth of field, figures blur and morph into abstracted forms, and bodies are layered within contained action, discipline and restriction. Karimah Ashadu's measured pans across backs, chests and arms imbue the Black male body with a visibility, without rendering it singular or fixed. Our attention is drawn to embodiment, representation and the complexities therein. The metallic clang of barbells in what we discern as a makeshift outdoor gym is punctuated with sounds of exertion and of the nearby street. Breath and muscle move in syncopated sonic choreography, and the men's commitment to the ritual of maintaining the body is evident. At intervals,

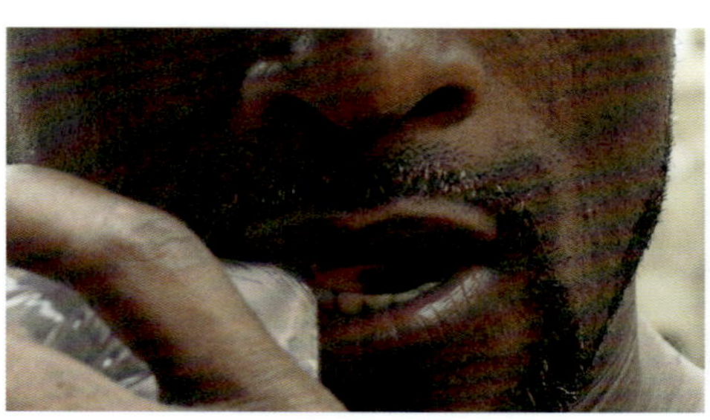
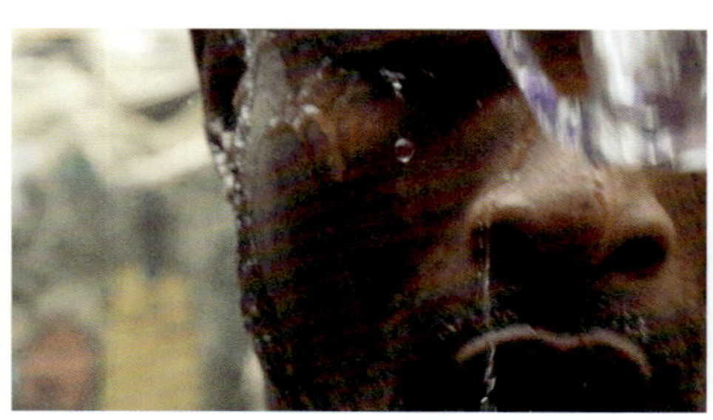
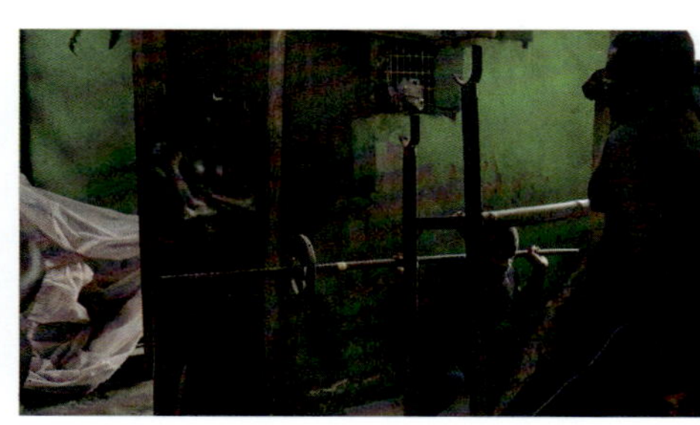
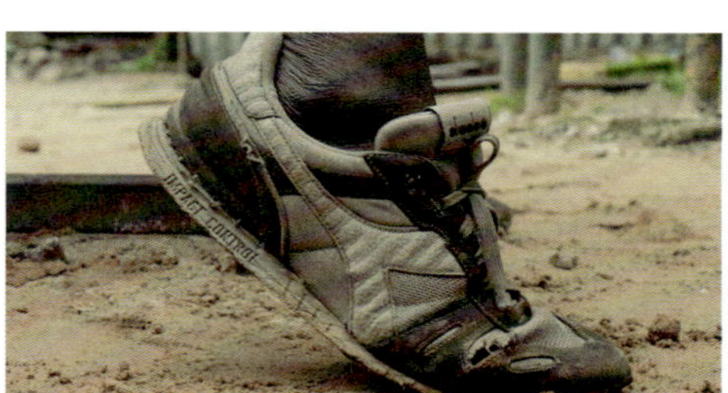
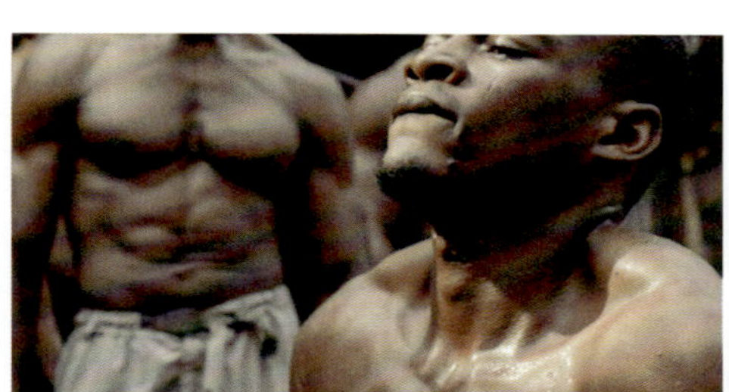
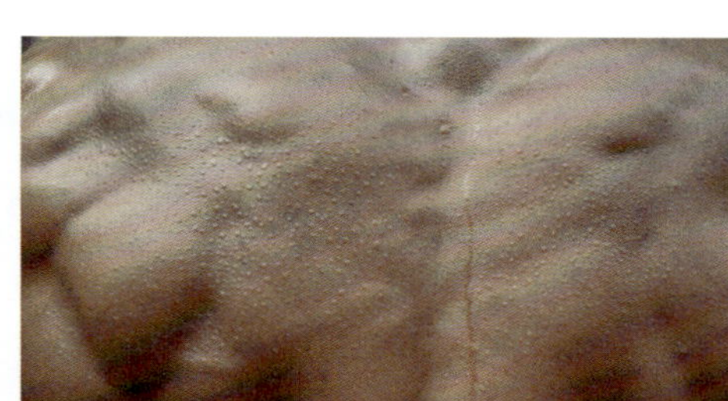

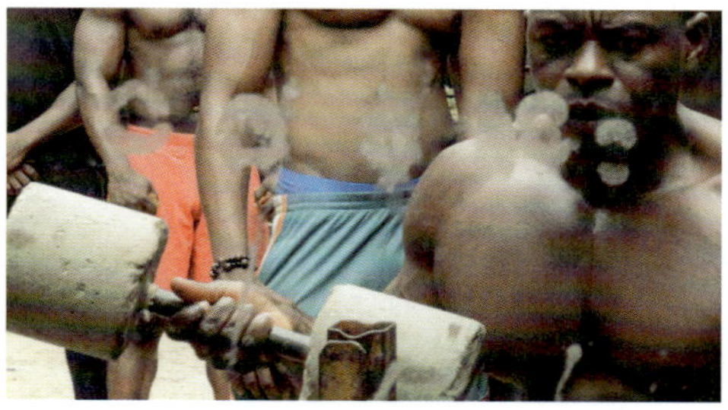

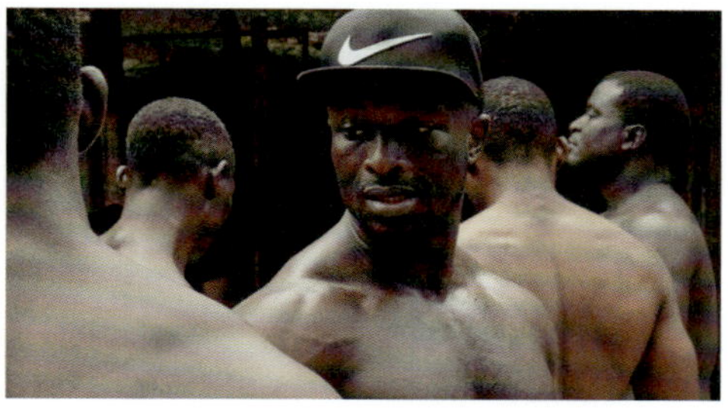

they drink sachets of 'pure water', framed with the precision of a commercial product placement that underscores their class-coded significance within capitalism. In patriarchal societies like Nigeria, the construction of masculine identity and its accompanying constraints necessitate performance, and the validation of an audience. As the men work to refine their bodies, we witness their desires imbricate and manifest in physical form, and gain insight into the immaterial realm of affect that resides in each of them.

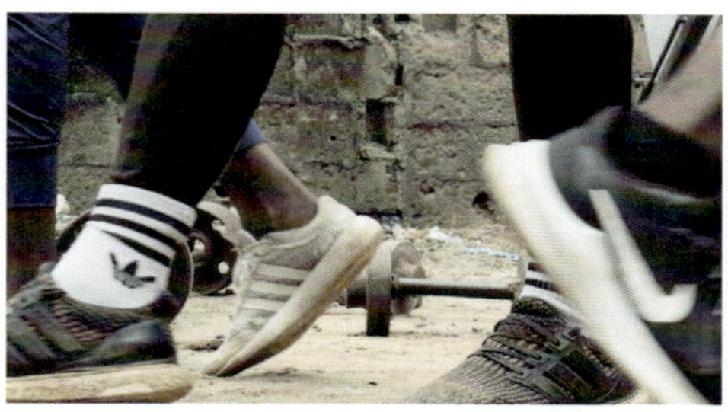

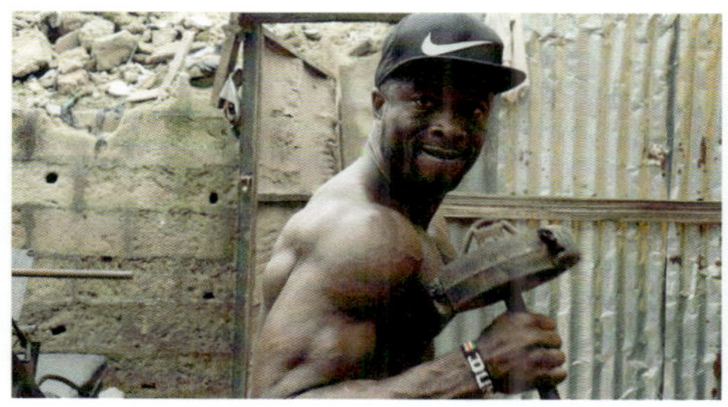

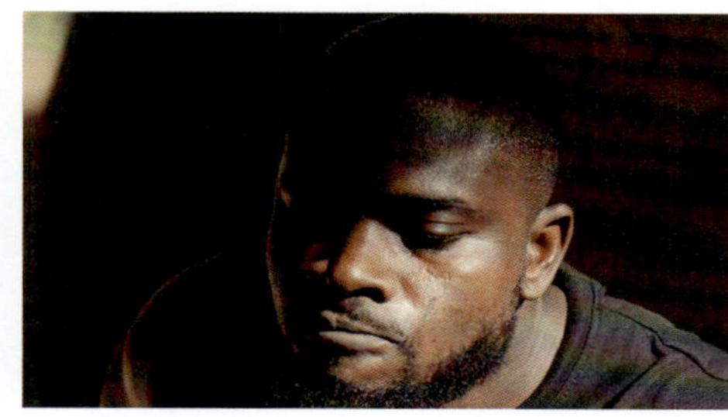

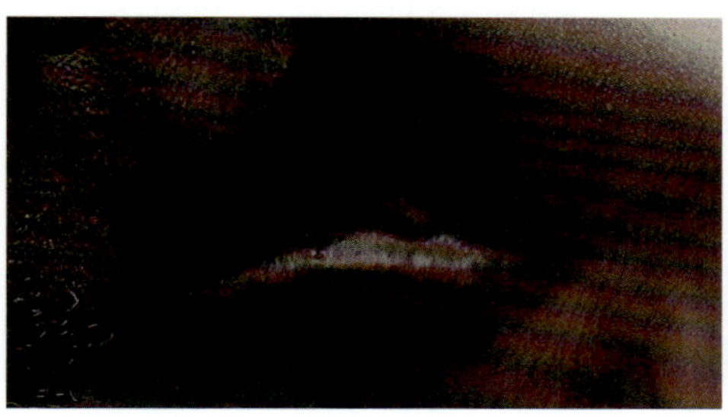

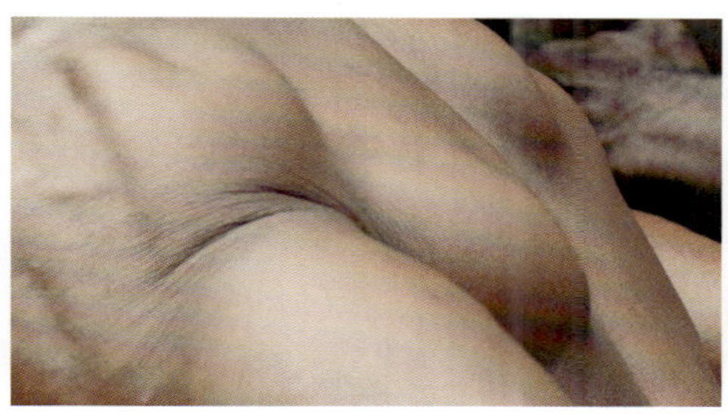

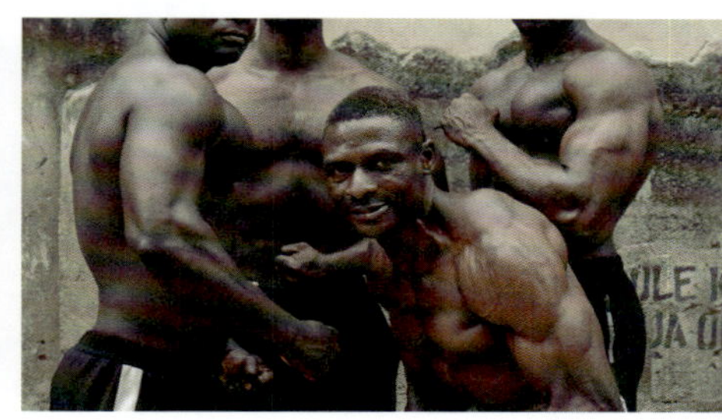

Director and Editor
Karimah Ashadu

Camera and Production Coordinator
Aigberadion Israel Ikhazuangbe

Sound Recordists
Onu Rosemaryjoy Chiwendu
Joseph Eyo Edem

Audio Post-Production
Jochen Jezussek

Colour Grading and Graphic Design
wave-line GmbH

Production Assistants
Ibrahim Babatunde Adebayo
David Olamide Lawson

Commissioned and Produced by
Camden Art Centre, London; Fondazione In Between Art Film; the Renaissance Society at the University of Chicago

Creative Producers
Leonardo Bigazzi
Alessandro Rabottini

Co-produced by
Golddust by Ashadu

With special thanks to
The bodybuilders and crew; Marie Becker and Gianna Furia; Camden Art Centre; Fondazione In Between Art Film; Sadie Coles HQ, London; the Renaissance Society at the University of Chicago; my family

Gazes Back and Collectivity

Karimah Ashadu

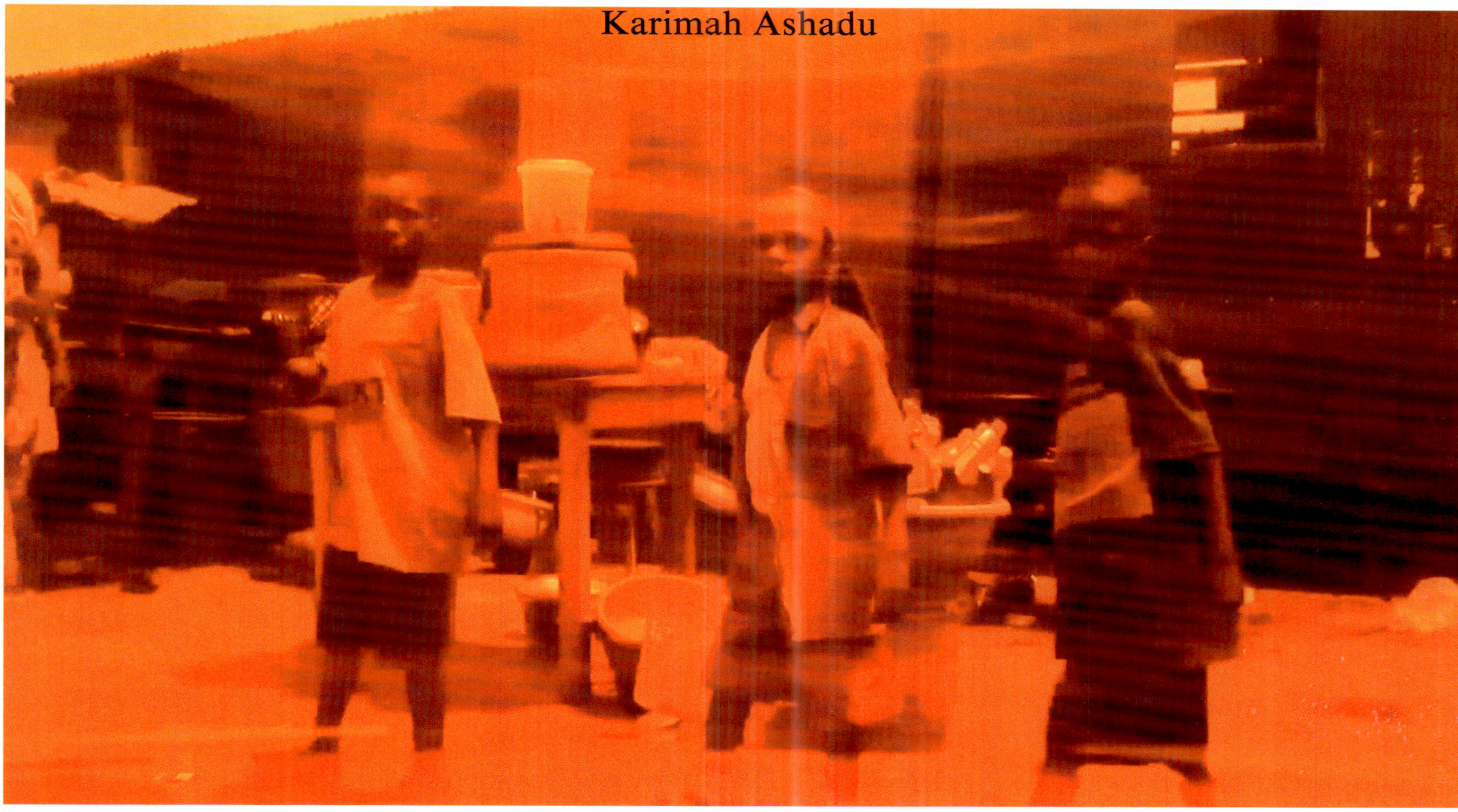

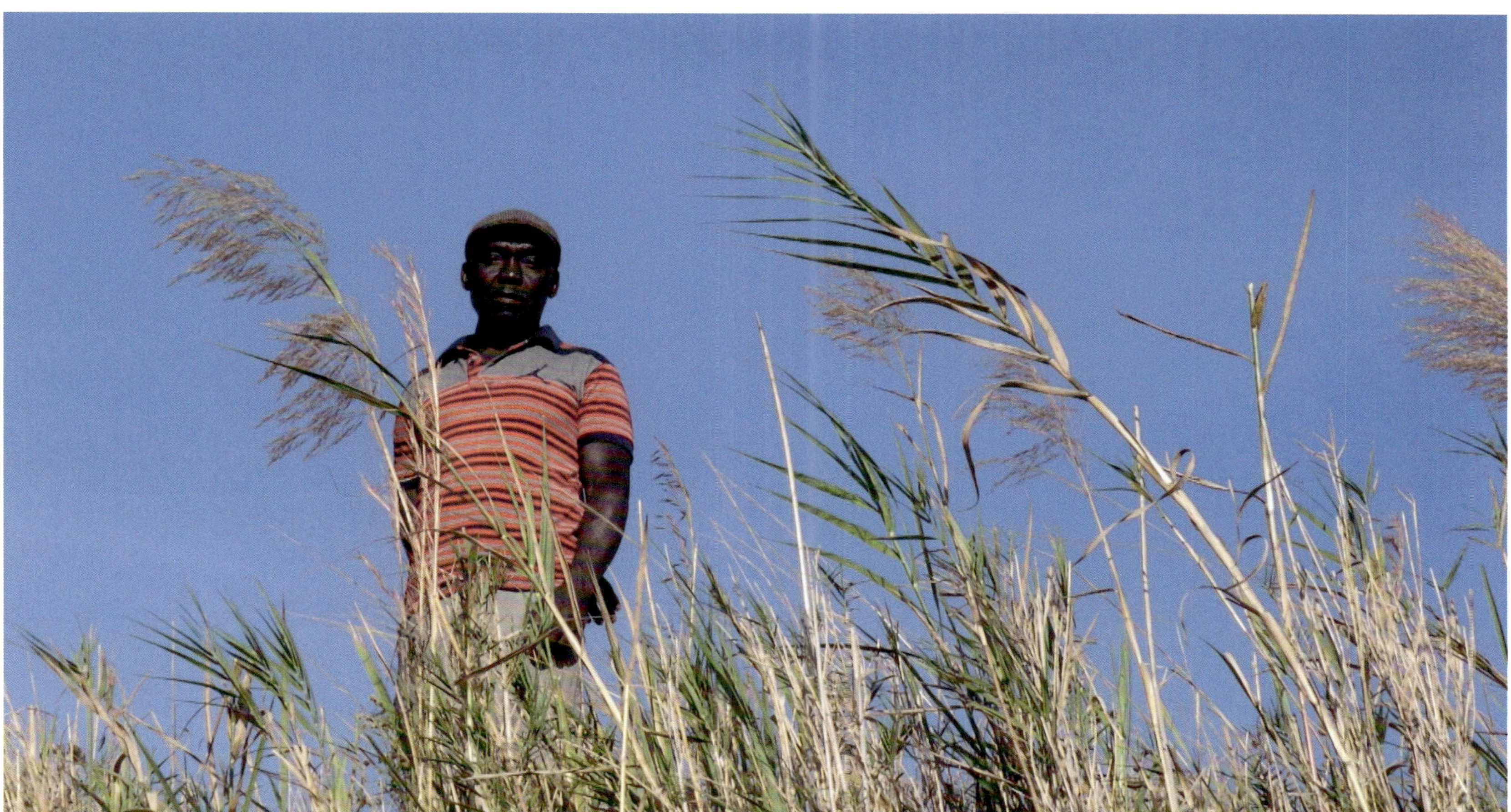

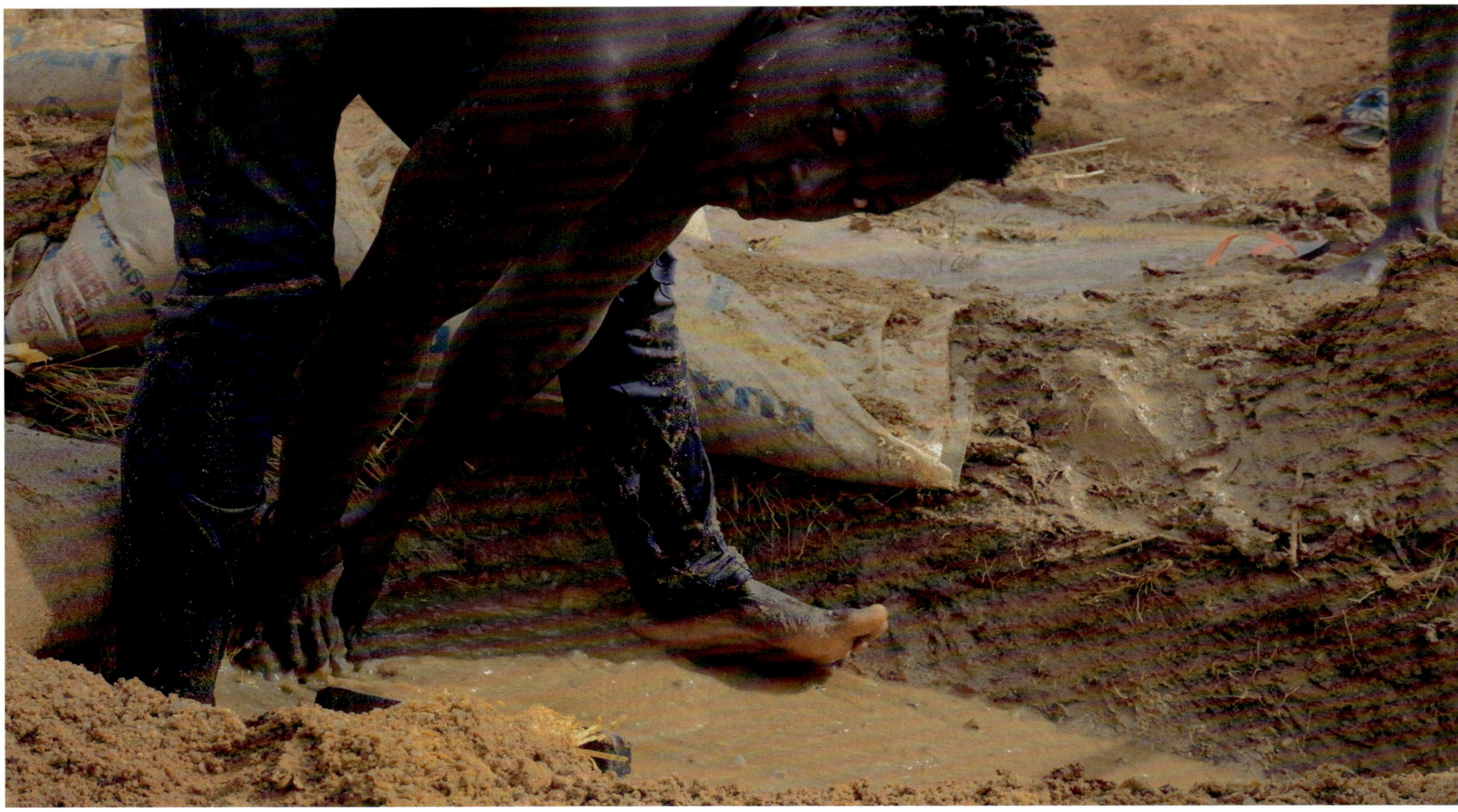

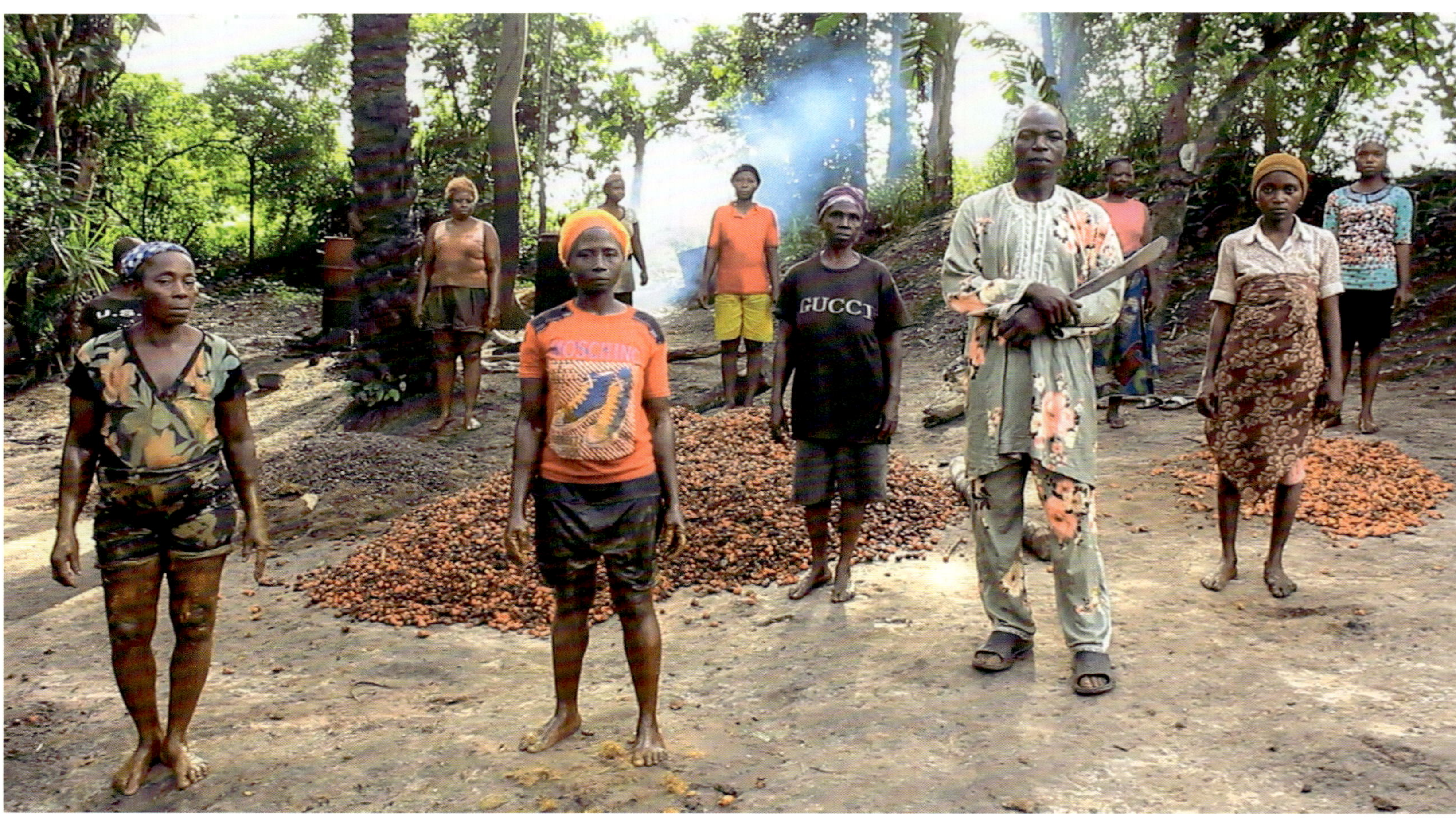
GUCCI

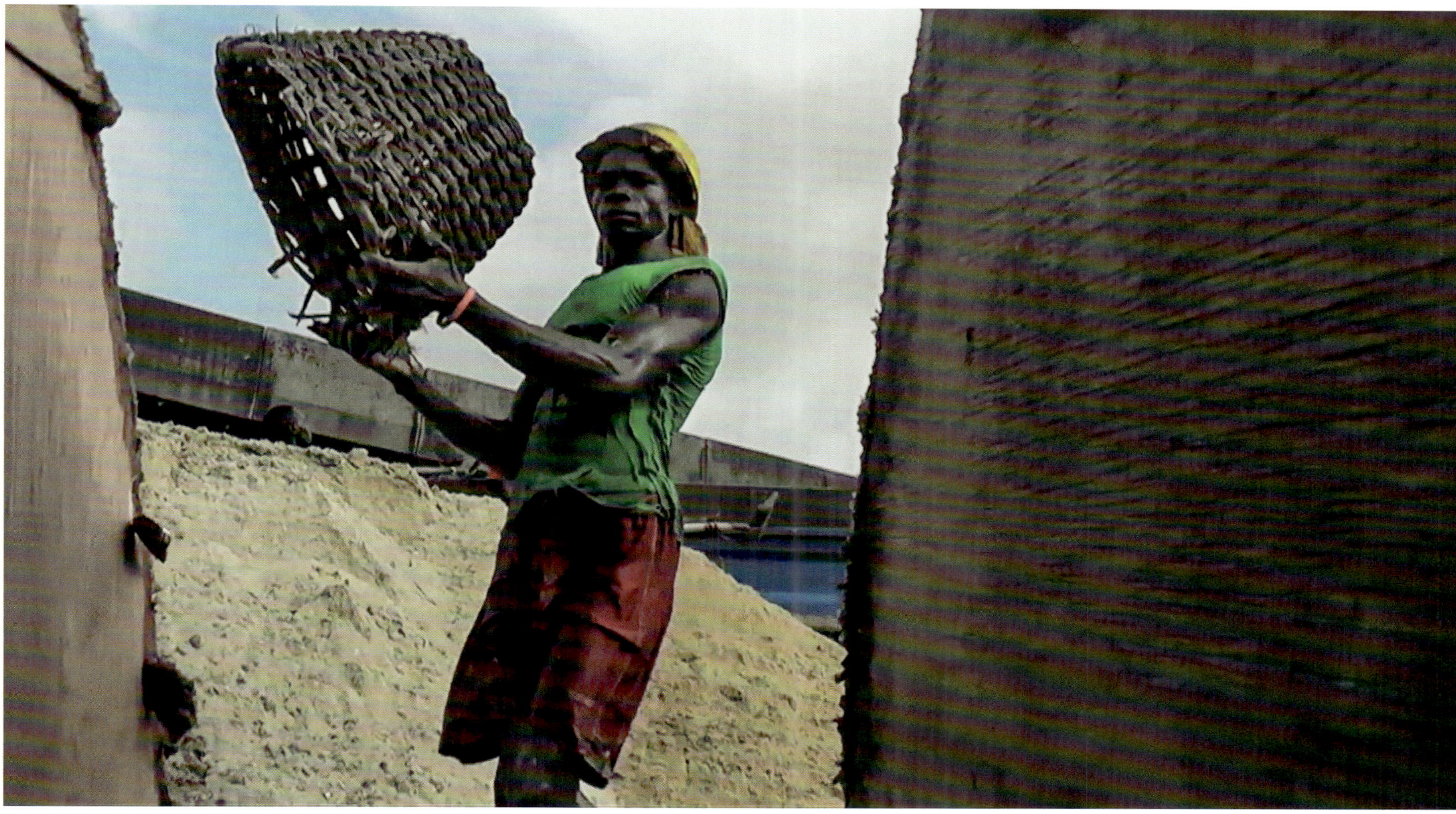

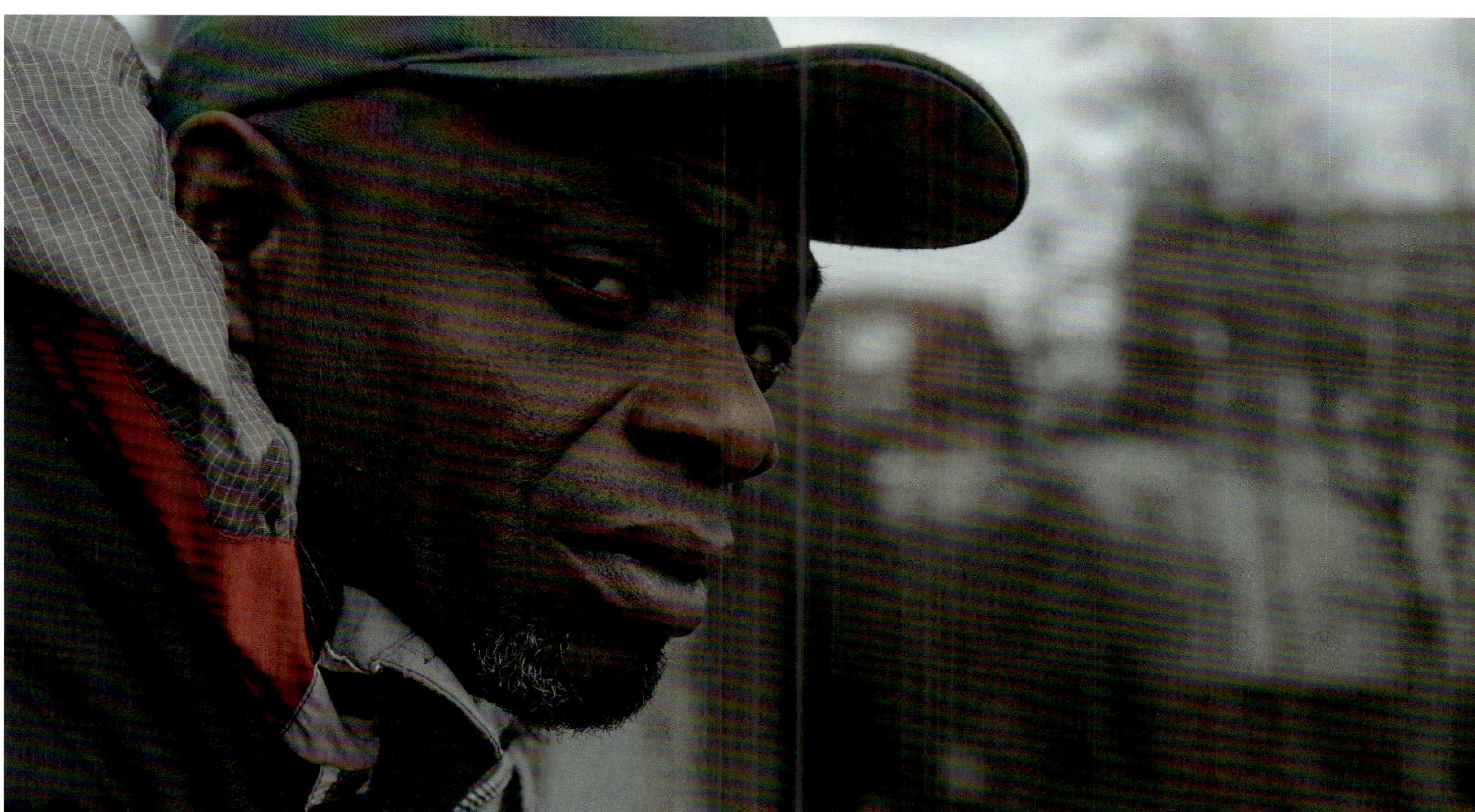

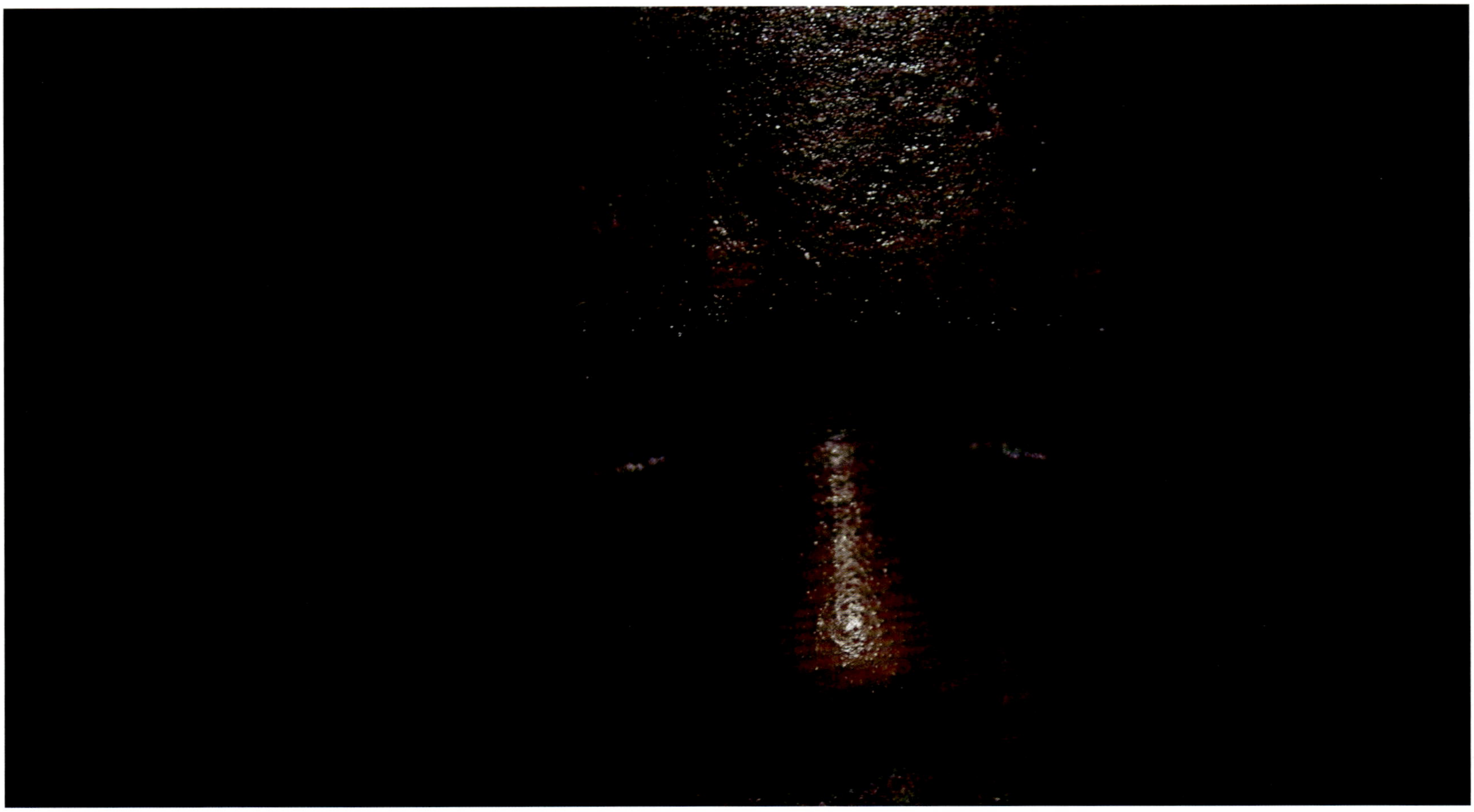

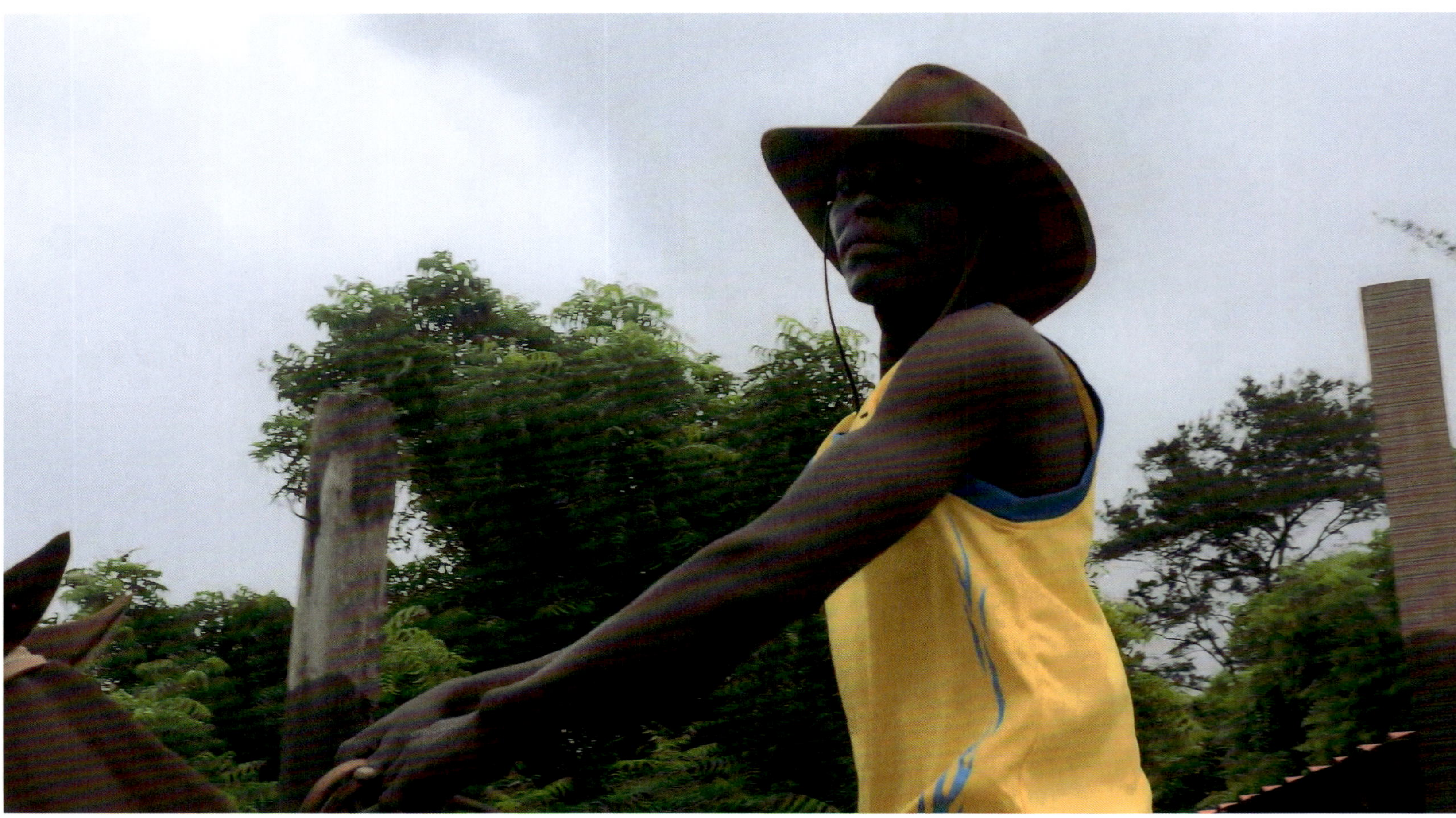

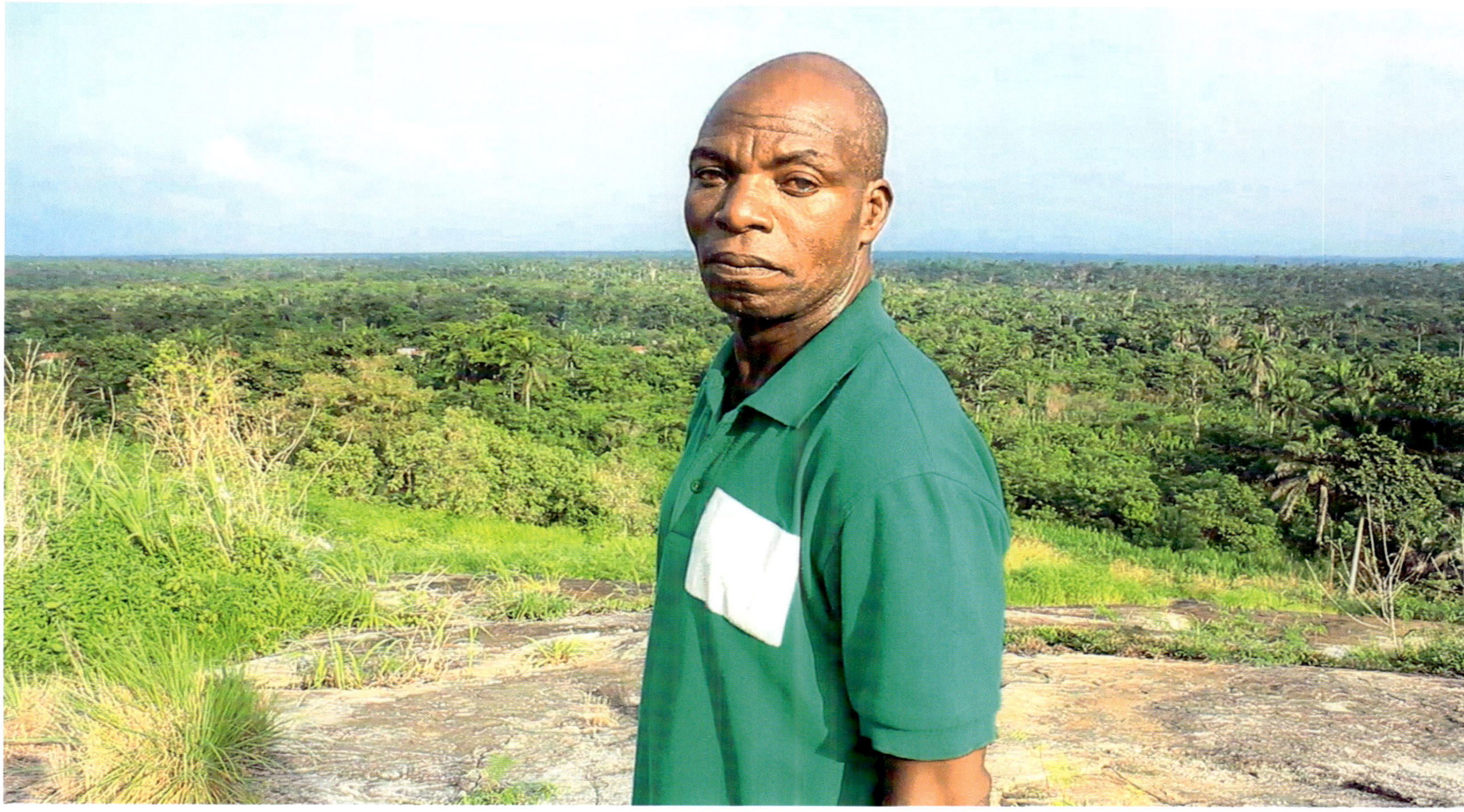

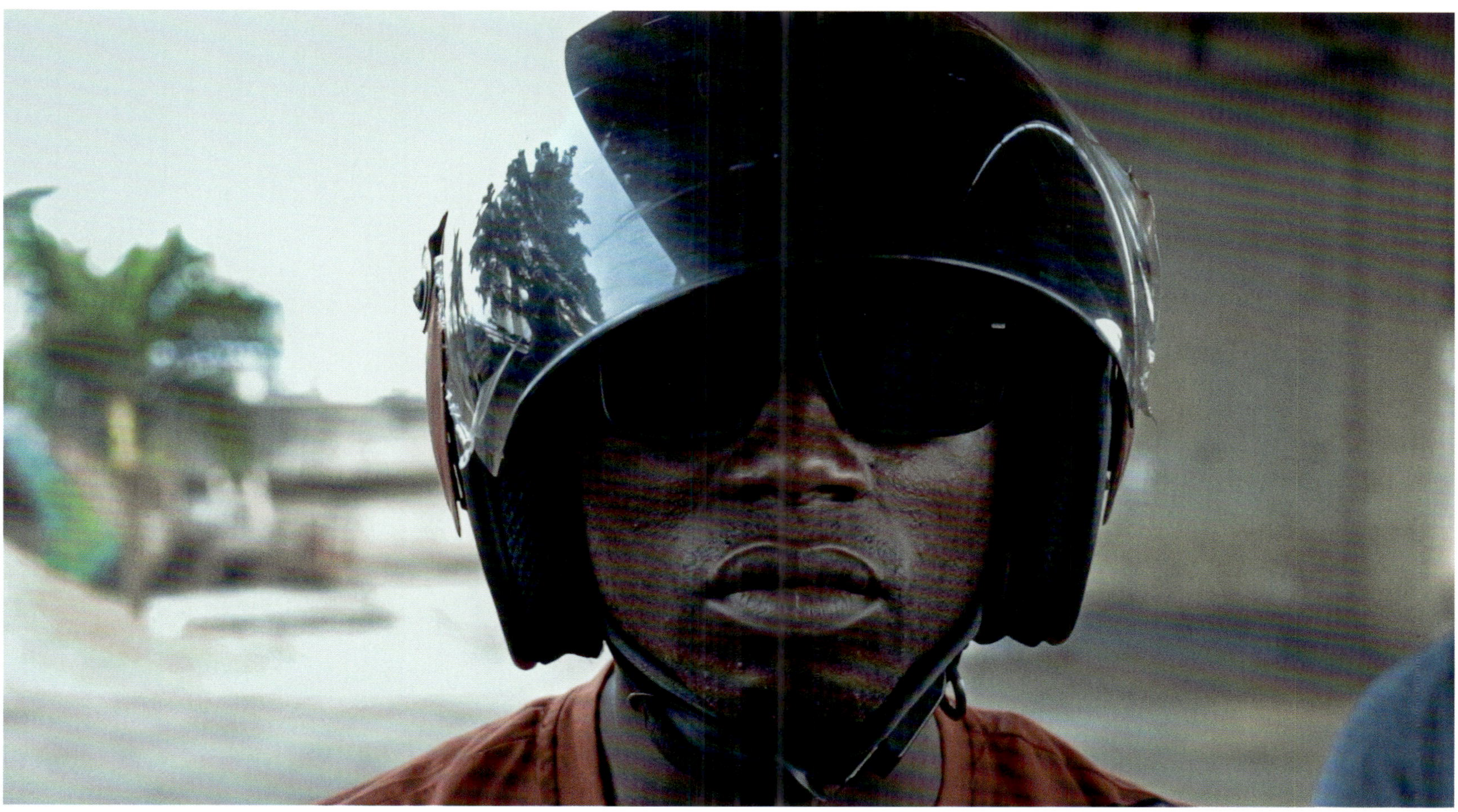

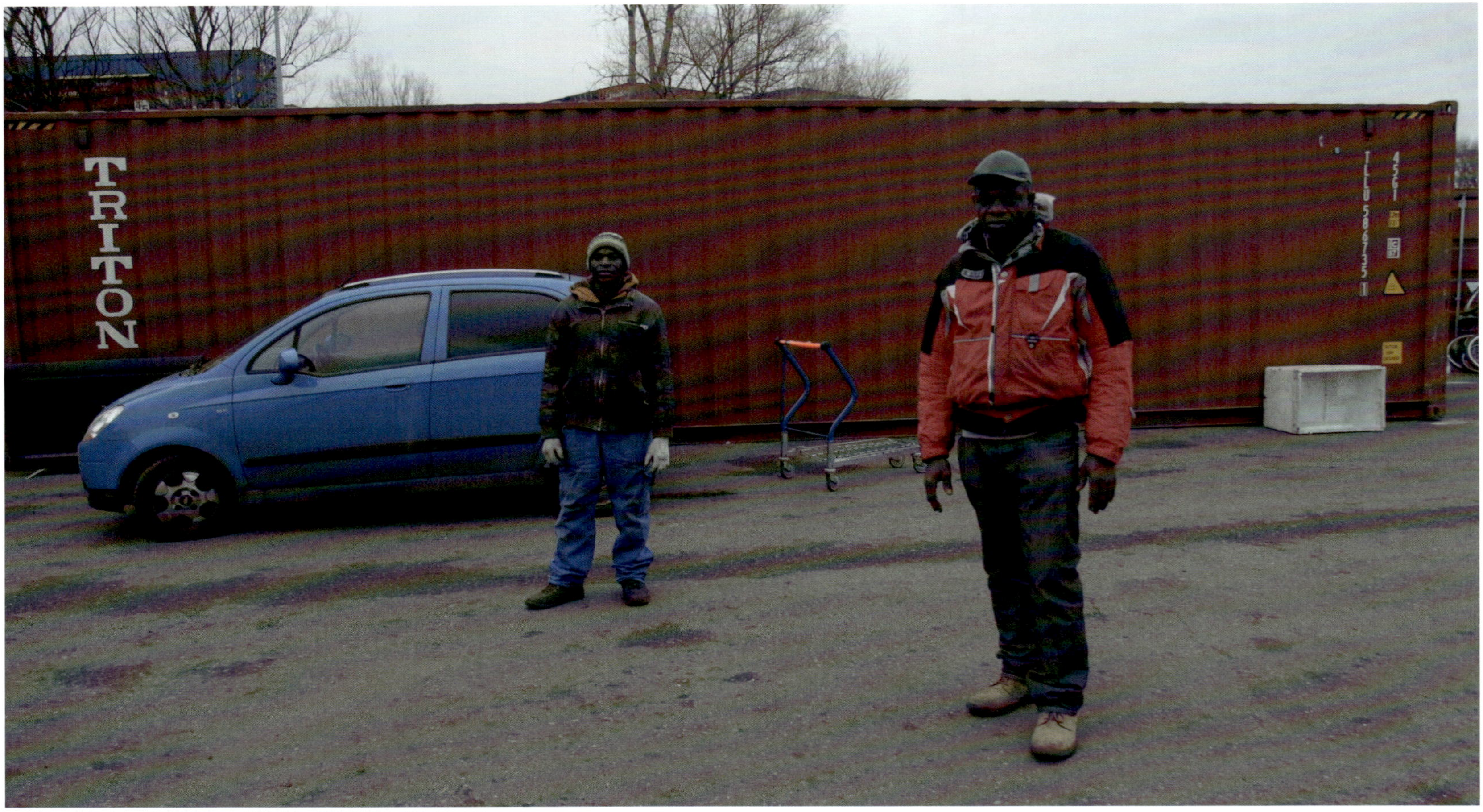
TRITON

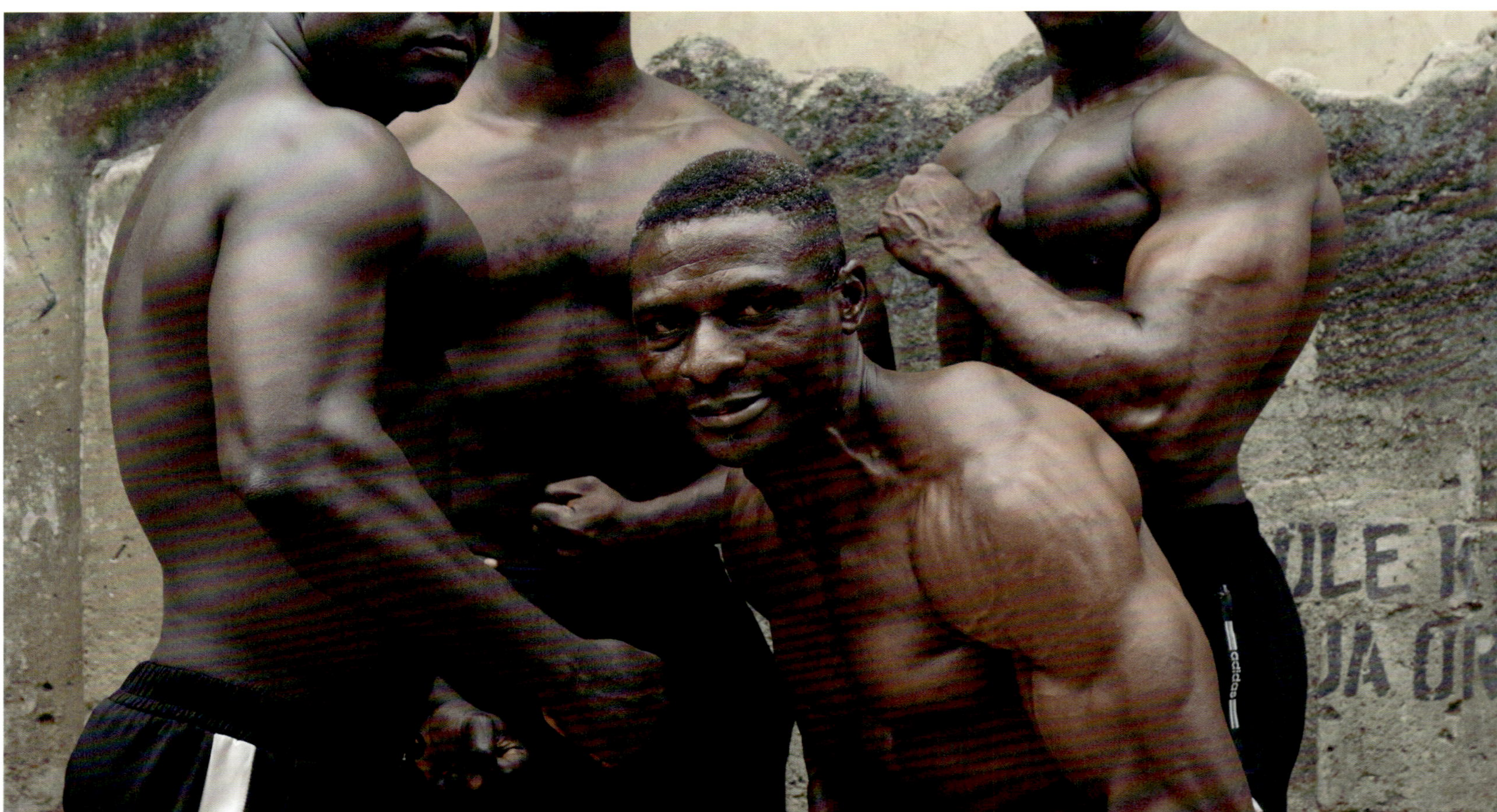

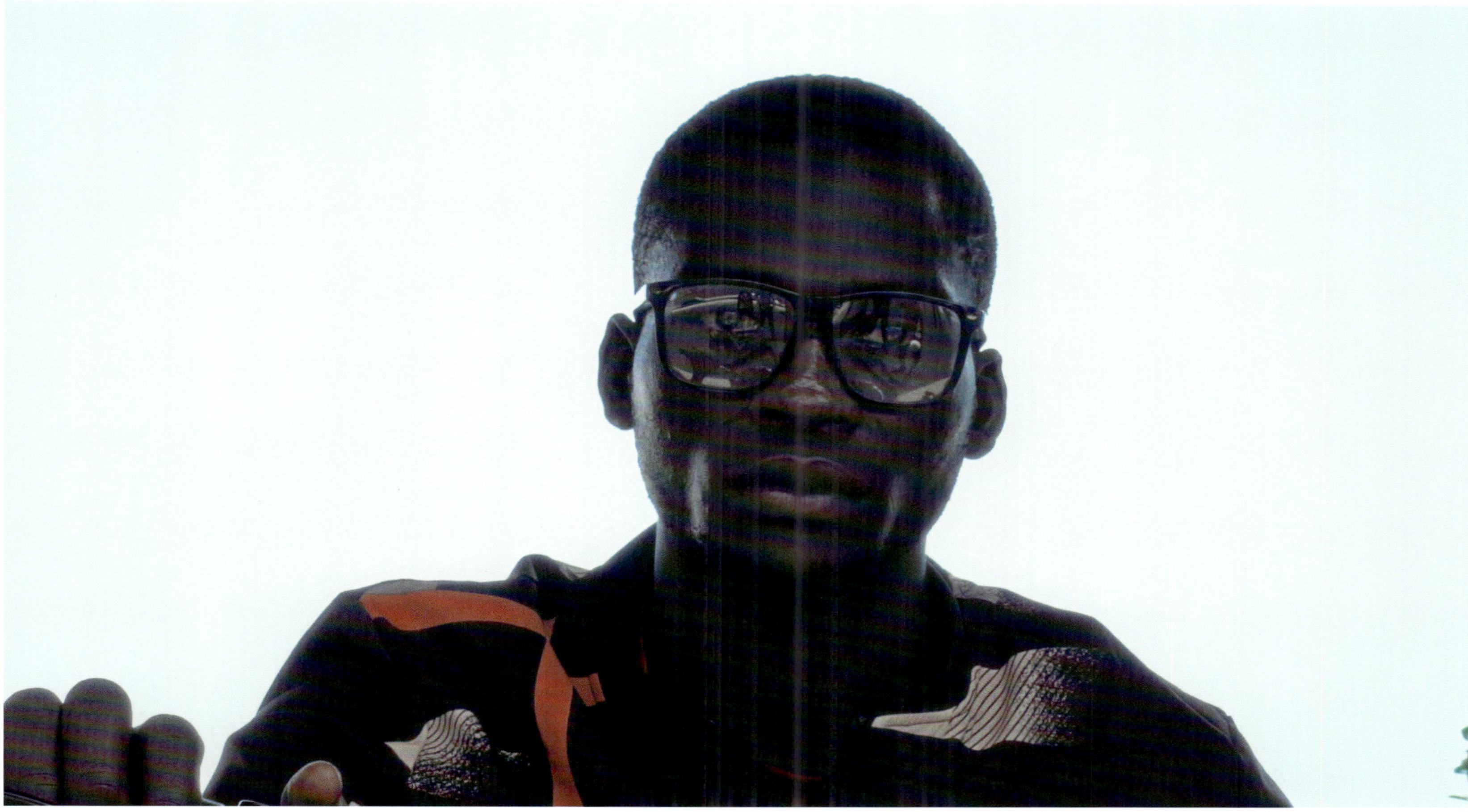

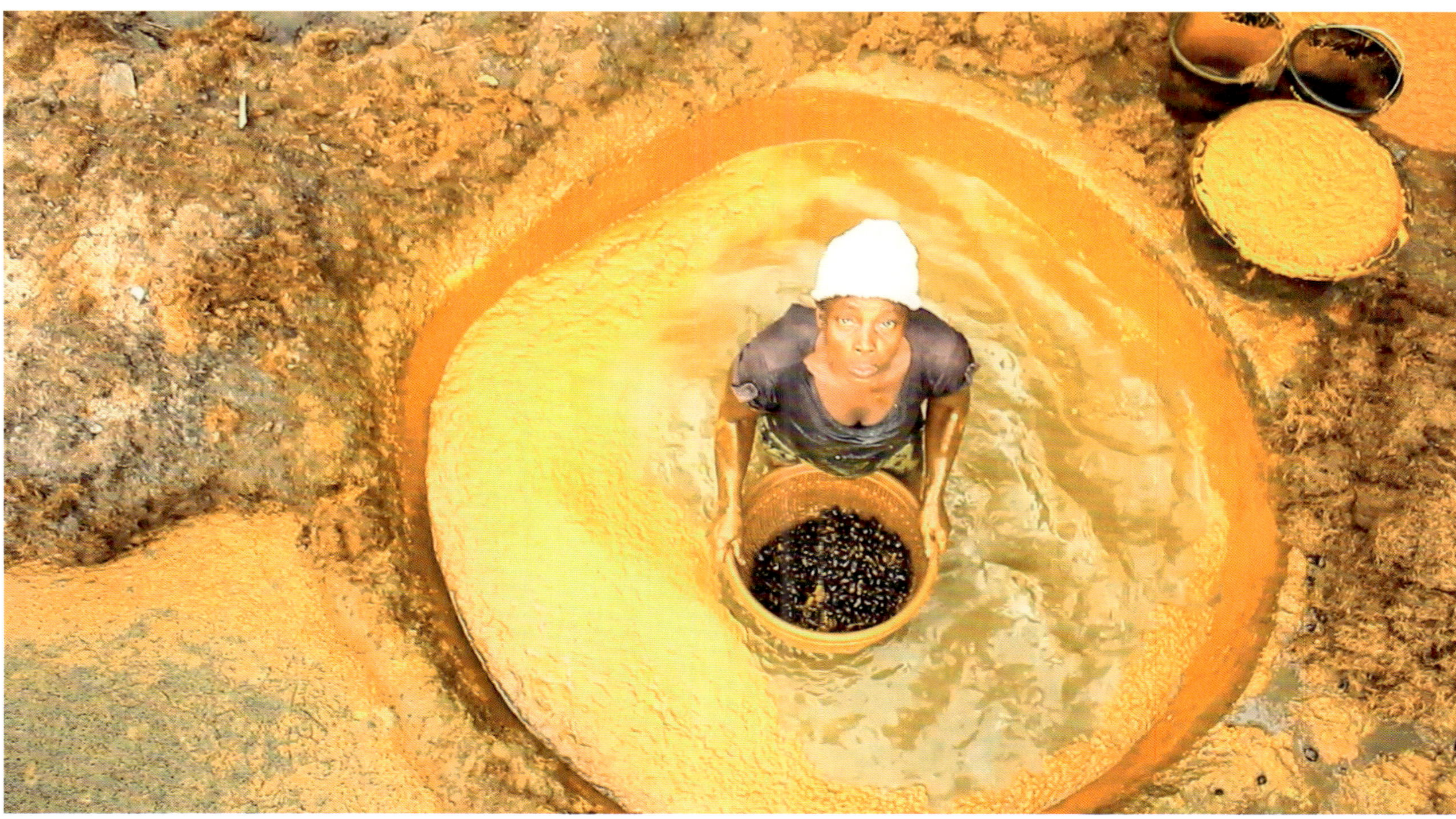

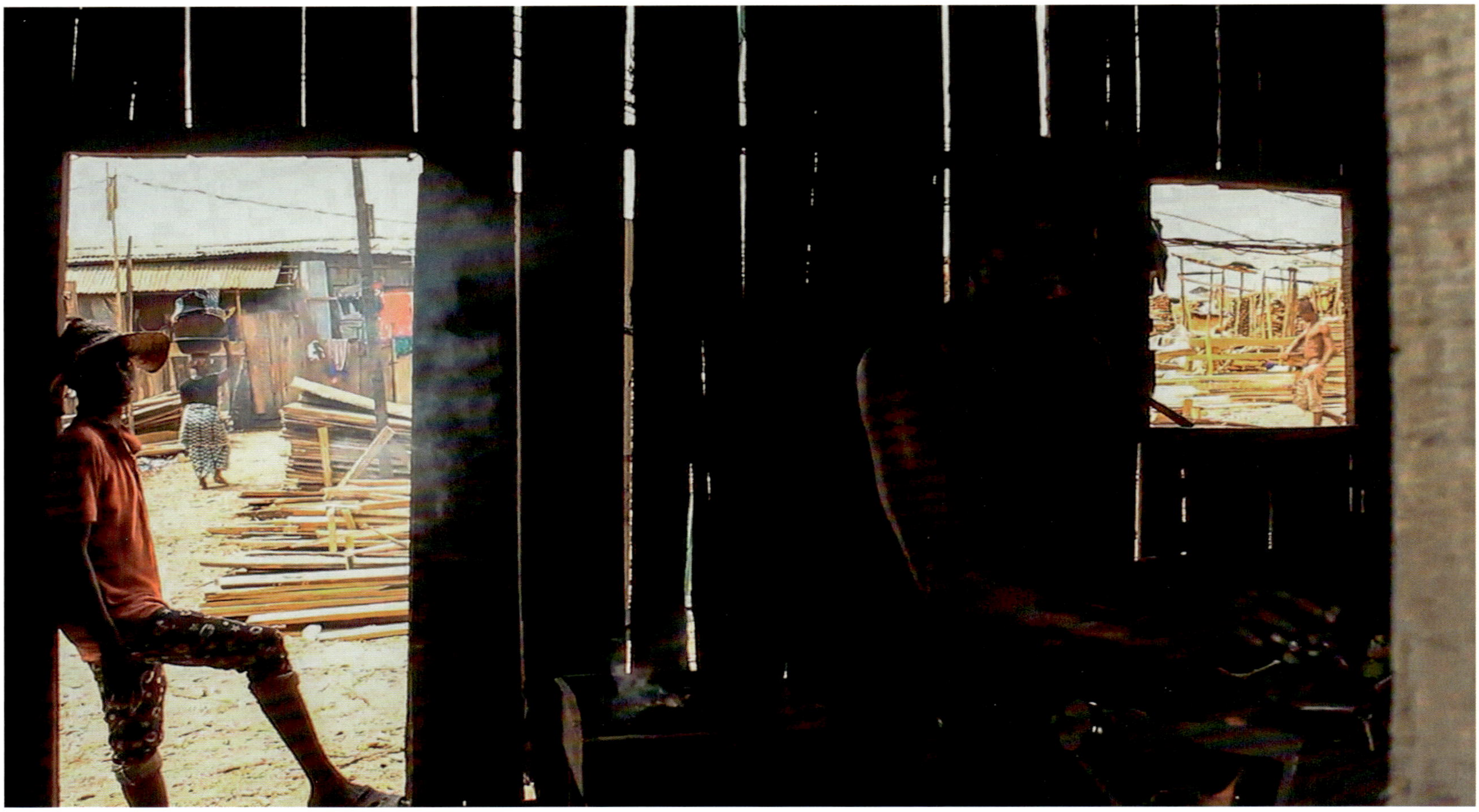

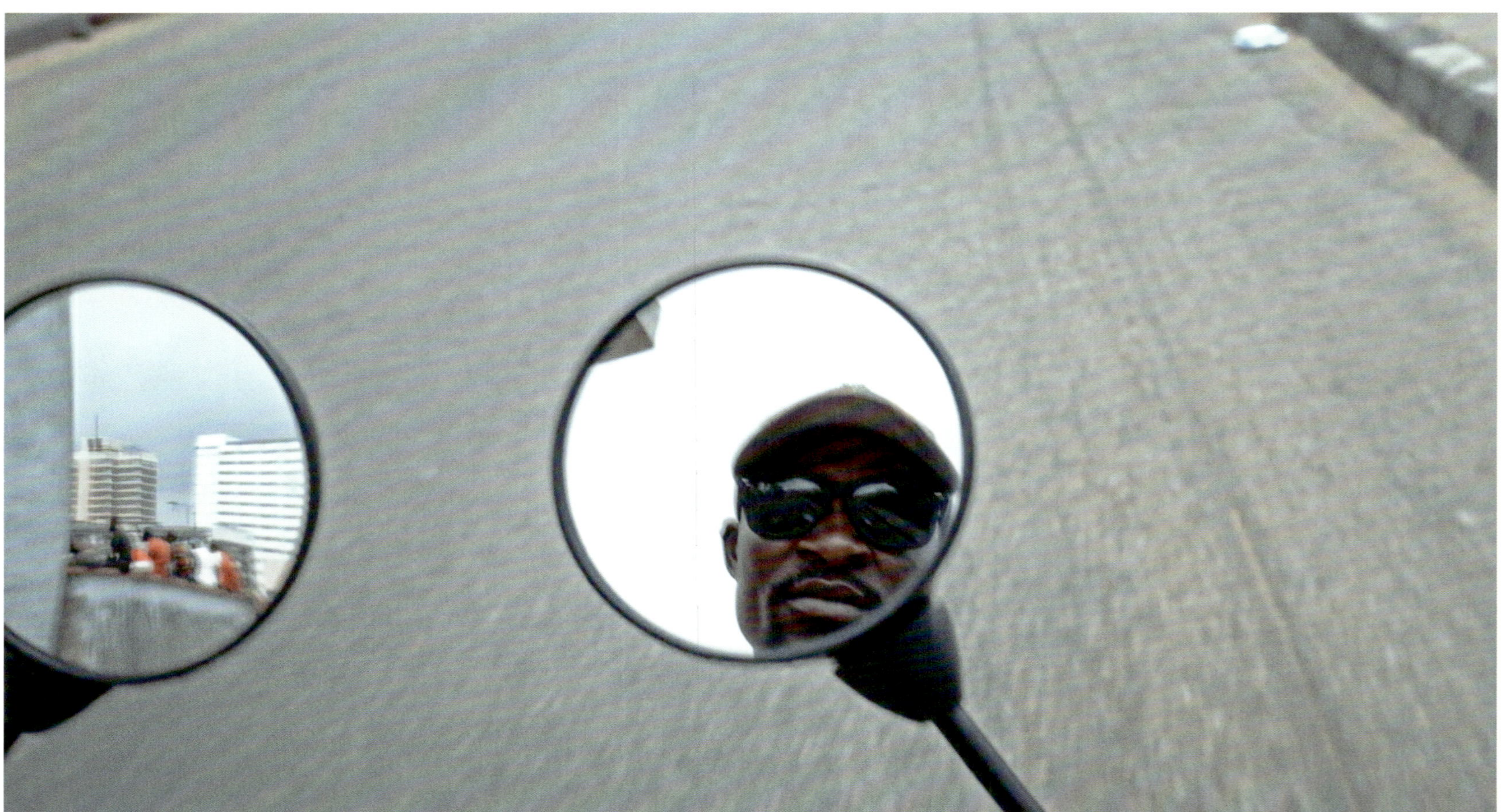

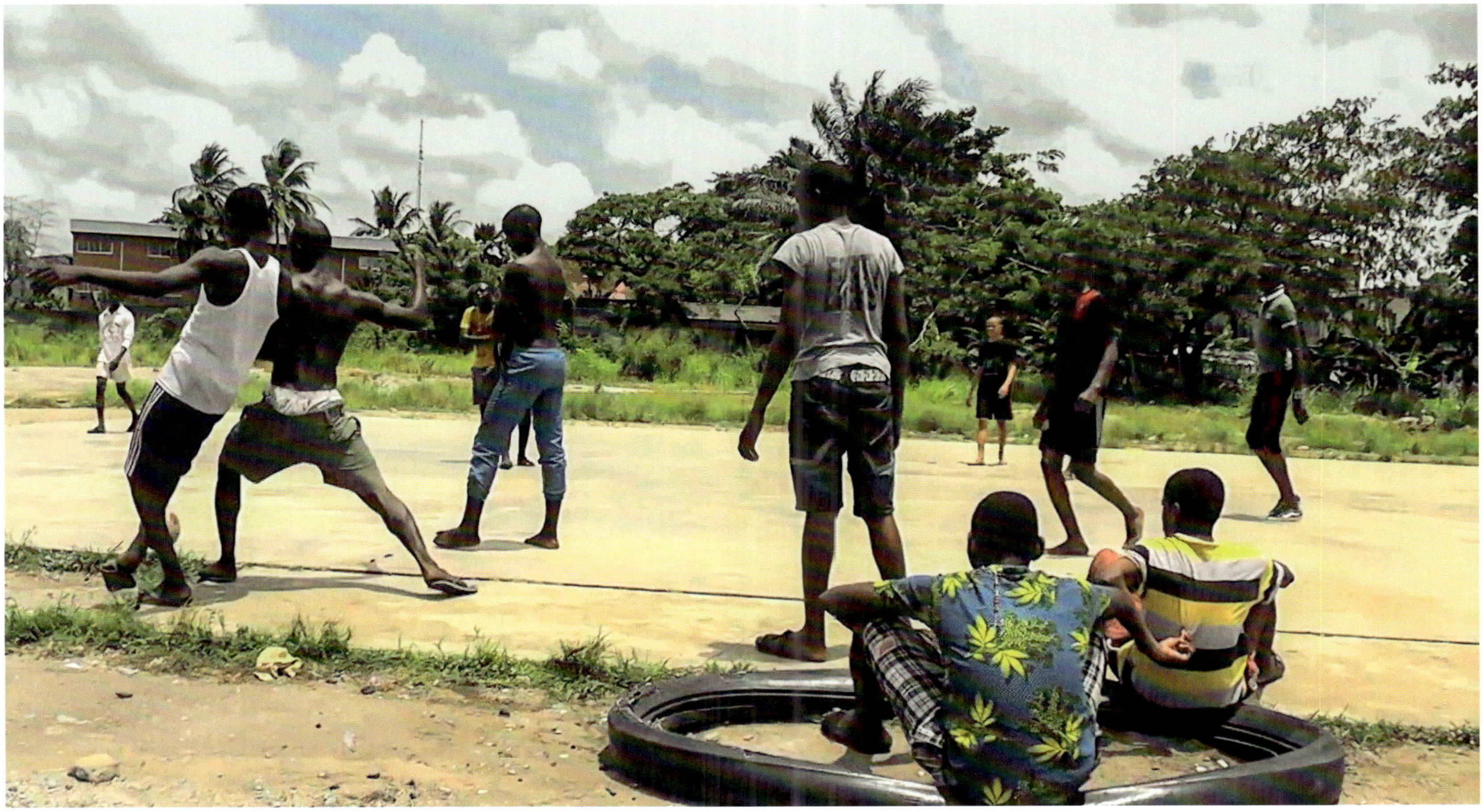

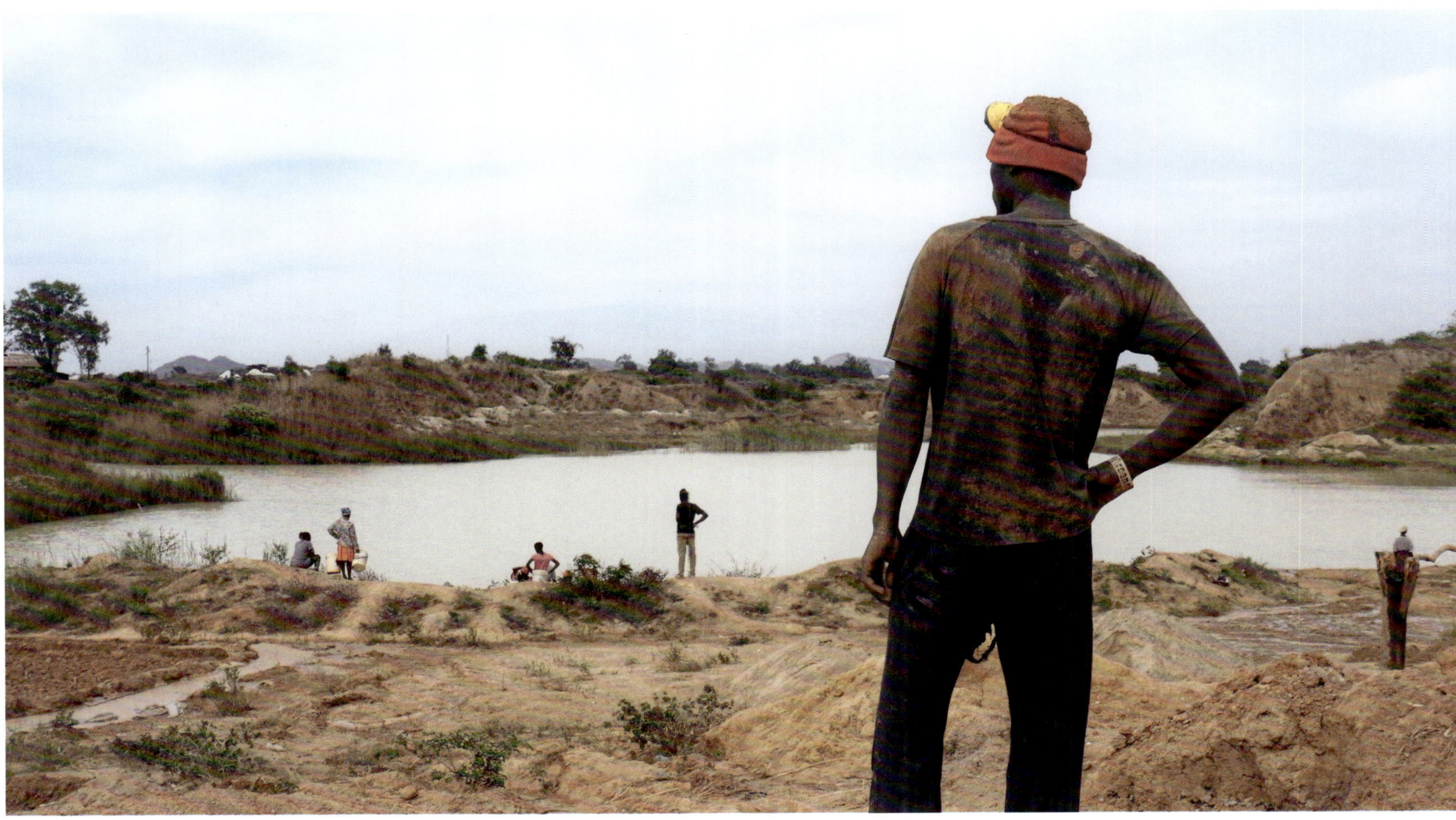

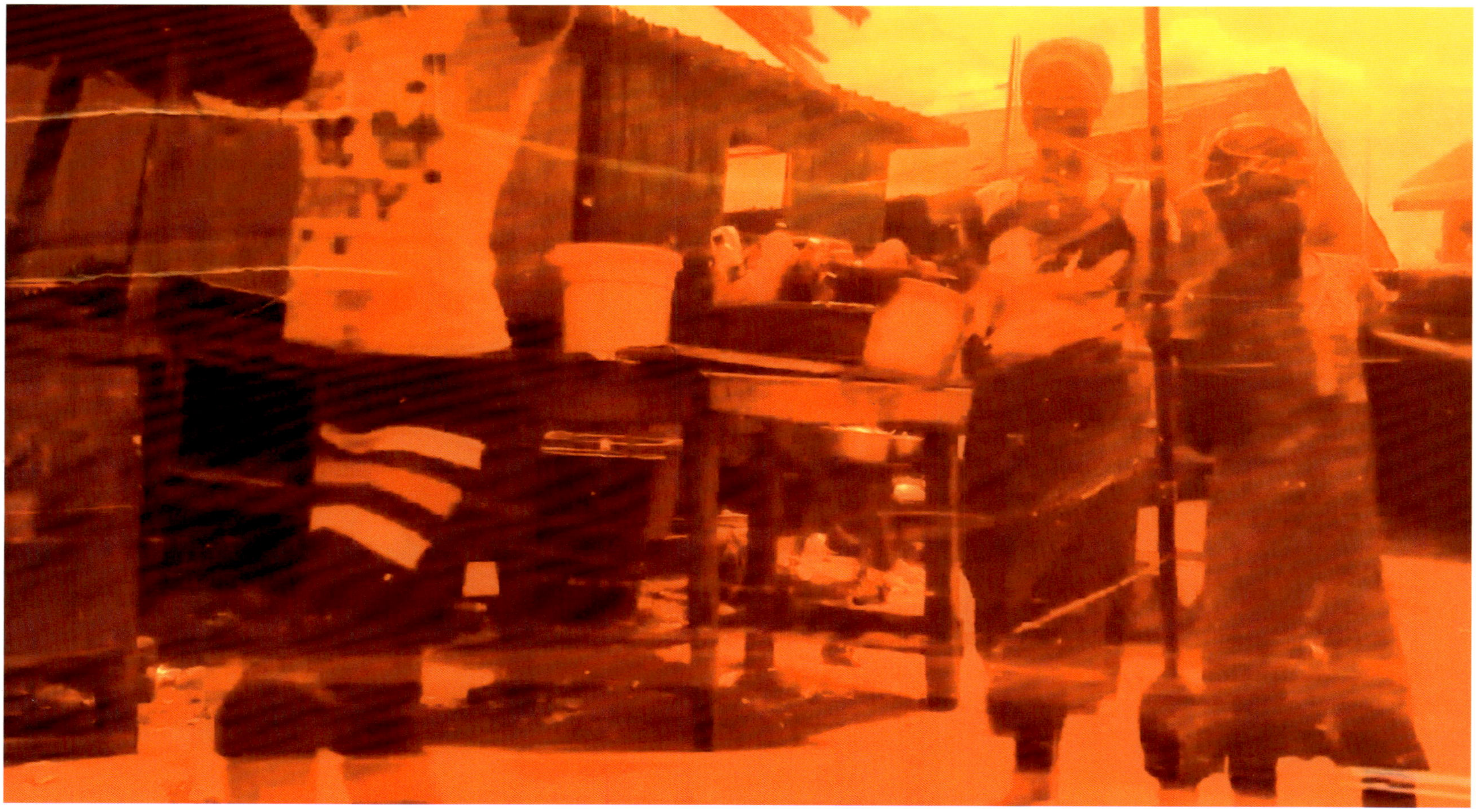

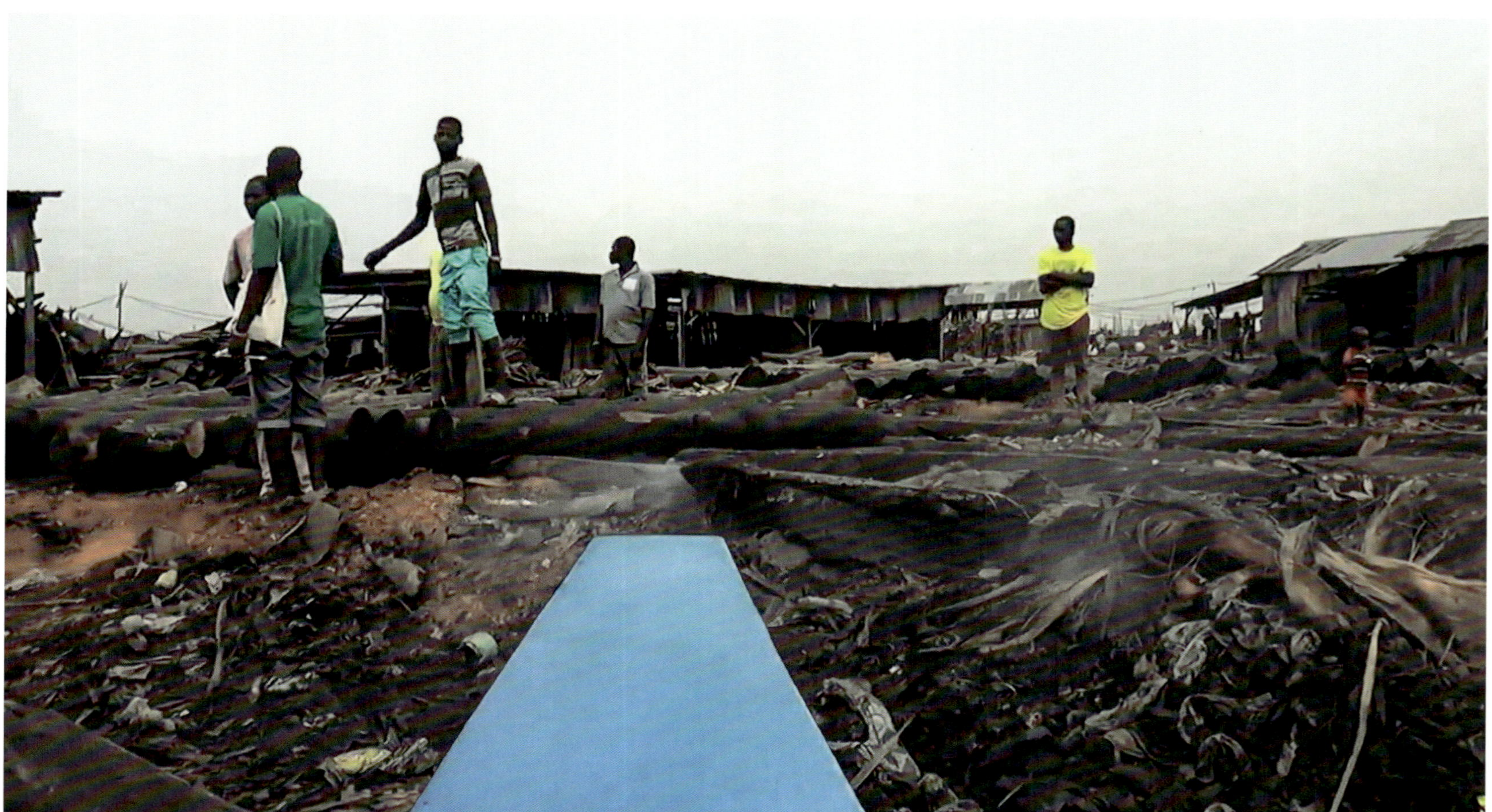

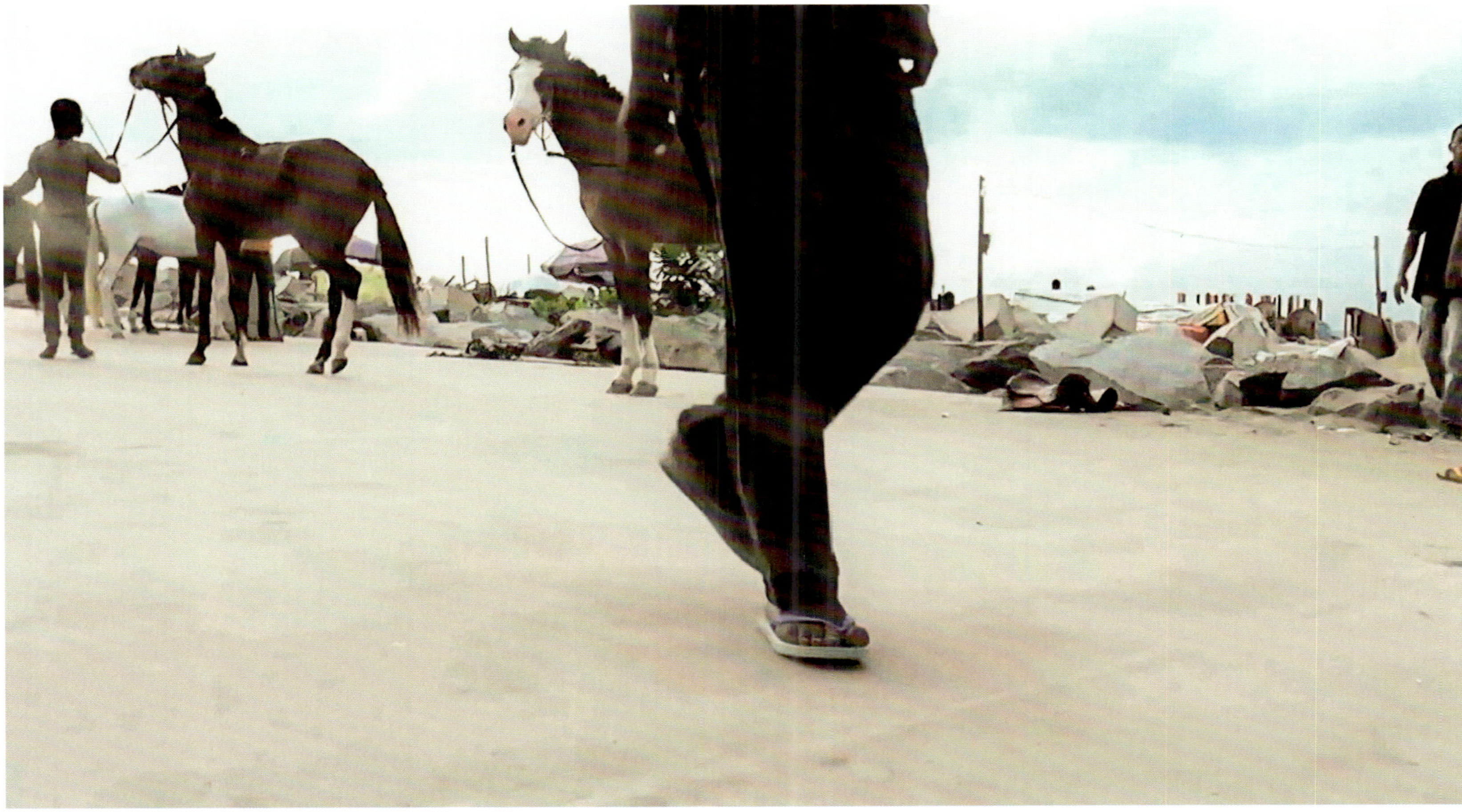

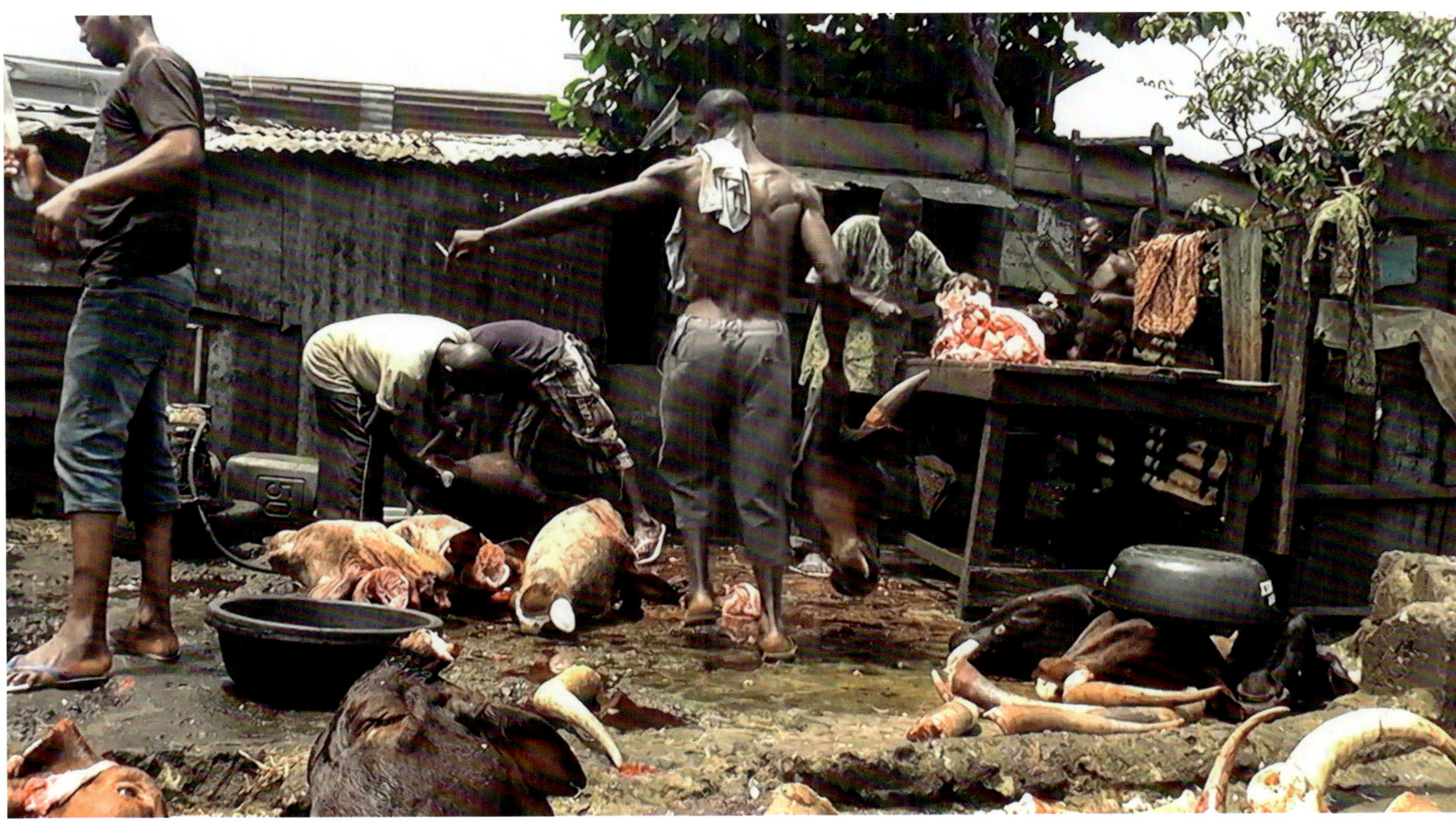

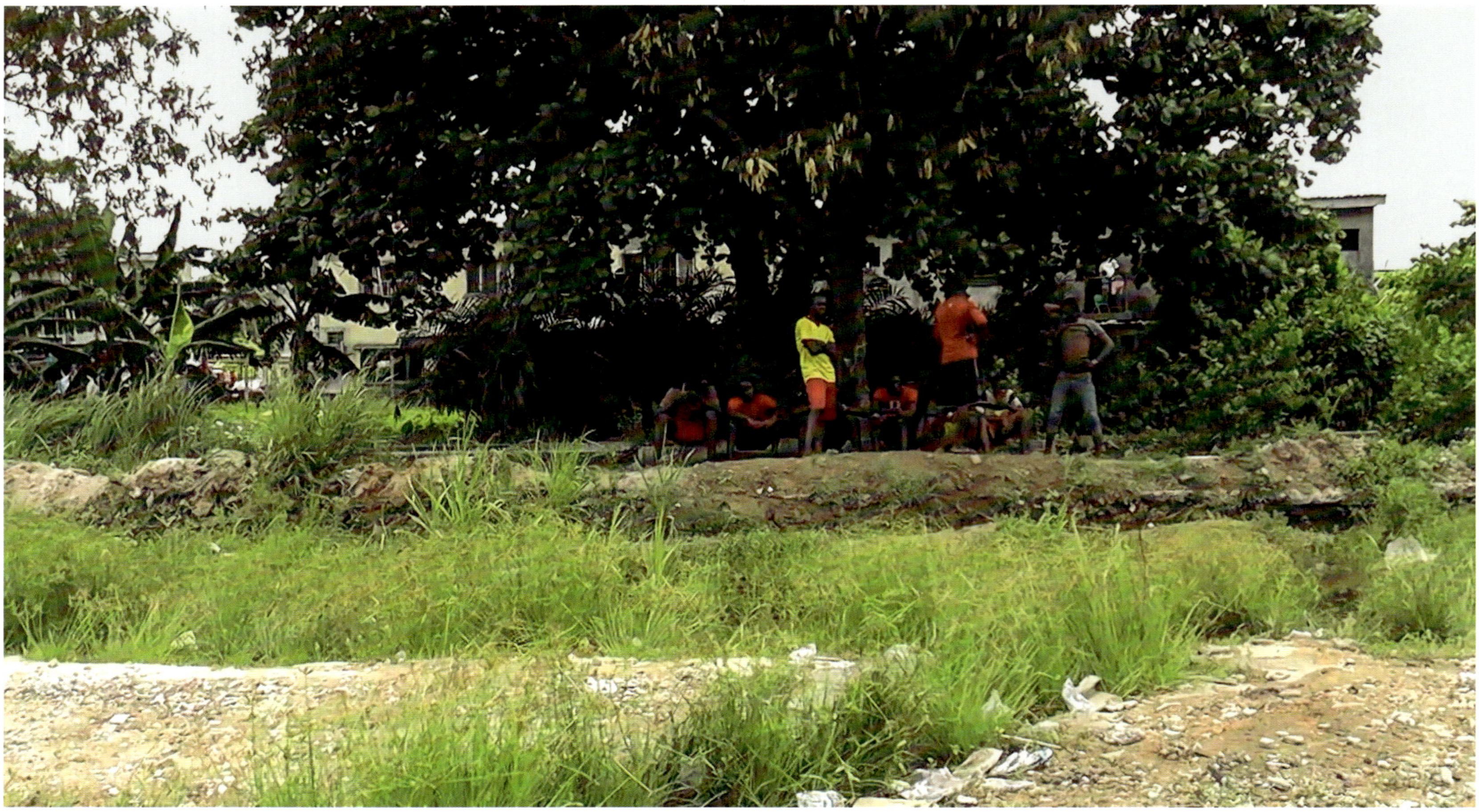

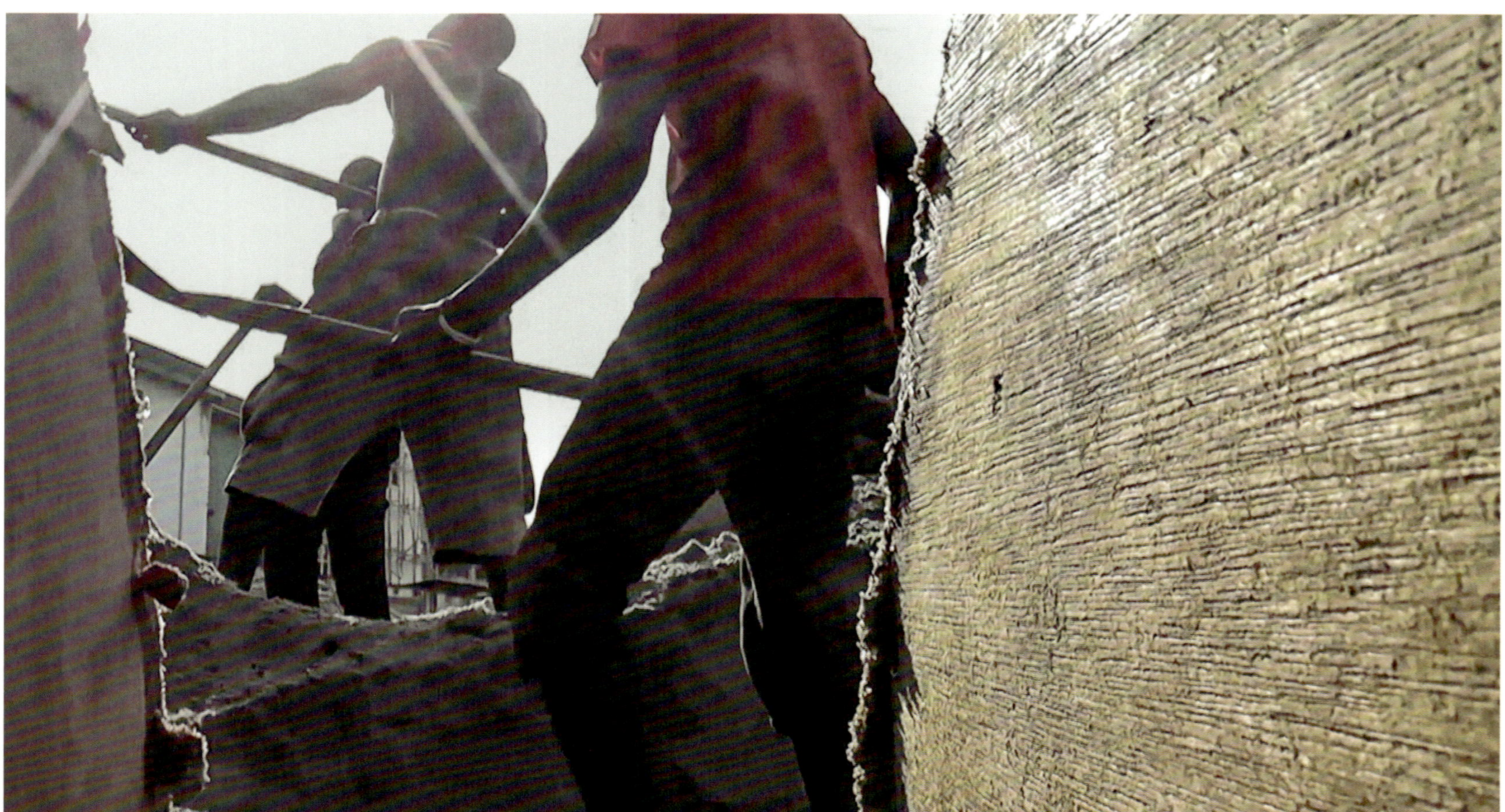

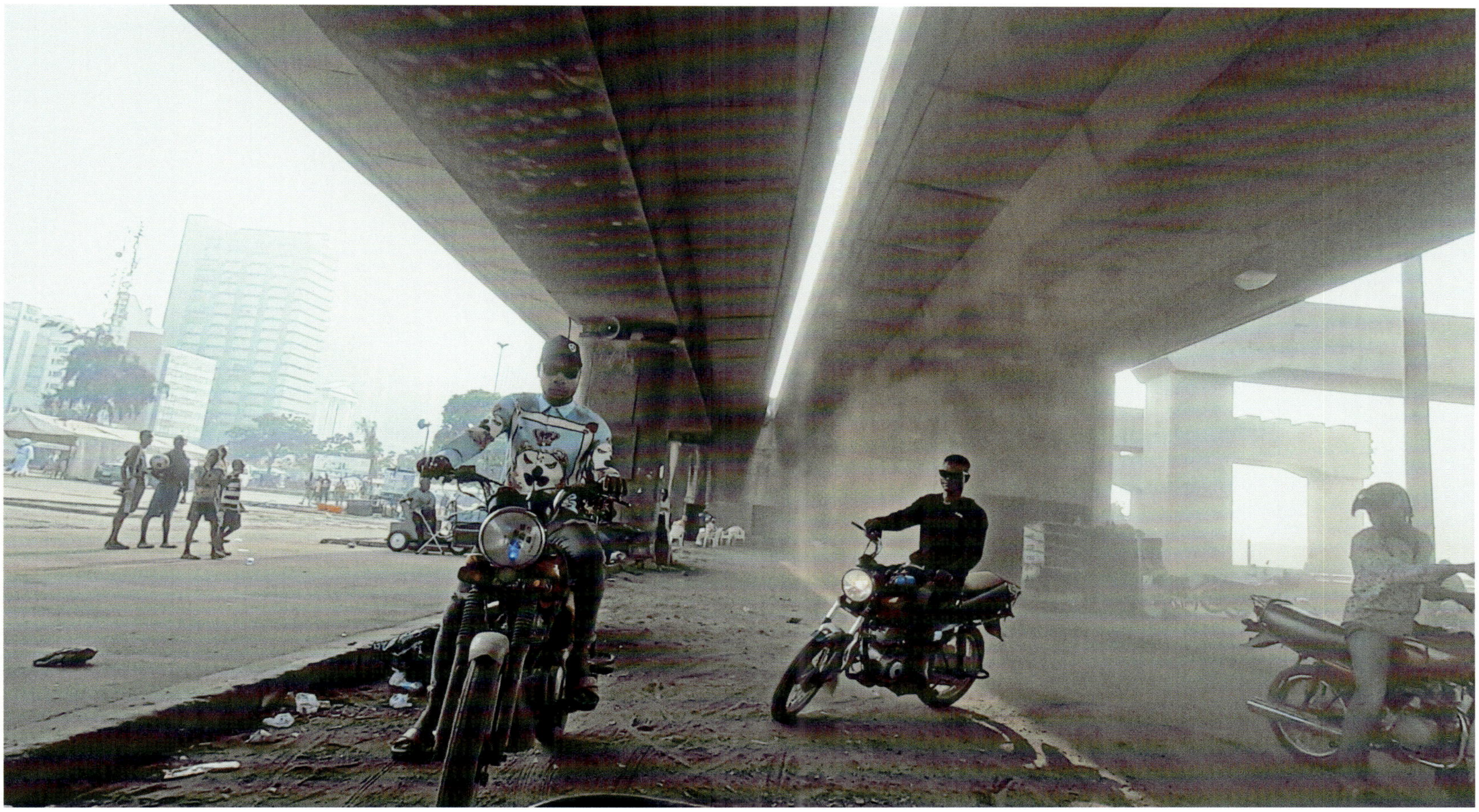

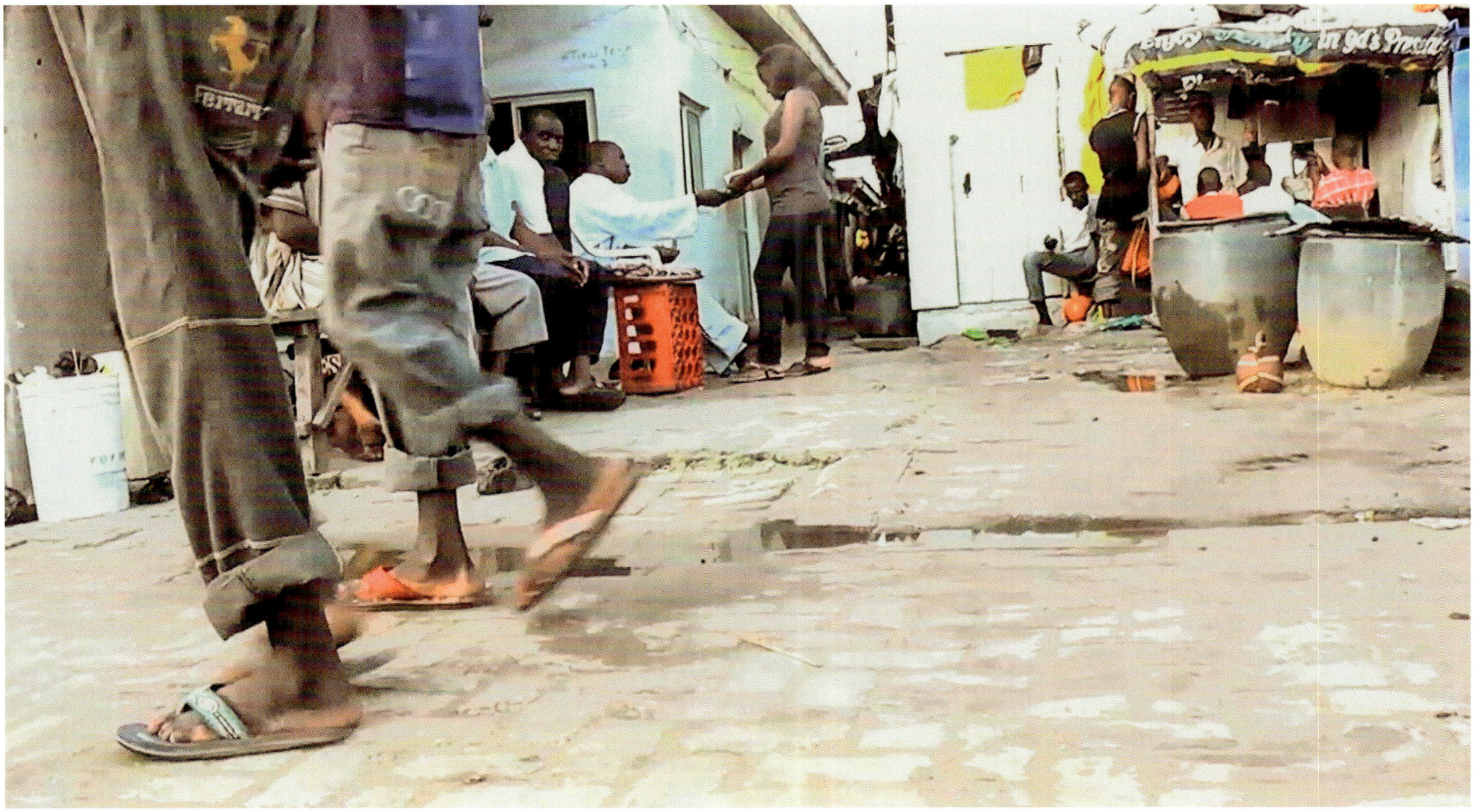

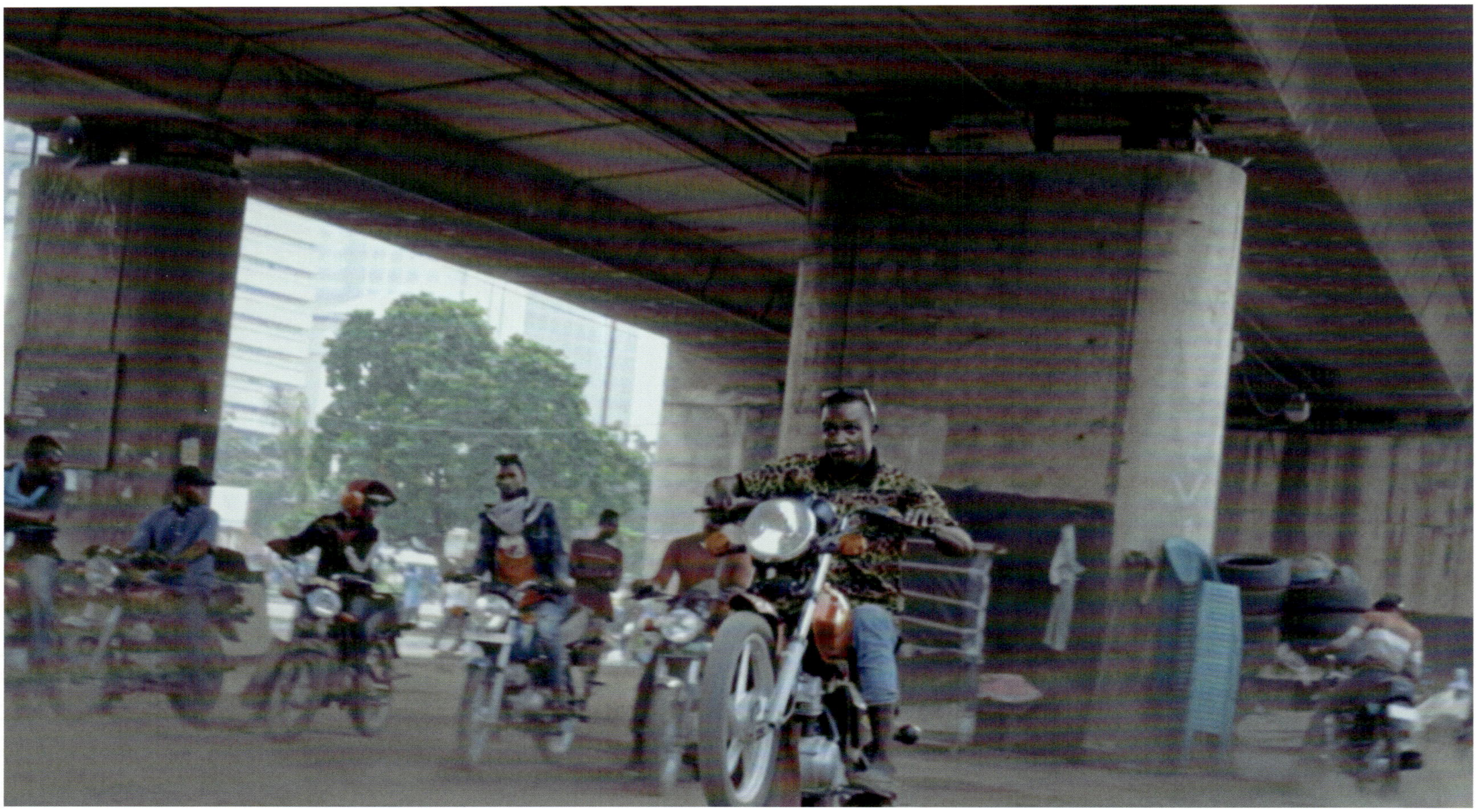

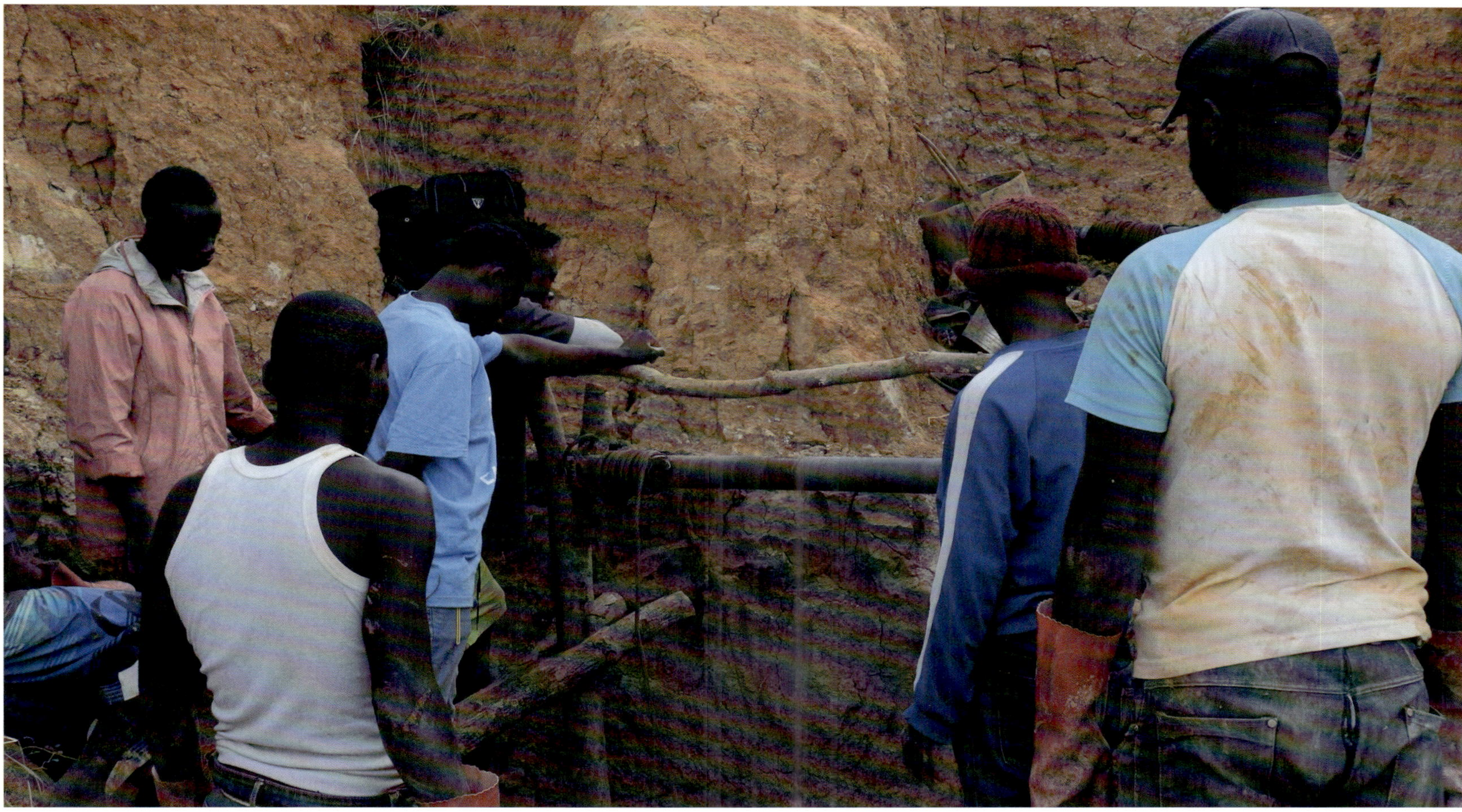

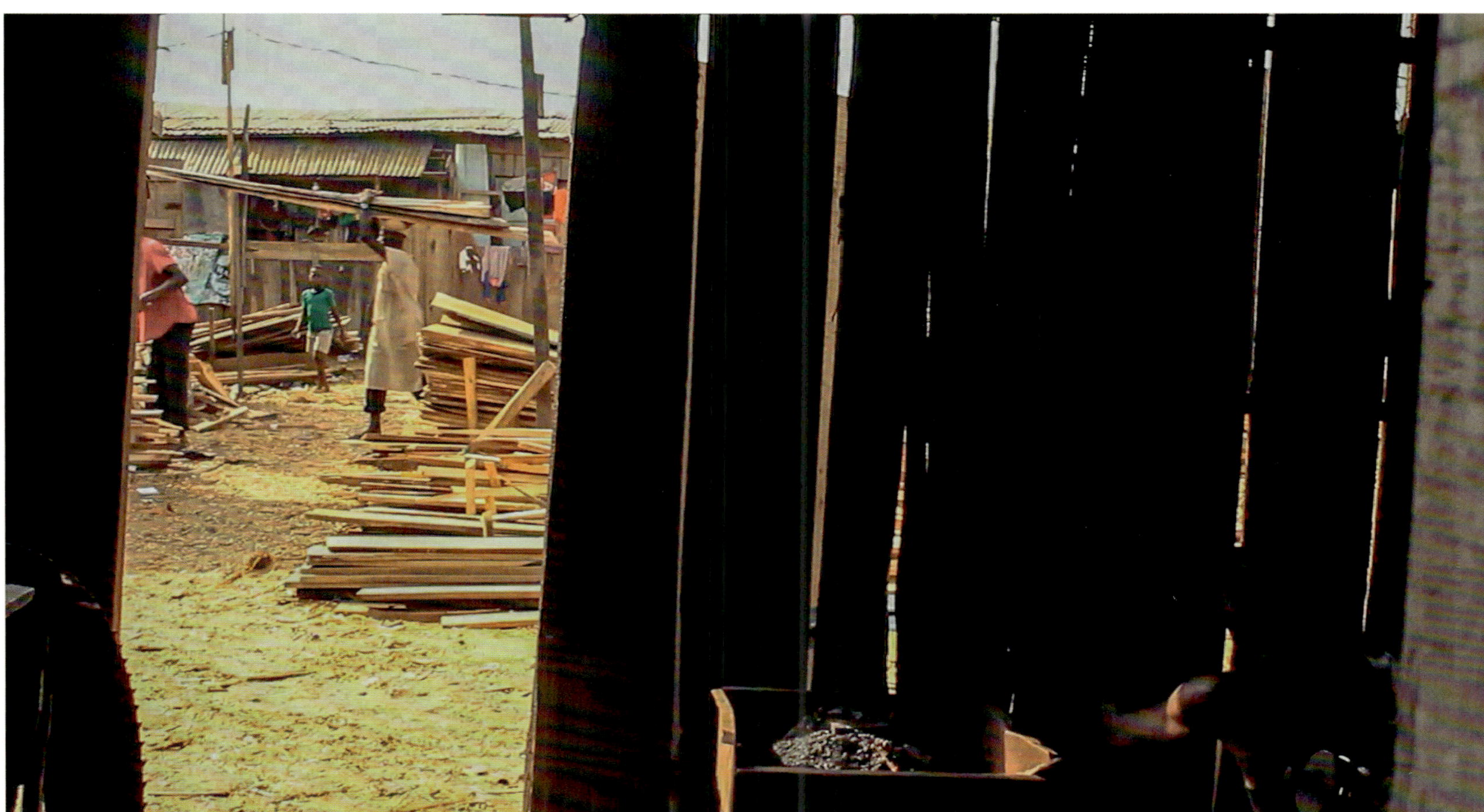

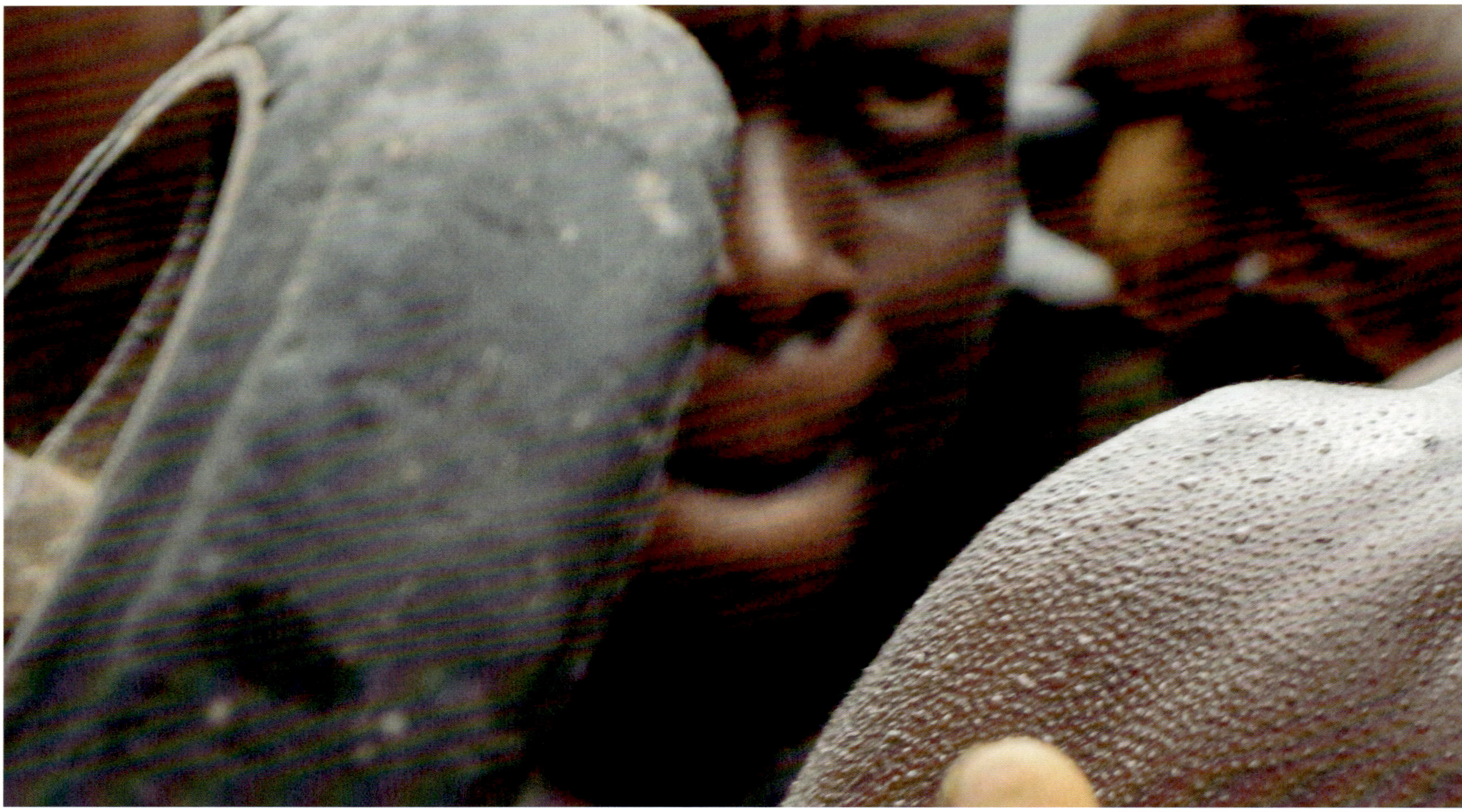

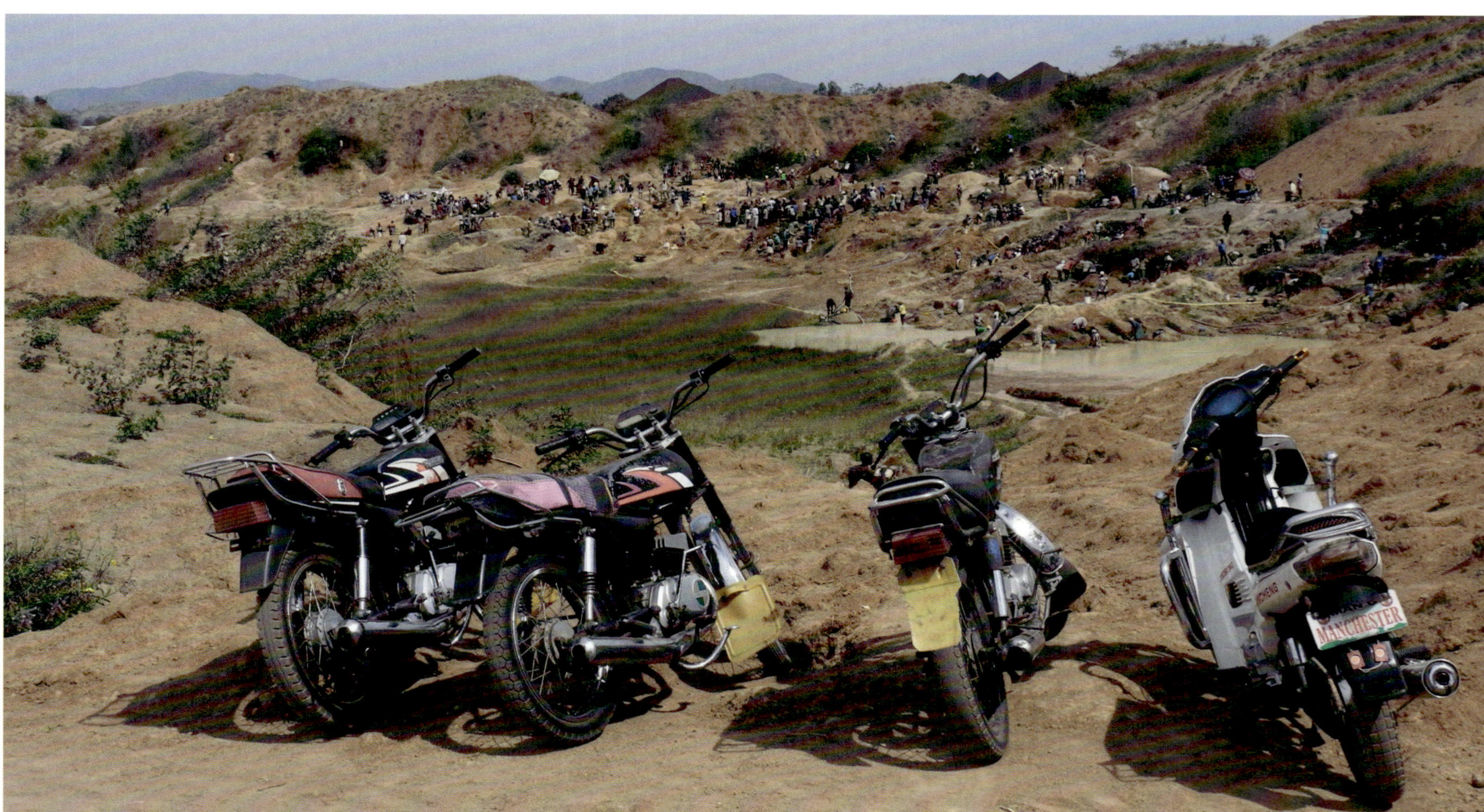
MANCHESTER

Muscle Memory: The Black Atlanticist Form of *MUSCLE*

Dr. Clive Chijioke Nwonka

The Black Atlantic, Paul Gilroy's foundational theory on Black modernity, refers to a Black identity and culture born not from disparate national cultures, but from a boundless, transcendent Black history and culture. It arises from an innate social and cultural knowledge that connects the Black diaspora across Africa, the Americas, Europe and the Caribbean. The Black Atlantic – as an intellectual intervention, a way of being, a concept and a framework of perception and interpretation – has been applied to a heterogeneous range of cultural experiences, processes, artworks and creative practices. What remains constant is Black culture as a composite of historic points of exchange. The legacies of slavery and movement across the Atlantic Ocean retain textualities that can be consistently identified within and across Black vernacular cultures. And in *MUSCLE* (2025) – Karimah Ashadu's essayistic film concerned with Nigerian masculinity, the debris of postcoloniality, Lagos as a city that opens up to the Atlantic and the visuality of Black skin – we again find the Black Atlanticist form.

While marginal life in Nigeria is a recurring thematic interest for the filmmaker, it is in *Machine Boys* (2024), another examination of the contours of identity, nationhood and masculinity, where *MUSCLE* finds its most reliable analogue within Ashadu's oeuvre. Exploring the human textures of *okada*, Lagos's informal and outlawed motorcycle taxi industry, the film is a documentation of an impoverished underclass and the hazards involved in casual labour deemed outcast by the government. *Machine Boys* opens to a medium close-up of heads, helmets and eyes, and the revving of bike engines. Then it goes on to depict *okada* as a muscular Black masculine practice through a number of narrative means and audiovisual strategies, but also through the capturing of subjective Nigerian masculine identities. For some of the riders, *okada* is their sole means of survival, while others simply see it as a means of funding higher education.

But despite these important heterogeneities, the men are all bound and unified by a certain fugitivity, congregating as they do at the city's edges and underpasses. Their involvement is the outcome of the collective experience of marooned Black identities made so by economic precarity, the actions of the police and a diurnal and everyday system of bribery, all of which mark *okada* as a decidedly edge economy.

Here I rely on a definition drawn from the discipline of urban sociology, specifically the concept of edge economies as advanced by Suzanne Hall. Hall discusses peripheral and denigrated street vendors, informal traders and hustlers, often operating at the boundaries of legality, and the centrality of such trades to the formation of street existences within the divided metropolitan cities that become rendered as the urban margins. The sense of *okada* as an edge economy is aestheticised by Ashadu's dramatic cutting across the scene to capture its kinetic energy, made all the more impactful when framed within the confined space of Lagos's underpasses, all affirming *okada* as an outcast economic activity of street livelihood. However, in her depiction of the riders in a congregational space dislocated (albeit temporarily) from the city's mainstream economic energy, the expressions here are decidedly *non*-street. In other words, we witness the *okada* drivers in their collective, but subterranean and invisible, existence.

The camera focuses in on a Black fist gripping and revving motorbike handlebars, and from among the collective of riders in motion we locate the film's main protagonist. He laments a system of habitual confrontations and agitations: "Area boys harass us. The police harass us. My mind is only at peace when I'm lying down. We are always restless." A multitude of bidirectionalities are in operation throughout. As we observe the bike handles as held by the rider, framed by a close-up, the fist is distressed, its lacerations and scarring narrating a literal history of austerity and struggle, but equally one of uninterrupted mobility and transit. *Okada* drivers are compelled to assert a defensive posture – a stance that may appear confrontational and dominating, but one that is born from social marginality and physical jeopardy.

The film's characterisation of *okada* as a necessary danger is visually corroborated at the point where it relocates its story to the Lagos roads and highways. We, just as the riders, are now confronted with the inevitability of death via fatal police pursuit, a circumstance itself motivated by the reality of Nigeria's economic and social situation as the centripetal force propelling these men from the margins into the centre. Such vicissitudes are encoded in the narrator's complaint that "a lack of industry makes us do *okada*." *Okada* riders are also required to navigate the hazards of Nigeria's rainy season, which features as a recurring and potent antagonist just as much as law and order (either formal or, in many cases, informal). As the camera tracks the riders in transit through the rain, a heightened sense of jeopardy and imminent capture emanates from the screen and produces a haptic affect upon the audience.

This bidirectionality (as a visual and narrative project) is further evidenced in the film's final scene. Despite the *okada* drivers being previously framed in a much more direct and overt mode, they now maintain a conspicuousness thanks to their uniform sunglasses. The protagonist aggressively growls directly at the screen, a display of gnashing teeth that may appear to satisfy a pathology of Black male menace. But such a demonstration of rage should be understood not as a contradiction, a departure from the fugitive human status we witnessed moments before, but rather as one facet of a human and social condition, as multi-constitutional. It is a demonstration of aggression that only temporarily betrays the vulnerability that structures the riders' daily existence, the expression of a suppressed and now-combusting pressure created by *okada*, the police and the city of Lagos.

MUSCLE, as *Machine Boys*' thematic progenitor, equally depicts Black masculine identities in a state of contradiction, paradox and multiplicity, replacing *okada* with bodybuilding. In this way, such a practice can also be interpreted primarily as a defensive posture. Ashadu perennially captures the quotidian experiences and forms of labour that structure Lagosian normality, and here, weightlifting is conceived as a simple variant of such Lagosian labour, in that it can also be a process of self-actualisation. The backdrop is in this case a number of determinants that lie outside of the film's narrative and visual frame but are nevertheless negotiated as part and parcel of socioeconomic realities in the slums.

Despite the film's short duration, we are given a clear sense of repetitiveness. Bodybuilding is presented as a daily experience, and the film succeeds in its aestheticising of mundanity as a simple variant of marginal existence and subjugation, although it is marked aesthetically by a certain departure, and is situated in a much more historical context of masculinity, Black men and racism. *MUSCLE*'s thematic interest in the relationship between Nigerian hypermasculinity and peripheral labour as a postcolonial condition asks us to consider the social histories that underpin the men's recourse to a patriarchal orthodoxy that is not seen or referenced, but is very present, with the Black hauntological experience of violent white othering also beyond the film's frame but likewise alive and perceptible. It directs a specific audience, one of Black cultural knowledge and memory, toward the legacies of colonial possession and the persistent traumas of transatlantic slavery and ultra-violence.

While the branding and mutilating of Black people was a brutality meted out to both men and women, there is a specific textual haptic affect in recalling the practice of human castration as the primary modality of control, rebuke and punishment directed at Black men during Jim Crow, a procedure that would result in the deaths of many Black men across the southern United States. Castration was directly related to mythic ideas of an inescapable Black male hypersexuality *as* hypermasculinity, one that would propel the punishment of an act, either alleged or imagined, which white supremacy regarded as the ultimate racial transgression: romantic desire and inference both toward and between white females.

The castration of Black males was therefore practiced to attend to white masculine anxiety toward Black male identity, and the more fundamental purpose of castration, namely to demasculinise Black men, is an epistemic residue of slavery that casts a hauntological spectre over Black life across global contexts and temporalities. It reoccurs as the claimed social and psychological impotence of Black men, through which they are consigned to inextricable racial, economic and social vicissitudes across geographies. Black men remain afflicted by a set of historical emasculating technologies that are met with the thrust of *re*-masculation across the Black Atlantic, inducing in Nigeria, that manifests, among so many other things, in Black women being subjected to patriarchal domestic and social existences. As we see in *MUSCLE*, weightlifting as a practice of strengthening bodily construction for such men in Lagos's modern society is a protracted process of *re*-masculinisation, and at its core, self-esteem building and the accrual of symbolic, domestic and social power though physical power. The film asks us to understand the culture of *MUSCLE* building as a hauntological form of hypermasculinity in its most physical and patriarchal manifestation.

MUSCLE's multilayered thematics encourage a reading of the film as governed by three planes of audiovisual interpretation. My reading of the film in such a way is concerned not with the appreciation of such. These planes are hardly independent, but rather overlap and interweave as part of a specific aesthetic strategy. First, we find a preoccupation with the image of collective Black men operating within an edge existence not simply through images of muscle, but also through imagery of human sweat, which functions as an independent form of narration, and as a result, contributes to a more capacious interpretive surface. Visually, Ashadu's aestheticisation of sweat produces a refractive quality upon Black skin – here, its layering over Black muscle works to a dramatic optical effect of masculine domination. We find, however, that in the context of Ashadu's general interest in Black men and labour practices in Nigeria, *MUSCLE* is

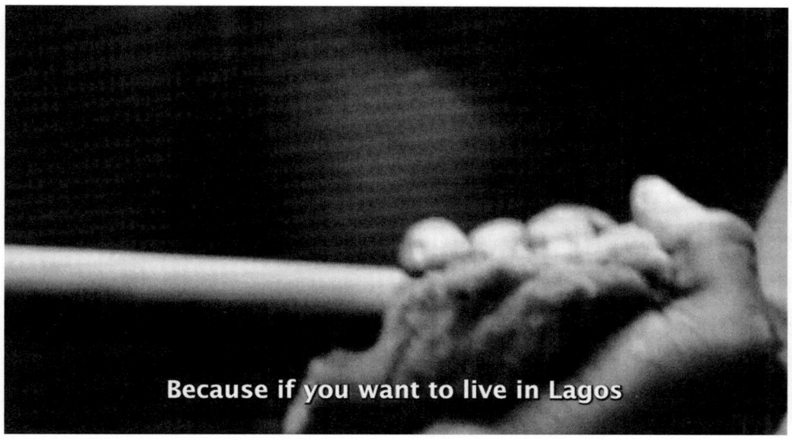

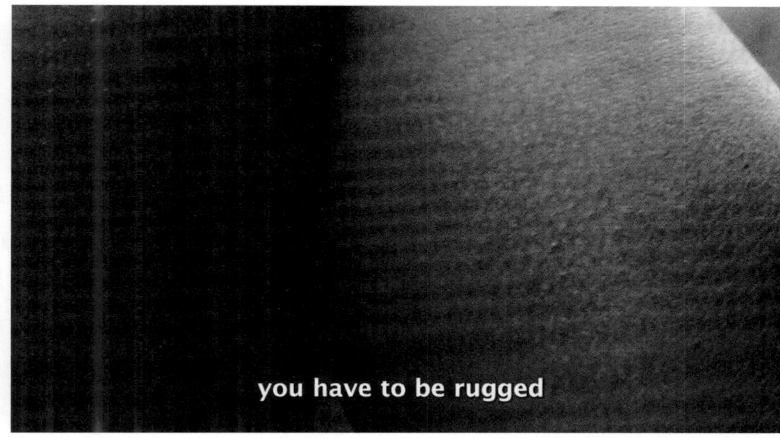

equally marked by a certain bidirectionality. *MUSCLE* visualises the filmic function of sweat as a bodily response to physical exhaustion, expenditure and labour that illuminates the sharpness and density of the bodybuilders. *MUSCLE* indeed uses sweat as an aesthetic device to accentuate the subject's muscle definition. This being so, and considering the film's attempts to weave the textures of Black intergenerational memory, trauma and injustice to the question of labour as *MUSCLE*'s audiovisual and contextual manifesto, sweat in the film reconfigures both the denotative and connotative meaning of Black muscle as a Black pictorial experience. The film lexicalises the image of Black perspiration as an index of not just physical exertion, but also mental strain, stress and unease. In doing so, it confronts us with anti-Black racism and racialisation, recalling an intergenerational experience of socially induced pressure. Weightlifting is literalised as physical development, as a pathway toward self-determination, but is a more substantive outcome of Black struggle, a struggle to be identified and recalled across and within Black diasporic cultural memory.

MUSCLE's affect as a filmic Black diasporic encounter is also made meaningful through a specific audio register. Throughout, the scenes are continuously punctuated by the sound of clanging metal as the bodybuilders work out in the searing Nigerian heat. The coming together of weights produces a dramatic sound effect, a repetitive but non-uniform intonation of sorts that performs as the diegetic soundtrack to the history and present of Black contestation, combat and conflict. As the bodybuilder declares, "If you want to live in Lagos, you have to be rugged." Such a declaration of the need for human durability suggests that his daily activities can be understood not simply as a culture of weightlifting, but as a compelled and essential labour of survival. As a result, the film possesses a visceral and haptic affect that renders the sound of clashing metal much more than a diegetic backdrop, or even simply a metaphor. It asserts an audial continuity with the very physical bondages of transatlantic slavery that unify Black cultural histories of the regions of the Black Atlantic.

There is a final plane of audiovisual interpretation that, somewhat paradoxically, is identified not through a single aesthetic feature, but via a more phenomenological engagement with the film. I am reluctant to particularise this phenomenology as germane only to *MUSCLE*, as it can be observed across all of Ashadu's film practice, which as a broader oeuvre explores the contours of West African labour practices, socio-spatial formations, identifications and self-identifications, affirmations and crises of masculinity and, crucially, racial systems of signification. It is this particular context to the consumption of *MUSCLE* – a text situated within an inescapable framework of representation – that necessitates an understanding of the cinematic screen, particularly when concerned with Black identities, as constituted by racial and gendered divisions of looking. Black audiences will bring expectations to the screen that differ from white normative expectations, and will be the recipients of different filmic affects, a spectatorial partition further fragmented by gender. The work's pictorial focus on Black masculinity opens us to something about Black womanhood. Such a position requires an interest in how Ashadu's films are circulated and consumed outside of the depicted geographies. In turn, my reading of the film as accommodated within the expansive cultural projects of the Black Atlantic draws from my contention that Black filmic visuality and moving images possess a limited meaning or materiality *prior* to their being processed by their primary (white) audience. I am thinking of the range of irresolvable cultural, political, social and industrial factors imbricated in the struggle over their ownership and propriety that are energised in the cultural process of the film becoming prefixed as Black film, as Black representative and of Black social value.

For the Black diaspora – be this located in the backyards of Lagos, or among the Black people dispersed across the geographies that unify the Black Atlantic – the film's depictions of both the possession and the swelling of Black muscle carries with it a multiplicity of meanings and elicitations. I draw our attention back to the bidirectional characterisation of *okada*'s Nigerian masculinity as one of external power and internal fugitivity, a state that I defined above as a posture of defense. This is highly valuable in both my interpretation of *MUSCLE* as having a Black Atlanticist aesthetic, and what I read as the film's consonance between muscle and Black identity, for muscle is both a physical, bodily construction of strength and power and a social pseudonym, a fiction, a characterisation. I want to suggest that the film's aestheticisation of muscle, when considered through a number of provenances, is also sociologically, psychologically and systemically *implied*. Muscle, when situated within the historic categories of race, is also an imaginary, an external construction, something assumed, an illusion and an illumination. For muscle, as a racial synonym, has and continues to be inscribed onto the Black male body as an incessant form of social hauntology.

Muscle, as a reliable derivation and inference of physical strength, is inculcated within ossified white optics, where it (as physical strength, rather than alternately contracting and relaxing fibrous tissue) is made indissociable from the identification of blackness and the Black physical form, even where Black people are devoid of the literal density of such human tissue. This points to the permanency of scientific racism at the basis of the justification for subjecting the heterogeneous identities of the Black Atlantic to an undifferentiated racialisation – where, for instance, Black children are unjustly and prematurely reclassified as adults and targeted for

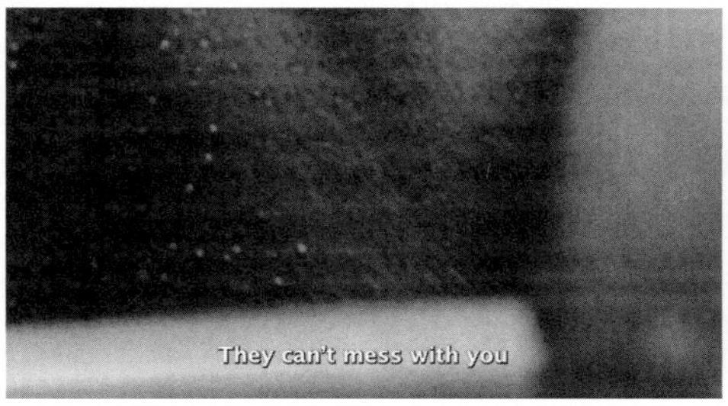

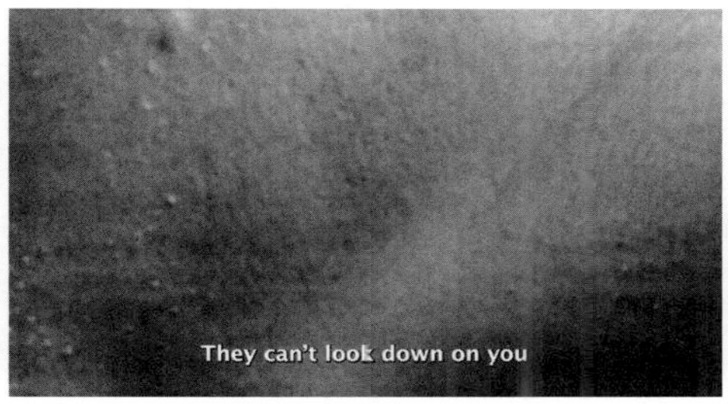

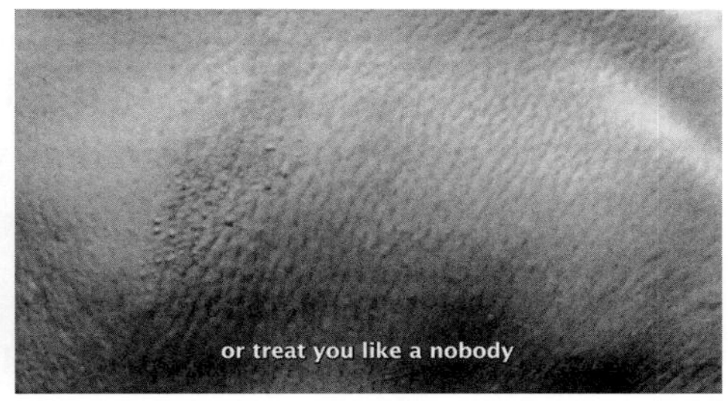

violent and mortal policing; where Black men and women are consigned to fatal enslaved and subjugated labour and incarceration systems, or generally relegated to the status of the infrahuman through white idealisations of a genetic Black physical capability and, as its inevitable binary, Black mental and emotional incapability; and where Black men are conceived as animalistic and savage in nature, as a deviant threat, as discorded beings. *MUSCLE* insists upon the reversal of the looking systems so inscribed within the white normative frame, where Black men's fates and freedoms are predetermined by the imaginary possession of muscle as a powerful, atemporal signifier of malevolent blackness.

MUSCLE's ability to unify these three interpretive planes, and further affirming its Black Atlantic form, lies in how it captures the bodybuilder's own competing sense of identity, social perceptions and self-perceptions. As the film's narrator asserts in describing his purpose for the building of muscle, "They can't mess with you, or look down on you, or treat you like a nobody." Just who or what is being referred to in this comment, which can be understood as both a lament and a statement of intent, is never specified, and in many ways is immaterial. It is the resistant command of modernity to construct the real and imagined 'veils', the social and psychological barriers, dividing the men from mainstream society that becomes their primary agitator, and positions the men in a state of mental and spatial subjugation and fugitivity that only accumulates and ossifies over time.

I want to pay attention to the film's physical arranging of Black men, one that indeed performs as a visual schema. For the vast majority of the film, the bodybuilders are framed in profile, and this directs our focus toward their muscle, their dynamic motions; as a result, they remain bound in inconspicuousness. We rarely see the faces of our filmic subjects, which, Ashadu is keen to remind us, are neither protagonists nor antagonists. The film eschews the positioning of the bodybuilders, at least dialectically, as malevolent, a circumventing of the casual binaries that define the conventions of a linear narrative. It is precisely as a result of Ashadu's approach, utilising as it does both a visual and a narrational schema of nonlinearity, that we are purposefully denied visual access to the full panoply of Black humanness that would be achieved by the full framing of the Black body.

I identify a didactic purpose for the film: to mirror the optic of racism from the vantage point of white normativity, where proximal confrontation with the physicality of Black male skin evokes a reductive and instantaneous fear of the unknown – one of the central tenets of anti-blackness as a global technology. On the rare occasions when we are given access to the facial features of the bodybuilders, these again are rarely fully formed faces but rather vignettes obscured by baseball caps, or close-ups of the textures of the physical facts of Black skin, for instance sweat or Afro-textured hair. Eventually, the film does offer a medium close-up of one of the bodybuilders, revealing not just bodybuilding but the building of the *Black* male body, in full motion. Momentarily isolated visually in frame, he is shown from the shoulder up, side on, as he performs arm curls.

The voice-over narration provides a greater sense of Black Atlanticism, and renders the screen as highly penetrable. The narrator asserts, "They're afraid of the guy with the big body [. . .] We don't know what he can do, we don't know what he has in mind." The scene's bidirectionality is located in how the men exhibit a reversed fear toward society; in a sense, the bodybuilding is propelled by a fear of *being* feared by another. Phenomenologically, this points to the dual perceptions of self that occupy the bodybuilders' minds, an internal contestation in navigating one's own identity and the identity ascribed to them by the dominant society. I am identifying the outcome of the protracted process of double consciousness that has spirited their desire to accrue an unassimilable fearfulness to the level of a collective manifesto. We see how muscle building possesses a broader ambition for the citizens, more a social than a physical purpose.

I use the term 'double consciousness' in a capacious manner to accommodate the heterogeneous interpretations of W. E. B. Du Bois's foundational concept that have accrued across different generations, social

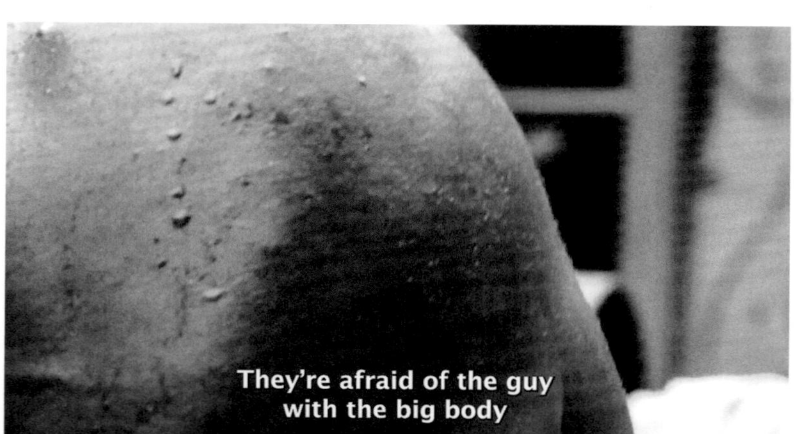

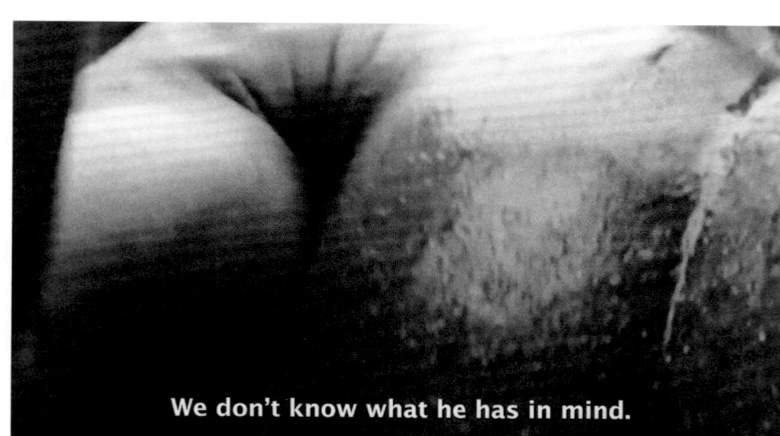

conditions and intellectual cultures and paradigms. At its most rudimentary application, double consciousness is the internalisation by Black men of the dominant structures of racial ordering and othering – the very psychological position of white normativity that continues to instruct Black modes of existence. Such a condition as identified in *MUSCLE*, and reminding ourselves of the film's Black diasporic intentions, has a permeation beyond the immediate context of the work's framing of the makeshift gyms of Lagos. It refers to a more historic, current and planetary framework through which the presence of Black male identity is subject to violent colonial pursual. Here, Black men are compelled to acquiesce to the visual allure of the unknowable and unassimilable Black male body, upon which a set of reviving racial imaginaries can be conferred, and which positions *MUSCLE* within the visual cultures of the Black Atlantic. Resultingly, once shorn of all the sensory elements, what remains latent across the film's surface is a visual and visceral encounter with the most historic, contemporary and racially focused interpretations of Black muscle: as an external defensive posture, and an internal imposition.

P. 117, 119–20: Karimah Ashadu, stills from *MUSCLE*, 2025. See pages 94–95.

Discipline of Desire

A Conversation with Karimah Ashadu, Myriam Ben Salah, Martin Clark and Gina Buenfeld-Murley, Moderated by Leonardo Bigazzi

Leonardo Bigazzi

I would like to start with how Lagos – and Nigeria more broadly – often serves as a point of departure in your work. You were born in London, but grew up in Lagos until the age of ten, then moved back to the UK. You now live in Hamburg, Germany. How does this personal geography intertwine with the narratives in your work?

Karimah Ashadu

Those years in Nigeria were so formative. They instilled a Nigerian-ness in me, and a great sense of pride as well, which was tested when I moved back to the UK in my youth and suddenly realised that there was something 'Other' about me. I had to quickly learn 'Britishness', and relocate not only my physical being, but my thinking and my sensibility as well. Nowadays, in the UK, I don't feel 'Other'. But that 'Otherness' stayed with me. It became acutely evident again when I moved to Germany, whose cultural heritage, as I learned, has little reconciled with its colonial past.

Martin Clark

How do you think that informs your practice? Are there specific works that address this?

Karimah Ashadu

I think that my discomfort in Germany is something I probed and continue to probe, and my films are, to an extent, self-portraits. With *Brown Goods* (2020), I tried to understand how I could contribute to that society in any way that felt worthy, as a Black and African woman. When I met Emeka, the film's protagonist, and saw his work in the export of second-hand electrical goods to Africa, and that he was doing it with such pride, that struck a chord in me. With every film I make, I'm trying to understand where I fit in, either in the European landscape where I live now, or in the grander scheme of things. I'm also trying to understand my relationship with Nigeria, and the broader socio-political and economic structures that shape it. I'm interested in how history unfolded to bring us here – how colonialism imposed borders, collapsed tribes into one nation and gave us a name that distanced us from our origins.

Leonardo Bigazzi

I find that much of your work renegotiates the idea of distance – for example, the distance between you, your protagonists and the work's (often Western, white) audience. I'm curious to discuss how distance and the perspective you hold by being embedded in the realities you portray – such as the slums in Lagos – shapes your practice and the work you create. Class difference plays a significant role in the Nigerian context, but you also bring the experience and knowledge of observing these dynamics from Europe.

Karimah Ashadu

It's a bit complicated to answer, and I'm thinking of an answer visually. In *Makoko Sawmill* (2015), for instance, the mechanisms I employ make proximity tangible. In later works, the breaking of the fourth wall, where subjects confront the viewer directly, creates a dialogue around proximity. Proximity, though, is never only physical; it is also structured by class. The act of bringing these communities into view inevitably exposes the economic and social dynamics between subject, filmmaker and audience. At the same time, I'm aware of my own distance as a filmmaker. Once the film is completed, I leave, and that can mark the end of my connection with those I've worked with. So I recognise the complexity of these relationships. The work is at once deeply personal, yet also marked by a certain detachment.

Gina Buenfeld-Murley

I've been thinking about your early experiments with the camera, the rudimentary adaptations you made to the technology. It brought to mind Jean Rouch and his idea of direct cinema, those experiments with the technology to make it more portable, attempting to get as close as possible to the subject. This feels especially relevant in the new film *MUSCLE* (2025) that we commissioned for this exhibition, which has quite an extreme proximity to the body. But what you just described diverges from Rouch's primary motivation of a kind of cinematic realism that allows the camera to be as objective as possible, without the bias of the director. You are deliberately acknowledging your authorship, the perspective you bring, and this comes through in the range of approaches to the camera frame you've used, from the travelling shot in *Cowboy* (2022) to the panning shot in *Makoko Sawmill*. With each of these approaches to the camera there comes a sense, for the viewer, of a relationship to the subject, and an intention toward what is revealed, whether that's up close and intimate, or more distant, and perhaps imposing.

Karimah Ashadu

When I made my earlier works, I had started returning to Nigeria after having been in the UK for a long time. I was trying to figure out and understand the many things that had changed. So these mechanisms were a way to put something in front of myself while trying to figure out not only where I fit into this new landscape, but also what was going on around me. Over the length of my practice, that 'figuring out' has been reflected in my personal life. Many things have also changed in my life, and with the person I identify as being now. So that 'up close and personal' that you see in *MUSCLE* makes a lot of sense. There's been a long journey, quite difficult and often painful, to arrive at a sense of self. *MUSCLE* is entirely intimate; you're confronted with Black skin so close-up that it looks completely abstract. You're not quite sure at times what you're seeing, but how close would you get to Black skin like that?

Myriam Ben Salah

That abstraction you mention feels also intentionally protective. What role does opacity or misrecognition play in your work?

Karimah Ashadu

It is a form of care. It creates space for the possibility that something doesn't have to be fully known in order to be felt. When I crop the frame tightly or allow the image to drift out of focus, it's not necessarily about withholding, but about protecting the subject's right to complexity. Historically, Black and African bodies have been overexposed and exploited. So there's something radical, and also compassionate, about allowing a subject to evoke the very mystery it holds.

Myriam Ben Salah

Many of your works are set in geographies marked by colonial afterlives – Jos Plateau, Makoko, Billstraße in Hamburg. How do you navigate these places as both insider and observer? What's your compass in that in-between space?

Karimah Ashadu

My compass is curiosity, and a deep awareness of how colonial and imperial histories continue to shape the present. I'm drawn to places where those legacies are a tangible echo in the everyday. I was drawn to Jos because of tin mining and how British rule transformed the landscape for industrial gain. The remnants of extraction are still visible and continue to impact daily life in the region. In Makoko, I encounter a different kind of survival, a community built largely by migrants from neighbouring countries. Its precariousness reflects the resilience of a marginal existence. In Hamburg, Billstraße reveals another postcolonial dimension – a corridor of labour, commerce and racial tension. Migrants, particularly those of African descent, gather there, often working for store owners from other migrant communities in conditions that reflect broader hierarchies of value and visibility.

I navigate these spaces as a Nigerian woman, shaped by the country of my upbringing, carrying a British passport and now living and working in Germany. This layered position allows me to move with both intimacy and critical distance. The places I encounter are active sites of historical and socioeconomic entanglement – spaces through which I trace the residues of the past in order to understand how they relate to the present. The work becomes a way to hold these complexities and to understand my position in it all.

Leonardo Bigazzi

Nigerian society is deeply rooted in patriarchal structures, and your work often centres on male communities operating in physically demanding environments. As a female artist, how challenging is it to access and engage with these spaces? And what strategies do you use to build trust and establish a dialogue with your subjects?

Karimah Ashadu

Fundamentally the only reason I might think about my gender in a particular circumstance is because people remind me of it. Of course it's not always as easy as I'm making it seem; a lot of groundwork goes into it. I'll have an idea and share it with my production team, and my fixer might go and start talking to people on a very basic level. And then I'll get to meet them, and spend time with them, and it just goes from there.

With a work like *Plateau* (2021–22), I started by reading about communities of undocumented tin miners working in the Jos Plateau. I came across some academic papers, and then I went down a rabbit hole and started making some inquiries.

Martin Clark

I'm curious why you seem to be drawn again and again to very male spaces, whether the street abattoir of *King of Boys (Abattoir of Makoko)* (2015), the Makoko sawmill in the work of that title, the motorbike taxis in *Machine Boys* (2024), the miners in *Plateau*, and now the bodybuilders for the new film, *MUSCLE*. It can't be a coincidence that you are going, again and again, into such macho spaces.

Karimah Ashadu

It's personal. As a child, I knew very early on that I didn't think the same way as other children. Part of it was a kind of inner authority, which was challenged by my father, always trying to tell me what to do and how to move in the world as a woman. Restrictions came with how I was supposed to live my life. I understood that he's my father, but how does a man get to tell me what to do, and how to be, just because of my gender? I challenged him in a lot of ways – we had that kind of relationship – but I also learned that it wasn't entirely safe for me to be myself, and therefore I had to retreat, and that meant that I isolated myself a lot. Then I discovered films, and that was my safe place. Nigerian society is entirely patriarchal. There is a way according to which you should conduct yourself in order to be respected and taken seriously, even today. It's absurd, and hypocritical.

Gina Buenfeld-Murley

What I find so compelling about your work is that in many ways it's positioned as a counterpoint to dominant narratives around these issues. There's a well-established discourse of critique and a deconstruction of patriarchy, but your work approaches notions of masculinity with such tenderness. In *Machine Boys*, for example, the men are also labouring under those patriarchal values. At worst, for women, it can create a kind of sublimated misogyny, where you actually end up aligning with that value system. For both men and women, it can elicit a performance of masculine ideals or behaviours in order to be accepted and recognised in the culture.

Karimah Ashadu

I think the social performance of gender is a vulnerable dynamic. It's something that requires a lot of love and compassion, because that's how we change things. We need to question the traditionally gendered meanings of strength and weakness. Women are strong too, not only in what our bodies have to do if we choose to have children, but also in the social weight we have to carry. And through all of that, we keep on showing up to break those glass ceilings.

Myriam Ben Salah

It seems you think about masculinity not just as subject, but as material, posture or pressure point.

Karimah Ashadu

I am interested in how masculinity is navigated and worn, in its sociocultural construct, because the existence of a societal standard of masculinity invites its performance. Especially in contexts like *MUSCLE*, where strength becomes social capital, I'm compelled by the underlying framework that sustains the performance – the strain of repetition, the determination, the intimacy of training collectively toward the same goal and the unspoken codes of brotherhood and camaraderie. The work also reveals the tension in how the men carry themselves, the weight of expectation, the way that their particular performance of masculinity requires an audience to activate it, otherwise it's flaccid. There's a vulnerability beneath the toughness, a precarity beneath the image of masculinity as something fixed, and I'm interested in that slippage. Society hasn't really allowed men to be soft, or 'weak', so I'm interested in what that does, and how that repression is embodied.

Myriam Ben Salah

More specifically, what drew you to this ecology of performance and precarity in *MUSCLE*? The film seems to hover between bodily excess and structural lack – hypervisible muscles, minimal equipment, heat as atmosphere.

Karimah Ashadu

I was drawn to the tension – this vulnerable spectacle of strength shaped by scarcity. And scarcity not only in the material sense that the gym itself is improvised with rusted and unfinished equipment. The bodybuilders wear branded sportswear with logos of global athleticism, and these symbols of prestige and power place them within a capitalist structure they're striving to belong to, even as it exploits and excludes them. There's something performative about this too – how value is symbolised and worn, how power is assumed through appearance, even when the socioeconomic infrastructure is broken.

Myriam Ben Salah

MUSCLE has no single protagonist, no neat narrative arc. How did you envision its structure – if not through plot, then through sensation, accumulation, fatigue?

Karimah Ashadu

I like my films to feel open, in the sense that they're nonlinear and you don't have to watch them the whole way through – for me, there is no beginning, middle or end. In *MUSCLE*, the structure is repetition and rhythm. The work builds with cumulative intensity; it is layered and unfolds through sweat, breath, sets and reps. The bodybuilders are driven by desire, and that desire encourages discipline. The monotony of this physical attainment of strength, this performance that becomes a form of endurance, is for me where the beauty lies. An undulation where the body builds and wanes under duress, constantly edging exhaustion. The film mirrors this monotony and shapes it so that it morphs into something quite ambiguous – especially with its suggestive soundtrack of panting, heavy breathing and groans of exertion. It is shot with a lot of very tight close-ups, and positions the audience in such a way that they begin to feel embedded in the work.

Leonardo Bigazzi

Your work consistently returns to themes of labour survival and economic struggle, particularly in the West African context. But while your narratives often expose harsh realities around precarious working conditions and informal economies, or the quest for financial independence, your portrayal of the individual is never reduced to victimhood. Instead, your protagonists are marked with dignity, strength and an unwavering sense of self-determination. What drives your commitment to telling these stories in such a way, and how do you navigate the responsibility of representing them?

Karimah Ashadu

The story of the Black struggle has been told *for* us, and that's problematic. It's only recently that we have African and Black historians starting to grasp the implications of a history that made colonisers look like they did Africa a favour, and make the truth known. I'm thinking of a book I read recently, Max Siollun's *What the British Did to Nigeria* (2021), one of the first books told from the perspective of a West African person.

Don't get me wrong – I'm entirely proud to be also British – but a lot of ancestral knowledge has been wiped out and African history could not be taught, to the extent that some Nigerian people think that the dominant (albeit misrepresented) history is correct. That is mind-blowing to me. Although things have been dire, we are entirely empowered, and resilient. No matter what you do to us, we'll not only to survive, but thrive. So my commitment, even though I'm not an activist, comes from the ownership of this trauma, and from shifting the narrative therein.

Myriam Ben Salah

I would like to expand upon Leonardo's question. Much of what we call contemporary art still carries the burden of explanation – especially for artists working in or from the Global South. How do you navigate that demand to be 'legible' to certain audiences?

Karimah Ashadu

I'm not making work to explain or justify who we are. For too long, Black and African cultures have been appropriated without context or credit. My intention is to tell stories from within – to affirm what's already ours. The Global North was built in large part through extraction from the Global South. In Nigeria's case, the British Empire grew rich from what it took. My work won't resonate with every viewer, and that's okay.

Martin Clark

What led you to begin working with the moving image? I know you studied art, as well as art history and spatial design, and you worked for a while in an architectural office.

Karimah Ashadu

I'm a painter; I started from that place. But it soon became clear that it was quite easy for me, and I suppose I always like to feel challenged. Having spent my youth watching films so much, I guess I was thinking filmically without even realising it. At the beginning, I was very interested in performance painting, in artists like Carolee Schneemann, Janine Antoni or even Hannah Wilke, who would put things on her body and so on. But I didn't want to be a performance painter, because there was something about the two that just wouldn't fit for me. I tried picking up a camera and performing for the camera, but that didn't feel quite right, either.

When I did my degree in spatial design at Chelsea College of Arts in London, I started thinking spatially. I would attach a camera to my body, perform in the space and see what I could discover. The camera was an extension of my body. And then when I started putting the camera in mechanisms, taking away that sense of control, not knowing what it was capturing, that was exciting for me. The outcome wasn't entirely as I had imagined it would look, and that sense of surprise and discovery was very refreshing for me, and something that at the time painting couldn't offer.

Myriam Ben Salah

Do you think of the camera as an agent? A collaborator? A witness? Or something more bodily, like a pulse? What's your relationship to control in the filmmaking process?

Karimah Ashadu

The camera shifts between roles, initiating, listening and responding. In *Plateau*, it has corporeal qualities and moves in a disembodied way, reflecting the displacement of the landscape and its people, while in *King of Boys* it alerts the viewer to my presence as a filmmaker. In *MUSCLE*, it's nearly still, or it moves softly, like breath on skin. In my early works, the choice to relinquish control was also a way to resist certain cinematic conventions. There's a freedom in that, but also rigour. Because letting go is about trusting the process, the camera and the idea. My practice is an investigation, and the camera teaches me something through each work.

Martin Clark

This makes me think about structuralist filmmakers like Tony Conrad, Stan Brakhage, Bruce Conner, Michael Snow or Hollis Frampton, who (albeit in very different ways) foregrounded the physicality of the camera, the materiality of the medium and its relationship to our own bodies and subjectivities. In your own work, there's the production of the film as a kind of moment of performance, and, as we've discussed, the camera itself is a central and very active element in the way you deploy it. But then there's the subsequent installation of the work, and the opportunity to stage a second encounter for the audience. Can you say a little bit about how you think of the work being spatialised and installed?

Karimah Ashadu

I want to create an environment for the audience to engage with the work, to feel held in its container. For instance, in *Machine Boys*, there's a moment where headlights flash purple, and I thought it would be amazing if even for a second the whole space was a synchronisation of that purple. That's why I chose that colour for the room where it was presented at the Venice Biennale in 2024. Sculptures also function as extension of the film. In Venice, *Wreath* (2024) – a brass bas-relief of interwoven tyres – invited the audience into the space to discover the film. Upon watching *Machine Boys*, they realised that the sculpture is a motif that emerges from the moving-image work.

Gina Buenfeld-Murley

In *King of Boys*, the chromatic treatment in parts of the film with a red filter felt, to me, intoxicating. It drew me into the work's atmosphere while creating some distance where things got quite graphic and hard to watch. It's interesting to hear how that extends into your choreography of the physical space that holds the work. Could you talk about how you made *King of Boys*?

Karimah Ashadu

When I had the idea for it – I'm so grateful for instinct! – I was riding my bicycle in Amsterdam past this plastic red container, and I decided to take it to my studio. There was a side of me that wondered what was I supposed to do with it, but I grabbed it anyway, and then I thought it would be interesting to place my camera in it, but not have it static, because I wanted it to be clearly analogue, bringing a sense of performance into it. In hindsight, it was how I discovered the narrative layer that colour would add to the work. Together with the camera shifting in and out, it breaks the mysticism around the filmmaking process.

Martin Clark

In *King of Boys*, you feel that red filter going across the lens in an incredibly physical way – it's like a prosthetic or a visor being drawn across your vision. I've always had this curiously uncanny feeling when watching home videos from the 1980s and 1990s. Not just the image – which is peculiarly intimate in the way it moves with the operator's body, wobbling and juddering and twitching with every tiny movement – but also, perhaps even more so, with the sound. There's an unsettling proximity produced by the sound of the camcorder rubbing up against the operator's hand and face – the abrupt violence of a gust of wind, or the sound of breathing on the inbuilt microphone. To me, it always feels queasily intimate and intense, almost like being in someone else's head, the camcorder as a kind of surrogate consciousness, an analogue to our own clumsy perception.

Karimah Ashadu

I think of the camera as a way to get as close as possible to things – to confront and engage us. I always think about that proximity and how I can make it clear. You talked about the formalities of my filmmaking, and I wanted to touch a little bit on that, because even though I make my films in a way that's quite abstract, and at times maybe nonlinear and experimental, they are informed from that place very early on in my studies when I explored rhythm, pace, colour and spatiality.

Leonardo Bigazzi

We first worked together in 2016, almost ten years ago. That year feels like an important moment in your practice, as it marked a shift from your earlier works, produced from 2012 to 2015, where you often used handheld, self-made camera devices that acted as viewfinders. But in 2016, *Red Gold*, initially presented at the Biennale de l'Image en Mouvement in Geneva, for the first time used voice-over and adopted a more narrative structure. You also began developing an approach that continued in later works, namely portraying communities and individuals, and bringing their voices directly into the piece. I wonder if you remember what led to that shift.

Karimah Ashadu

The two years I spent in residency at De Ateliers in Amsterdam, from 2014 to 2016, were such an intense time of experimentation and understanding – it was almost like a sketchbook. Once I finished it, I had arrived at a basis for my practice, and I started to make longer works. It became clear to me that they needed another layer, and that became the narrative aspect. I also wanted to understand what voice and spoken narrative could do to an image, how they could work together in a way where you never see the protagonist speaking – it just comes in a stream of consciousness and then it's gone, and you don't know when to expect it again.

Gina Buenfeld-Murley

That comes through – that there's the image and there's so much, as the viewer, you can project onto it. I'm thinking in particular about *Cowboy* and *Plateau*, where the mystery of an individual world – with its complex feelings and memories and histories and aspirations – is skilfully brought forward.

Karimah Ashadu

That direct telling of stories, whether of individuals or communities, is very important because it's about shifting the narrative and the ownership of history.

Martin Clark

There's something else within all of these films that has to do with the way people reclaim spaces. The idea that there is a sort of mainstream or dominant culture – which can be seen as a colonial culture – being reclaimed and redeployed by communities. It comes back to something you said earlier: that even if something is being done to you, an oppression – a violence, often – there's a resilience, and a creativity, in the way that aspects are then assimilated or subverted. Whatever the conditions economically or culturally, whatever you have access to, you take what you want, what you can, and create something rich and specific to your own community and your own place. There's something very moving and celebratory about that, but also very defiant and powerful. And it's not just specific to Nigeria or Lagos, of course. These communities could be kids in London who have nothing, but take what they need from the dominant culture and create something from it that is even more rich and beautiful.

Karimah Ashadu

Absolutely. Even though, as you said, that can be quite a universal thing, I think it comes down to a very Nigerian spirit of being resourceful, because we've had to be. I think it's also about taking part in an economy that you don't have access to on your own terms. For instance, buying a knockoff at the market: you still feel that by wearing that brand, you're in some way part of its idea and culture. It speaks about the value we ascribe to things.

Gina Buenfeld-Murley

Thinking about the protagonists of *Machine Boys*, they wear knockoffs of high-fashion brands – which are mainly about monetary status – to express something quite at odds with the position they actually occupy. There's a kind of mimetic desire at play, in the sense that it's not the thing itself that you desire; it's the fact that other people desire it. It speaks to what you just described, a kind of value system that we all uphold, yet it's only because of the circling of desire that the illusion is sustained.

In relation to this idea, I'm interested in the sculptural works that accompany *MUSCLE*: garden chairs made from resin and covered in a patchwork of recycled sportswear logos (*Cotch*, 2025), and glass sculptures of the ubiquitous plastic water pouches used in the kinds of gyms where the film was shot (*Pure Rugged Water*, 2025). To my understanding, there are many packaged water brands in Nigeria, generically labelled 'pure water', made with somewhat dubious methods of purification. The commodification of this natural, vital resource is obviously absurd. This new series of sculptures also includes your own patented logo and very directly confronts the language of brand identity as a signifier.

Karimah Ashadu

Desire is universal in the human experience. A sense of wanting is something that we all contend with in some way. And for me, this translates into a desire to belong, which is almost tribal. If we take a deeper look at desire, it's never really the thing itself that we're desiring. It's about a feeling, it's about how this thing is going to make me feel. I want to make people feel that my works mirror that feeling.

Leonardo Bigazzi

We've touched on the idea of collective history and representations of communities, but with other works, such as *Cowboy*, you felt the urgency to tell more intimate and personal stories, focusing on individual portraits. Let's delve a little deeper into the character in *Cowboy*. What interested you in his life as a horse rider and caretaker?

Karimah Ashadu

The word that comes to my mind is 'nurture'. Lagos, as you know, is a very aggressive place, very fast and hard, whereas the cowboy was this character who is soft and gentle, so he stood out to me. I wanted to understand this soft power that I hadn't seen in this way before. When I made the work, I was in a very specific place in my life, namely I was pregnant, and when I was editing it, I had my baby, so I was in a place that was quite soft and nurturing, but at the same time I was having a lot of personal struggles. Something beautiful came out of this place of struggling and striving.

Leonardo Bigazzi

There's a very powerful moment when Cowboy arrives at the beach and we see the ocean filled with container ships. It lasts only a few frames, but it brings into focus Nigeria's role in West Africa as a port of entry and therefore a major economic force. It also evokes a body of water that is historically charged – especially in light of the legacy of the Atlantic slave trade. I wonder if you could elaborate on how this fluid landscape intertwines with the palm tree in the two-channel structure of the film, and the symbolic value you associate with these natural elements.

Karimah Ashadu

I often come back to a notion of nature as a silent witness. It's been here before us, and will remain afterward. I think of it as a motif. In *Cowboy*, there are the palm trees and the sea, with the interplay between the two channels adding a lot of depth. The image in one channel fades in and out – I wanted to play with that technique and create the feeling of time slowing down. We often think of time as linear, but I think of it as several things happening simultaneously.

Gina Buenfeld-Murley

It seems to me that your approach is to create a kind of counterpoint – that you occupy a somewhat adjacent perspective on a subject or discourse that's otherwise familiar to audiences.

Karimah Ashadu

There is always a lot of symbolism in my work, but in *Cowboy* much more so because it comes from a soft place. For example, the motif of the palm trees gently fluttering in the wind: If we go back in West African history, palm fronds signified peace during times of strife, but also resilience, since they were used to camouflage buildings during times of war, for instance during the Biafra War. Or, the cowboy is shot a lot from the back – he's on his horse, and he almost seems to be led, or even chased – and that image, particularly with a Black man, is historically charged. But then if we think of the image of the cowboy in mainstream culture, there isn't really any such thing as an African cowboy, especially a gentle one. I wanted to subvert that.

Leonardo Bigazzi

Talking about how you play with multiple temporalities and narratives, there's a moment in the film when the cowboy looks at the audience and breaks the fourth wall. You intentionally fade the other screen to black to heighten the impact of this moment of encounter between the gaze of the audience and that of the protagonist. You often use the gaze as a tool to shrink the perceived distance between the viewer and the characters on screen. In *Plateau*, this moment happens roughly halfway through. The audience has had time to settle in – to feel safe, and to become aware of the distance between their own privilege, their own geographies, and those of the characters – then, suddenly, this man looks directly at them and clearly seems aware that he's being watched. In *Machine Boys*, this gaze is even more confrontational. For me, this is a very powerful moment when your audience becomes vulnerable. Can you talk about how you use this tool, and why you choose to place it either in the middle or at the end of a film?

Karimah Ashadu

The placement comes from a gut feeling, but also from the energy and length of the work, and it certainly comes from how I want the audience to feel. With *Machine Boys* I wanted to ramp things up – it opens with a motorcyclist staring into the audience, and it continues very much like that. In *MUSCLE*, it happens a few times, and more toward the end. I always like to consider the audience as actively encountering my films. They're not passive, and I think installation has a part to play. This is why I never like people to sit and passively watch my work. I want you to feel your body while watching, and maybe the discomfort of not sitting. And the breaking of the fourth wall adds another layer. It jolts you. It makes you think of your position.

Leonardo Bigazzi

There's a long tradition of African artists engaging with the idea of returning the gaze, and also reflecting on the use of the camera directed at Black bodies on the African continent. I'm thinking of artists like Zanele Muholi, for example. Do you see yourself as working within this tradition? Or is it more about a kind of performativity – something you want to create specifically in relation to your audience?

Karimah Ashadu

It stems from the dialogue I want to have with my audience. I'm speaking with them, I imagine, and it's about how to take that conversation one step further, or how to inspire that conversation to stay with them once they leave. In my films, when someone turns to look at you like that, it's not something you'll likely forget.

Myriam Ben Salah

Your work returns to labour insistently – not just as content, but as form. What does labour mean to you in relation to cinema, to spectatorship, to survival?

Karimah Ashadu

There's something deeply cinematic about labour, because it reveals time. It conveys repetition, resilience and endurance. In a Nigerian context, where labour is ubiquitous – especially in a fast-paced megacity like Lagos – I want to draw attention to it not just as toil, but as ritual, as performance, as presence. I've always maintained that when someone's body has done the same thing for a long time, as in the case of physical labour, there's a fluidity and muscle memory to it that I find rather beautiful. Of course the kind of labour that I portray isn't something that late capitalist societies, often in the Western part of the world, are as familiar with, even if it's the backbone of their economies. So there is some discomfort in witnessing it, especially when it comes to black bodies labouring. My films ask you to stay with that discomfort, to question what you're witnessing and how you're positioned in relation to it.

Martin Clark

Sound plays an important role in the work as well, again around experiences of distance and proximity. How do you think about sound in relation to the work?

Karimah Ashadu

I consider sound, and experience sound, in a highly sensitive way. One of my ears is not quite the same as the other, so I receive sound very specifically. I can hear the tiniest things, and so I guess that comes through in my work. I love background noise, it calms me. In *King of Boys*, there's the background noise of the TV playing a Nollywood film, providing almost an accidental soundtrack. I thought that was something magical to keep in, because certain exact moments in the soundtrack coincidentally complement what's going on with the image. The art historian Gabe Beckhurst recently wrote that often in my works, you experience the sound before the image, which creates a space of expectation. You hear before you see.[1] Sound is very visceral; it places you, and then your brain is able to understand what's happening.

Myriam Ben Salah

Sound in your films isn't just atmospheric – it's architectural. Metal clangs, language speeds, heat hums.

Karimah Ashadu

Indeed, sound in my work is structural. It reaches into places the image alone cannot – into memory, into mood – giving the work depth by allowing us to feel emotions.

In *MUSCLE*, the sound makes you feel close to the skin and the sweat you're seeing. The clatter of weights, the primal sounds of the men training, the cadence of Yoruba. The soundtrack envelops the image like a cloud or a second skin. In *Cowboy*, the meditative crashing of waves and the curious

1 Gabe Beckhurst, 'Follow My Lead', *Camera Austria International*, no. 170, 2025: 7–18.

rustling of palm fronds in the second channel create a kind of sonic imprint – a sensory anchor that roots the viewer in place and feeling, yet feels expansive.

Leonardo Bigazzi

I was also thinking about how you play with the contrast between moments of silence and moments where the background noise is incredibly rich. I'm thinking of the constant sound of machines in the mine in *Plateau*, or the layered, chaotic noise of the abattoir in *King of Boys*. But then there are these moments of calm where the contrast becomes even more striking. Often it comes when you're showing a landscape. So I'm curious about how you use this contrast. As you said, the word 'visceral' captures the experience of your sound design, and the way sound becomes a tool to locate the viewer within the scene. There's never a moment when we're outside of it. We're always immersed in the reality you're portraying.

Karimah Ashadu

I like to use sound to pace a work. There are moments when the sound overlaps, accelerates, then slows down. Moments where you're confronted with an intense cacophony of noise, then plunged into silence and stillness. I enjoy this spontaneity because it adds dynamism and a sense of the unexpected. For me, silence is sanctuary, a moment of respite. We're so overstimulated that when we have moments of absolute silence – of being able to hear and process our own thoughts – it's magical. Maybe it goes hand in hand with the way I like to bring nature into the works; this is also very much bringing us back to ourselves. We've created this world, and in it so many different experiences, but ultimately the thing we enter and leave with is ourselves, and in certain works I'm able to bring that in through silence – moments of meditation, almost.

Myriam Ben Salah

Your production company, Golddust by Ashadu, feels like more than infrastructure. Is it a kind of refusal? A form of protection? A proposal for another way of working?

Karimah Ashadu

Golddust by Ashadu is about legacy building and ownership – of process, of narrative, of archive. It's a platform to nurture our stories from the inside, without distortion or dependence. For me, it's vital that Black and African histories are told on our own terms, and produced and treated with care. When I began making films, it was difficult to find the right support. There weren't many frameworks for the kind of work I was making, and I had to believe deeply in myself to propel forward. Golddust is a way to invest in the next generation of artists working in moving image. It aims to support those who lack access to funding or creative infrastructure by offering support for complex, self-defined work that's rooted in our culture.

Landscapes
Karimah Ashadu

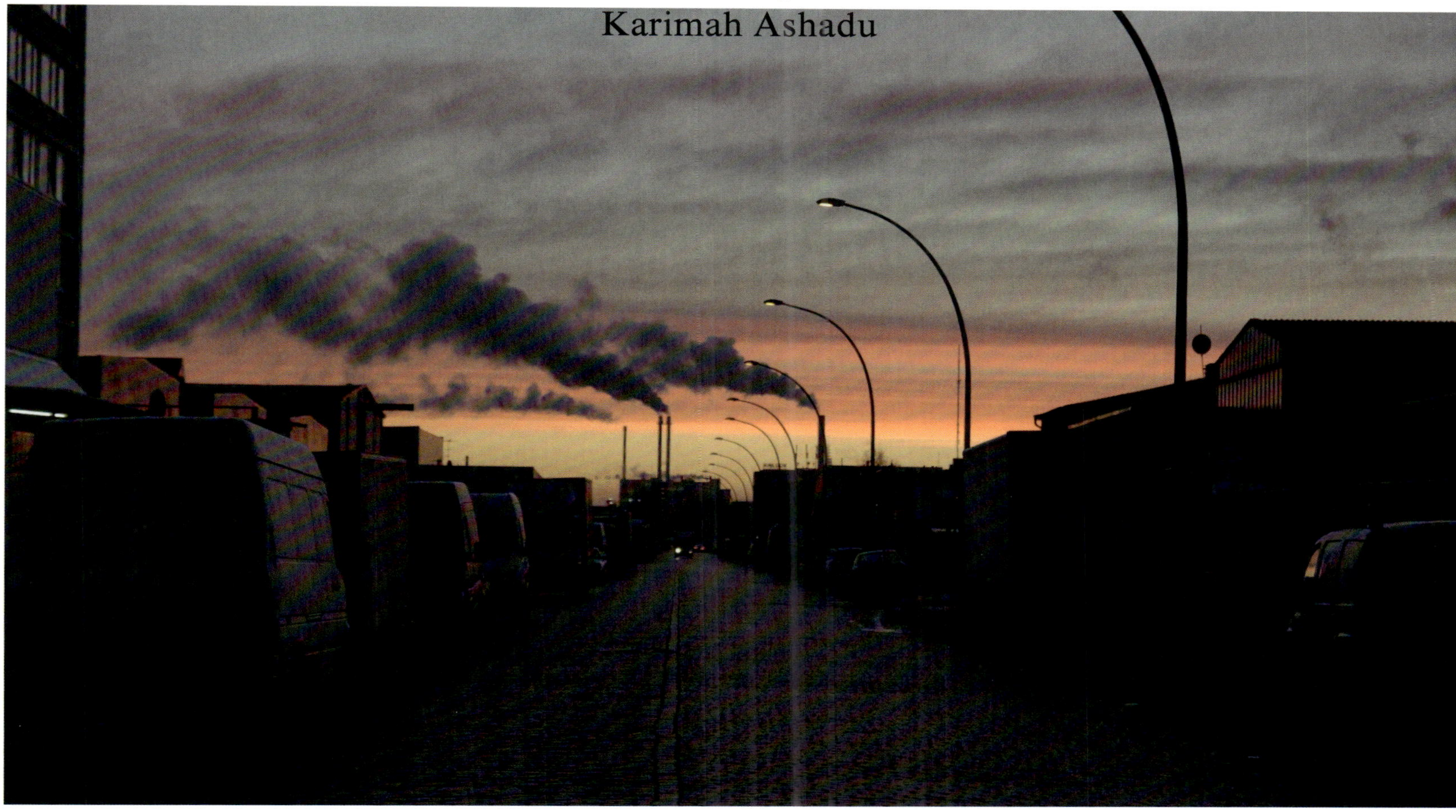

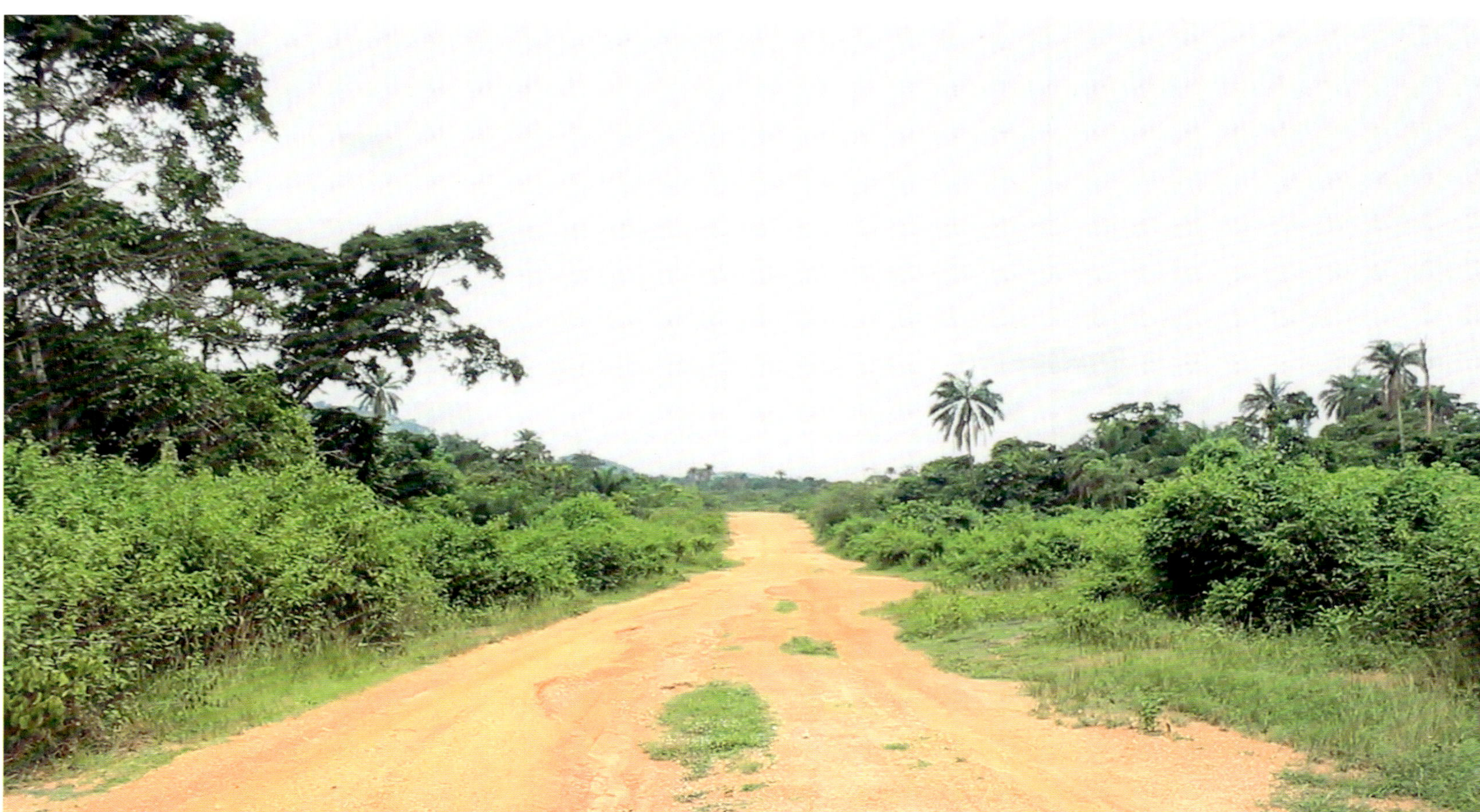

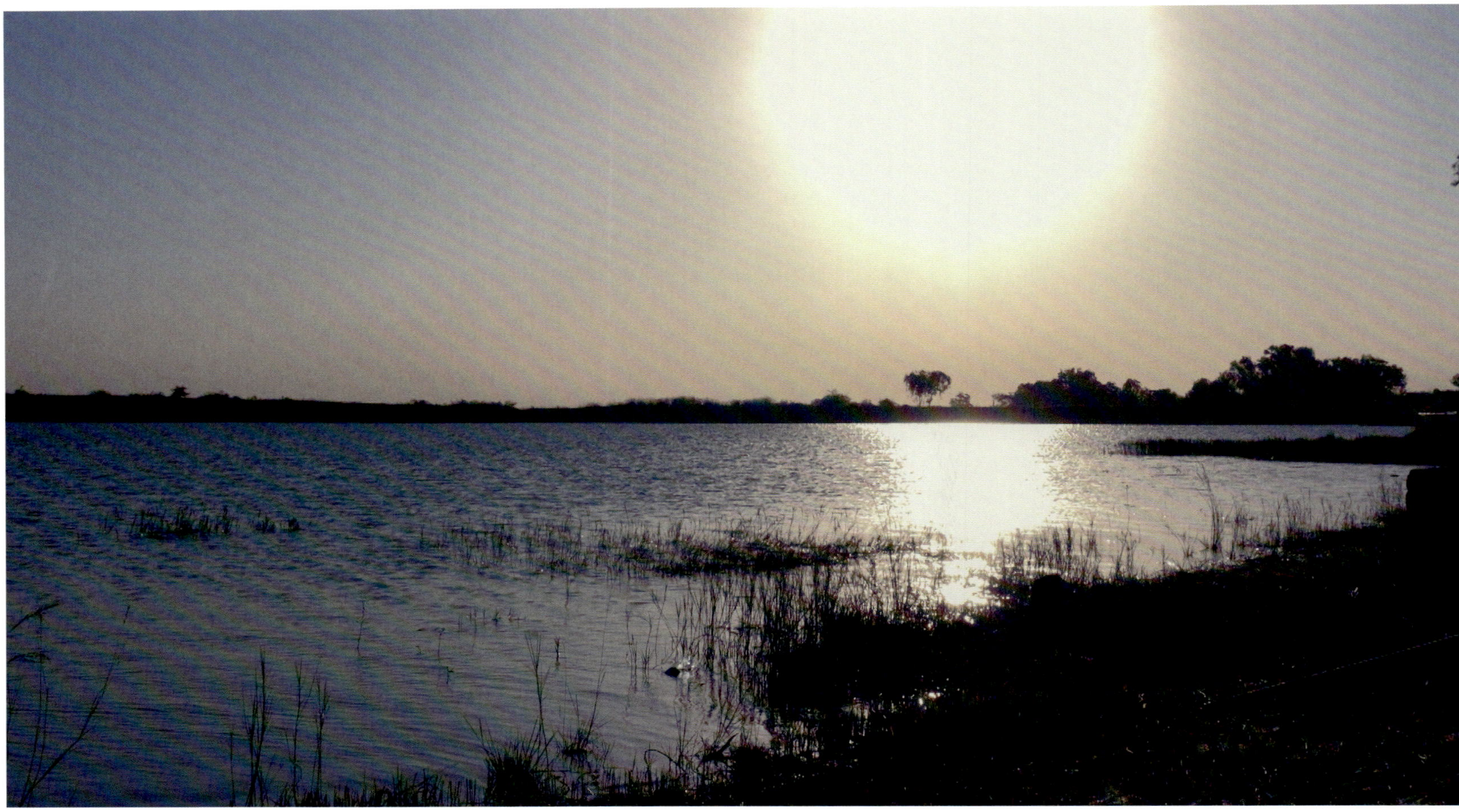

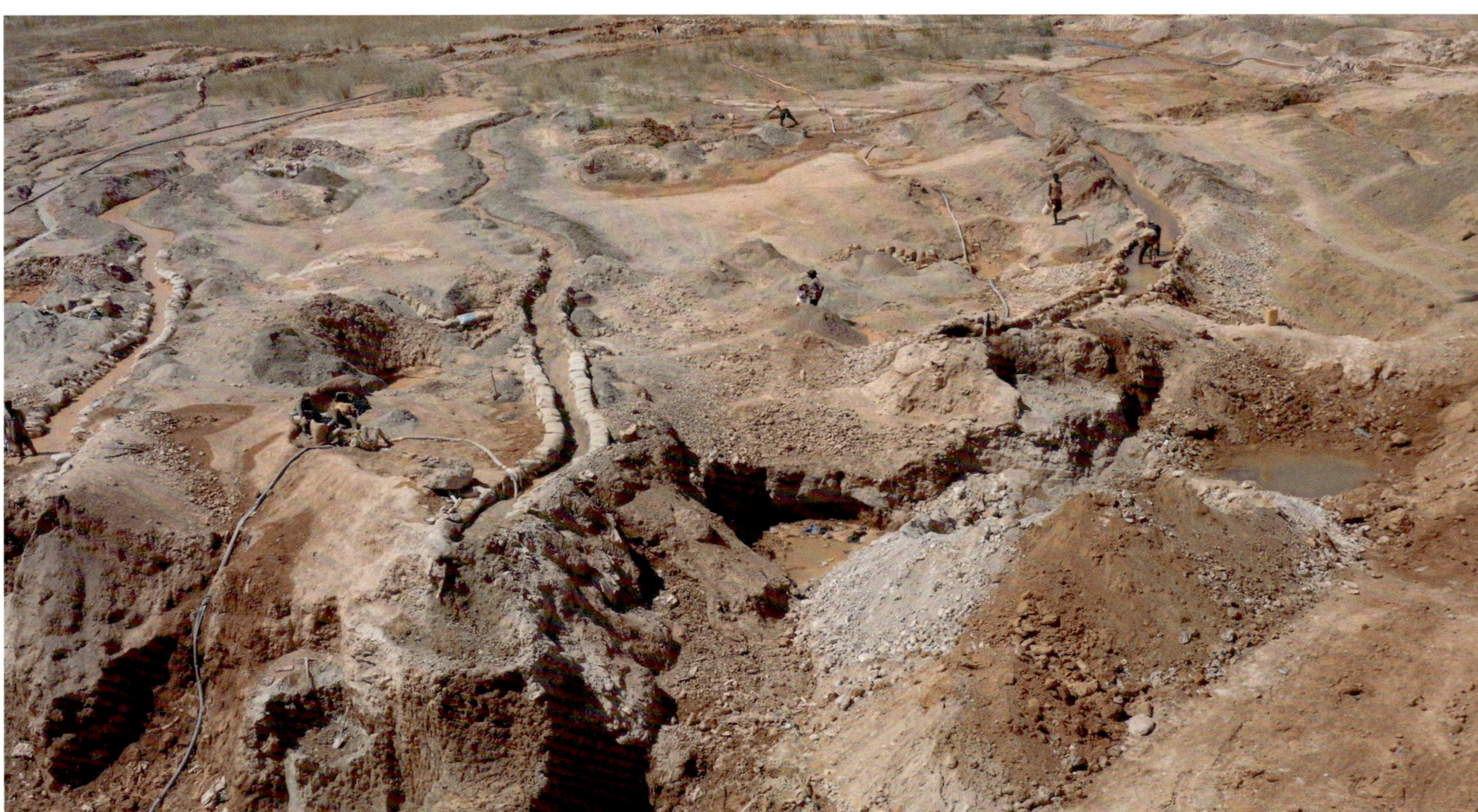

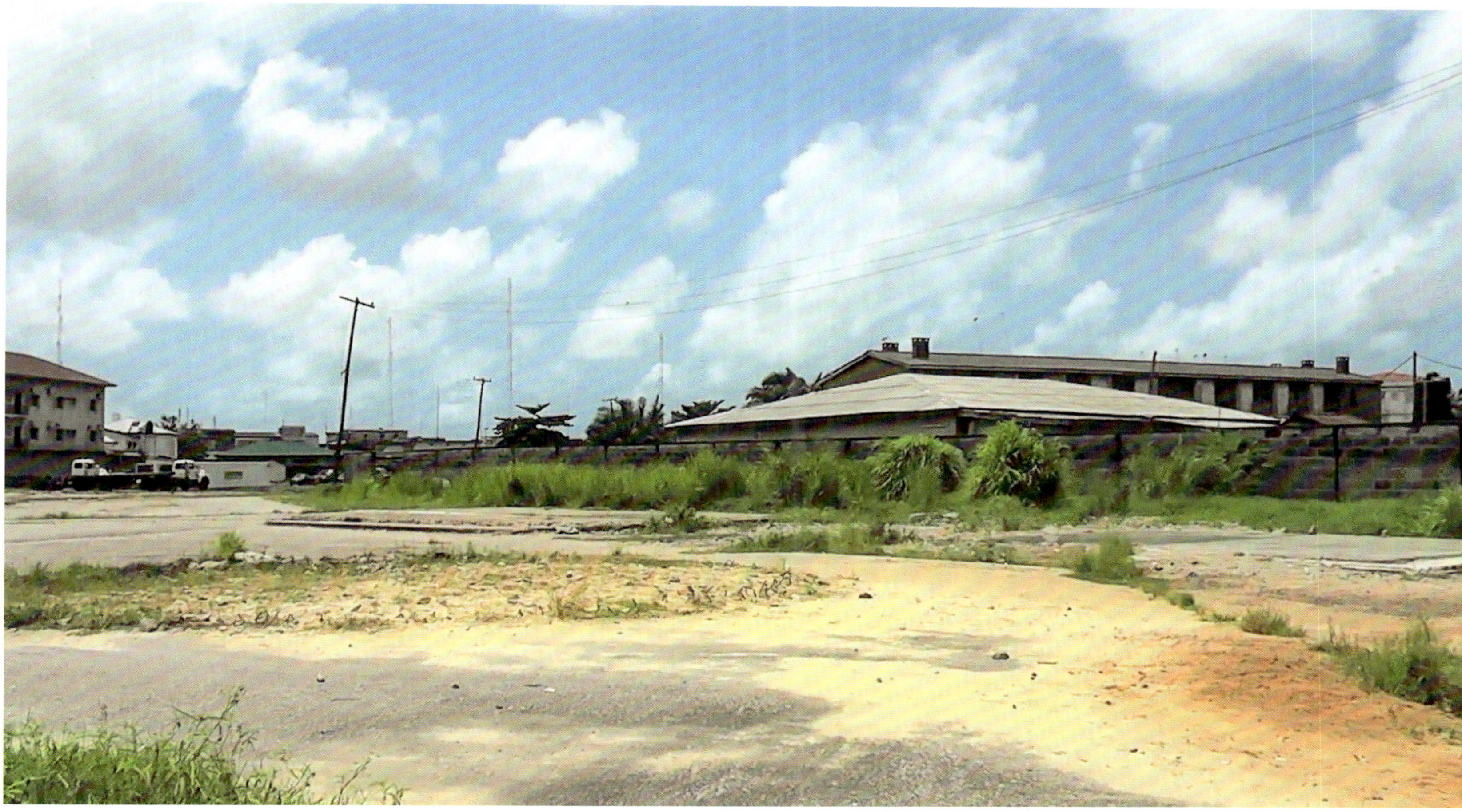

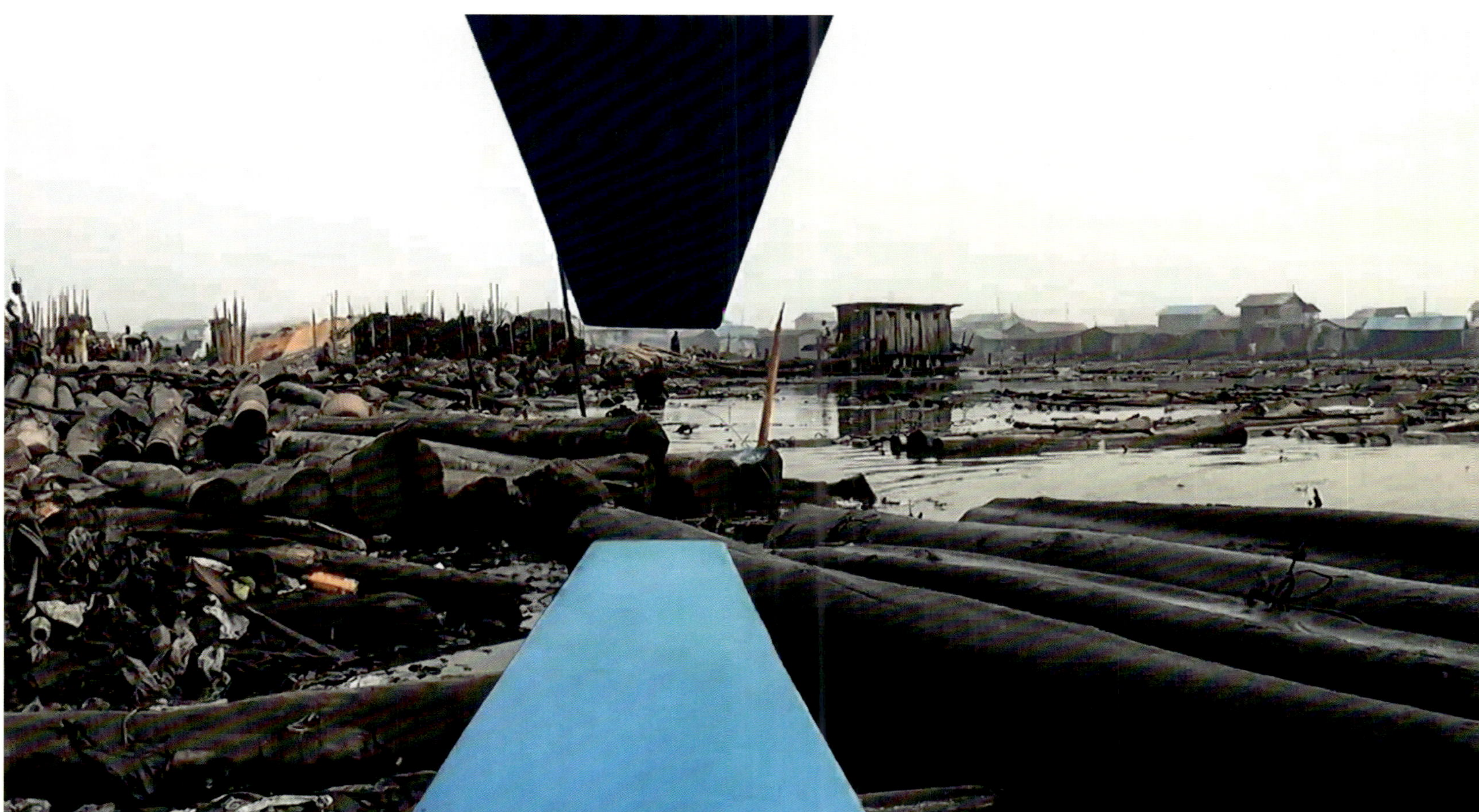

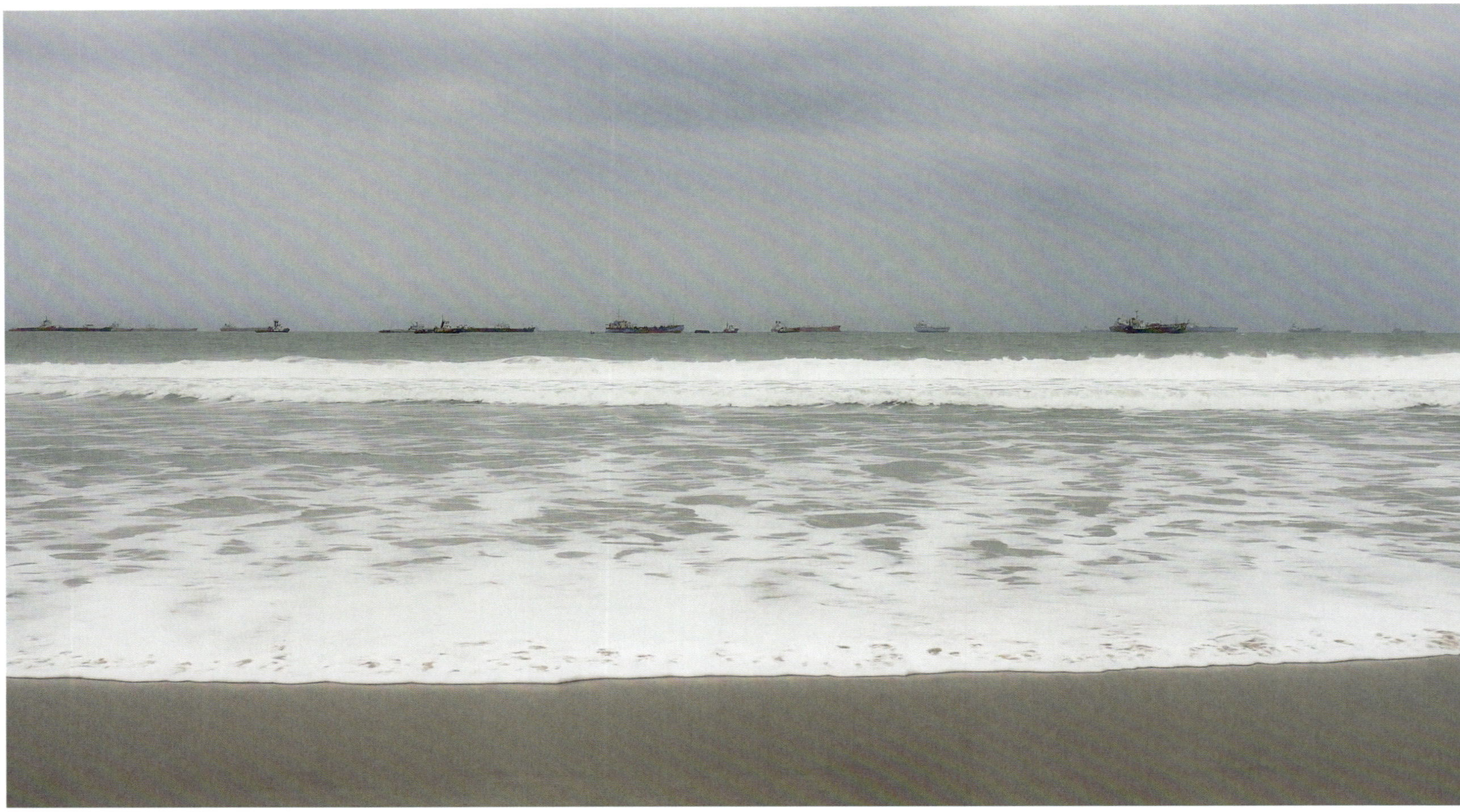

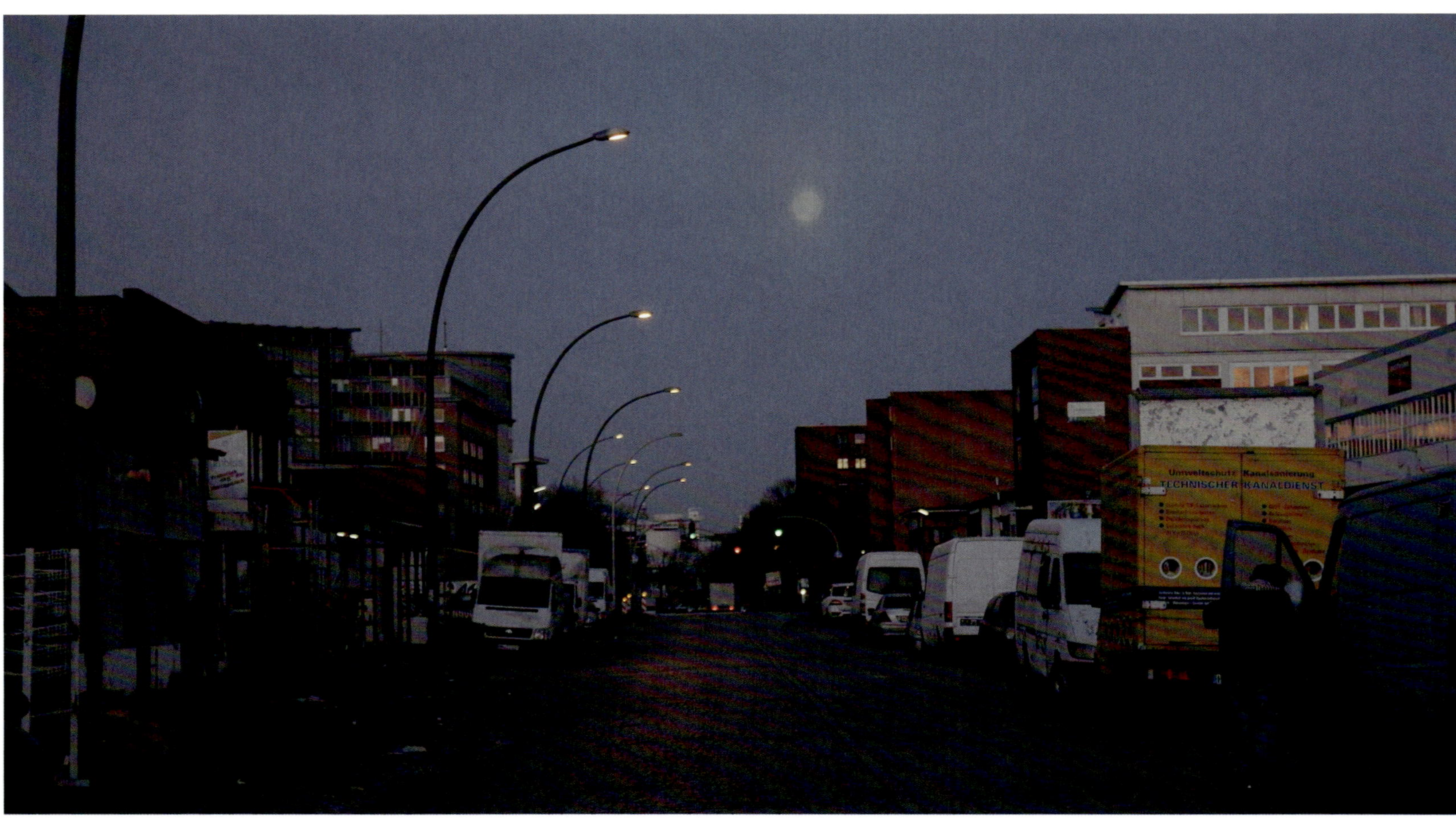
TECHNISCHER KANALDIENST

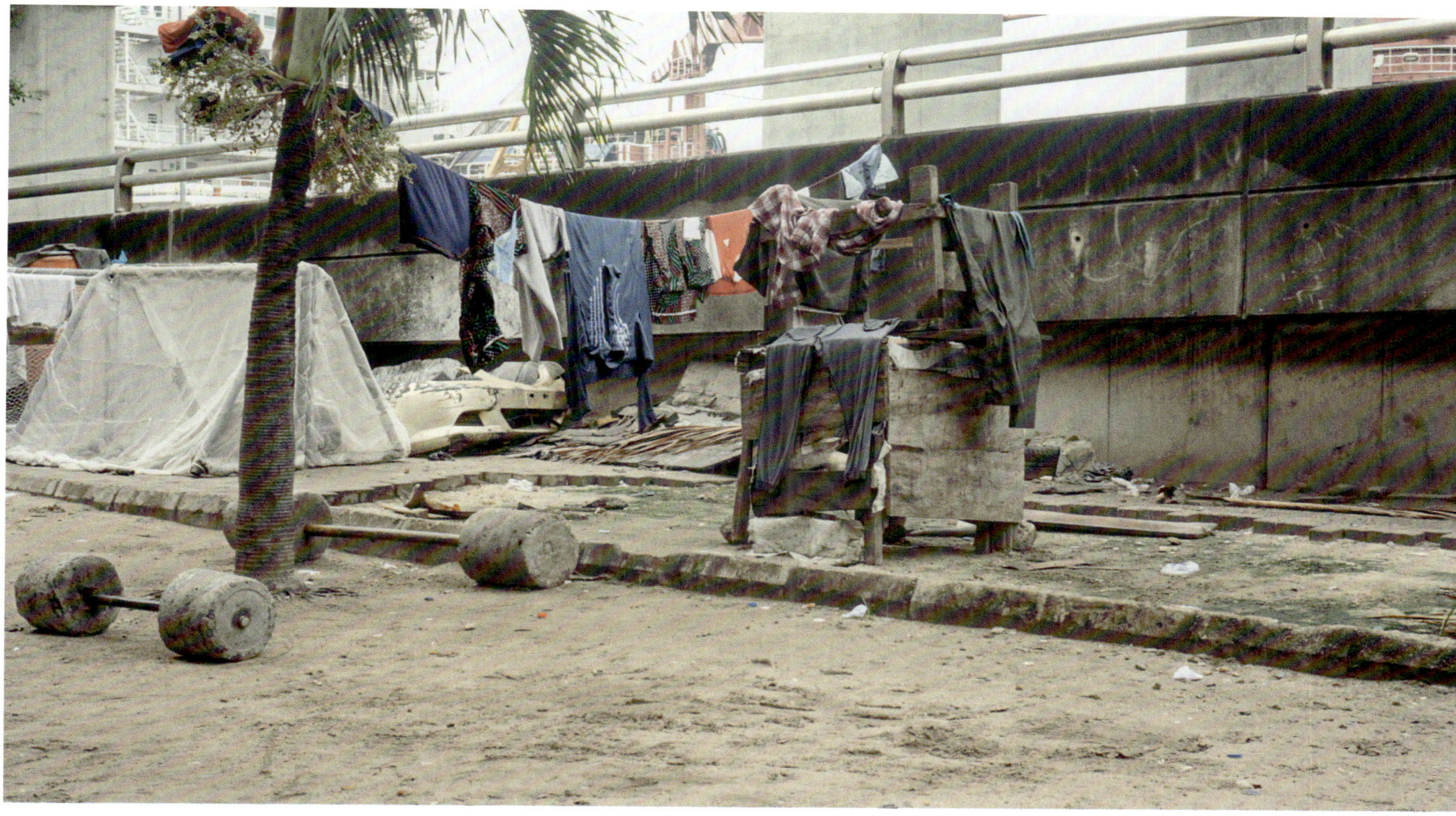

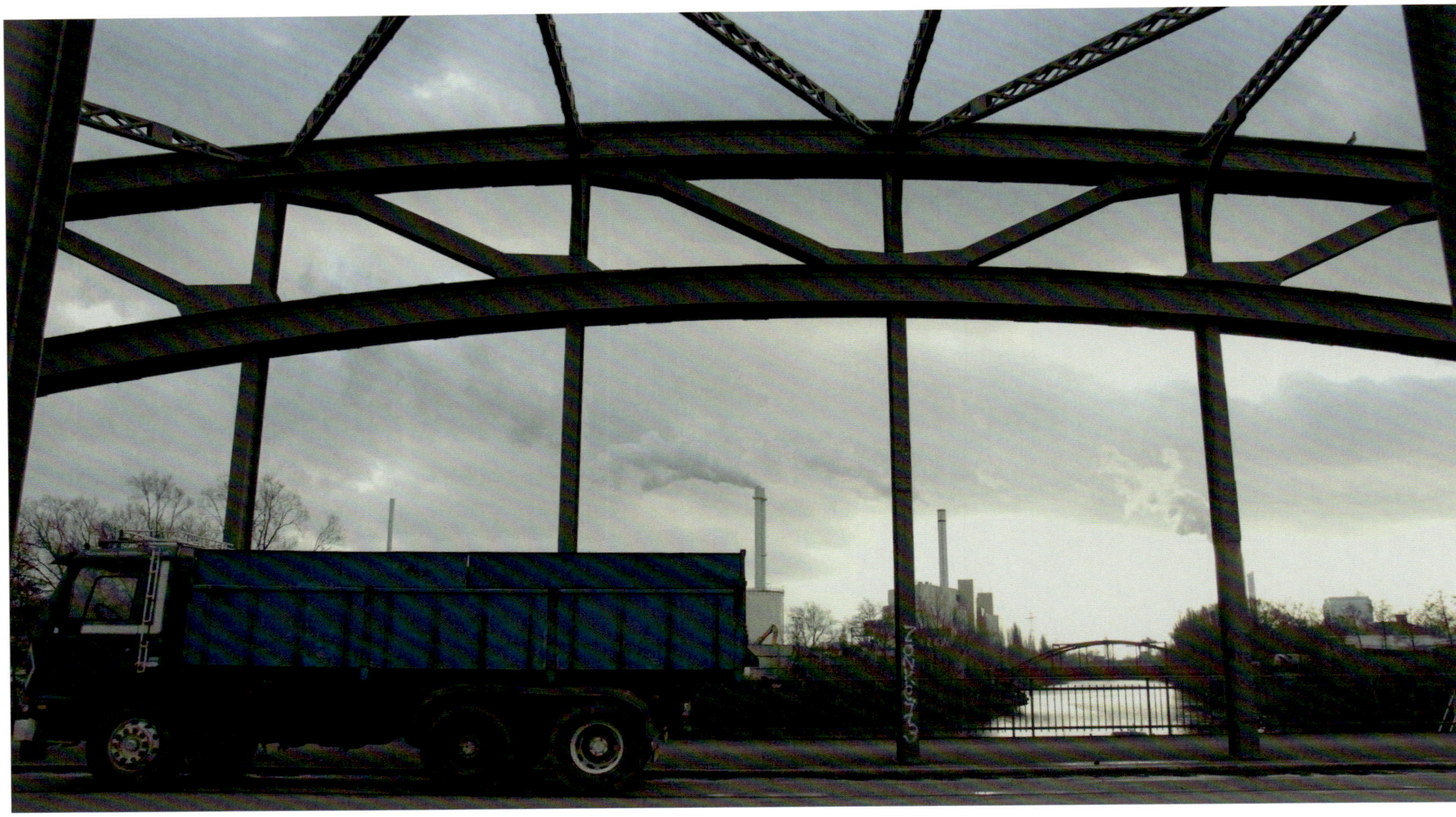

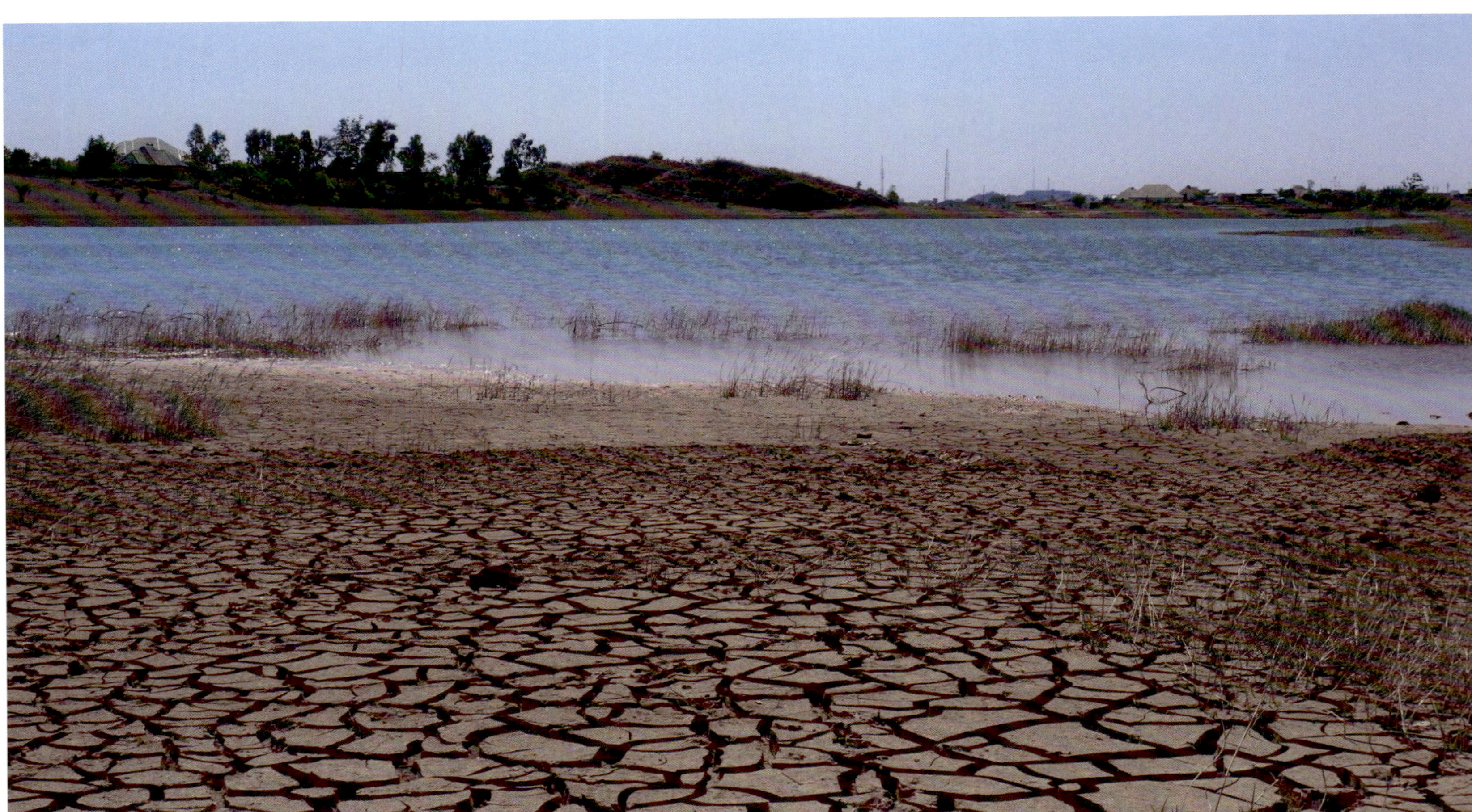

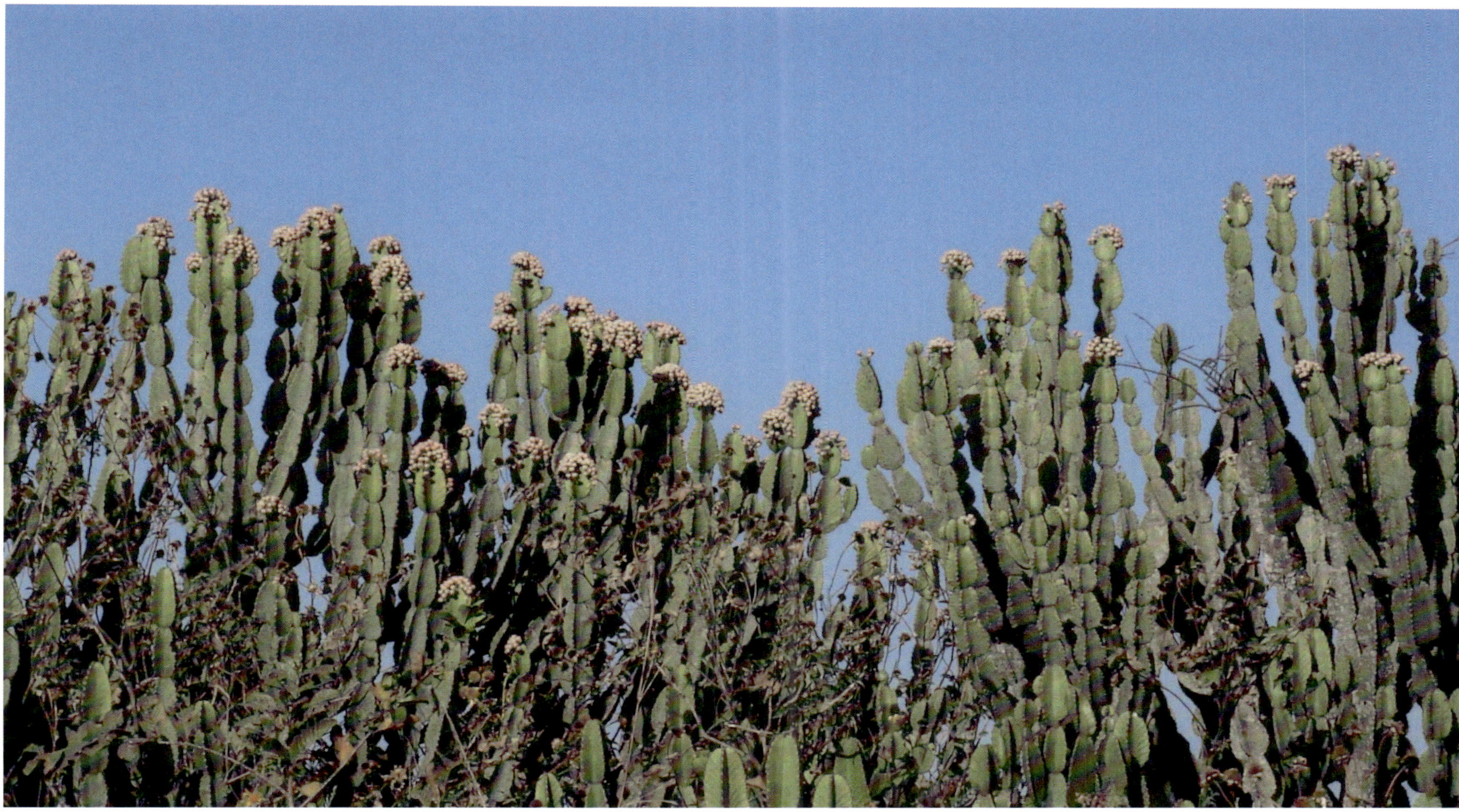

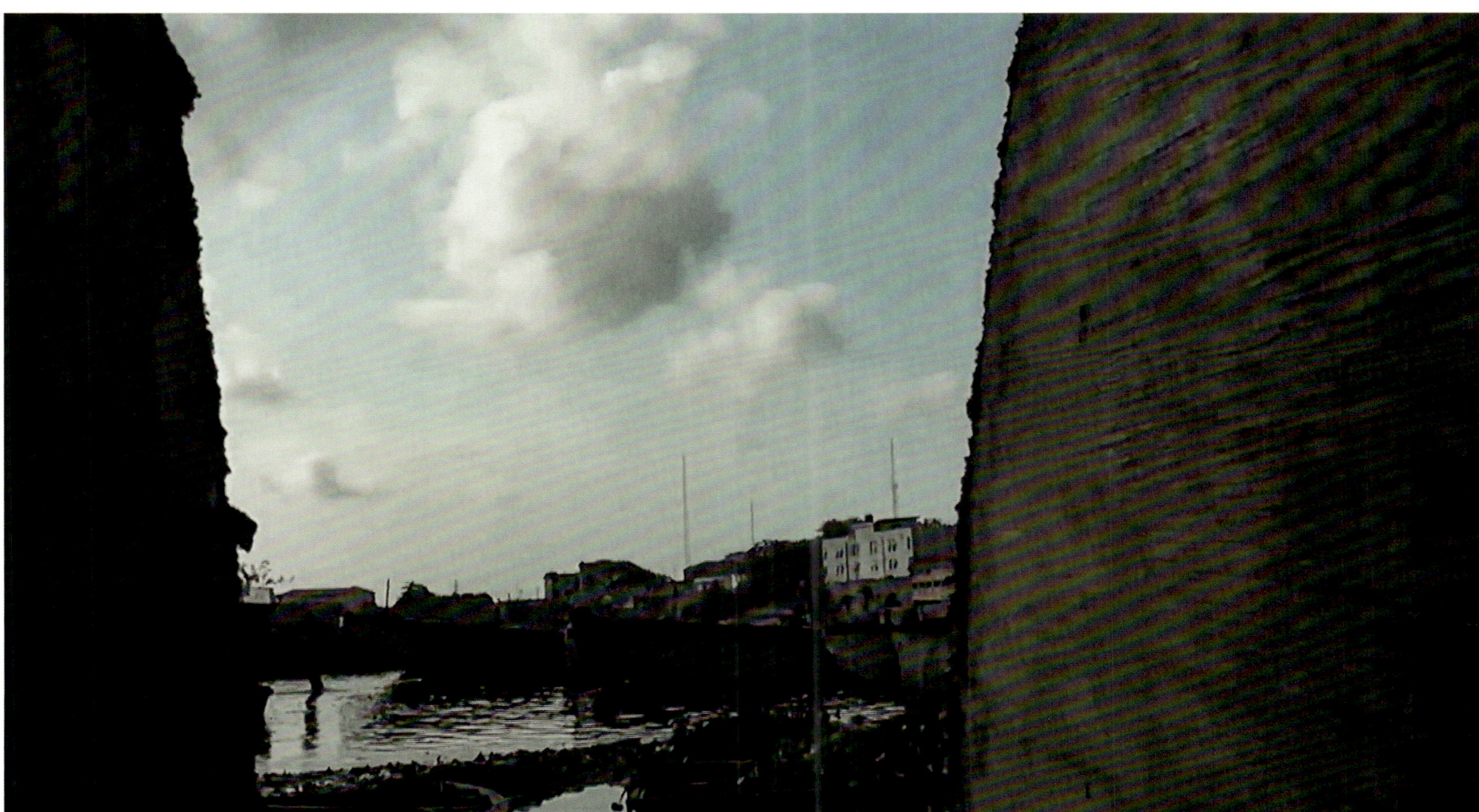

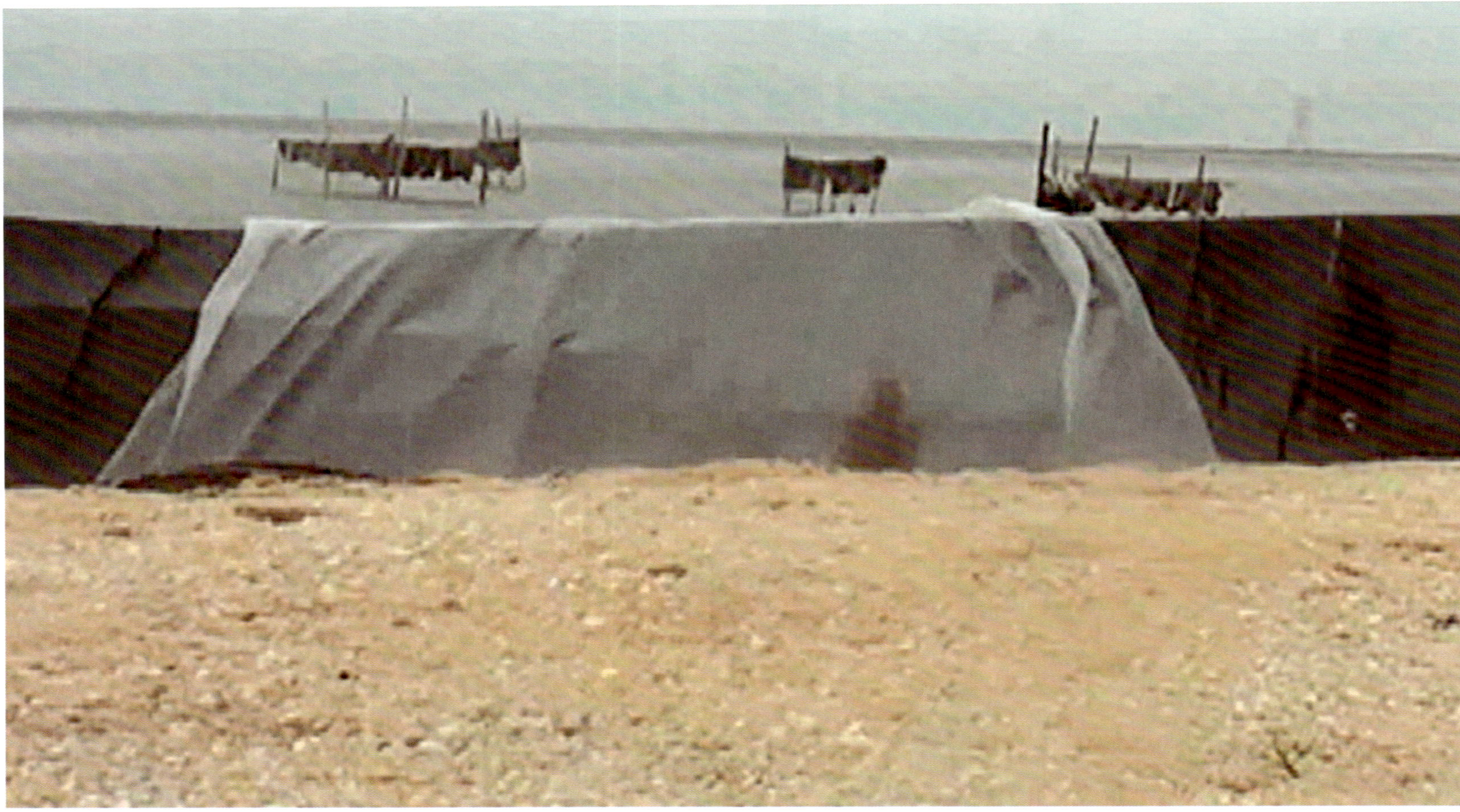

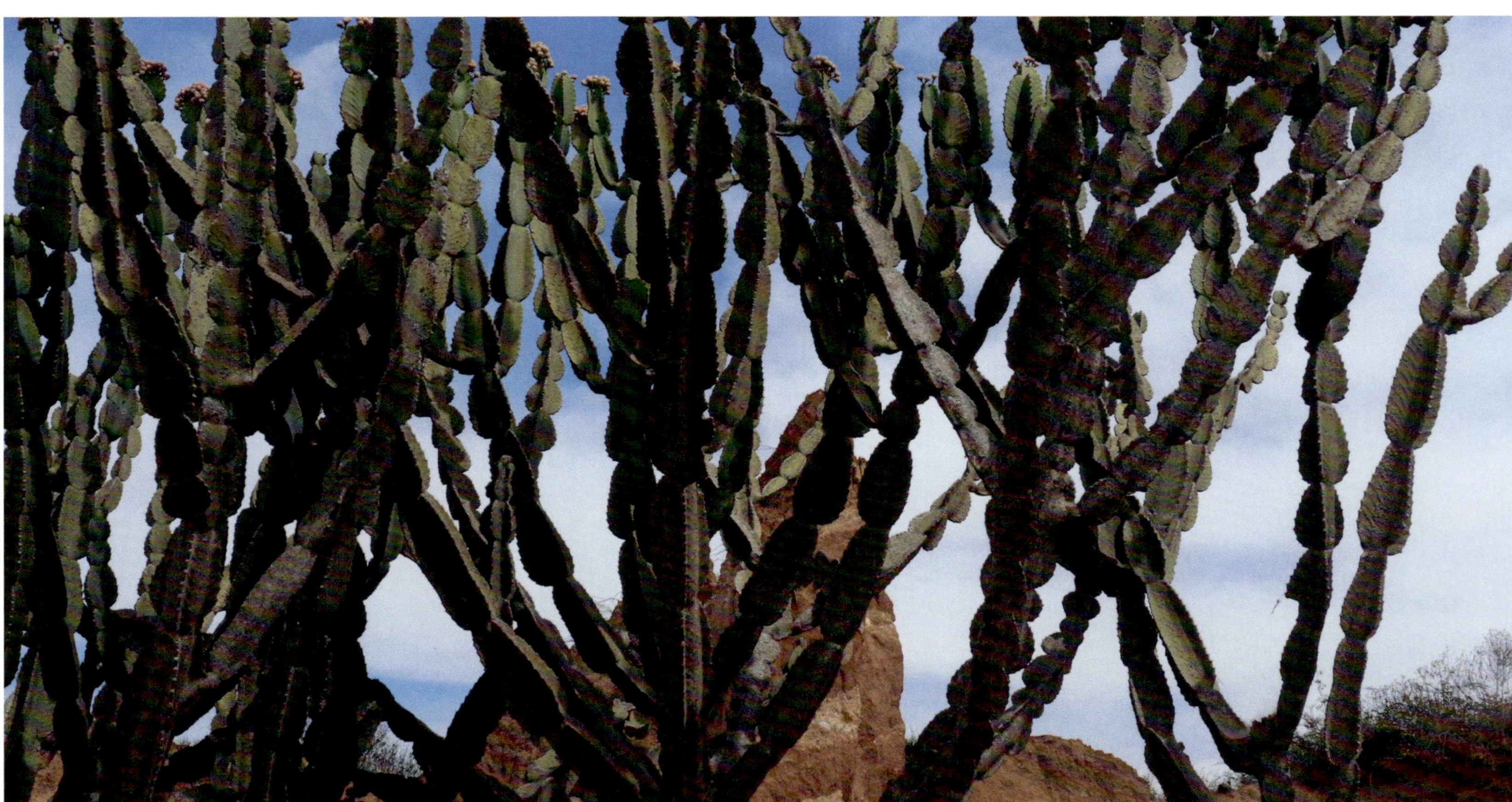

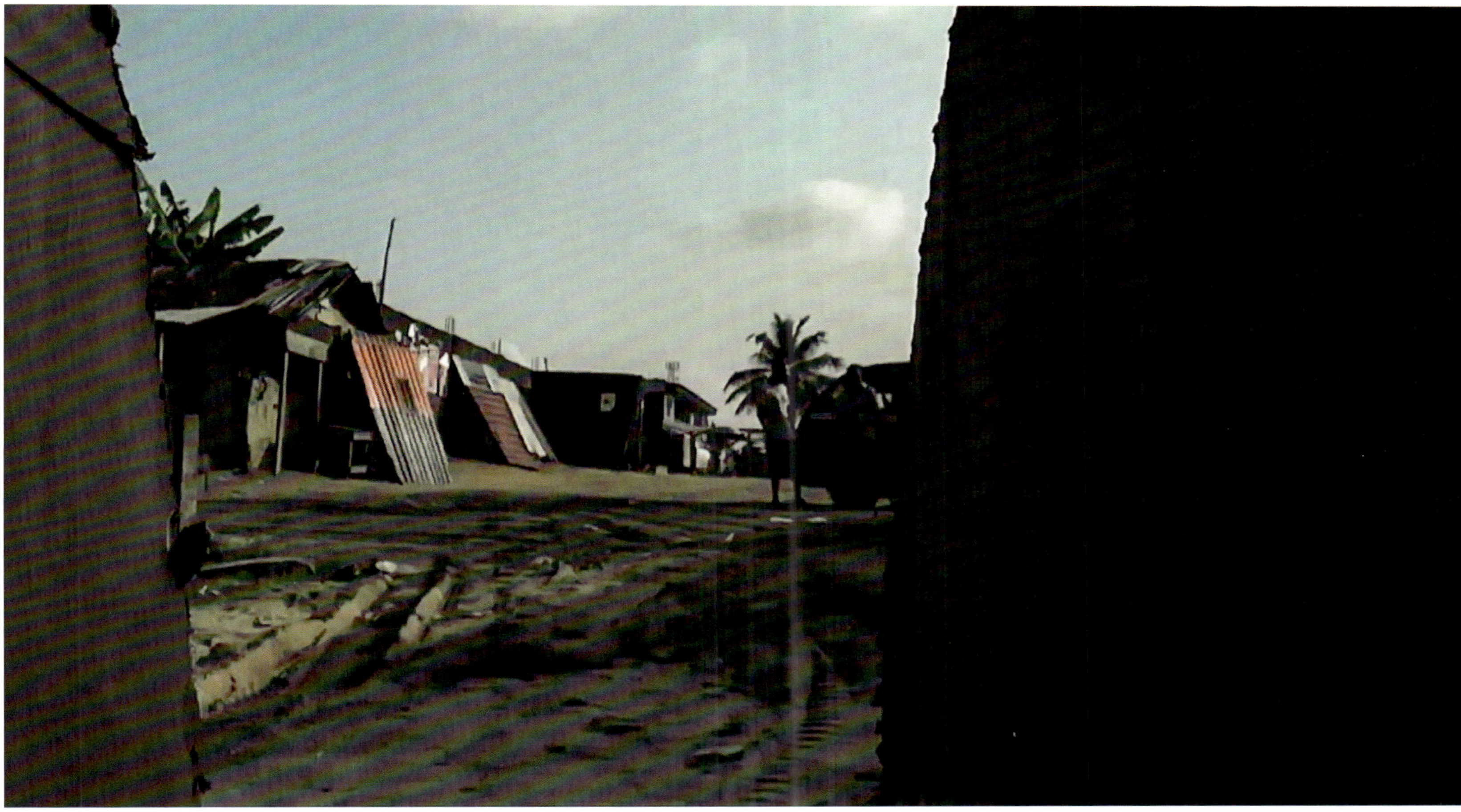

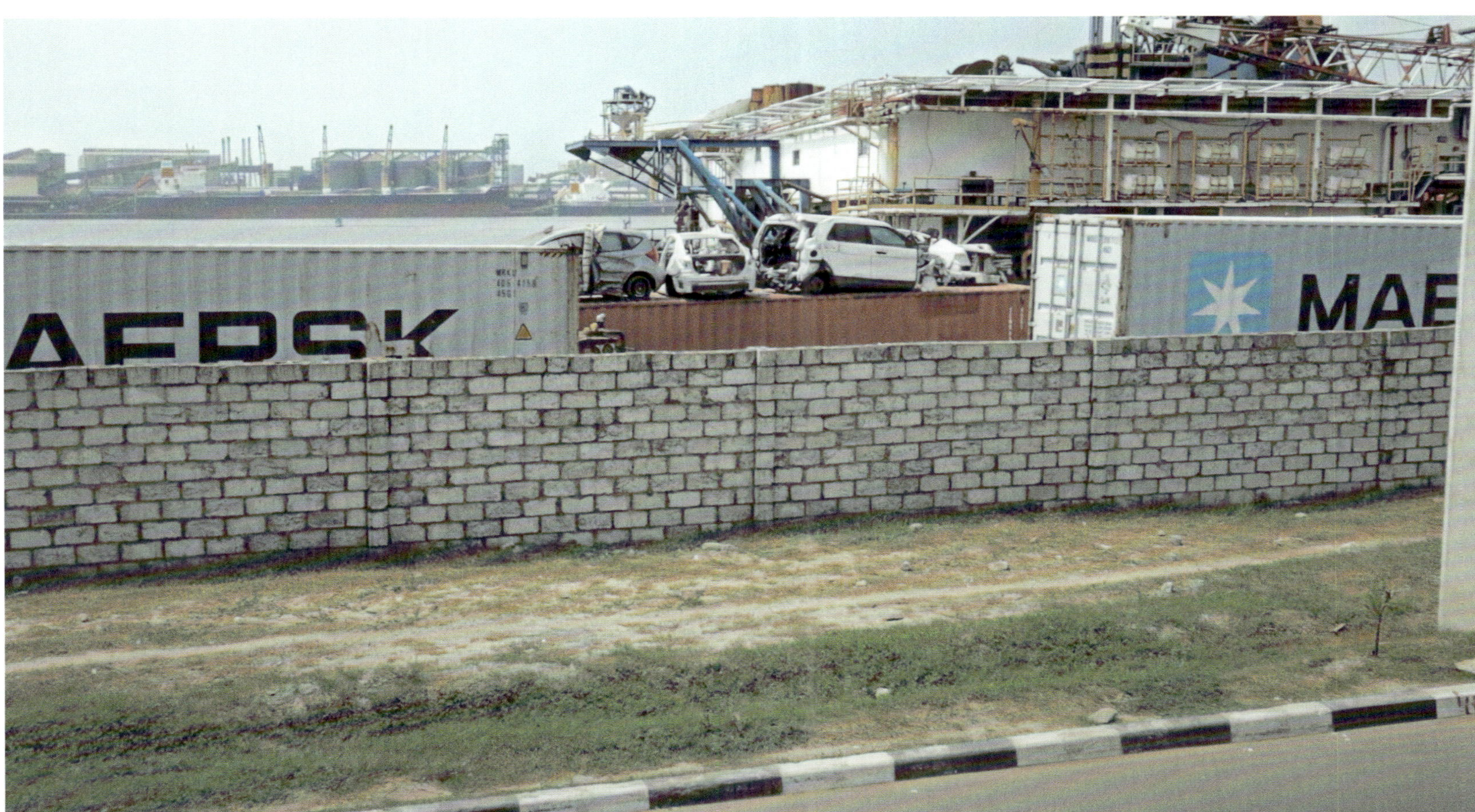
MAE

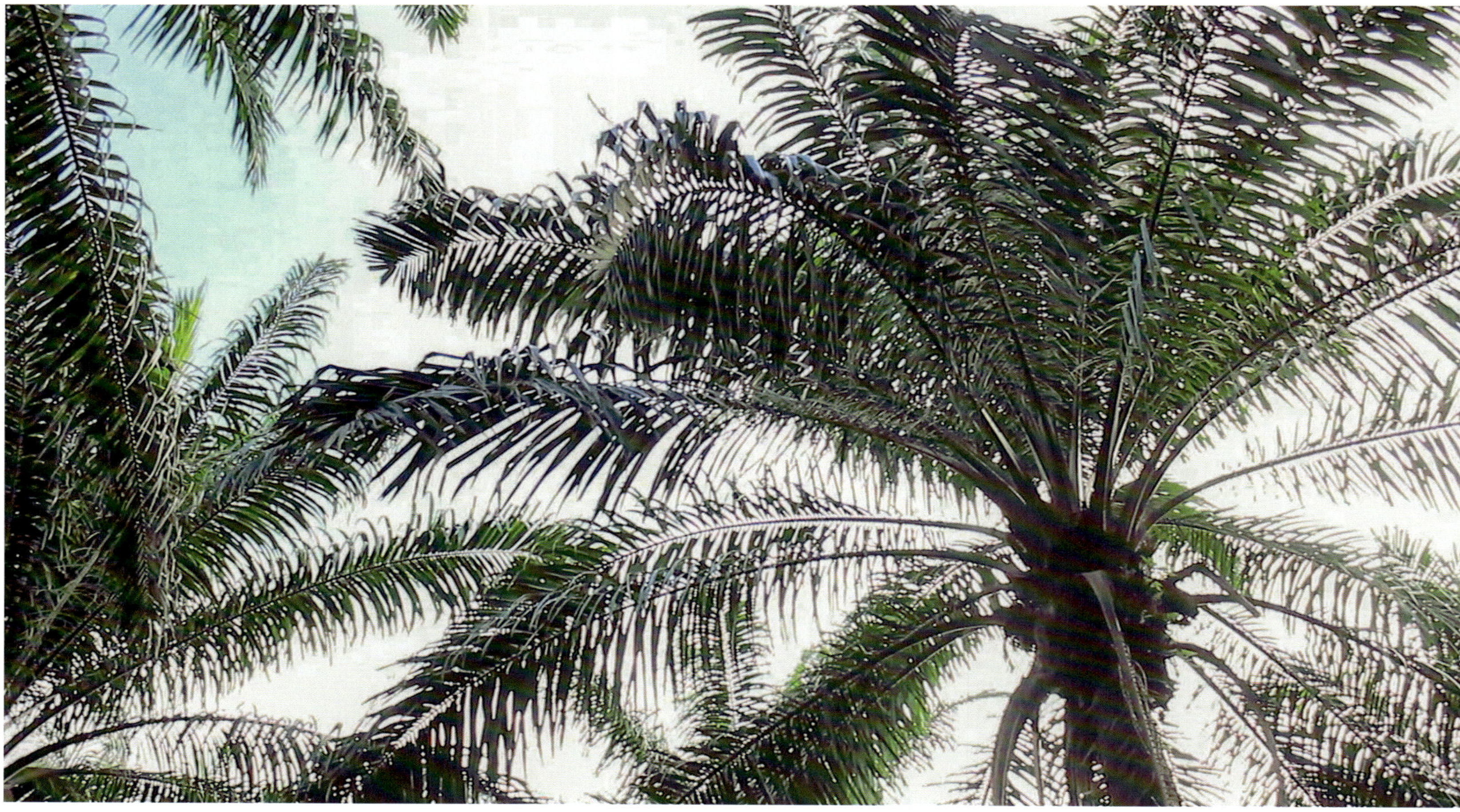

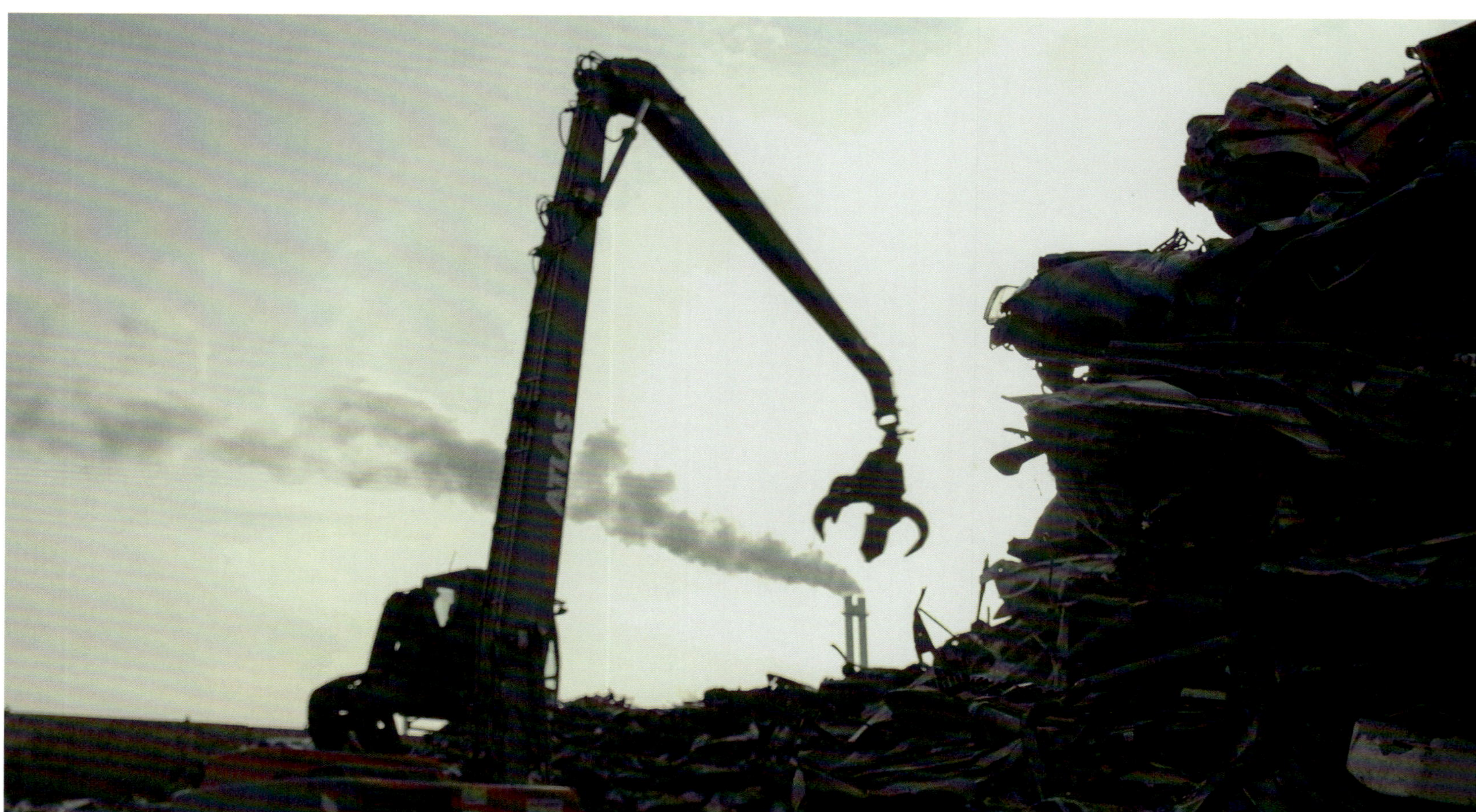
ATLAS

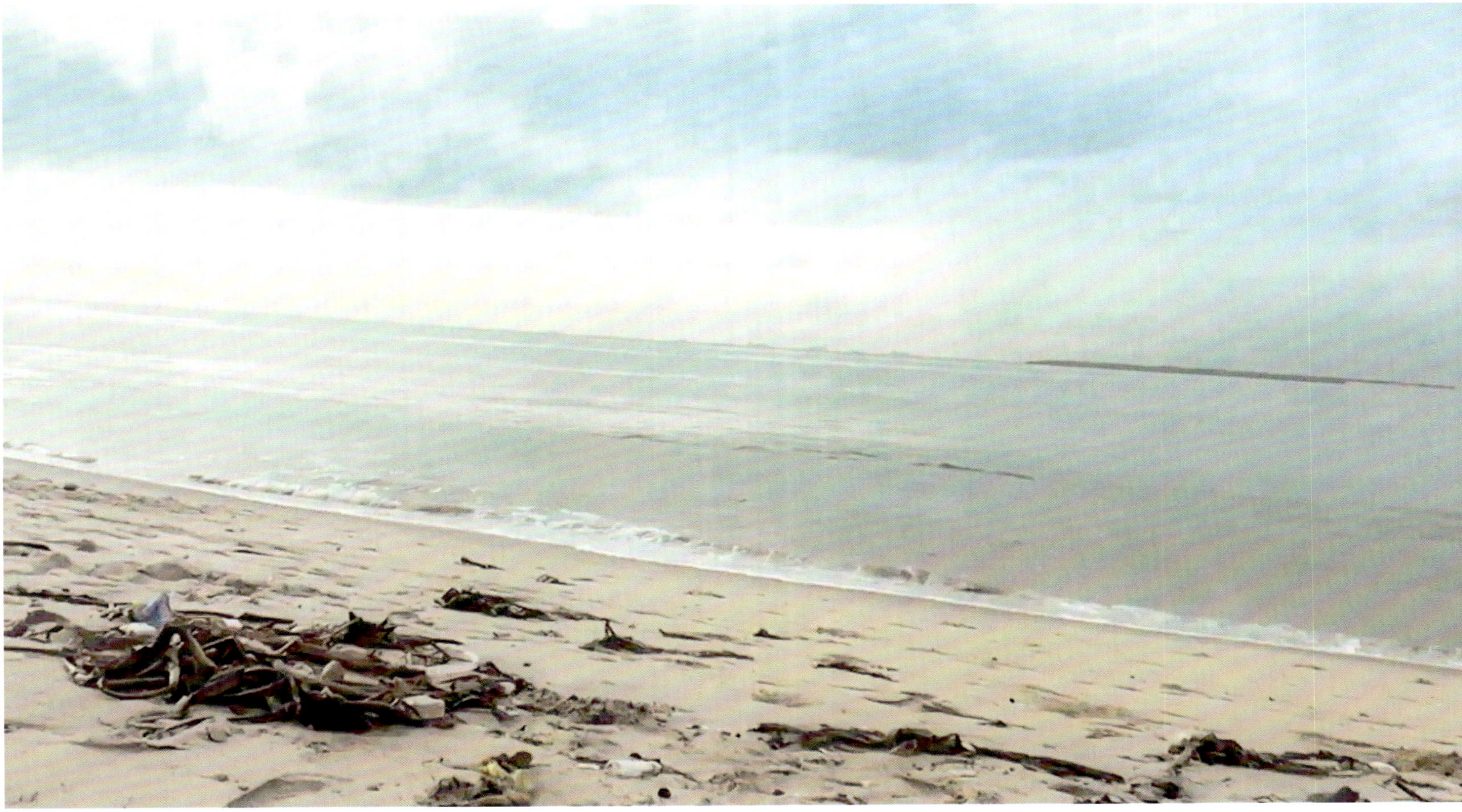

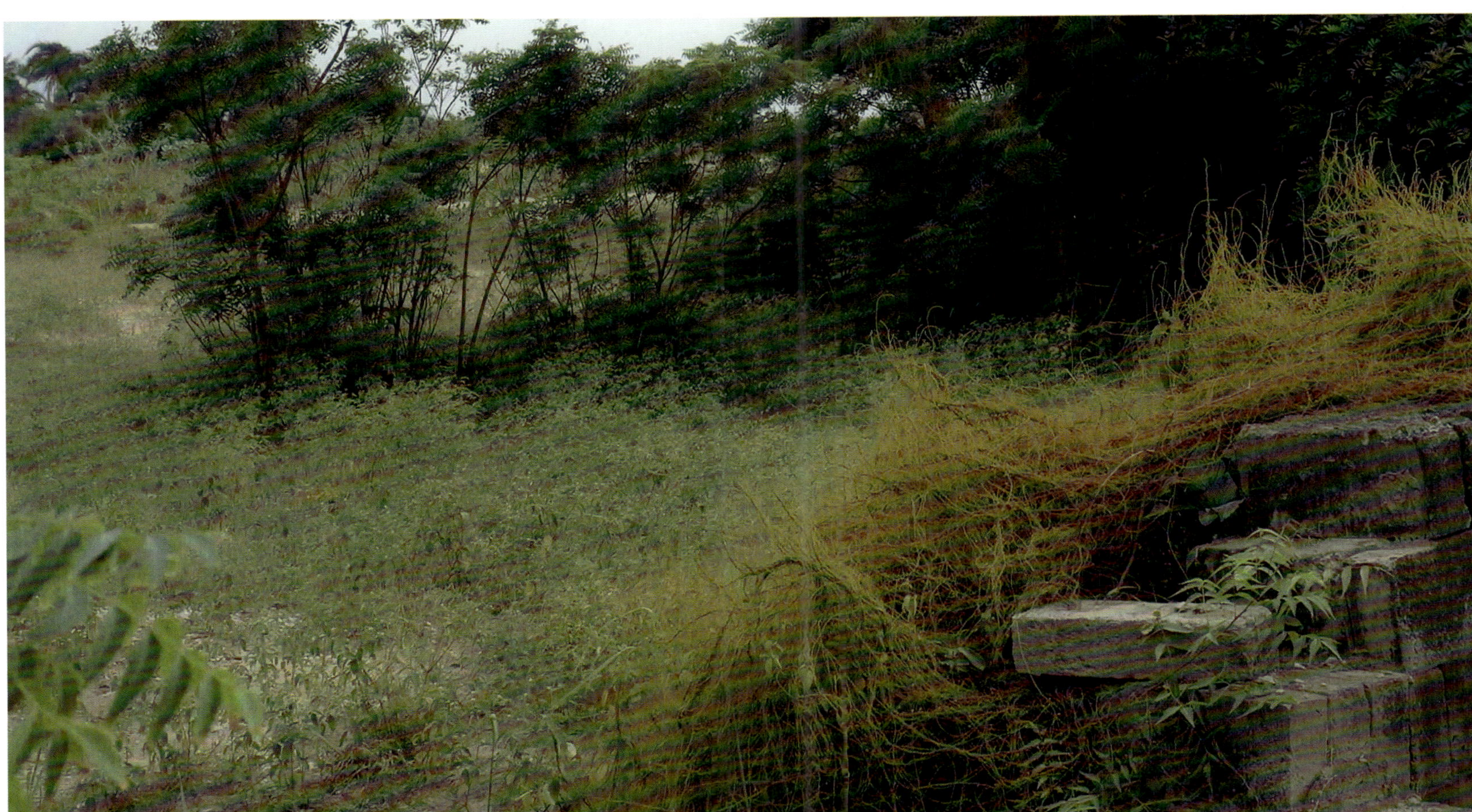

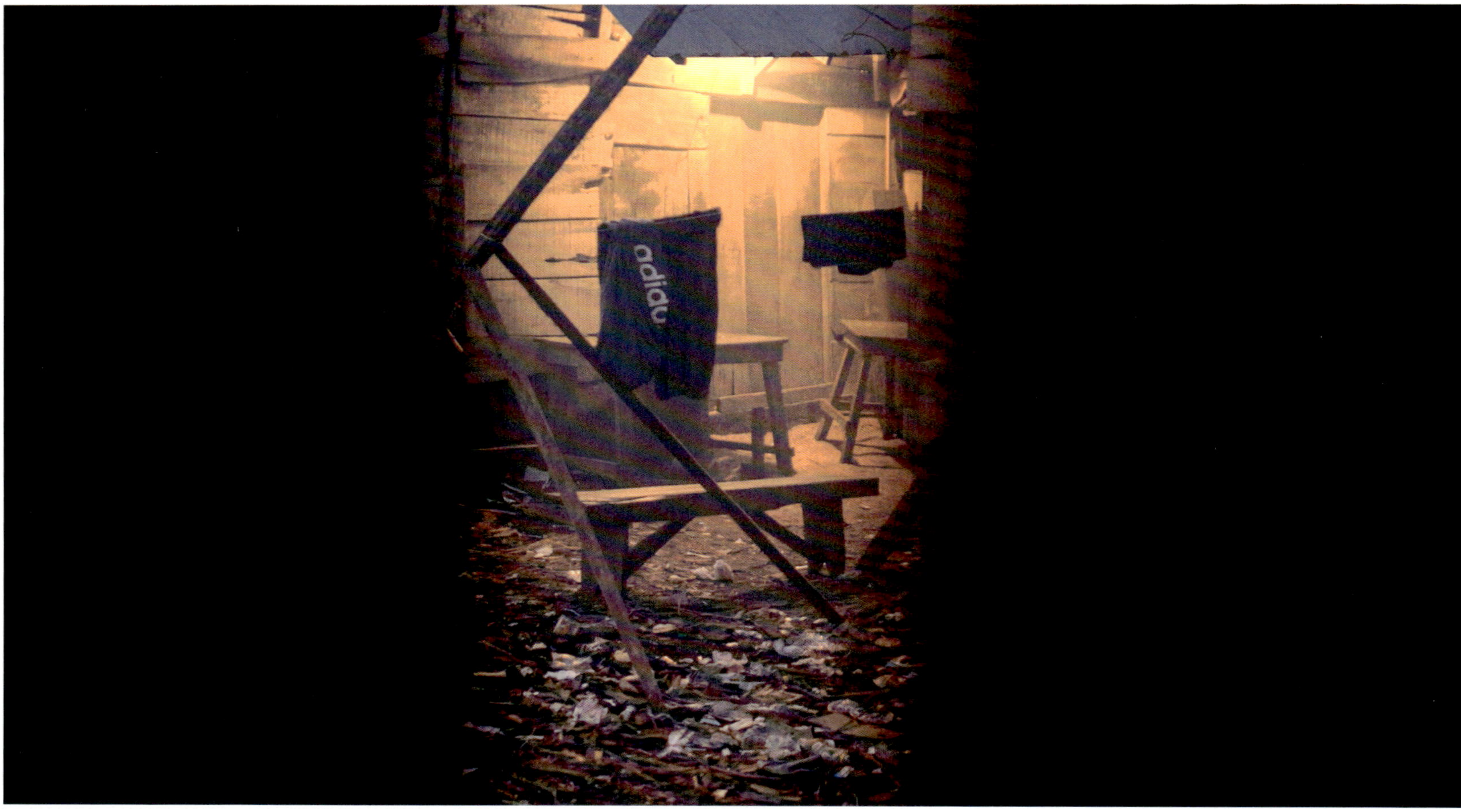

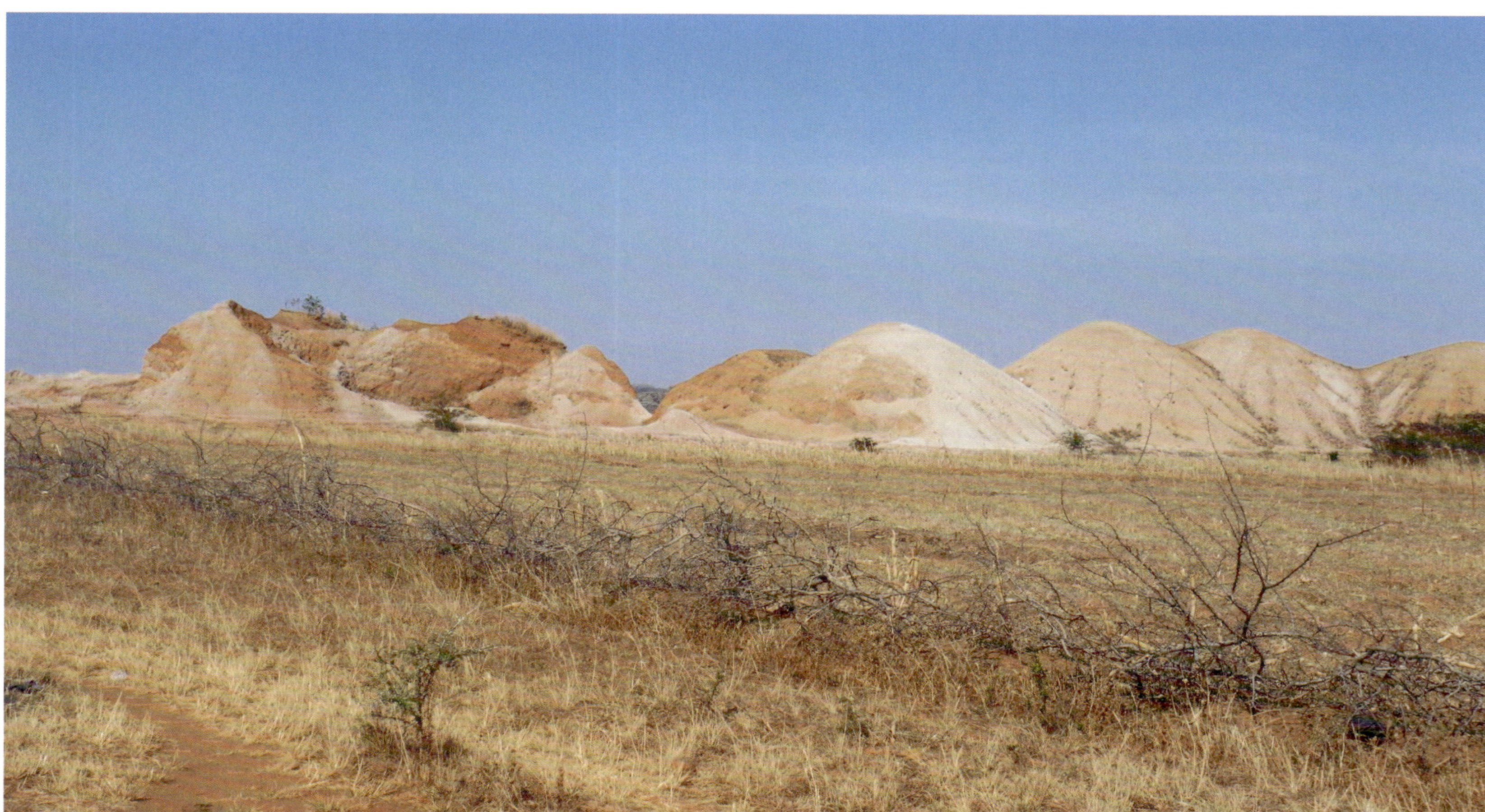

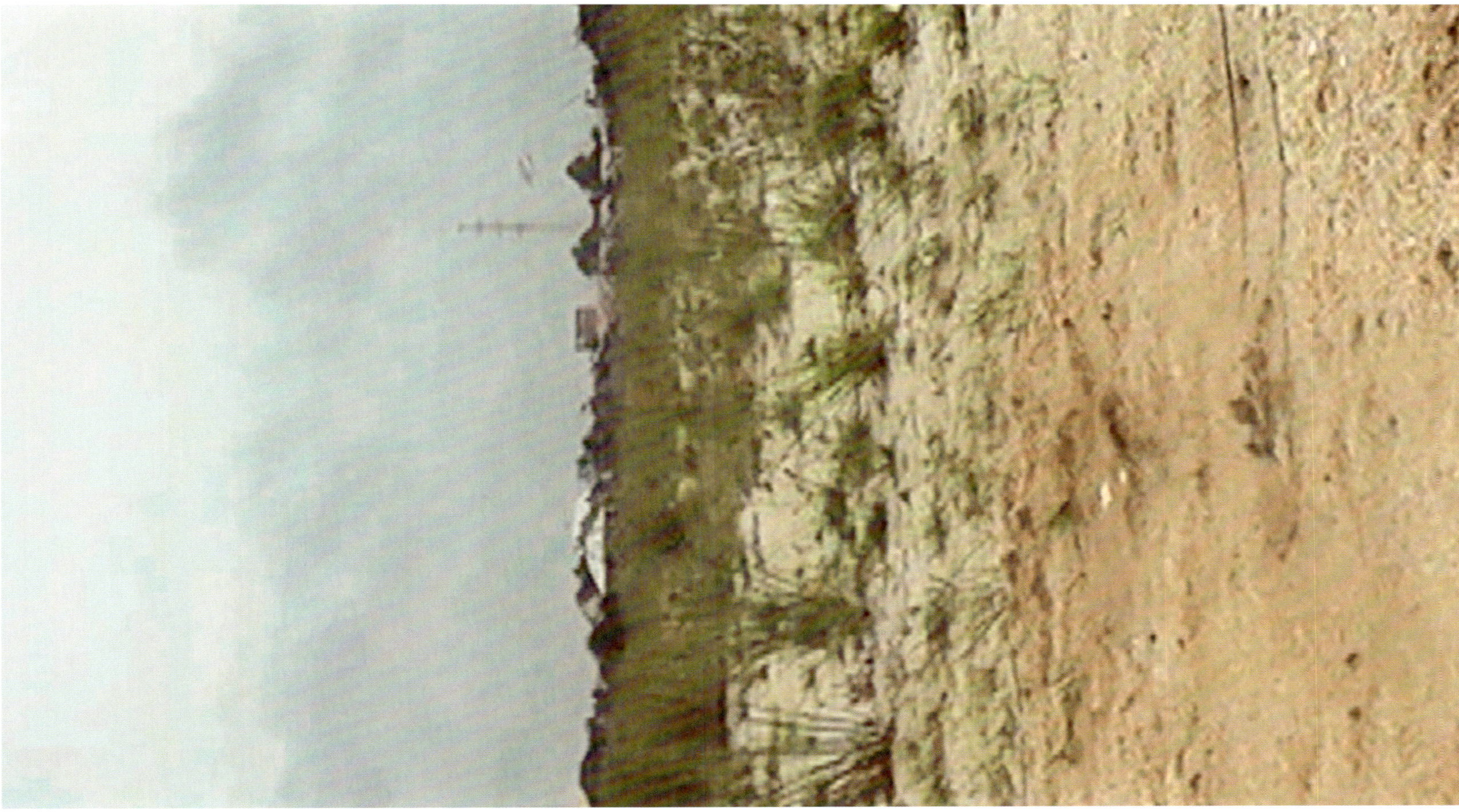

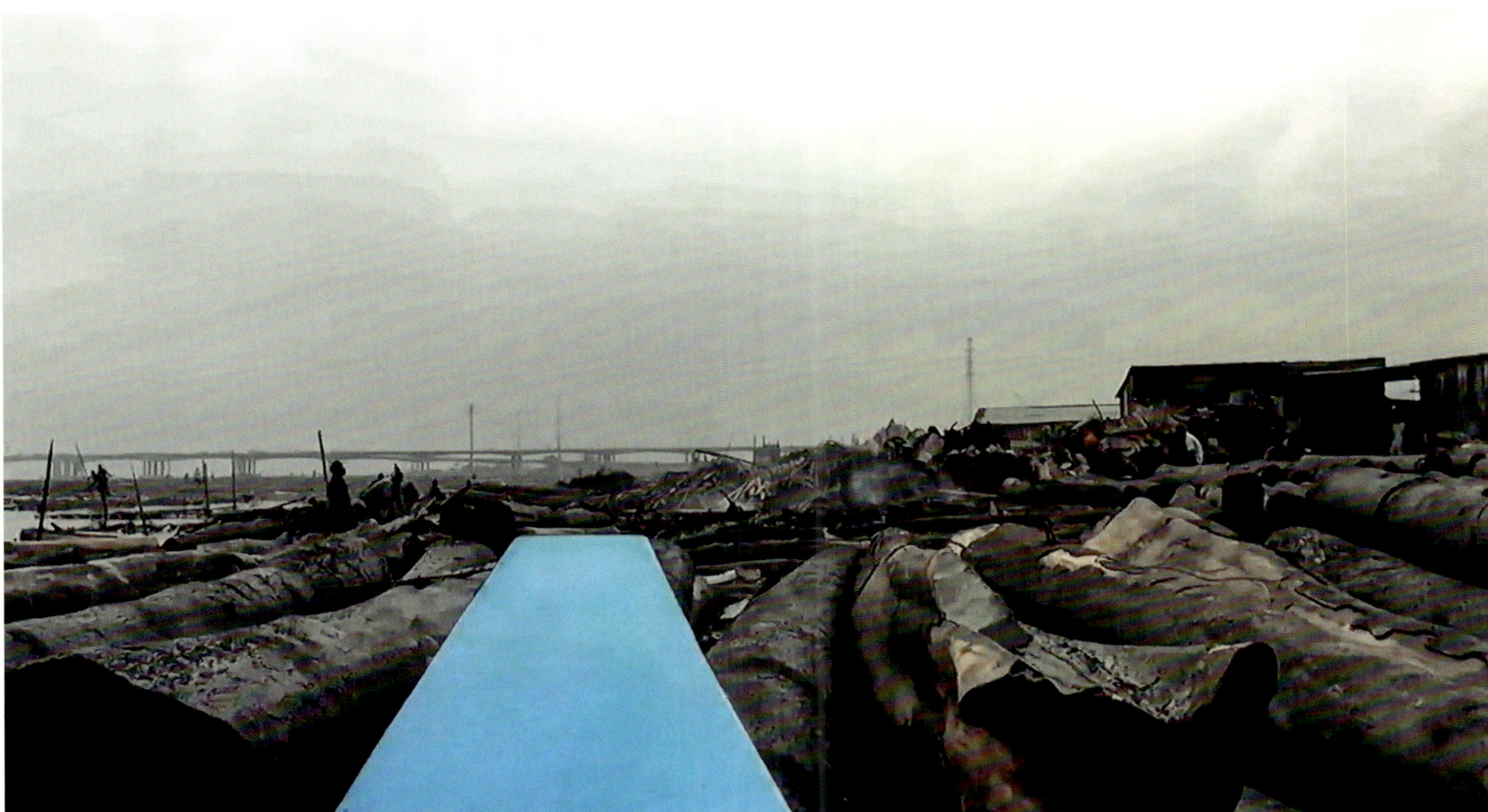

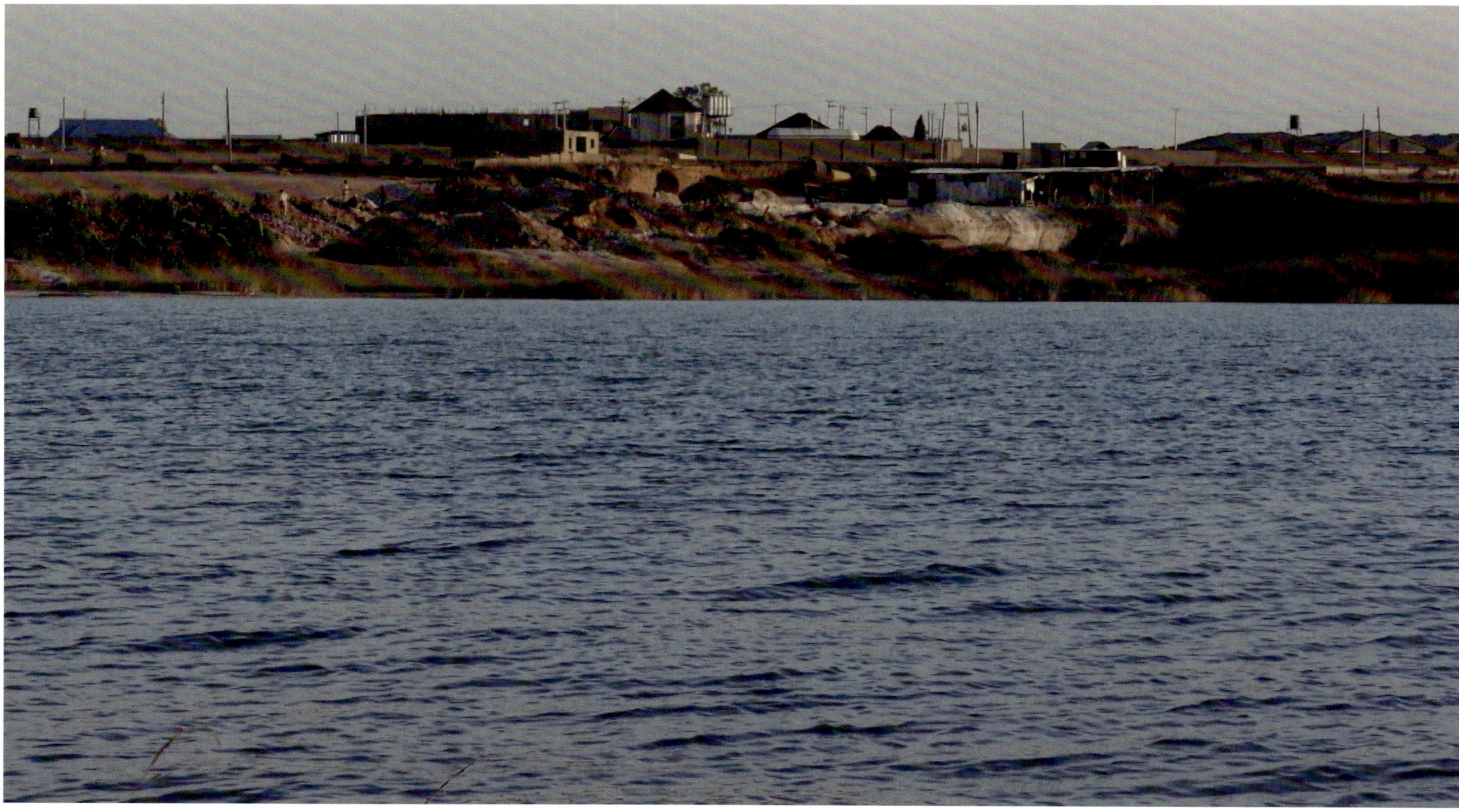

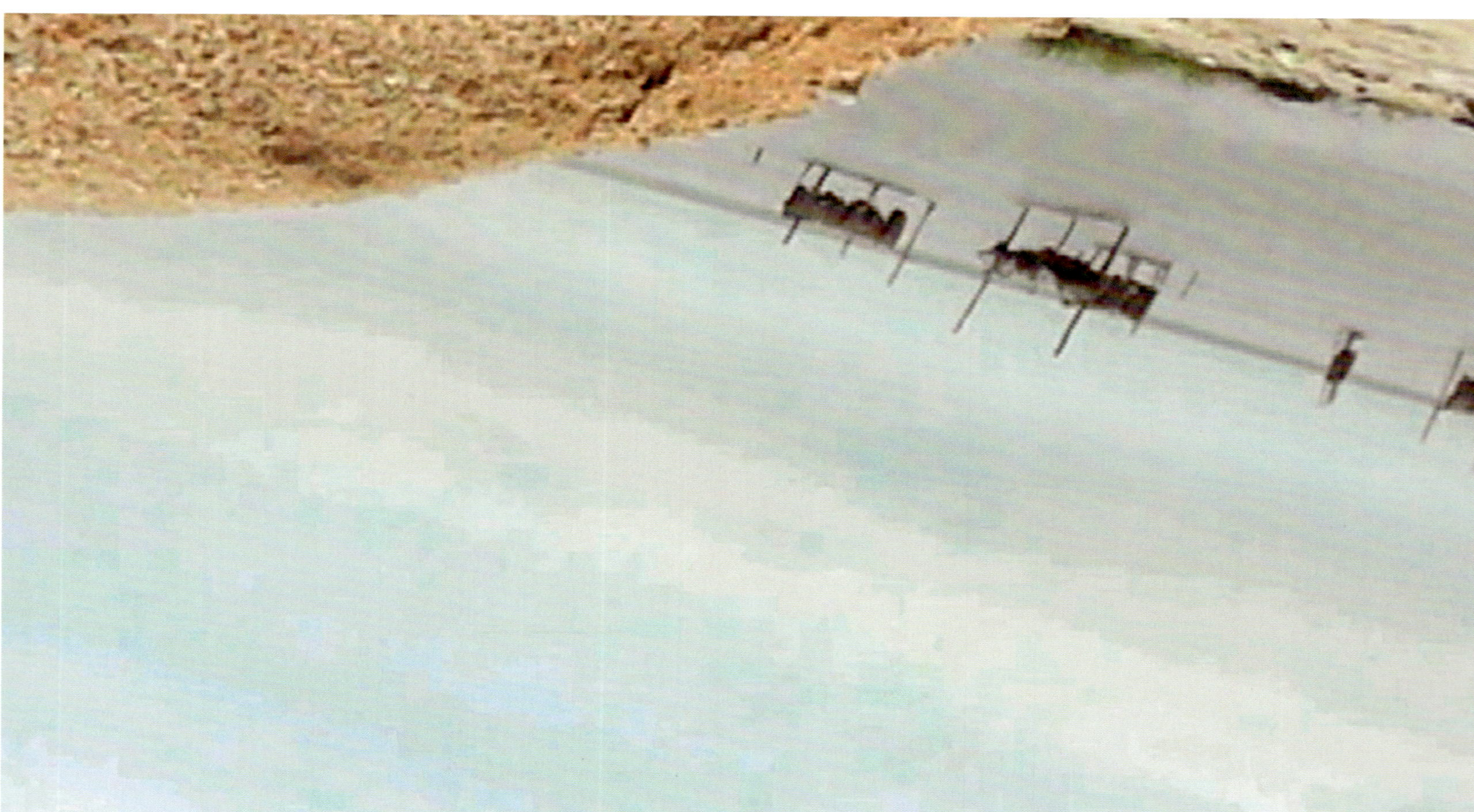

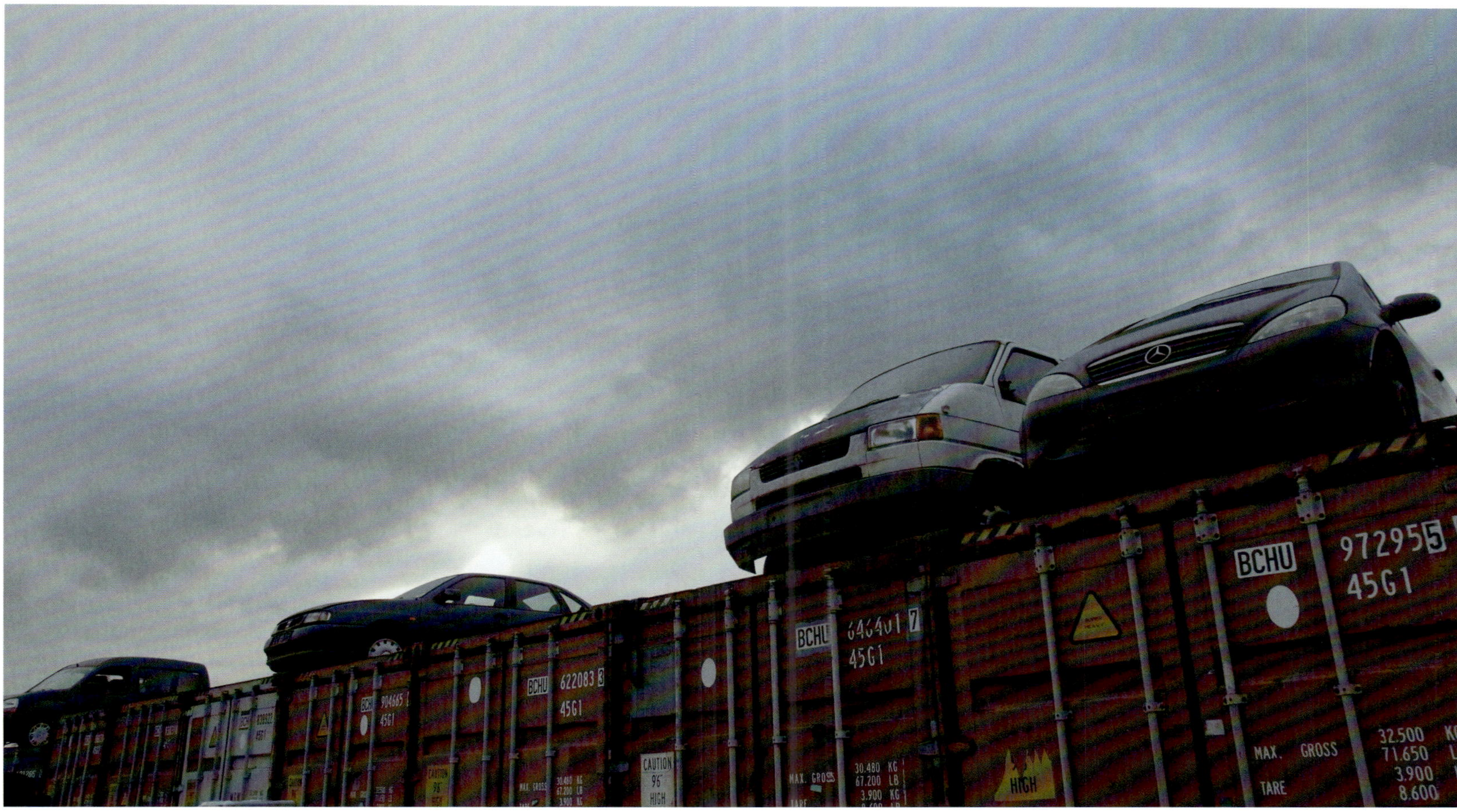
BCHU 972955
45G1
MAX. GROSS
32.500 KG
TARE
3.900 KG
HIGH

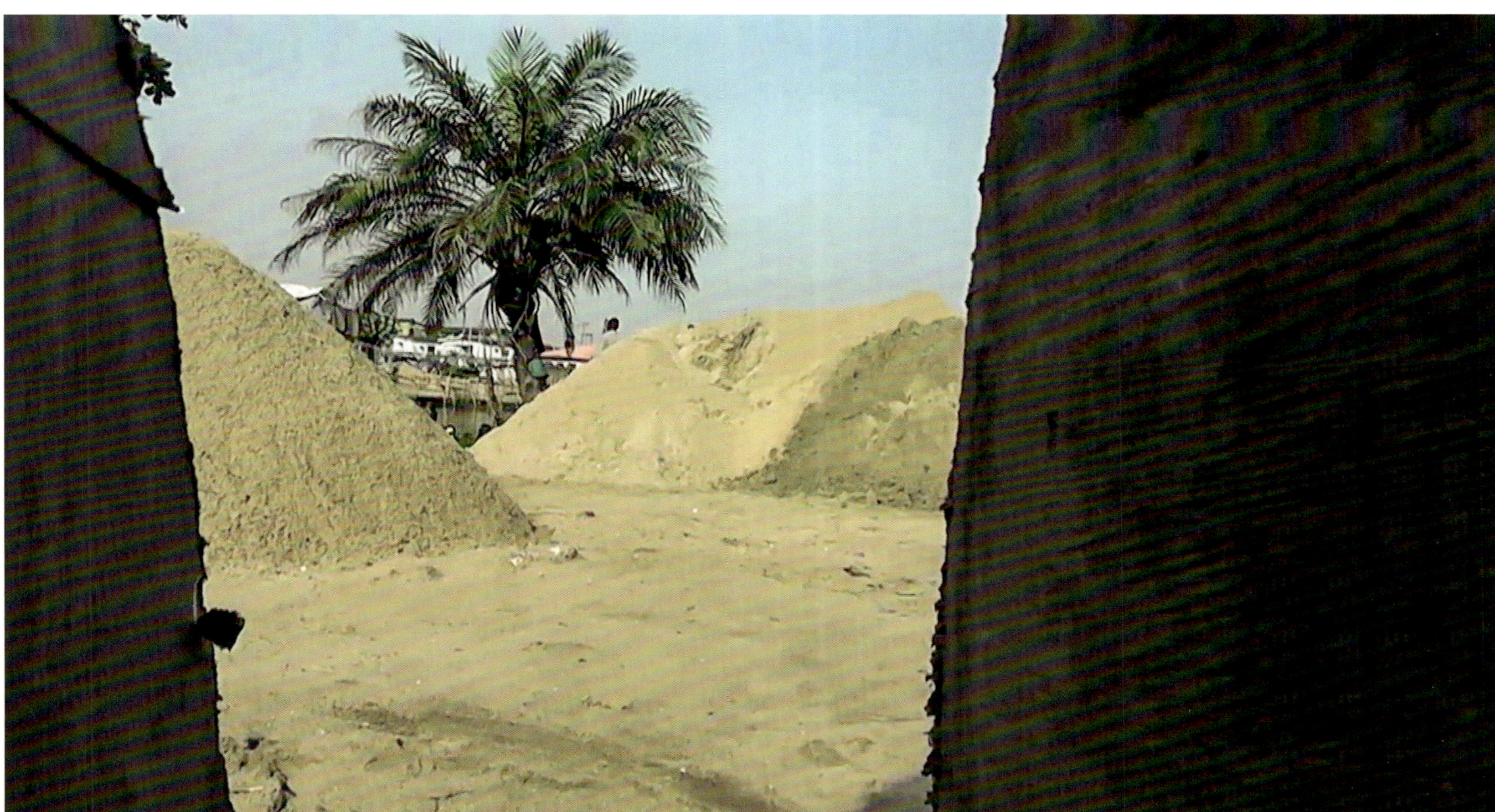

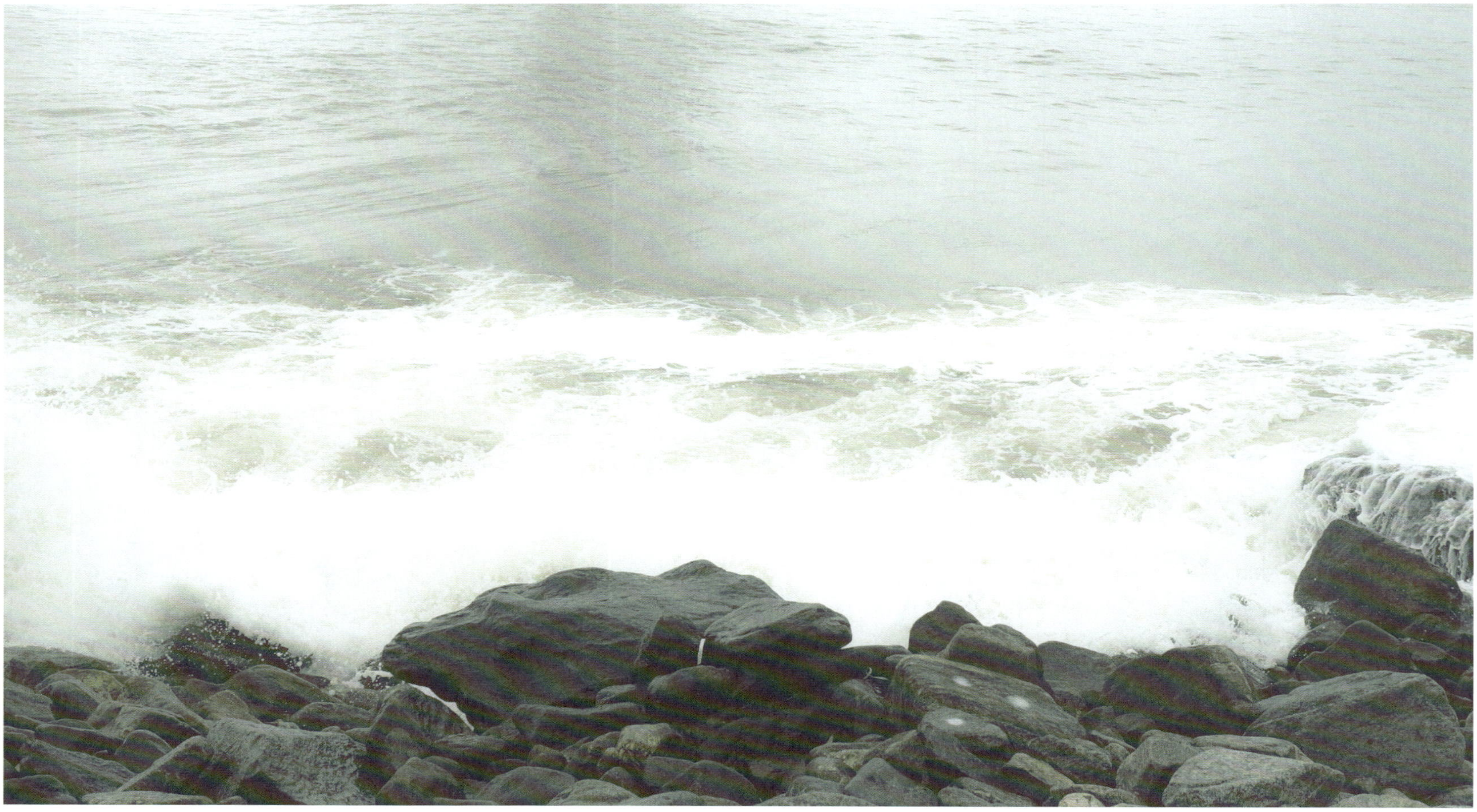

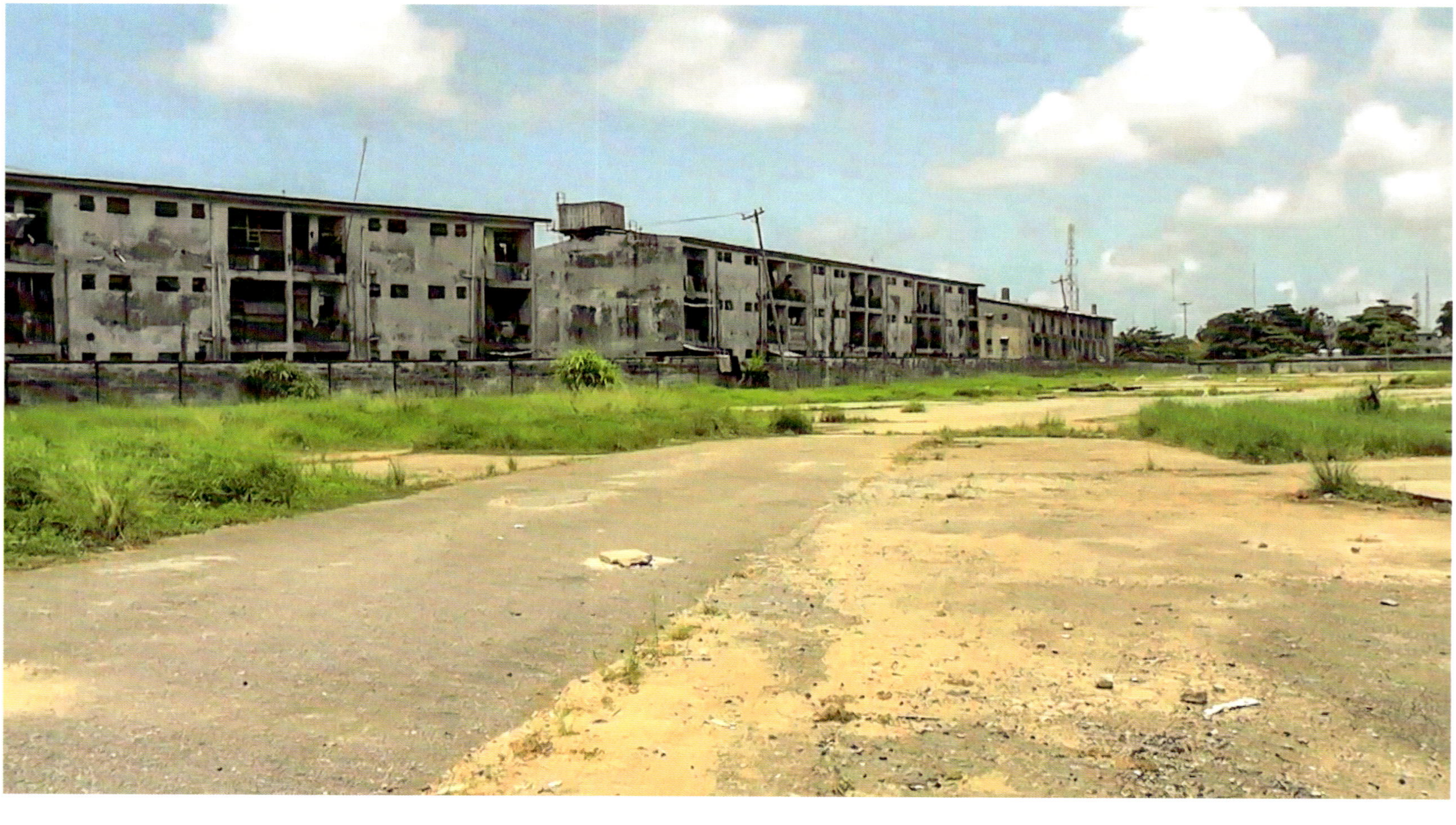

Myriam Ben Salah
is a Tunisian French curator and executive director and chief curator at the Renaissance Society in Chicago. She is the curator of the French Pavilion at the Biennale Arte 2026 with a project by artist Yto Barrada. She co-curated *Made in L.A. 2020* at the Hammer Museum, Los Angeles. Ben Salah served as the editor in chief of *Kaleidoscope* magazine between 2016 and 2020, and as curator of special projects and public programs at the Palais de Tokyo, Paris, from 2009 to 2016. In 2018 she was the guest curator of the 10th Abraaj Group Art Prize, Dubai. Ben Salah's projects encompass exhibitions and programs organised at such institutions as the Kamel Lazaar Foundation, Tunis; the Institute of Contemporary Arts, London; Beirut Art Center; Kunsthall Stavanger; Kadist Foundation, Paris and San Francisco; Pejman Foundation, Tehran and DESTE Foundation, Athens. She sits on the scientific committee of Mudam Luxembourg, on the commissioning committee of the Hartwig Art Production/Collection Fund and on the 2025 jury of the American Academy in Berlin.

Leonardo Bigazzi
is a curator and artist's film producer based in Florence. Since 2020, he has been a curator at Fondazione In Between Art Film, co-curating the exhibitions *Penumbra* and *Nebula* for the Biennale Arte 2022 and 2024 in Venice, and *Ali Cherri: Dreamless Night* at GAMeC, Bergamo, and FRAC Bretagne, Rennes. Since 2008 he has been the curator of Lo schermo dell'arte – Contemporary Art and Cinema Festival, Florence, and since 2012 the founder and curator of VISIO – European Programme on Artists' Moving Images. He has commissioned and/or produced more than forty artists' films, which have been presented at Tate, London; the Museum of Modern Art and MoMA PS1, New York; Centre Pompidou, Paris; the Venice Biennale; and Manifesta, among others. He produced Karimah Ashadu's *Machine Boys* (2024), which was awarded the Silver Lion for a Promising Young Artist at the Biennale Arte 2024 in Venice. He has contributed to and edited several publications, including *VISIO – Moving Images in Europe since the 2010s* (Lenz Press). Most recently, he curated *Iván Argote: Radical Tenderness*, Galerie Rudolfinum, Prague, and *Aziz Hazara: Nightfall*, coleção moraes-barbosa, São Paulo.

Gina Buenfeld-Murley
is exhibitions curator at Camden Art Centre, London, where she has curated solo shows with Jack O'Brien, Lonnie Holley, Tamara Henderson, Marina Xenofontos, Olga Balema, Adam Farah, Athanasios Argianas, Wong Ping, Yuko Mohri, Joachim Koester, and João Maria Gusmão & Pedro Paiva. She recently co-curated a major Nicola L. survey, and has organised exhibitions on a number of important twentieth-century artists, including Martin Wong and Grace Pailthorpe & Reuben Mednikoff. Her research with Indigenous communities in the Amazon rainforest led to a series of thematic exhibitions in 2019 and 2020, including *The Botanical Mind: Art, Mysticism and The Cosmic Tree*, Camden Art Centre; *Gäa: Holistic Science and Wisdom Tradition*, Newlyn Art Gallery and The Exchange, Penzance;

and *Origin Story*, Wäinö Aaltonen Museum of Art, Turku. She regularly writes on contemporary art and artists, including recent essays on Lonnie Holley, Donald Locke, Nicola L., Emma Talbot, Raven Chacon and Cui Jie.

Martin Clark
is director of Camden Art Centre, London. Previously he was director of Bergen Kunsthall, Norway; artistic director of Tate St. Ives and curator of exhibitions at Arnolfini, Bristol. Over the last twenty-five years, he has curated and organised more than one hundred exhibitions, including recent solo shows devoted to Richard Wright, Nicola L., Lonnie Holley, Gregg Bordowitz, Matthew Krishanu, Mohammed Sami, Allison Katz, Forrest Bess, Lily van der Stokker, Walter Price, Jesse Darling, Julien Creuzet, Amy Sillman and Vivian Suter. Group exhibitions he has curated include *The Botanical Mind: Art, Mysticism and the Cosmic Tree* (with Gina Buenfeld-Murley), Camden Art Centre, London; *Up, Down, Top, Bottom, Strange and Charm*, Art Sheffield; *The Noing Uv It* (with Steven Claydon), Bergen Kunsthall; *The Dark Monarch: Magic and Modernity in British Art* (with Michael Bracewell and Alun Rowlands), Tate St. Ives and Towner Eastbourne; and *Pale Carnage*, Arnolfini, Bristol, and Dundee Contemporary Arts. He writes widely on modern and contemporary art, including recent essays on Yuko Mohri, Nicola L., Thomas Nozkowski and Richard Wright.

Dr. Clive Chijioke Nwonka
is an associate professor of film, culture and society in the School of European Languages, Culture and Society within University College London's Faculty of the Arts and Humanities, and a faculty associate of the Sarah Parker Remond Centre for the Study of Racism and Racialisation at University College London. Nwonka's scholarship broadly centers on race and the humanities, with a particular focus on Black film, culture and identity. He is a co-editor of *Black Film British Cinema II* (MIT Press); author of *Black Boys: The Social Aesthetics of British Urban Film* (Bloomsbury), which was longlisted for the 2024 Kraszna-Krausz Moving Image Book Award; co-editor of *Black Arsenal: Club, Culture and Identity* (Weidenfeld & Nicolson) and author of the forthcoming *James Baldwin: On Film*. In 2025 he was appointed a professor in practice at the British Film Institute.

Alessandro Rabottini
is an art writer and curator who lives in London. Since 2020, he has been the artistic director of Fondazione In Between Art Film. In this role, he co-curated the exhibitions *Nebula* and *Penumbra* for the Biennale Arte 2022 and 2024 in Venice, and *Ali Cherri: Dreamless Night* at GAMeC, Bergamo, and Frac Bretagne, Rennes. Rabottini has also curated exhibitions at other venues, including MAXXI L'Aquila; Center d'Art Contemporain, Geneva; Bergen Kunsthall; Le Consortium, Dijon; Triennale di Milano; PAC, Milan; Villa Medici, Rome; Museo MADRE, Naples and GAM, Turin. He has contributed to museum catalogues on the practices of Uri Aran, Rosa Barba, Cecily Brown, Formafantasma, Thao Nguyen Phan, Dana Schutz, Piotr Uklański, Paloma Varga Weisz and others. He has edited books and catalogues on the work of Gianfranco Baruchello, Andrea Branzi, Latifa Echakhch, Giuseppe Gabellone, Massimo Grimaldi, Elad Lassry,

David Maljković, Victor Man, Luca Monterastelli, Oscar Murillo, Robert Overby, Tim Rollins and K.O.S., Sterling Ruby, Ettore Spalletti and Tris Vonna-Michell, among others.

Bettina Steinbrügge
is director of Mudam Luxembourg – Musée d'Art Moderne Grand–Duc Jean. From 2014 to 2022, she was the director of Kunstverein in Hamburg and a professor of art theory at the Hochschule für Bildende Künste (HfBK) in Hamburg. She has directed Halle für Kunst Lüneburg; was a curator at La Kunsthalle Mulhouse; was a senior curator and collection director at Belvedere Wien, Vienna and has taught at Leuphana University Lüneburg and HEAD in Geneva. From 2007 to 2017, she was a member of the program team of the Forum Expanded at the Berlin International Film Festival. Steinbrügge has contributed to and edited numerous publications, most recently *A Model* (Roma & Mudam); *what looks good today may not look good tomorrow: The Legacy of Michel Majerus* (Mudam and Sternberg Press); *Korakrit Arunanondchai: Songs for Living / Songs for Dying* (Mousse Publishing) and *Proof of Stake: Technological Claims* (Lenz Press). Steinbrügge is a member of the board of directors of Villa Romana, Florence; the advisory board of the Museum of Progress, Vienna and the advisory board of the Saarland Cultural Heritage Foundation, Saarbrücken.

Bianca Stoppani
is an art researcher who does writing and curatorial work around deviant beings and emancipatory politics. Their writings have appeared in artists' catalogues, art magazines and newspapers. They have edited publications, organised reading groups and given talks at art institutions, artist-run spaces and universities. In their role of curator for the editorial and discursive projects at Fondazione In Between Art Film, they have co-edited the exhibition catalogues *Nebula* (Marsilio Arte); *Ali Cherri: Dreams of a Dreamless Night* (Lenz Press) and *Penumbra* (Mousse Publishing), and curated the exhibition-related public programs *Thick Atmospheres*, Teatrino di Palazzo Grassi, Venice (2024) and *Vanishing Points*, Complesso dell'Ospedaletto, Venice (2022).

Arese Uwuoruya
has been the assistant curator at Camden Art Centre, London, since 2023, during which time she has worked closely on solo exhibitions devoted to Matthew Krishanu, Andrew Omoding, Lonnie Holley, Jack O'Brien, Tamara Henderson and Marina Xenofontos. She holds an MA in art history from the Courtauld Institute of Art and has previously held positions at the Studio Museum in Harlem, New York; Christie's Education and the Yale University Art Gallery, New Haven (CT).

Visitor Assistants
Alisa Aistova, Maria Andrade, Nick Bradford, Davide Caprioli, Cat Feliciano, Sylvie Field, Sophie Northcott, Max Peters, S. Rajah, Begoña Tormo

Communications Manager
Margarida Amorim

Gallery Manager
Alejandro Ball

Technician
Milo Brennan

Exhibitions Curator
Gina Buenfeld-Murley

Director
Martin Clark

Learning Curator Children and Young People
George Collum

Finance Manager
Izabela Czop

Trusts and Foundations Manager
Kate Ferrie

Head of Development (Maternity Cover)
Kathryn Gigler

Commercial and Events Coordinator
Jenny Hernu

Retail and Editions Manager
Jacqueline Jeffries

Development Manager
Clementine Langley

Deputy Director
Moya Malekin

Residencies Curator
Nisha Matthew

Gallery Technician and Duty Manager
Ezgi Bayazit

Communications Coordinator
Sarena Moss

Office Coordinator
Mikun Oluwayemi

Assistant Retail Manager
Pablo Otero

Head of Development (Maternity Leave)
Ruth Piper

Front of House Coordinator
Stefania Rosi

Head of Commercial
Andrew Smith

Development Researcher and Executive Assistant to the Director
Ellen Smith

Administration and
Personnel Manager
Fay Tsorapa

Assistant Curator
Arese Uwuoruya

Public Programme Assistant
Didi Wambugu

Public Programme Curator
Matt Williams

Learning Coordinator Children
and Young People
Stephanie Wong

Digital Content Producer
Patrick Young

FONDAZIONE IN BETWEEN ART FILM

President
Beatrice Bulgari

Artistic Director
Alessandro Rabottini

Curators
Leonardo Bigazzi
Paola Ugolini

Project Manager
Alessia Carlino

Editor
Bianca Stoppani

Administrative Office
Simona Iandoli

Collection Manager
Chiara Nicolini

THE RENAISSANCE SOCIETY AT THE UNIVERSITY OF CHICAGO

Executive Director and Chief Curator
Myriam Ben Salah

Deputy Director
Jessica Cochran

Communications Manager
Margaret Crowley

Curatorial Associate and
Program Manager
Michael Harrison

Associate Director of Major
Gifts and Individual Giving
Polina Kasian

Senior Curator
Karsten Lund

Associate Director of Development
Programs and Events
Joshi Radin Flores

Director of Publications and Registrar
Karen Reimer

Exhibitions Manager
Pierre Sondeijker

Communications and
Development Coordinator
Eleonore Zurawski

This book has been published on the occasion of the exhibition *Karimah Ashadu: Tendered*

Camden Art Centre, London
October 10, 2025–March 22, 2026

The Renaissance Society at the University of Chicago
September–November 2026

Karimah Ashadu: Tendered is organised by Camden Art Centre, Fondazione In Between Art Film and the Renaissance Society within the framework of *Unison*, a biennial initiative created by the Fondazione to commission and produce moving image-based exhibitions together with international institutions.

Curators
Alessandro Rabottini
Leonardo Bigazzi

With Martin Clark and Gina Buenfeld-Murley for the iteration at Camden Art Centre

With Myriam Ben Salah and Karsten Lund for the iteration at the Renaissance Society

Research
Bianca Stoppani

Acknowledgments

Karimah Ashadu
To my dear family, I am deeply grateful for your immense support and invaluable encouragement. You are a constant source of strength, love and joy. To my son, thank you for being my little ray of light.

Special thanks to Camden Art Centre: Martin Clark, Gina Buenfeld-Murley, Arese Uwuoruya, Alejandro Ball, the Karimah Ashadu Exhibition Circle; Fondazione In Between Art Film: Beatrice Bulgari, Leonardo Bigazzi, Alessandro Rabottini, Bianca Stoppani; The Renaissance Society at The University of Chicago: Myriam Ben Salah, Karsten Lund; Bettina Steinbrügge, Dr. Clive Chijioke Nwonka, Yasmina Price, Lorenzo Mason Studio and Mousse Publishing.

To my studio team, Marie Becker and Gianna Furia, thank you for your unwavering support and commitment.

Many thanks to Sadie Coles, Laura Lord, Connor Linskey and the team at Sadie Coles HQ.

Camden Art Centre
The Karimah Ashadu Exhibition Circle

Camden Art Centre Artists' Circle

Sadie Coles HQ

Arts Council England

All Renaissance Society publications are made possible by The Mansueto Foundation Publications Program

The Editors
Paola Mirashi, Livia Polacco, David J. Sheldon, Camilla Toschi

PUBLICATION

Edited by
Bianca Stoppani with
Alessandro Rabottini
and Leonardo Bigazzi

Visual essays
Karimah Ashadu

Texts
Karimah Ashadu
Myriam Ben Salah
Leonardo Bigazzi
Gina Buenfeld-Murley
Martin Clark
Dr. Clive Chijioke Nwonka
Alessandro Rabottini
Bettina Steinbrügge
Arese Uwuoruya

Publishing Editor
Agnese Cantelmi (Mousse)

Copy-editing and Proofreading
Agnese Cantelmi
Lindsay Westbrook
Joanne Laws

Translations
Ben Bazalgette-Staples

Design
Lorenzo Mason Studio,
Michele Bellinaso
Lorenzo Mason
Simone Spinazzè

Colour Reproduction and Printing
Grafiche Veneziane, Venice

First edition
October 2025
ISBN 978-88-6749-708-9
€ 35 / £ 30 / $ 40

Published and distributed by
Mousse Publishing –
Contrappunto srl
via Piercandido Decembrio 28
20137, Milan–Italy
moussemagazine.it

Images Credits

P. 44: Michael Snow, *La Région Centrale*, 1971. 16mm film, 190', colour, sound. Courtesy of Michael Snow Studio and Jack Shainman Gallery, New York

P. 45: Chantal Akerman, *News from Home*, 1977. 16mm film, 89', colour. Belgium-France-Germany. Cast: Chantal Akerman. Production: Unité Trois / INA (Paris), Paradise Films (Brussels), Z.D.F. (Mainz). Sound: Dominique Dalmasso, Larry Haas. Editing: Francine Sandberg. Photography: Babette Mangolte, Jim Asbell. © Chantal Anne Akerman, by SIAE 2025. Courtesy Fondation Chantal Akerman & CINEMATEK

P. 48: *Workers Leaving the Factory* © Harun Farocki, 1995